R62175A0098

1998 SND Officers:

President
Lynn Staley
Newsweek

First Vice President
Ed Kohorst
The Dallas Morning News

Second Vice President
Jean D. Dodd
Kansas City Star

Treasurer
Lucie Lacava
Lucie Lacava Pub. Design, Inc.

Secretary
Svenåke Boström
Sundsvall, Sweden

Past President
Neal Pattison
Seattle Post-Intelligencer

Executive Director
Dave Gray
The Society for News Design

Special Thanks:
S.I. Newhouse School of Public Communications
Syracuse University

Judging Assistants:

Jay Anthony, associate professor, University of North Carolina at Chapel Hill, N.C.
Stephen Cavendish, page one designer, San Jose Mercury News, San Jose, Calif.
Elizabeth Cromer, SND membership assistant, Providence, R.I.
G.W. Babb, design director, Austin American-Statesman, Austin, Texas
Steve Dorsey, presentation editor, Herald-Leader, Lexington, Ky.
Kelly Frankeny, AME/design, San Francisco Examiner, San Francisco, Calif.
Carolyn Flynn, AME/photo & design, Albuquerque Journal, Albuquerque, N.M.
Scott Goldman, assistant sports editor, Charlotte Observer, Charlotte, N.C.
Dave Gray, SND executive director, Providence, R.I.
Barbara Hines, associate professor, Howard University, Washington, D.C.
Jim Jennings, vice president & editorial director, Thomson Newspapers
Adriana Libreros, page designer/illustrator, Asbury Park Press, Neptune, N.J.
Marshall Matlock, associate professor, School of Public Communications, Syracuse University, N.Y.
Jim Michalowski, photography director, The Citizen, Auburn, N.Y.
Kenny Monteith, news designer, Savannah Morning News, Savannah, Ga.
Kim Parson, design desk chief, The Orlando Sentinel, Orlando, Fla.
Andrew Phillips, staff artist, Home News & Tribune, East Brunswick, N.J.
John Sherlock, graphics editor, Philadelphia Daily News, Philadelphia, Pa.
Harris Siegel, ME/design, Asbury Park Press, Neptune, N.J.
Randy Stano, professor, University of Miami, Miami, Fla.
Shamus Walker, SND judging auditor, Syracuse University, N.Y.

S.I. Newhouse School of Public Communications Students – Kannan A.M.R.,
Taylor Atseff, Lauren Biddle, Sara Bines, Kat Fahrer, Reneé Henrich, Shane Kite, Heather
Knoll, Colleen McDaniel, Christopher Page, Courtney Robinson, Susanna Virden, Jennifer
Waddell, James Weber

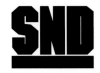

The Society for News Design
129 Dyer Street
Providence, R.I. 02903-3904
Telephone: 401•276•2100
FAX: 401•276•2105
snd@snd.org
http://www.snd.org

First published in the United States of America by:
Rockport Publishers, Inc.
33 Commercial Street
Gloucester, Mass. 01930-5089
Telephone: 978•282•9590
Fax: 978•283•2742

Distributed to the book trade and art trade in the United States by:
North Light Books, an imprint of
F & W Publications
1507 Dana Avenue
Cincinnati, Ohio 45207
Telephone: 800•289•0963

Other distribution by:
Rockport Publishers, Inc.
Gloucester, Mass. 01930-5089

ISBN 1-56496-489-2 (Hardcover edition)
ISBN 1-878107-09-7 (Softcover edition)

THE BEST OF NEWSPAPER DESIGN

NINETEENTH EDITION

Book Credits

Designer & Editor
C. Marshall Matlock
S.I. Newhouse School
of Public Communications
Syracuse University

Associate Designer
Shamus Walker
Syracuse, N.Y.

Associate Copy Editor
Barbara Hines
Silver Spring, Md.

Cover & Chapter Illustrations
Debra Page-Trim
Providence, R.I.

Production Consultant
David Gray
Providence, R.I.

Contents

We don't design for contests.

You've heard it. You've probably even preached it. But still the content of this book always fascinates us — and sometimes drives us — towards the goal of building the better newspaper.

With an increase of nearly 25 percent in the number of entries from the last judging, the quality of work has never been more vast.

Judges awarded 165 publications from 19 countries a total of 826 awards. If you don't finish this, I wouldn't blame you since the work that follows is the reason you are looking at this book's content.

This has always been a contest about excellence, but I have found the judges to be as much a part of that process as the art directors, designers and illustrators who loyally submit their best of the best.

The judges who assembled in Syracuse in February were a diverse, talented, multi-national group. But they had in common one critical element — a passion for the profession.

After seeing the work and spending long days with the judges, I felt rejuvenated by both the work and the company.

Although the judges are the key to the process, the behind-the-scenes personnel provide the all important supporting cast. The professional assistants who forgo long work days for even longer competition days included: Jay Anthony, Stephen Cavendish, G.W. Babb, Steve Dorsey, Kelly Frankeny, Carolyn Flynn, Scott Goldman, Barbara Hines, Adriana Libreros, Jim Michalowski, Kenny Monteith, Kim Parson, Andrew Phillips, John Sherlock and Randy Stano.

Also, a special thanks to:
• David Gray and Elizabeth Cromer from the SND office;
• Jim Jennings for his help in coordinating the World's Best-Designed Newspapers judging;
• Marshall Matlock for making the contest run so smoothly (as usual!) and to Shamus Walker for everything from proper lighting at the judging site to designing the "big board" that kept us on track;
• the Syracuse University students who helped us and will help us define our industry over the next few years;
• the S.I. Newhouse School of Public Communications at Syracuse University and Dean David Rubin and his staff for being our gracious host and cosponsors for the tenth time.

Finally, thanks to my colleagues at the Asbury Park Press who understood and tolerated the time away from my job I spent on this judging.

As for me, I couldn't be more thrilled that my alma mater would support the industry in such a great way.

Now read on!

Harris G. Siegel
19th Edition Coordinator

No diseñamos para los concursos.

Ya lo hemos oído. Probablemente hasta lo hayamos predicado. Pero aún el contenido de este libro nos sigue fascinando — y a veces nos impulsa — hacia el objetivo de lograr un periódico mejor.

Con un aumento de casi un 25 por ciento más en concursantes desde el último concurso, la amplitud del trabajo de calidad jamás ha sido tan vasta.

Los jueces otorgaron un total de 826 premios a 165 periódicos de 19 países. Si no termina de leer, no se lo reprocho. El trabajo que sigue es la razón por la cual está viendo el contenido de este libro.

Éste siempre ha sido un certamen sobre excelencia, pero he descubierto que los jueces son tan partícipes de dicho proceso como los directores de arte, los diseñadores e ilustradores que fielmente producen lo mejor de lo mejor.

Los jueces reunidos en Syracuse en febrero componían un grupo diversificado, talentoso y multinacional de todos los rincones del mundo. Todos ellos tenían un elemento en común: la pasión por su profesión.

Luego de examinar el trabajo y pasar largos días y noches junto a los jueces, me sentí rejuvenecido tanto por el trabajo como por la compañía.

Si bien los jueces tienen un rol clave en el proceso, el personal detrás de la escena constituye el elenco de reparto. Los asistentes profesionales que reemplazan largas jornadas de trabajo por días de certámenes aún más largos incluyen: Jay Anthony, Stephen Cavendish, G.W. Babb, Steve Dorsey, Kelly Frankeny, Carolyn Flynn, Scott Goldman, Barbara Hines, Adriana Libreros, Jim Michalowski, Kenny Monteith, Kim Parson, Andrew Phillips, John Sherlock y Randy Stano.

Además, debo agradecer especialmente de:
• David Gray y Elizabeth Cromer de la oficina de SND;
• veterano Jim Jennings por su ayuda en la coordinación del jurado de Los Periódicos Mejor Diseñados del Mundo;
• Marshall Matlock por lograr que el certamen sea taneficiente (como siempre) y a Shamus Walker por todo desde la iluminación adecuada en el salón del jurado hasta el diseño del "cartelón";
• la Universidad de Syracuse que nos ayudaron y quienes contribuirán a definir nuestra industria en los próximos años;
• gracias a la Facultad de Comunicaciones Públicas S.I Newhouse de la Universidad de Syracuse y a su Decano David Rubin y su personal por ser nuestro anfitrión y patrocinador por décima vez.

Finalmente, gracias a mis colegas de Asbury Park Press quienes comprendieron y toleraron el tiempo que dediqué a este concurso.

En cuanto a mí, no podría estar más emocionado de que mi alma mater apoyara a la industria de manera tan excelente.

¡Ahora, continúen leyendo!

Harris G. Siegel, Coordinador de la 19na Edición

Chapter One

WORLD'S BEST-DESIGNED NEWS-PAPERS

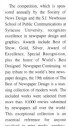

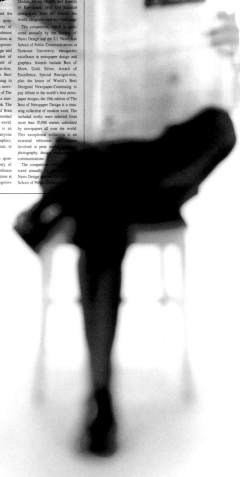

The competition, which is sponsored annually by the Society of News Design and the S.I. Newhouse School of Public Communications at Syracuse University, recognizes excellence in newspaper design and graphics. Awards include Best of Show, Gold, Silver, Award of Excellence, Special Recogni-tion, plus the honor of World's Best Designed Newspaper.Continuing to pay tribute to the world's best news-paper designs, the 19th edition of The Best of Newspaper Design is a stun-ning collection of modern work. The included works were selected from more than 10,000 entries submitted by newspapers all over the world. This exceptional collection is an essential reference for anyone involved in print media, graphics, photography, design, journalism, or communications.

The competition, which is spon-sored annually by the Society of News Design and the S.I. Newhouse School of Public Communications at Syracuse University, recognizes excellence in newspaper design and

graphics. Awards include Best of Show, Gold, Silver, Award of Excellence, Special Recogni-tion, plus the honor of World's Best Designed Newspaper.Continuing to pay tribute to the world's best news-paper designs, the 19th edition of The Best of Newspaper Design is a stun-ning collection of modern work. The included works were selected from more than 10,000 entries submitted by newspapers all over the world. The competition, which is sponsored annually by the Society of News Design and the S.I. Newhouse School of Public Communications at Syracuse University, recognizes excellence in newspaper design and graphics. Awards include Best of Show, Gold, Silver, Award of Excellence, Special Recogni-tion, plus the honor of World's Best Designed Newspaper.Continuing to pay tribute to the world's best news-paper designs, the 19th edition of The Best of Newspaper Design is a stun-ning collection of modern work. The included works were selected from more than 10,000 entries submitted

The competition, which is spon-sored annually by the Society of News Design and the S.I. Newhouse School of Public Communications at Syracuse University, recognizes excellence in newspaper design and graphics. Awards include Best of Show, Gold, Silver, Award of Excellence, Special Recogni-tion, plus the honor of World's Best Designed Newspaper.Continuing to pay tribute to the world's best news-paper designs, the 19th edition of The Best of Newspaper Design is a stun-ning collection of modern work. The included works were selected from more than 10,000 entries submitted by newspapers all over the world. This exceptional collection is an essential reference for anyone involved in print media, graphics, photography, design, journalism, or communications.

The competition, which is spon-sored annually by the Society of News Design and the S.I. Newhouse School of Public Communications at Syracuse University, recognizes excellence in newspaper design and

newspapers from all around the world.

The competition, which is spon-sored annually by the Society of News Design and the S.I. Newhouse School of Public Communications at Syracuse University, recognizes excellence in newspaper design and graphics. Awards include Best of Show, Gold, Silver, Award of Excellence, Special Recogni-tion, plus the honor of World's Best Designed Newspaper.Continuing to pay tribute to the world's best news-paper designs, the 19th edition of The Best of Newspaper Design is a stun-ning collection of modern work. The included works were selected from more than 10,000 entries submitted by newspapers all over the world. This exceptional collection is an essential reference for anyone involved in print media, graphics, photography, design, journalism, or communications.

The competition, which is spon-sored annually by the Society of News Design and the S.I. Newhouse School of Public Communications at Syracuse University, recognizes

pay tribute to the world's best news-paper designs, the 19th edition of The Best of Newspaper Design is a stun-ning collection of modern work. The included works were selected from more than 10,000 entries submitted by newspapers all over the world. This exceptional collection is an essential reference for anyone involved in print media, graphics, photography, design, journalism, or communications.

judging include overall page design, portfolio, magazine cover design, art and illustration, photo journalism, and informational graphics.

This nineteenth edition presents the finest newspaper design in the field.

Selected by a panel of judges of the Society of News Design, the award-winning newspapers featured in this nineteenth edition were chosen for excellence in design.

Selected by a panel of 21 judges of the Society for News Design, the award-winning pub-lications featured in this nineteenth edition were chosen for excellence in design.

The Best of Newspaper Design, 19th edition, featured text in English and Spanish; more than five hundred awards: Best of Show, Judges' Special Recognition, Gold Medals, Silver Medals, and Awards of Excellence over five hundred newspapers from all around the world, categories such as overall page

The competition, which is spon-sored annually by the Society of News Design and the S.I. Newhouse School of Public Communications at Syracuse University, recognizes excellence in newspaper design and graphics. Awards include Best of Show, Gold, Silver, Award of Excellence, Special Recogni-tion, plus the honor of World's Best Designed Newspaper.Continuing to pay tribute to the world's best news-paper designs, the 19th edition of The Best of Newspaper Design is a stun-ning collection of modern work. The included works were selected from by newspapers all over the world. This exceptional reference for anyone involved in print media, graphics, photography, design, journalism, or communications.

The competition, which is spon-sored annually by the Society of News Design and the S.I. Newhouse School of Public Communications at

What did we learn?

Two days and 291 newspapers later, the judges sat around newsprint stained tables discussing what they had seen and why 14 newspapers were named the World's Best-Designed Newspapers in category 1.

They also noted what they did see in many of the category 1 entries: a lack of surprises, innovation, attention to detail and thoughtful writing.

"I am really amazed at the sameness of it all," one judge said.

"There was very little to differentiate one newspaper from another. Many entries felt the same. There was no sense of community about them. I had no idea who they were writing to."

The winning entries, the judges said, represented a holistic approach to the design process: One that considered voice and texture of a story within the context of the readership as much as it did typography or color usage.

"The winners were filled with really good content. If it did not read well, I couldn't vote for it," said one judge. "Too many of the papers presented a lot of flash, but very little substance," responded another.

"That's right. Great design without great content is something of an oxymoron," said a third.

You be the judge.

The judges for Category 1, which is the World's Best-Designed Newspapers entries, recognized publications that excel at presenting the news. Judges were asked to evaluate overall content as well as the design of the newspaper — how well the newspaper tells stories, communicates the news and conveys ideas to its readers.

The judges set the standards. The following items were included on a form which judges could use at their discretion.

• **Content:** How are stories told and presented? Are the headlines informative? Do photographs convey information? Are graphics explanatory?

• **Usefulness:** Is the information presented valuable to the reader? Is the newspaper filled with material that engages the reader? Is this a newspaper that is, or should be, a part of the reader's daily routine?

• **Structure & organization:** Do the pages invite readers in? Does the design steer the reader through the page? Is the newspaper well indexed or signposted? Is it easy to follow and use?

• **Storytelling:** Does the newspaper use all storytelling elements — narrative, text, photos and graphics — to tell stories?

• **Clarity:** Is information presented clearly and simply? Is it easy to access, to understand?

• **Creativity:** Does the newspaper approach its story selection, presentation and design in a routine or creative way?

• **Impact:** Do pages and packages appropriately capture the importance of the news? How does the newspaper react to the news?

• **Detail:** Does the newspaper pay attention to detail in the execution of reporting, writing, copyediting, design, typography and the rest of the storytelling elements?

• **Use of resources:** How does the newspaper use its resources — staff, newshole, time, etc.?

• **Sense of community:** Do the content and design reflect and, or capture the character of the community?

¿Y qué aprendimos?

Luego de dos días y 291 periódicos, los jueces se sentaron alrededor de mesas manchadas de tinta para discutir lo que habían visto y por qué 14 periódicos fueron nombrados los Periódicos Mejor Diseñados del Mundo en la categoría 1.

También notaron lo que no vieron en muchos de los concursantes de la categoría 1: falta de sorpresas, innovación, atención al detalle y redacción cuidadosa.

"Realmente estoy sorprendido de que todo sea tan igual," comentó uno de los jueces.

"Había muy poco que diferenciara a un periódico del otro. Muchos concursantes parecían lo mismo. No tenían sentido comunitario. Realmente no sé a quien le escribían."

Los concursantes ganadores, según los jueces, representaron el enfoque holístico al proceso de diseño. Los que tuvieron en cuenta la voz y la textura de un artículo dentro del contexto de los lectores al igual que la tipografía y el uso del color.

"Los ganadores presentaron un contenido realmente bueno. Si un concursante no valía la pena leerse, no podía votar por él," dijo uno de los jueces. "Demasiados periódicos presentaron mucho impacto, pero poca sustancia," respondió otro.

"Es verdad. Un excelente diseño sin contenido es como una paradoja," dijo un tercero.

Juzgue usted mismo.

Los jueces de la Categoría I, que son quienes concursan para los Periódicos Mejor Diseñados del Mundo, reconocen aquellas publicaciones que se destacan en la presentación de las noticias. Se pidió al jurado que evalúe el contenido general además del diseño del periódico — cuán bien los periódicos relatan las historias, comunican las noticias y transmiten las ideas a los lectores.

Los jueces establecieron los parámetros. Los siguientes elementos fueron incluidos en un formulario que los jueces podían usar a su discreción.

• **Contenido:** ¿Cómo se presentan las historias? ¿Los titulares son informativos? ¿Las fotografías son informativas? ¿Los gráficos son explicativos?

• **Utilidad:** ¿La información presentada es valiosa para el lector? ¿El periódico está lleno de material que atrapa al lector? ¿Es este un periódico que constituye, o debería hacerlo, parte de la rutina diaria del lector?

• **Estructura y organización:** ¿Las páginas invitan a los lectores a leer? ¿El diseño guía al lector a través de la página? ¿El periódico cuenta con un buen índice o indicaciones? ¿Es fácil de seguir y usar?

• **Relato de las historias:** ¿El periódico utiliza todos los elementos que integran el relato de historias — narrativa, texto, fotografías y gráficos- para contar las historias?

• **Claridad:** ¿La información es presentada de manera clara y simple? ¿Es fácil de acceder y de comprender?

• **Creatividad:** ¿El periódico encara la selección de sus historias, la presentación y el diseño de manera rutinaria o creativa

• **Impacto:** ¿Las páginas y los paquetes capturan de manera adecuada la importancia de las noticias? ¿De qué modo el diario reacciona a las noticias?

• **Detalle:** ¿El periódico es detallista en la ejecución de la nota, la redacción, la corrección, el diseño, la tipografía y el resto de los elementos que hacen a un artículo?

• **Uso de recursos:** ¿De qué modo el periódico usa sus recursos: personal, fuente de noticias, tiempo, etc.?

• **Sentido de comunidad:** ¿El contenido y el diseño reflejan y/o capturan el perfil de la comunidad?

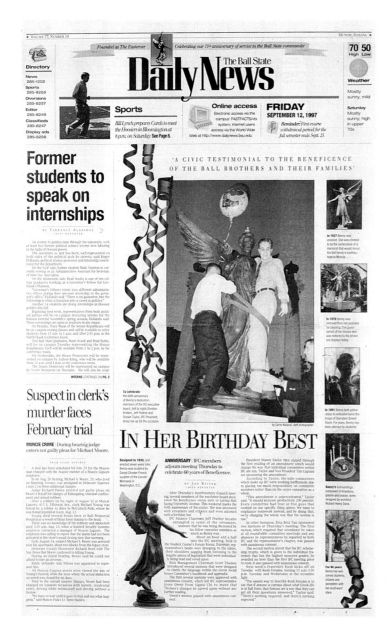

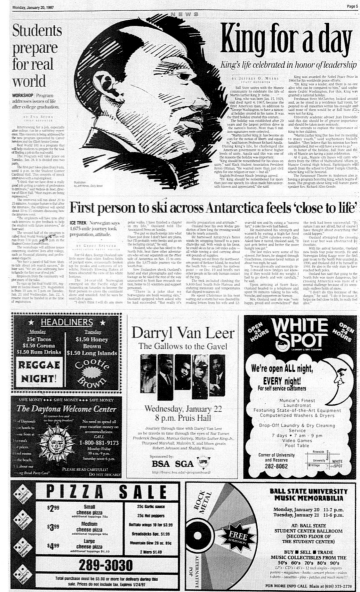

The Ball State Daily News
Muncie, IN

"This is a controlled, clean newspaper that hits the market perfectly. There is a real clarity of content here that was missing in many of the papers that didn't make it to the table. Professionals could learn a few things from this newspaper. It is very polished. The staff pays a lot of attention to the little things that really set it apart from the rest. The News has wonderful finishing touches to its pages. The typography is very good. This is a very nice piece of work."

The Ball State Daily News
Muncie, IN

"Éste es un periódico controlado, límpido que llega al mercado perfectamente. Posee una perfecta claridad de contenido ausente en la mayoría de los periódicos que no llegaron a calificar. Los profesionales podrían aprender unas cuantas cosas de este periódico. Es muy pulido. El plantel de periodistas dedica gran atención a ciertos detalles que realmente lo distinguen del resto. Sus páginas tienen fabulosos detalles de terminación. La tipografía es muy buena. Es una gran obra."

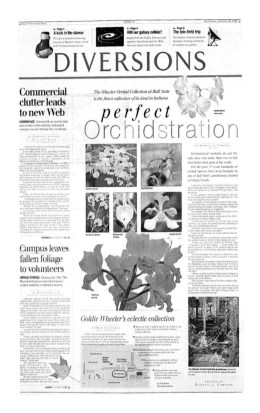

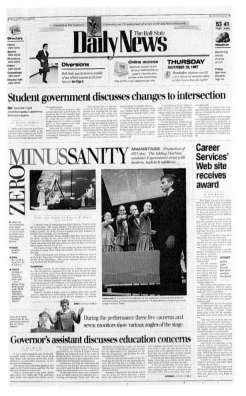

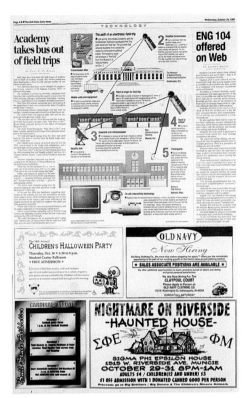

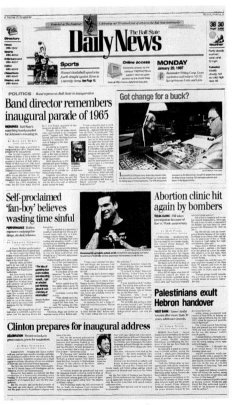

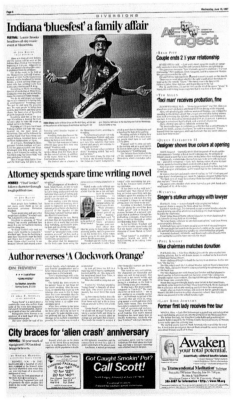

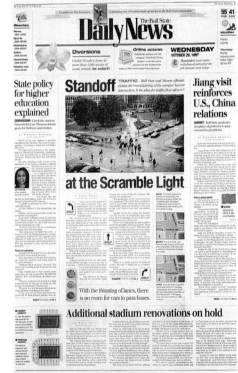

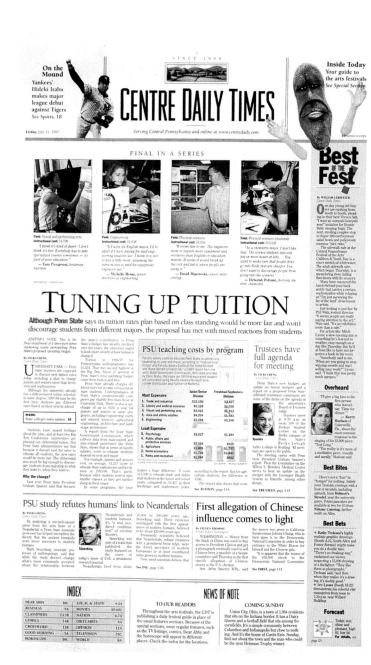

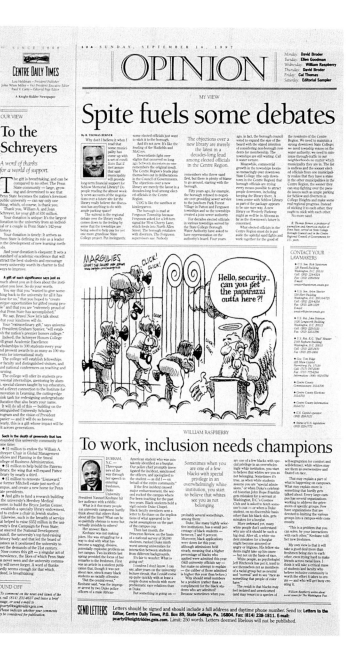

Centre Daily Times
State College, PA

"This is a well-crafted newspaper that is not afraid to take some risks. It is well organized, but not overly formatted. The staff is willing to be flexible to adapt its design to the news of the day and not try to force things into a pre-determined mold. The paper has a sense of flair about it using all of its resources to tell its stories. The paper is very well layered and has some very good headlines throughout. It has a refined look about it. Its typography is elegant. The entire package gives one a sense of who its readers are."

Centre Daily Times
State College, PA

"Éste es un periódico bien realizado que no teme asumir ciertos riesgos. Está bien organizado, pero no tiene demasiado formato. El plantel está dispuesto a ser flexible y adaptar su diseño a las noticias del día sin tratar de forzar las cosas en un molde predeterminado. El periódico tiene la sagacidad de aprovechar todos sus recursos para contar las historias. Está muy bien diagramado y cuenta con algunos titulares muy buenos. Tiene un aspecto refinado. La tipografía es elegante. Se puede saber claramente quiénes son sus lectores."

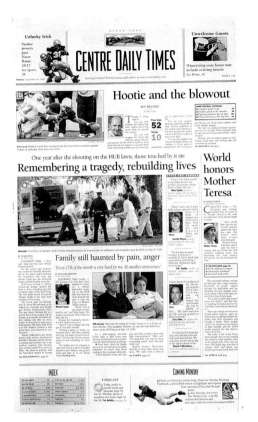

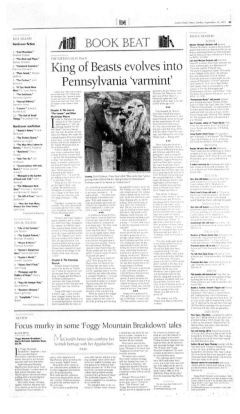

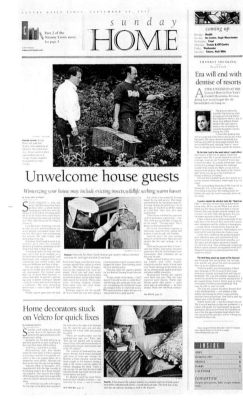

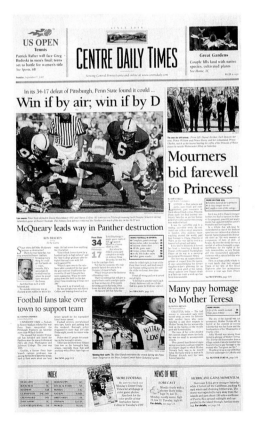

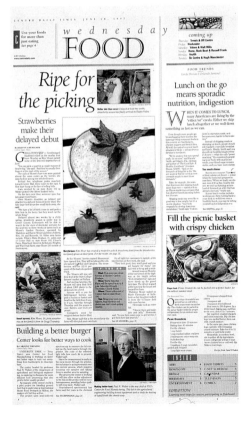

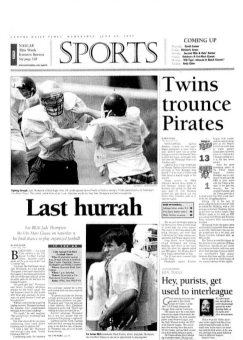

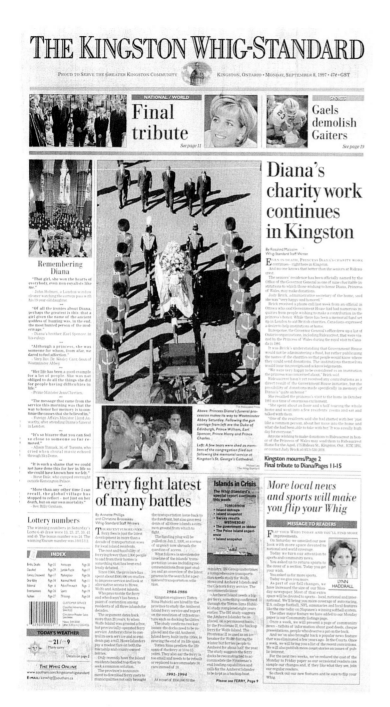

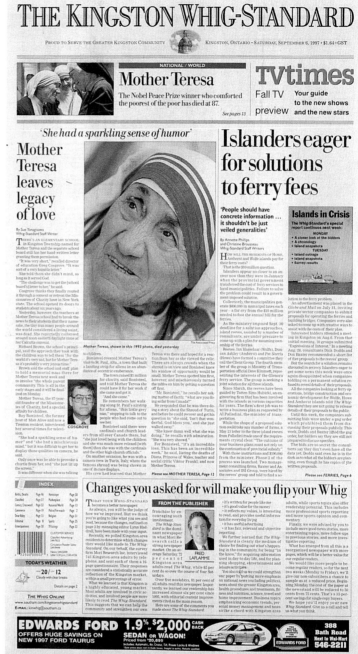

The Kingston Whig-Standard
Kingston, Canada

"This is a newspaper that has listened and responded to its readers. It is not afraid to have a dialog with the readers on the front page. The design is extremely consistent from page to page. The paper has a restrained, clean design that has a pleasant, organized feel about it. Nothing is left half-done inside this newspaper. It is sign posted very well to make it easy to navigate. The writing is well done. This is nicely done."

The Kingston Whig-Standard
Kingston, Canada

"Éste es un periódico que ha sabido escuchar y responder a sus lectores. No teme dialogar con los lectores en la primera plana. El diseño es extremadamente uniforme de una página a la otra. Su diseño es recatado y limpio, y da una agradable sensación de orden. En este periódico nada está hecho a medias. Cuenta con muy buenas indicaciones que lo hacen sumamente fácil de hojear. Está bien escrito. Un trabajo bien realizado."

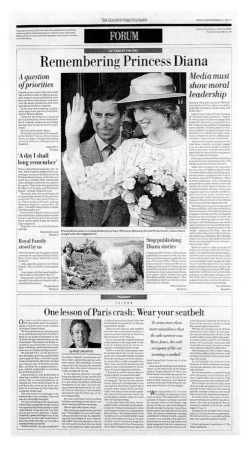

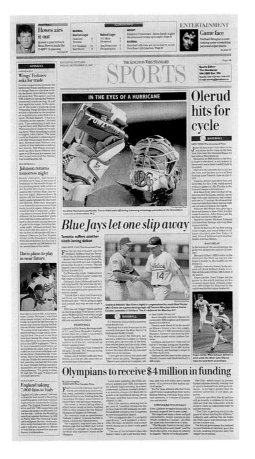

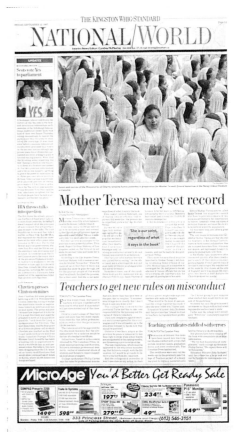

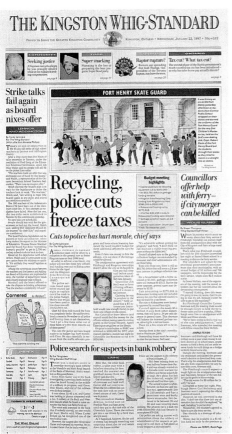

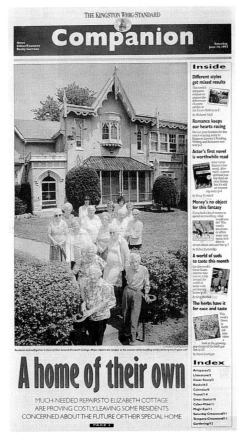

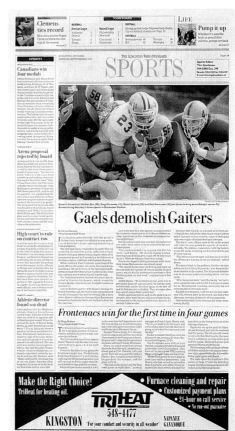

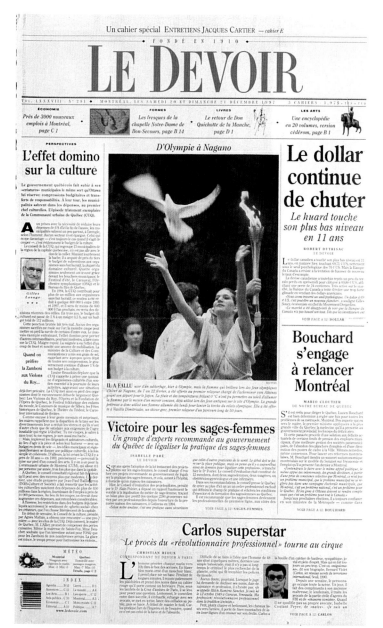

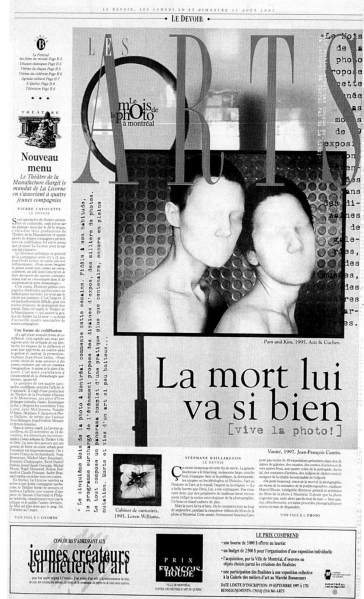

Le Devoir
Montreal, Canada

"This is a stunning piece of work. It's another paper that really hits its target audience. It is not afraid to speak directly to its readership. The paper has a lot of type, but it is very well organized. Its design is simplicity itself with a wonderful mix of elegant typography, nice use of photography and simple, but effective, color. The paper has a true sense of sophistication in its presentation. Nicely done."

Le Devoir
Montreal, Canada

"Un trabajo asombroso. Éste es otro periódico que realmente llega a la audiencia a la que se dirige. No teme hablar directamente con los lectores. Es un poco verboso, pero muy bien organizado. El diseño es la simplicidad misma con una maravillosa mezcla de tipografía elegante, buen uso de la fotografía y una aplicación simple pero efectiva del color. El periódico es verdaderamente sofisticado en cuanto a su presentación. Muy bien hecho."

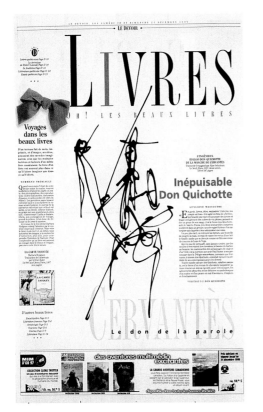

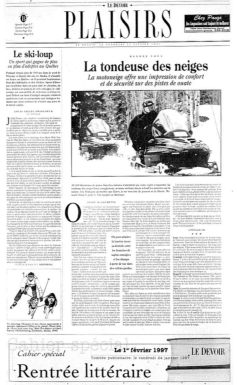

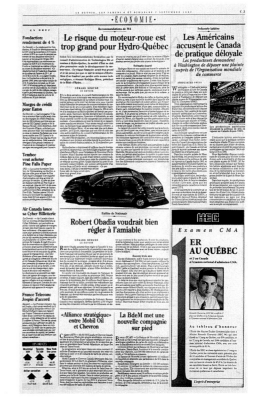

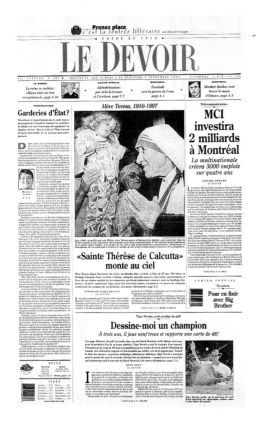

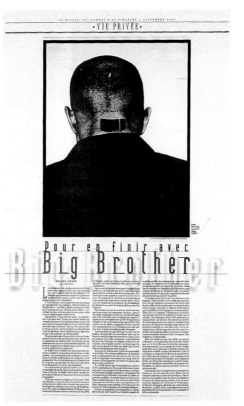

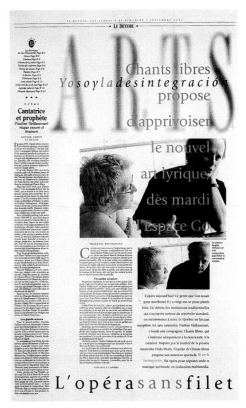

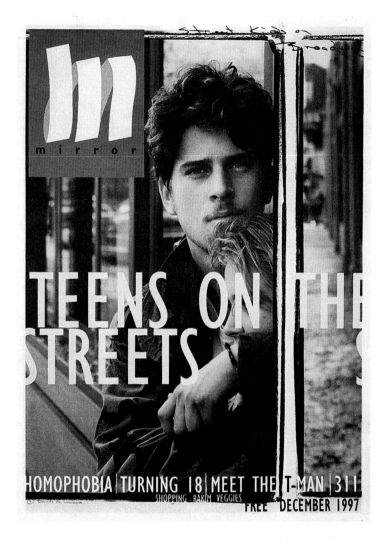

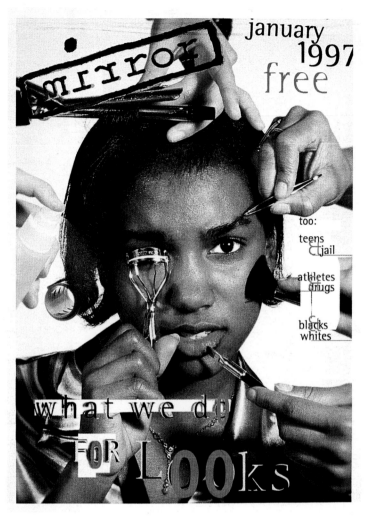

mirror
Seattle, WA

"This newspaper has a real edge to it. It stood out from all the others as trying to do something different to reach the target audience. The paper is packed with energy and lots of substance. The presentation is spirited and 'intentionally studiously un-slick.' The staff is willing to take some major risks with its packaging and seems to succeed more often than it fails. This is the most intriguing product we have seen yet."

mirror
Seattle, WA

"Éste periódico es un verdadero vanguardista. Se destaca de todos los demás por tratar de hacer algo diferente para llegar a la audiencia a la que se dirige. El periódico está cargado de energía y pleno de contenido. La presentación tiene personalidad y esta intencional y estudiosamente poco adornada. El plantel está dispuesto a correr ciertos riesgos en cuanto a la presentación y parece tener más éxitos que fracasos. Es el producto más intrigante que hemos visto hasta ahora."

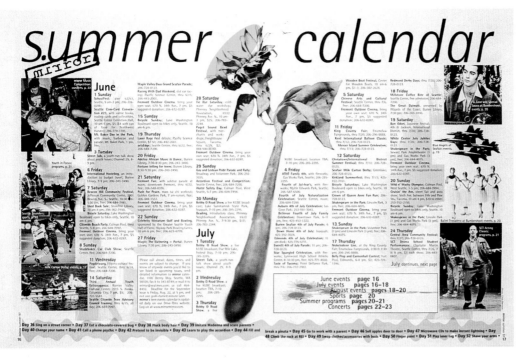

summer ✦ calendar

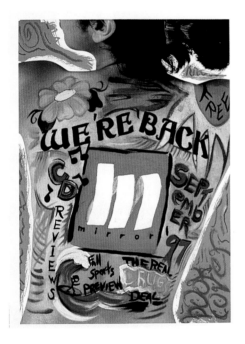

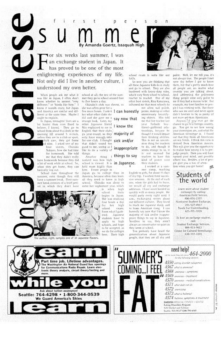

One Japanese summer

first person

By Amanda Goertz, Issaquah High

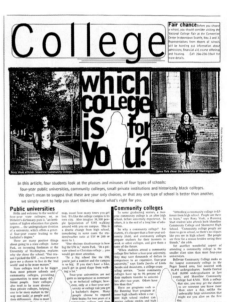

College

which college is for you?

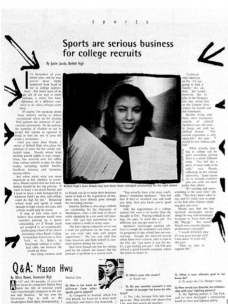

Sports are serious business for college recruits

By Justin Jacobs, Bothell High

Q&A: Mason Hwu

By Olivia Bowen, Shorecrest High

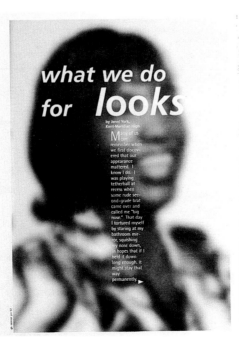

what we do for looks

by Jenni York, Kent-Meridian High

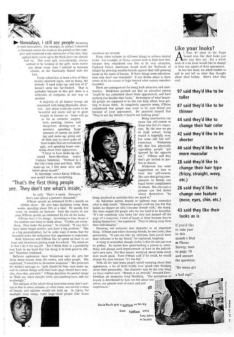

Like your looks?

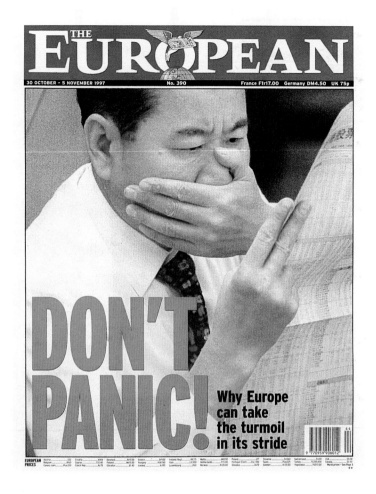

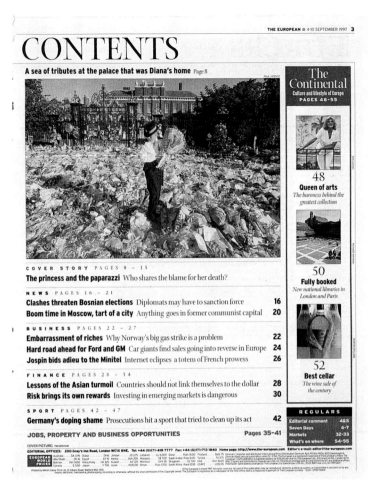

The European
London, England

"This newspaper feels like a paper that knows what it is and who its readers are. It has an identity, a personality and works to play it up. The paper covers all of the bases. It is packed with information presented in a very orderly fashion. The design is flexible, but is also lively, aggressive and energized. The typography has a sense of scale about it. The paper's use of color is very simple, but effective. This paper is really cool."

The European
London, England

"Este periódico da la sensación de saber quién es y quiénes son sus lectores. Tiene su propia identidad y personalidad y se esmera en destacarla. El periódico cubre todas sus bases. Pleno de información presentada de manera muy ordenada. El diseño es muy flexible, pero a la vez es vivaz, agresivo y enérgico. La tipografía tiene sentido de la proporción. El uso del color de este diario es muy simple pero efectivo. Es un periódico de onda."

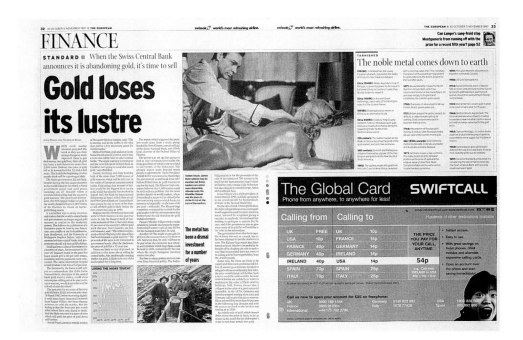

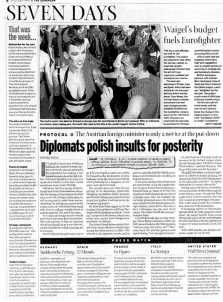

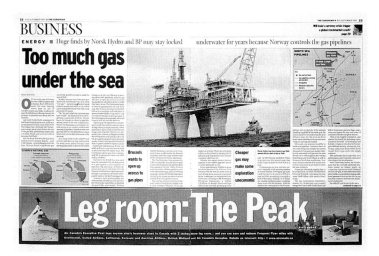

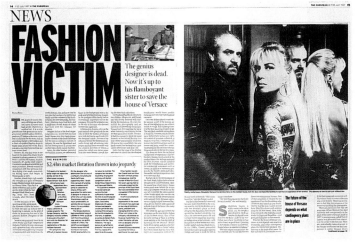

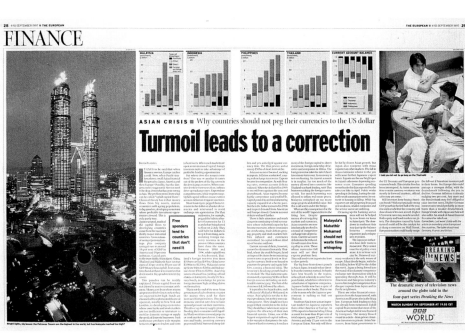

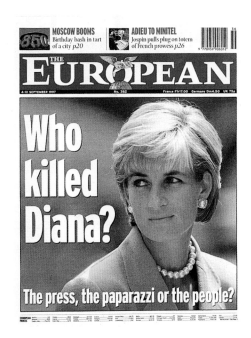

MAXIMUM SPORTS
TUCKER ENTEND GARDER
SA PLACE C 1

DIMANCHE MAGAZINE
PLUS EXOTIQUES
QUE JAMAIS B 1

LE QUOTIDIEN DE LA CAPITALE

LE SOLEIL

QUÉBEC, LE DIMANCHE 9 FÉVRIER 1997 · www.lesoleil.com

Une résurrection !

Un vrai défilé tout en couleurs qui a ravi la foule

LISE LACHANCE
Le Soleil

■ CHARLESBOURG — Une résurrection? Voilà le phénomène que 175 000 Québécois et Charlesbourgeois ont pu constater, hier soir, lorsque le défilé du carnaval leur en a mis plein les yeux avec sa quinzaine de chars allégoriques dont huit conçus par le dessinateur-humoriste Serge Gaboury. Quel contraste avec les quatre chars qui constituaient en tout et pour tout le défilé de l'an dernier dans la Haute-Ville, un défilé qui brillait d'ailleurs par son absence dans Charlesbourg!

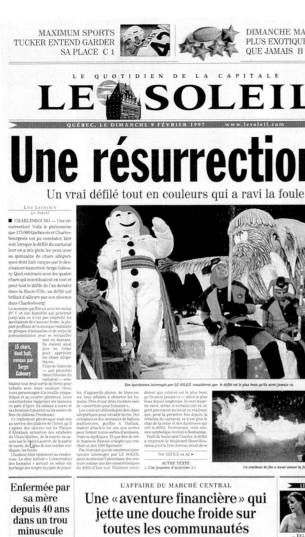

Des spectateurs interrogés par LE SOLEIL considèrent que le défilé est le plus beau qu'ils n'ont jamais vu.

Un cracheur de feu a aussi amusé la foule.

Voir DÉFILÉ en A2 ►

AUTRE TEXTE
● Une journée d'activités A 3

Enfermée par sa mère depuis 40 ans dans un trou minuscule

L'AFFAIRE DU MARCHÉ CENTRAL
Une « aventure financière » qui jette une douche froide sur toutes les communautés

DERNIER DE TROIS

QUÉBEC —

LE SECRET DES SOEURS DU BON-PASTEUR

Voir ENFERMÉE en A2 ►

Voir DOUCHE en A2 ►

LES ARTS

« Ridicule » en tête

« Ridicule » et « Microcosmos » en tête du palmarès des Césars 97.

Page A 11

LA MÉTÉO

Maximum -8, Minimum -23

A 10 · LE SOLEIL · LE VENDREDI 12 SEPTEMBRE 1997

LE MONDE

PROCHE-ORIENT

« La route est longue »

Madeleine Albright ne sait trop comment sauver le processus de paix du désastre

■ JÉRUSALEM (AP et AFP) — La « route » est encore longue » pour relancer le processus de paix, a reconnu hier le secrétaire d'État américain Madeleine Albright. Rencontrant Yasser Arafat à Ramallah, elle a une nouvelle fois exhorté à mener la guerre contre le terrorisme, tout en demandant aux Israéliens de faire une « pause » dans leur politique de colonisation.

BON CONTACT

Mme Albright demande l'arrêt de la colonisation juive

UN PAVÉ DANS LA MARE

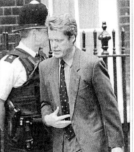

Des moines bouddhistes attendent leur tour à l'extérieur de l'église Saint Thomas, à Calcutta, pour rendre un dernier hommage à Mère Teresa, décédée d'une crise cardiaque vendredi dernier. Jusqu'ici, on estime qu'un demi-million de personnes ont défilé devant la dépouille de la sœur.

Mère Teresa reçoit l'hommage de la nation indienne

CALCUTTA (AFP) — Alors que l'Inde s'apprête à offrir des funérailles nationales à Mère Teresa, demain, l'hommage officiel de la nation a commencé. La dépouille mortelle de la fondatrice des Missionnaires de la Charité a été enveloppée hier dans le drapeau indien, au cours d'une cérémonie à la fois religieuse et militaire.

La NASA place une sonde en orbite autour de Mars

WASHINGTON (AFP) — La sonde Mars Global Surveyor (MGS) a été placée hier en orbite autour de la planète rouge « après l'allumage de son moteur principal, ont annoncé les responsables de la NASA au Jet Propulsion Laboratory de Pasadena (Californie).

Mars Global Surveyor est chargé de cartographier la planète rouge.

Diana est toujours aussi pleurée
Londres pourrait décréter un jour de congé annuel

LONDRES (AFP) —

28 JOURS DE PRISON

EN BREF

MEXIQUE

La Chambre en folie

CHILI
Bon anniversaire!

JAPON
Nomination choc

Le Soleil
Quebec, Canada

"This really knocks us out. It is intriguing how well this paper comes together. The paper is very well packaged, yet it is not a formula design. This is a paper that lives and changes every day. Everything is crisp. The design is vibrant and sophisticated in the way it uses color and typography. One comes away with a real sense of community here that was missing in some of the other entries. It is really beautiful."

Le Soleil
Quebec, Canada

"Éste verdaderamente nos dejó estupefactos. Es intrigante ver cómo está organizado este periódico. El diario está bien presentado, sin embargo no tiene un diseño preestablecido. Está vivo y cambia cada día. Todo es impecable. El diseño es vibrante y sofisticado en la manera en que utiliza el color y la tipografía. Posee un sentido de comunidad que faltó en algunos de los otros concursantes. Realmente hermoso."

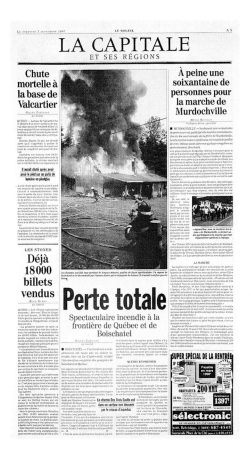

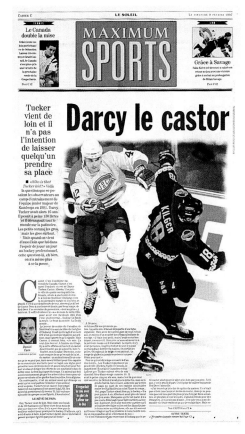

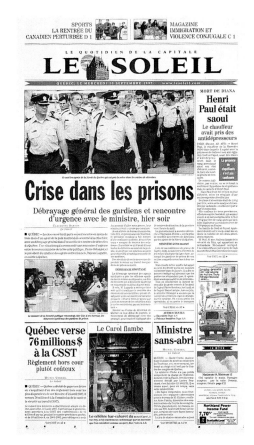

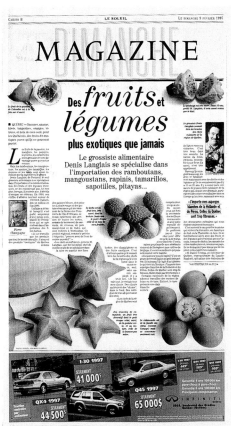

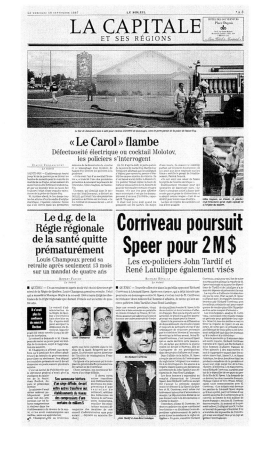

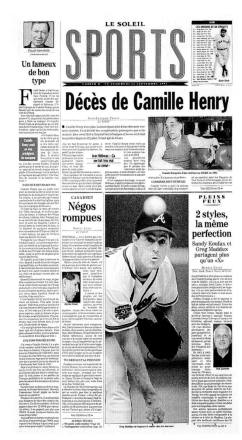

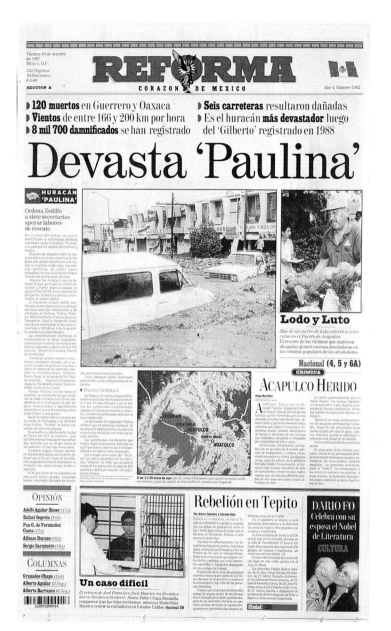

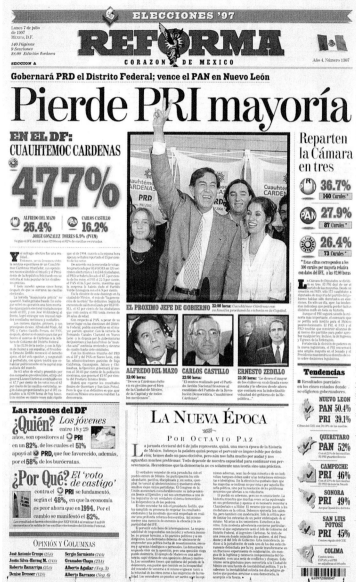

Reforma

México City, México

"There is a sense of authority mixed with excitement in this paper. It is a reflection of the Mexican way of life. It has the perfect mix of long and short stories. There is something for everyone and design has a lot of punch. The total package is sophisticated, dynamic, very easy to use and attractively put together. The paper is lively, colorful and has a wonderful sense of contrast about it. The paper is put together very well."

Reforma

México City, México

"Existe un sentido de autoridad y emoción a la vez en este periódico. Es un reflejo del estilo de vida mexicano. Tiene la mezcla perfecta de artículos largos y cortos. Hay algo para todos y el diseño tiene mucho empuje. La presentación en general es sofisticada, dinámica, muy fácil de usar y a la vez atractiva. Es muy viva, colorida y posee un maravilloso sentido de los contrastes. Es un periódico muy bien logrado."

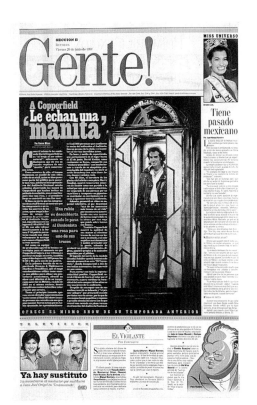

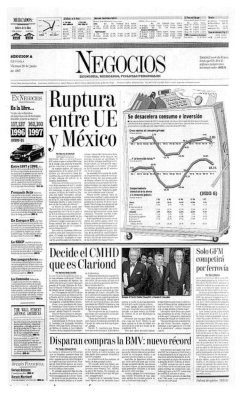

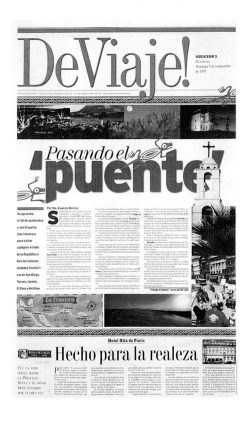

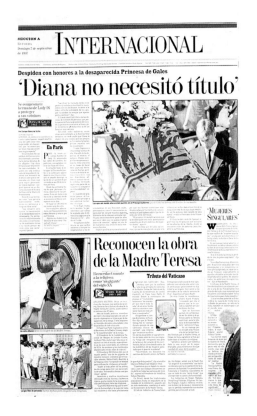

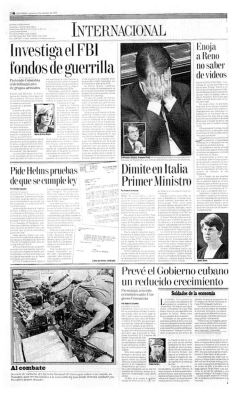

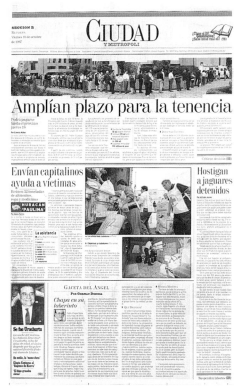

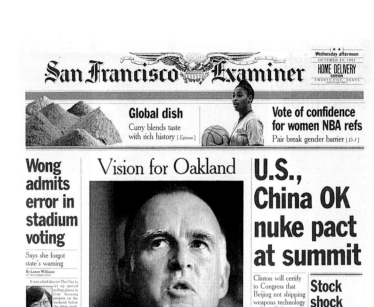

San Francisco Examiner
San Francisco, CA

"This is a very lively paper that is full of surprises. The staff has a real handle on who it is writing for. It screams, 'BUY ME!' 'READ ME!' It simply demands to be read. Its design is distinctive. The paper is very individualistic and unlike anything else in the group. It had the best Diana coverage in the competition. It is muscle in print; a tabloid done in broadsheet. The typography is fantastic. The paper is great. It is amazing how this is done."

San Francisco Examiner
San Francisco, CA

"Este es un periódico sumamente vivaz y lleno de sorpresas. Realmente sabe para quiénes escriben. A todas luces grita ¡CÓMPRAME! ¡LÉEME! Simplemente exige ser leído. Un diseño singular. Un periódico muy individualista y diferente de todos los demás del grupo. Ofreció la mejor cobertura de la Princesa Diana de todo el certamen. Es un músculo impreso, un tabloide en hoja sábana. La tipografía es fantástica. El periódico es excelente. Asombroso cómo está realizado."

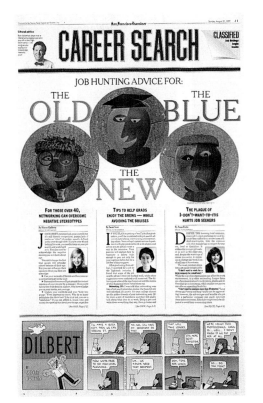

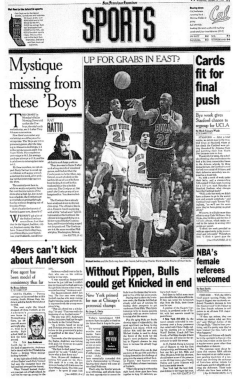

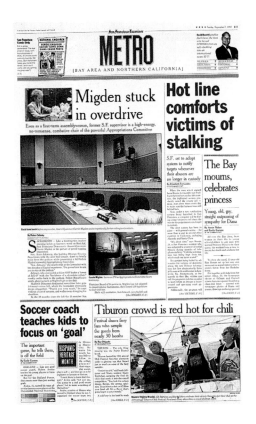

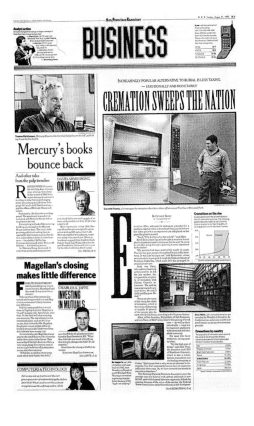

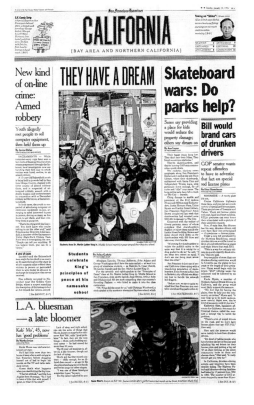

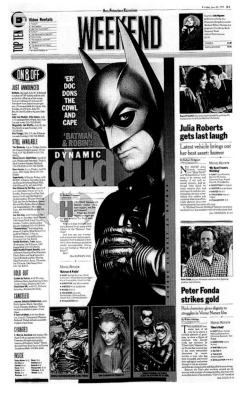

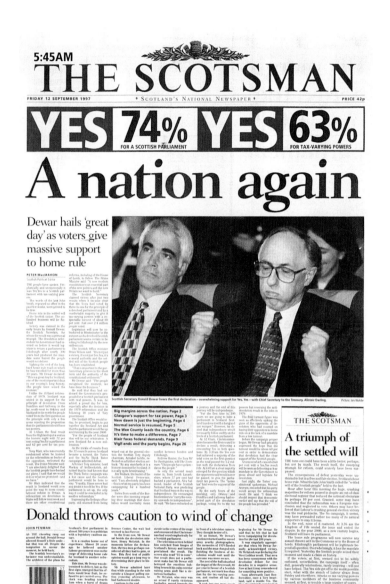

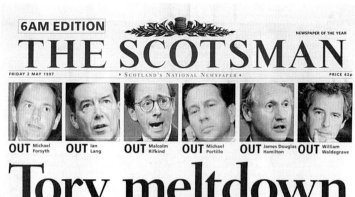

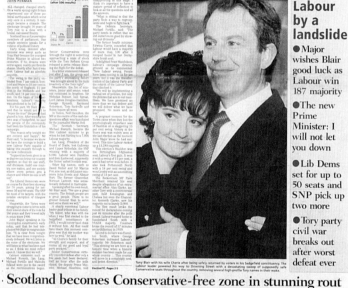

The Scotsman
Edinburgh, Scotland

"This is a newspaper that stood well above the rest. It has a sense of place about it. The paper seems to do everything well. The writing is wonderful. There is a surprise everywhere you look. The paper is consistent from beginning to end. The staff allows the design to flow with the news of the day. The staff pays attention to the details that kept many of the papers from making the grade. The inside pages are well thought out. Every page is packed with information with lots of entry points for the reader. The headlines are wonderful. Its typography is fantastic and the photography is well done. The only rule at this newspaper appears to be 'you can't be boring.'"

The Scotsman
Edinburgh, Scotland

"Este periódico se destacó muy por encima de los demás. Tiene un sentido de ubicación. Parece hacer todo bien. La redacción es maravillosa. Hay sorpresas por donde uno mire. Es uniforme de principio a fin. Permiten que el diseño fluya según las noticias del día. Prestan atención a aquellos detalles que por ignorarlos muchos periódicos no fueron calificados. Las páginas interiores están bien calculadas. Cada página está llena de información con muchos puntos de inicio para el lector. Los titulares son maravillosos. La tipografía es fantástica y la fotografía es correcta. La única regla para este periódico es 'usted no puede aburrirse.'"

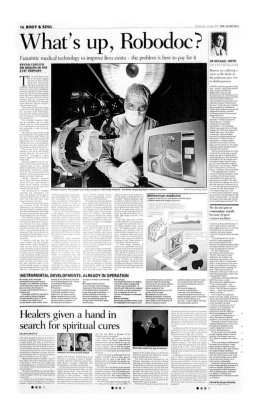

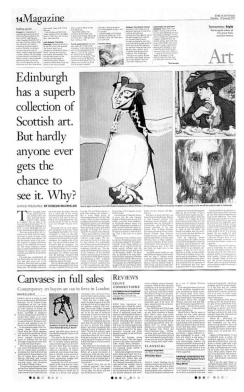

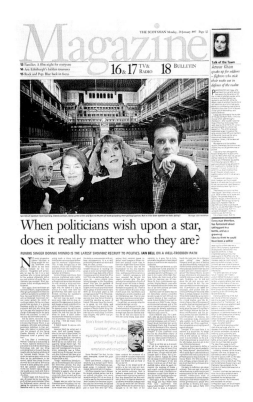

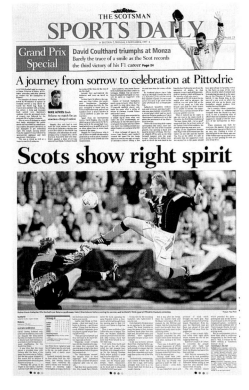

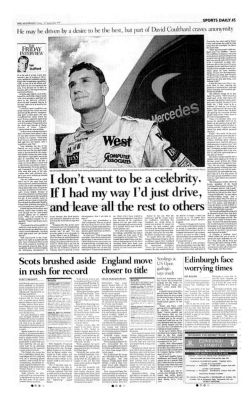

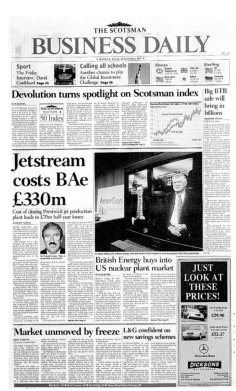

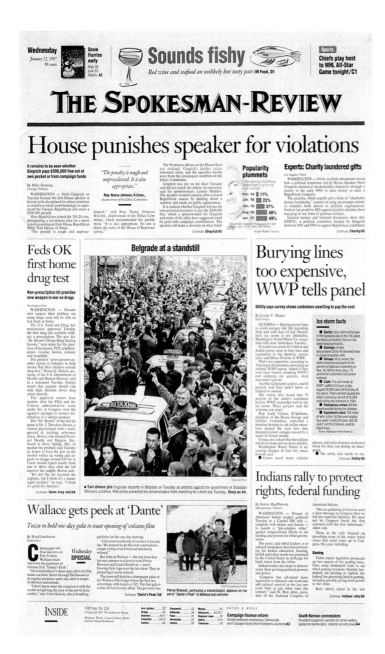

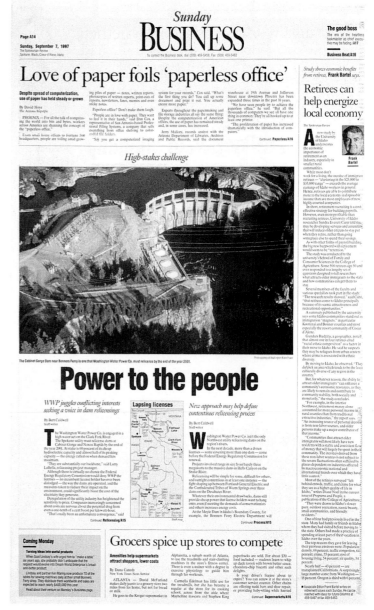

The Spokesman-Review
Spokane, WA

"This paper reflects its region and community perfectly. It is a very reader-oriented paper. It's a delightful newspaper that hits the audience where it lives. It is not afraid to openly discuss issues with its readers explaining why things are done the way they are. This is a paper that has fun, something we saw too little of in the entries. There is a tremendous amount of energy with lots going on visually in this paper. There are plenty of entry points on every page. The design is controlled and makes good use of its photography. The whole package leaves one with a comfortable feeling. It is energetic without being self indulgent."

The Spokesman-Review
Spokane, WA

"Este periódico refleja a su región y a su comunidad a la perfección. Es un periódico muy orientado hacia el lector. Es un diario encantador que apunta directamente a la audiencia del lugar. No teme discutir abiertamente los temas con sus lectores explicando por qué las cosas son como son. Éste es un periódico divertido, algo de lo que se vio muy poco entre los concursantes. Hay una tremenda cantidad de energía con mucho a su favor a nivel visual. Muchos puntos de inicio en cada página. El diseño es controlado y aprovecha bien la fotografía. La presentación total deja una sensación muy agradable. Es enérgica sin ser autoindulgente."

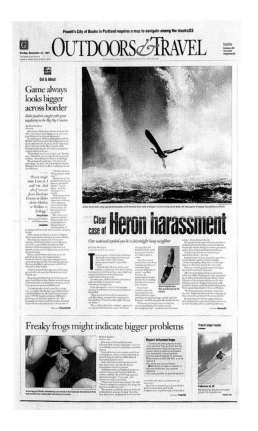

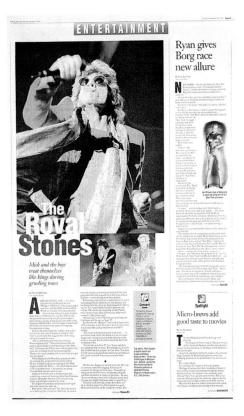

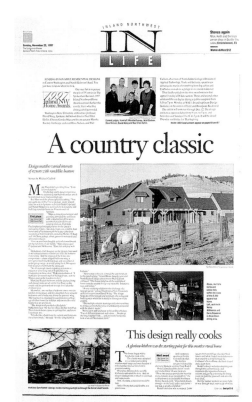

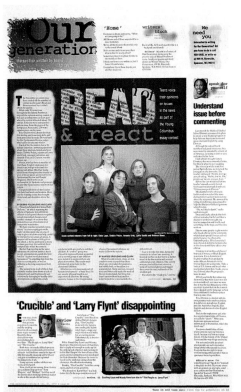

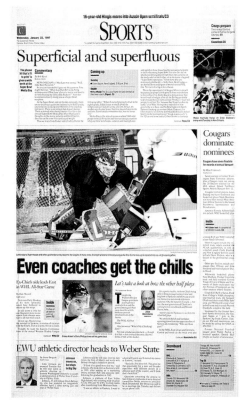

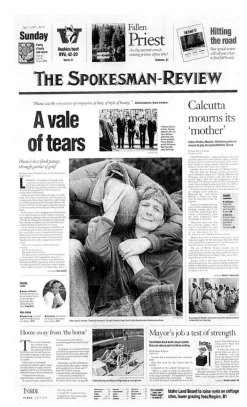

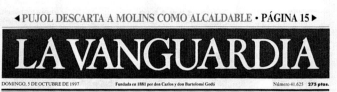

◄ PUJOL DESCARTA A MOLINS COMO ALCALDABLE · PÁGINA 15 ►

LA VANGUARDIA

DOMINGO, 5 DE OCTUBRE DE 1997   Fundada en 1881 por don Carlos y don Bartolomé Godó   Número 41.625   275 ptas.

BODA DE LA INFANTA CRISTINA E IÑAKI URDANGARIN

Princesa de Barcelona

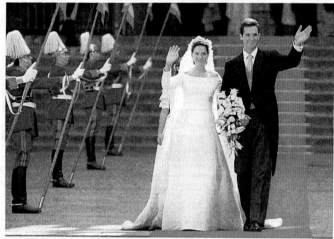

La infanta Cristina de Borbón y Grecia, segunda hija de los reyes de España, e Iñaki Urdangarin Liebaert corresponden a las aclamaciones de los barceloneses a la salida de la catedral.

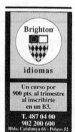

Brighton

idiomas

Un curso por
900 pts. al trimestre
al inscribirte
en un B3.

T. 487 04 00
902 200 600
Rbla. Catalunya 66 · Pelayo 52

El gran álbum
de la boda

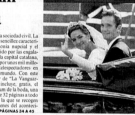

BARCELONA. – Más de doscientos mil barceloneses expresaron con espontaneidad su simpatía a la infanta Cristina –también Princesa de Barcelona, un reconocimiento popular compartido ayer con la patrona de la ciudad en la basílica de la Mercè– y a Iñaki Urdangarin después de contraer matrimonio en la catedral. Asistieron a la boda unos 1.500 invitados, entre miembros de las casas reales, representantes de las instituciones del Estado y de la sociedad civil. La solemnidad y la sencillez caracterizaron la ceremonia nupcial y el posterior recorrido por las engalanadas calles de la capital catalana, que fue seguido por unos mil millones de telespectadores en todo el mundo. Con este ejemplar de "La Vanguardia" se incluye, gratis, el gran álbum de la boda, una revista de 32 páginas a todo color en la que se recogen las imágenes del acontecimiento. **PÁGINAS 34 A 45**

LUNES, 1 SEPTIEMBRE 1997   LA VANGUARDIA SUPLEMENTO   1

Deportes

FÚTBOL
Brillante victoria del
Espanyol en San Mamés
4

FÚTBOL: El Mallorca se impone al Valencia en un bronco partido	7
FÚTBOL: Un suplente salva de la derrota al Inter de Ronaldo	7
BALONCESTO: El TDK Manresa se hace con la Lliga Catalana	8
AUTOMOVILISMO: Sainz abandonó en Finlandia a tres tramos del final	9

MOTOCICLISMO
Crivillé logra la cuarta
plaza en su reaparición
8

El Barça sigue aferrado al Brasil

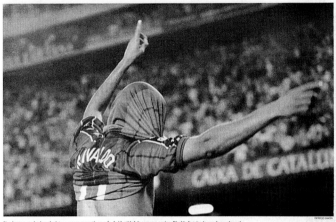

Una imagen que los barcelonistas esperan convertir en seña de identidad de su nuevo equipo; Rivaldo festejando uno de sus dos goles

BARCELONA, 3
REAL SOCIEDAD, 0

Goles: Final primera parte 1-0
1-0. Rivaldo (26 m.)
2-0. Giovanni (56 m.)
3-0. Rivaldo (61 m.)
Árbitro: Díaz Vega (Asturiano)
Tarjetas: Amarillas a De la Peña, De Pedro, Loren, Rivaldo, Kahhauer y Amor. No hubo rojas.
Campo: Camp Nou, 10.000 espectadores (?) V(t.)
Alineaciones:
BARCELONA: Hesp, Reiziger (Ferrer, 61 m.), Celades, Nadal, Luis Enrique, De la Peña, Serpi, Figo, Giovanni (Amor, 66 m.), Rivaldo y Anderson.
REAL SOCIEDAD: Alberto, López Rekarte, Loren, Pikabea (Mâd, 65 m.), Imanol, Gómez, De Pedro (Craioveanu, 65 m.), Imaz, Kahhauer, Idiakez y Rubén Vega.

ENRIC BAÑERES
Barcelona

N i en sueños podía imaginar Louis van Gaal un mejor comienzo de su equipo en la Liga: líder, dos puntos por encima del segundo, Atlético y Deport...a tres del Va-

LA FIGURA

Rivaldo comienza
a ser amortizado

■ Rivaldo había brillado en la segunda parte del partido de Supercopa ante el Madrid en el Camp Nou, pero reservó para ayer su mejor actuación como azulgrana. Bajó muchas veces a recibir el balón en su propio campo, no renunció a colaborar en tareas defensivas y se adueñó por completo de la banda izquierda. Trabajó sin arrugarse frente a la dureza con que se emplearon los defensas de la Real, salvo el escollo de un gran marcador, como Imanol, y combinó perfectamente tanto con Giovanni como con Iván de la Peña. Encima abrió pasillos para las subidas de un portentoso Serpi y firmó dos estupendos goles. Tiene que amortizar una fuerte inversión y llenar el inmenso vacío dejado por su precursor. Ayer, cumplió sobradamente con ambos compromisos.

lencia de Valdano y sólo inquietado en su jerárquica situación por su sorprendente Espanyol de Camacho, que hizo polvo al Athlétic en la catedral de San Mamés. Encima, un Camp Nou indulgente e ilusionado arropó en todo momento a su equipo, olvidó hacía otro lado cuando se cometía algún tropezón y descubrió lleno de gozo que la inversión realizada para tapar la profunda brecha dejada por la marcha de Ronaldo ha empezado a amortizarse. Tres goles brasileños –dos de Rivaldo y otro de Giovanni– y una satisfactoria actuación de De la Peña y Celades fueron detalles suficientes para que la hinchada azulgrana regresara a casa con la sensación de que la temporada promete mucho más de lo que dio el si la pretemporada.

Como no hay mal que por bien no venga, el Barça aprovechó la ausencia de Guardiola para jugar el mejor partido en lo que va de ejercicio. La baja del capitán y jugador mejor remunerado de la plantilla abrió la puerta de la titularidad a De la Peña o Celades. El otro sacrificado fue Amor. Pese a que el equipo tardó en adquirir su velocidad de crucero y acabó bastante encogido todo el primer tiempo, la segunda mitad del Barça fue más que aceptable y augura veladas muy felices. A partir de

que Giovanni instaló el gol de la tranquilidad en el marcador, el Barça brindó a sus seguidores una última media hora relajada, en la que buscó el preciosismo y abrió numerosas vías de agua en la defensa de una Real que, todo hay que decirlo, jugaba para entonces mucho menos organizada de como lo había hecho en un principio.

Los primeros minutos del partido fueron muy irregulares. Van Gaal recuperó su esquema de 3-3-3-1, el que le permitió al equipo jugar los mejores minutos en el amistoso de Palma y ante el Madrid y el Sampdoria en el Camp Nou. Un esquema que luego, en busca de una mayor solidez defensiva, desechó en la vuelta de la Supercopa en el Bernabéu, con el resultado de todos conocido, y en el tedioso partido de Riga. En cierto modo, el de ayer ante la Real fue el partido en el que Van Gaal retomaba sus orígenes, salvo la frivolidad de situar a Celades como defensa libre, una posición inadecuada a sus condiciones, el equipo parecía mejor plantado y más coherente que en ocasiones anteriores. La defensa de tres (Reiziger en su puesto, Celades libre y Nadal en la izquierda), garantizaba la vigilancia

Continúa en la página siguiente

La Vanguardia
Barcelona, Spain

"This is a superbly handled paper on just about all levels. The paper is very well done. It has a personality, a character about it. It is very authoritative and very literate. The staff knows how to market the news to its community. The paper's design is very well crafted. It seemed more inviting and more transparent in its use of typography and transition devices than many of the other papers. The staff makes excellent use of photography and graphics. It is willing to take more risks than some of the other papers we saw because of the use of color. Regardless, the staff succeeds more often than it fails. This is an example of what a quality newspaper can be. It is a classic."

La Vanguardia
Barcelona, Spain

"Éste es un periódico manejado soberbiamente en todos los niveles. Muy bien realizado. Tiene personalidad propia. Muy culto y conocedor. El personal sabe cómo vender las noticias a su comunidad. El diseño está muy bien realizado. Parece más atractivo y transparente en su uso de la fotografía y los dispositivos de transición que muchos de los otros periódicos. Excelente uso de la fotografía y los gráficos. Decidido a correr más riesgos que algunos de los otros periódicos que vimos en vista del uso que hacen del color. A pesar de esto, son más las veces que les sale bien que las que no. Éste es un ejemplo de lo que puede ser un periódico de calidad. Es un clásico."

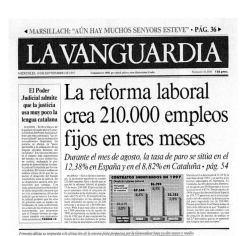
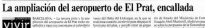

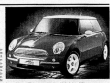
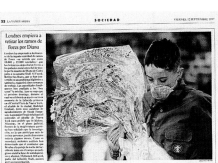
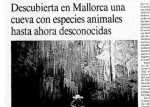
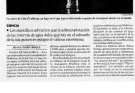
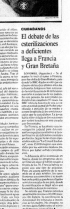
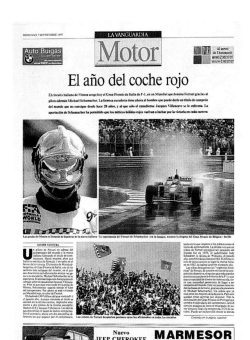
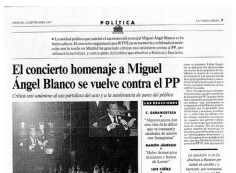

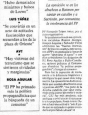
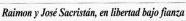
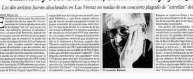
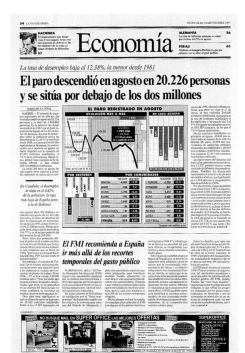
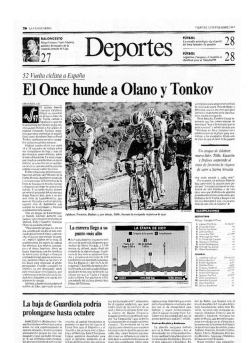

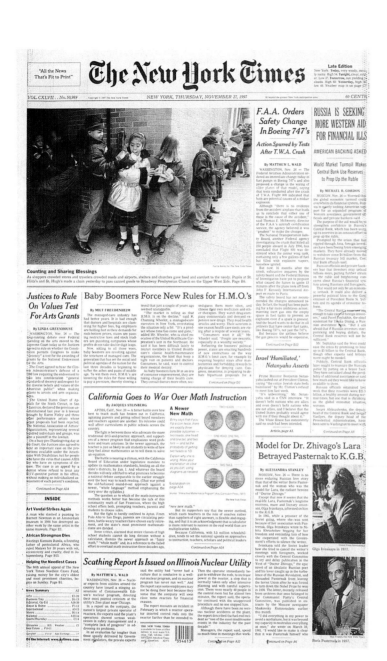

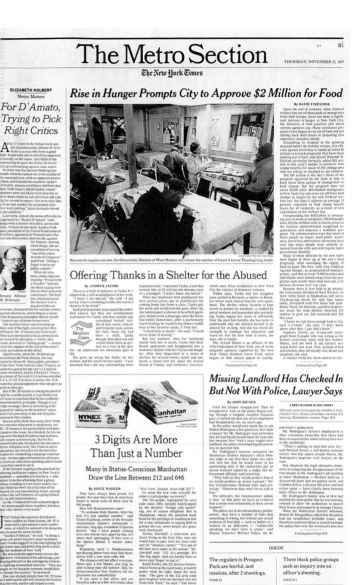

The New York Times

New York, NY

"We guess we expected this newspaper to be here in the end. This is an intelligent paper, with great writing that has shifted over the years to reflect its changing readership. It's got a feeling of credibility and weight about it. There is a lightness, a joy, a sense of fun about it. The paper is consistent from section to section. Half of the things we remember are the stories. There were some nice stories in here, very carefully packaged. It has managed its conversion to color very well. There have been some hiccups, but it worked out in the end."

The New York Times

New York, NY

"Supongo que esperábamos que este periódico llegaría a las finales. Es un periódico inteligente, con una redacción excelente que ha ido cambiando con los años para reflejar los cambios en sus lectores. Da una sensación de credibilidad y peso. Por otro lado es ligero, alegre y divertido. Es uniforme sección a sección. La mitad de lo que recordamos son los artículos. Había algunas buenas historias, muy bien armadas. Ha realizado muy bien su conversión al color. Han habido algunos tropiezos, pero finalmente funcionó."

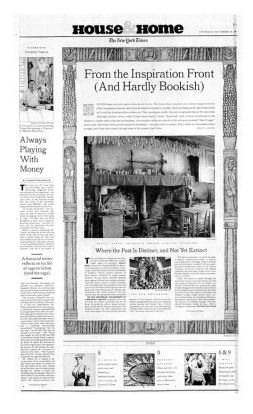

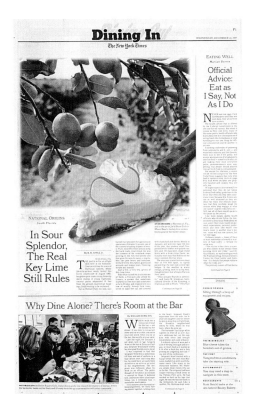

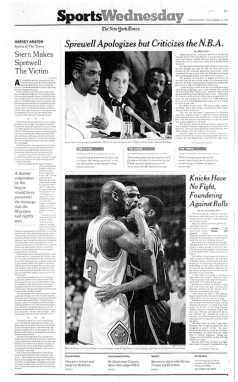

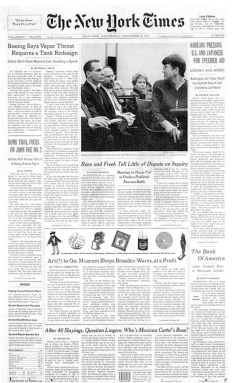

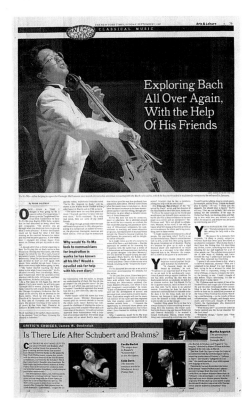

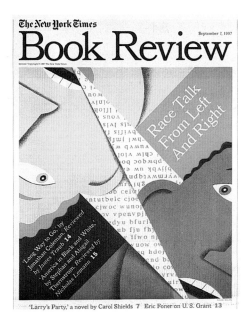

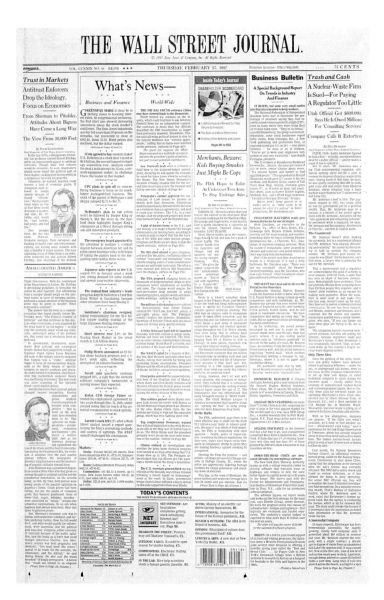

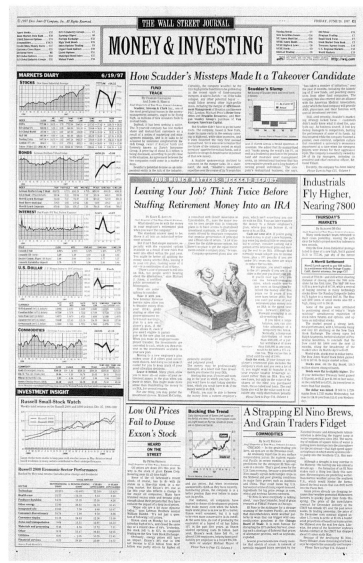

The Wall Street Journal
New York, NY

"This is a first-rate paper that knows its audience and delivers day after day. It is true to itself, while adapting to reflect the changing needs of its readers. The paper has the best news digest found anywhere. Its writing is superb. It provides a high story count without being ugly. The paper has a well organized, substantive and authoritative feel about it and still has fun with its coverage. It has fantastic special sections. It makes the design formula work for it and shows what one can do in black and white. The staff uses its creative resources for the reader. This is a great newspaper."

The Wall Street Journal
New York, NY

"Éste es un periódico de primera línea que conoce a su audiencia y cumple día a día. Es fiel a sí mismo, a la vez que se adapta para reflejar la cambiantes necesidades de sus lectores. Cuenta con el mejor compendio de noticias del mundo. Su redacción es magnífica. Ofrece un gran número de historias sin ser aburrido. Da una sensación de organización, sustancia y autoridad y aún se divierte con su cobertura. Tiene fantásticas secciones especiales. Hace que la fórmula de diseño se adapte y demuestra lo que se puede hacer en blanco y negro. Utilizan sus recursos creativos con miras al lector. Es un gran diario."

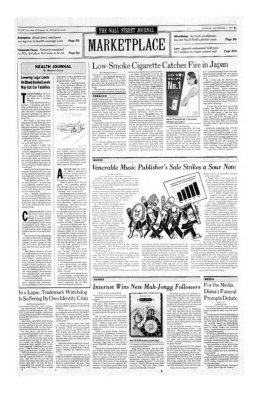

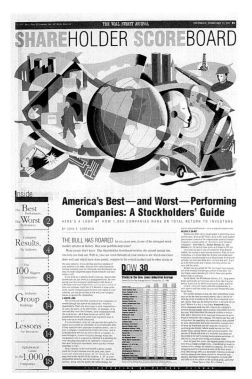

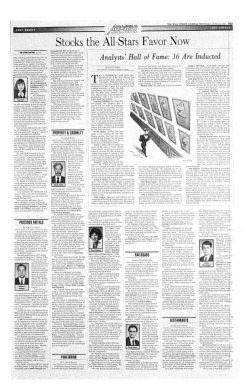

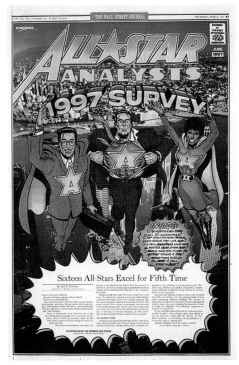

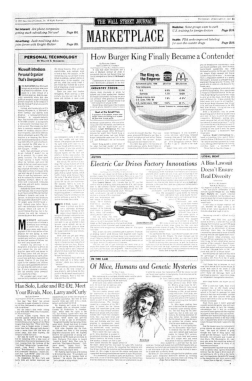

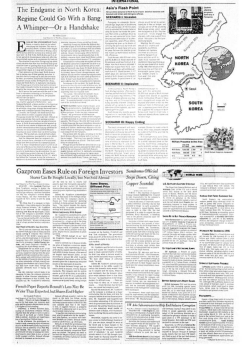

So, what lessons did we learn from the winners of the 19th Edition's World's Best-Designed Newspapers category?

1. Allow content to drive design: Structure and format are wonderful, but only so long as they allow the ability to react to the unexpected. The judges demanded flexibility, as much as innovation, in the winning designs. The winners selected made the tools of design — typography, illustration, infographics, photography, etc. — the most effective way to tell their stories based on the content.

2. Think like, not for, the reader: Superficial, institutional coverage presented without a sense of context was frowned upon. The winning papers dealt with relevant issues to the reader. The winners told the readers what they wanted to know, as well as what they needed to know. They worked to prioritize the material presented to the reader.

3. Reflect the community being served: The judges noted the lack of diversity in both the visuals and written content on the front pages of many of the papers in the competition. The winners were seen as inclusive of all demographic segments of their communities. "The world is far more diverse than the average white-male," one judge noted.

4. Develop a visual personality: The winners presented a sense of personality for the newspaper and the community. They noted, however, this did not begin or end with the inclusion of an icon of the community (building, animal, etc.) which was seen as a fad to be avoided. The judges decried the sameness that permeates North American newspapers. The winners were mirrors of their communities and not simply "recycled" copies of yesterday's editions.

5. Give the same care and attention to words as design: The judges found that headlines and cutlines in many of the entries were "dull, boring and lifeless," representing a hand-off effect where they became lost in the production process on the copydesk. Headlines and cutlines should say something and not be left to the end of the editing process.

6. Package information in a lively manner: The winning entries reflected the "urgency and vitality of daily life." They were the ones seen as willing to take risks with their design to communicate with their readers.

7. Keep it simple: Avoid the fads that interfere with the ability to communicate effectively with the reader. The judges suggested that working with every tool available (color, graphics, photographs, typography, etc.) did not require all of them to be used at once. Photography was seen as something of a lost art, overtaken by computer technology that masked the content of the original image.

8. Treat typography with respect: Remember the basics: Type is not, and never was, intended to be elastic.

9. Take care with the details: Remember that no matter how good the design, poor production values can destroy it.

10. Surprise the reader and have fun: Every day's paper should contain a surprise for the reader; something that should stop them and make them take notice. "We need to show the reader that we are enjoying our work," said one judge. "If we can do that, readers will enjoy spending time with the paper."

¿Qué lecciones hemos aprendido de la 19na Edición de la categoría Periódicos Mejor Diseñados del Mundo?

1. Permitir que el contenido guíe al diseño: La estructura y el formato son maravillosos, pero sólo en la medida en que permiten reaccionar ante lo inesperado. Los jueces exigieron flexibilidad, al igual que innovación, en los diseños ganadores. Demasiado formateadas, las soluciones estereotipadas no lograron captar la atención del jurado. Los ganadores seleccionados hicieron de las herramientas de diseño, tipografía, ilustración, infográficos, fotografía, etc., la manera más efectiva de contar sus historias basadas en el contenido.

2. Pensar como, no para, el lector: La cobertura superficial institucional presentada sin sentido de contexto fue vista con recelo. Los periódicos ganadores trataron los temas relevantes para el lector. Los ganadores contaron al ganador lo que ellos querían saber, así como lo que necesitaban saber. Trabajaron para poner prioridad en el material presentado al lector.

3. Reflejar la comunidad a la que se sirve: Los jueces notaron la falta de diversidad tanto en el contenido visual como escrito en las primeras planas de muchos periódicos del certamen. Los ganadores abarcaban todos los segmentos demográficos de las comunidades. "El mundo es mucho más diverso que el hombre blanco promedio," acotó uno de los jueces.

4. Desarrollar una personalidad visual: Los ganadores presentaron un sentido de personalidad del periódico y la comunidad. Los jueces desacreditaron la monotonía de los periódicos norteamericanos. Notaron, sin embargo, que esto no comenzaba ni terminaba con la inclusión de un símbolo de la comunidad (edificio, animal) lo que se percibía como una moda que debía ser evitada. Los ganadores fueron espejos de sus comunidades y no simplemente copias "recicladas" de las ediciones de ayer.

5. Poner el mismo cuidado y atención a las palabras que al diseño: Los jueces hallaron que los titulares y epígrafes en muchos de los concursantes eran "chatos, aburridos y sin vida", lo que representa el efecto de la falta de interés cuando se pierden en el proceso de producción. Los titulares y epígrafes deben tener contenido y no dejarse para el final del proceso.

6. Presentar la información de manera vivaz: Los concursantes ganadores reflejaron "la urgencia y vitalidad de la vida diaria." Fueron aquellos dispuestos a correr riesgos con su diseño y comunicarse con los lectores.

7. Simplificar: evitar las modas pasajeras que interfieren con la capacidad de comunicarse eficazmente con el lector. Los jueces sugirieron una mayor comprensión de que trabajar con todas las herramientas disponibles (color, gráficos, fotografía, tipografía, etc.) no significa usarlas todas al mismo tiempo. La fotografía fue percibida como una suerte de arte perdido, sobrepasado por la tecnología de la computadora que enmascara el contenido de la imagen original.

8. Tratar a la tipografía con respeto: Recordar lo básico: la tipografía nunca fue, si se pretendió que fuera, elástica.

9. Ser detallista: Recordar que independientemente de cuán bueno sea el diseño, puede ser destruido por valores de producción poco exigentes.

10. Sorprender al lector y divertirse: El periódico de cada día debería ofrecer una sorpresa al lector, algo que debería hacerle detenerse y notarlo. "Es necesario mostrar al lector que disfrutamos de nuestro trabajo," dijo uno de los jueces. "Si podemos lograr eso, los lectores disfrutarán el tiempo que dediquen a leer el periódico."

Chapter Two

BEST OF SHOW JUDGES' SPECIAL RECOGNITION

The competition, which is sponsored annually by the Society of News Design and the S.I. Newhouse School of Public Communications at Syracuse University, recognizes excellence in newspaper design and graphics. Awards include Best of Show, Gold, Silver, Award of Excellence, Special Recogni-tion, plus the honor of World's Best Designed Newspaper.Continuing to pay tribute to the world's best news-paper designs, the 19th edition of The Best of Newspaper Design is a stun-ning collection of modern work. The included works were selected from more than 10,000 entries submitted by newspapers all over the world.

The competition, which is spon-sored annually by the Society of News Design and the S.I. Newhouse School of Public Communications at Syracuse University, recognizes excellence in newspaper design and graphics. Awards include Best of Show, Gold, Silver, Award of Excellence, Special Recogni-tion, plus the honor of World's Best Designed Newspaper.Continuing to pay tribute to the world's best news-paper designs, the 19th edition of The Best of Newspaper Design is a stun-ning collection of modern work. The included works were selected from more than 10,000 entries submitted by newspapers all over the world.

The competition, which is spon-sored annually by the Society of News Design and the S.I. Newhouse School of Public Communications at Syracuse University, recognizes excellence in newspaper design and graphics. Awards include Best of Show, Gold, Silver, Award of Excellence, Special Recogni-tion, plus the honor of World's Best Designed Newspaper.Continuing to pay tribute to the world's best news-paper designs, the 19th edition of The Best of Newspaper Design is a stun-ning collection of modern work. The included works were selected from more than 10,000 entries submitted by newspapers all over the world.

The competition, which is spon-sored annually by the Society of News Design and the S.I. Newhouse School of Public Communications at Syracuse University, recognizes excellence in newspaper design and graphics. Awards include Best of Show, Gold, Silver, Award of Excellence, Special Recogni-tion, plus the honor of World's Best Designed Newspaper.Continuing to pay tribute to the world's best news-paper designs, the 19th edition of The Best of Newspaper Design is a stun-ning collection of modern work. The included works were selected from more than 10,000 entries submitted by newspapers all over the world. This exceptional collection is an essential reference for anyone involved in print media, graphics, photography, design, journalism, or communications.

The competition, which is spon-sored annually by the Society of News Design and the S.I. Newhouse School of Public Communications at Syracuse University, recognizes

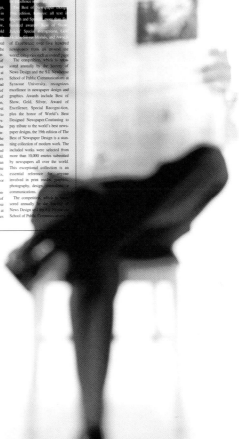

Introduction

It took five days, 21 judges and more than 40 assistants to sift through 12,137 entries from around the world to decide the winners in the 19th Best of Newspaper Design competition.

And after 250 hours of preparation and more than a thousand collective hours of judging, 140 newspapers from 19 countries received 826 awards.

Many of the winners are displayed in this book.

Judges use a complex system to decide winners. Balloting is secret; the system uses cups and chips so a judge does not know how others are voting until all votes are cast.

Almost as complex is the system to guard against conflicts of interest during the judging. Conflicts occur when a judge encounters an entry from his or her publication, a publication for which he or she has done recent consulting work (within an 18-month period immediately prior to judging) or a publication with which he or she directly competes. In these cases a "floating" judge is used to vote for or against the entry. A number of qualified "floating" judges were available on the judging floor to perform this duty.

Each panel consisted of five judges. At least three of them had to vote "yes" to grant an award. Entries receiving fewer than three votes were removed from the competition.
- Entries receiving three votes received an Award of Excellence.
- Entries receiving four or more votes in the first round advanced to the medal round.
- Entries receiving four votes during the medal round were awarded a Silver Medal.
- Entries receiving five votes (unanimous vote of the judging panel) earned a Gold Medal.
- At the end of competition judging, all judging panels came together to re-examine all Silver and Gold medal winners.

Sometimes, when confronted with the entire body of medal winners (rather than winners from just one or two categories), judges will re-vote on the worthiness of some of their choices.

Only the judges can move an entry up or down the awards scale.

SND presented three levels of awards:

An **Award of Excellence** was granted for work that was truly excellent. This award goes beyond mere technical or aesthetic competency. These entries need not be "perfect." It is appropriate to honor entries for such things as being daring and innovative if the entry is outstanding but less than 100 percent in every respect. This award went to 702 entries.

A **Silver Medal** was granted for work that went beyond excellence. The technical proficiency of the Silver Medal should stretch the limits of the medium. These entries are judged outstanding. Ninety-six Silver Medals were awarded.

A **Gold Medal** was granted for work that defines the state of the art. Such an entry should stretch the limits of creativity. It should be impossible to find anything deficient in a gold-winning entry. It should be near perfect. Twenty-one Gold Medals were awarded.

In addition to the Award of Excellence, Silver and Gold medals, two special honors are possible: the Judges' Special Recognition and the Best of Show. These honors are given only when specific, special circumstances warrant the awards.

A **Judges' Special Recognition** can be awarded by a team of judges or by all judges for work that is outstanding in an area not necessarily singled out by the Award of Excellence, Silver or Gold award structure. This recognition has been granted for such things as use of photography, use of informational graphics and the use of typography throughout a body of work. This body of work may be a particular publication, section or sections by an individual or staff. The special recognition does not supplant any Award of Excellence, Silver or Gold and should be seen as an adjunct. Six JSRs were awarded.

Best of Show is the best of the general competition winners. Discussion for this award takes place at the conclusion of the judging. Judges have an opportunity to view all Silver and Gold winners again at the same time. There is no limit as to the number of Best of Show awards that may be presented in one or more categories; however, in the past such awards were non-existent or very few in number. One Best of Show was given.

Introducción

Llevó cinco días, 21 jueces y más de 40 asistentes seleccionar entre 12.137 concursantes del mundo entero para elegir los ganadores del 19º certamen de Mejor Diseño de Periódico.

Y después de 250 horas de preparación y más de mil horas colectivas de juzgar, fueron, 140 periódicos de 19 países los que recibieron 826 premios. Catorce periódicos fueron nombrados los Periódicos Mejor Diseñados del Mundo.

Muchos de los ganadores aparecen en este libro.

Los jueces utilizan un complejo sistema para elegir a los ganadores. La votación es secreta; el sistema utiliza tazas y fichas para que un juez no sepa cómo votan los demás hasta que son emitidos todos los votos.

Casi igual de complejo es el sistema para evitar conflictos de interés durante la preselección. Los conflictos se dan cada vez que un juez se enfrenta a un concursante de su propia publicación, una publicación para la cual ha contribuido recientemente (dentro del período de 18 meses inmediatamente anterior a la competencia) o una publicación contra la cual compite directamente. En estos casos se lo reemplaza con un juez "flotante" para que vote a favor o en contra del concursante en cuestión. Existe una serie de jueces "flotantes" disponibles en el piso del certamen para realizar esta tarea.

Cada panel está conformado por cinco jueces. Al menos tres de ellos tienen que votar por el sí para otorgar un premio. Los concursantes que reciben menos de tres votos positivos son retirados de la competencia.

- Los concursantes que reciben tres votos recibieron un Premio a la Excelencia.
- Los concursantes que recibieron cuatro votos o más en la primera vuelta avanzaron a la vuelta de la medalla.
- Los concursantes que recibieron cuatro votos en la vuelta de la medalla ganaron la Medalla de Plata.
- Los concursantes que recibieron cinco votos (voto unánime del jurado) ganaron la Medalla de Oro.
- Al finalizar la selección de los ganadores, todos los jurados se reunieron para examinar nuevamente a los ganadores de medallas de plata y de oro.

Algunas veces, al enfrentarse a la totalidad de los ganadores de medallas (en lugar de ganadores de sólo una o dos categorías), los jueces votan nuevamente si los seleccionados realmente merecen el premio. Sólo los jueces pueden ascender o descender a un concursante en la escala de premios.

SND presentó tres niveles de premios:

Se otorgó un Premio a la Excelencia por trabajo que era realmente excelente. Este premio va más allá de la mera competición técnica o estética. Estos concursantes no necesitan ser "perfectos." Resulta apropiado honrar a los concursantes que se destacan por ser osados e innovadores, aunque no lleguen al 100 por ciento en todos los aspectos. Este premio se otorgó a 702 concursantes.

Se otorgó una medalla de plata por el trabajo que era más que excelente. La perfección técnica de los ganadores de medallas de plata debe sobrepasar los límites del medio. Estos concursantes son considerados sobresalientes. Se otorgaron noventa y seis medallas de plata.

La medalla de oro se otorgó por trabajo que define qué es de avanzada. El concursante debe sobrepasar los límites de la creatividad. Debe ser imposible hallar algo deficiente en un ganador de medalla de oro. Debe ser casi perfecto. Se otorgaron ventiuna medallas de oro.

Además del Premio a la Excelencia y las medallas de plata y oro, existen dos honores especiales: El Reconocimiento Especial del Jurado y el Mejor del Certamen. Estos galardones se otorgan solamente cuando circunstancias específicas justifican los premios.

El Premio de Reconocimiento Especial del Jurado (JSR) puede ser otorgado por un grupo de jueces o por todo el jurado por un trabajo sobresaliente en un área que no fue necesariamente distinguida por la estructura de los Premios a la Excelencia, las medallas de plata y de oro. Este reconocimiento ha sido otorgado por aspectos tales como el uso de la fotografía, el uso de gráficos informativos y de la tipografía en todo el cuerpo del trabajo. Este cuerpo de trabajo puede ser una publicación en particular, una sección o secciones de un individuo o del plantel. El reconocimiento especial no reemplaza el Premio a la Excelencia ni las medallas de plata y oro y debe considerarse como un adjunto. Se otorgaron seis JSRs.

El Mejor del Certamen es el mejor de los ganadores del certamen general. Este premio se debate al finalizar la selección. Los jueces tienen la oportunidad de ver a todos los ganadores de medallas de plata y de oro a la vez. No existe límite al número de premios "Mejor del Certamen" que se otorga en una o más categorías; no obstante, en el pasado estos premios prácticamente no se otorgaban o se otorgaban muy pocos. Se otorgó un sólo premio Mejor del Certamen.

El Mundo Metropoli
Madrid, Spain
Rodrigo Sanchez, Art Director

Awarded **Best of Show**, this is like fireworks. It's the brightest burst of energy in the contest. There's an incredible diversity of skill. In the black and white and red typography (see page 142), there is still balance in strong visual hierarchy. He works beautifully with type and conceptualizing. It's impressive and incredibly brave that he is reinventing a cover each week. This kind of depth is rare.

El ganador del premio Mejor del Certamen, es una fiesta. Es la mayor explosión de energía del concurso. Tiene una increíble diversidad de talento. Aún con la tipografía en blanco, negro y rojo (página 142) existe un equilibrio de fuerte jerarquía visual. Funciona maravillosamente con la tipografía y el concepto. Es impresionante y a la vez increíble que se re-invente una tapa cada semana. Este tipo de profundidad no es común.

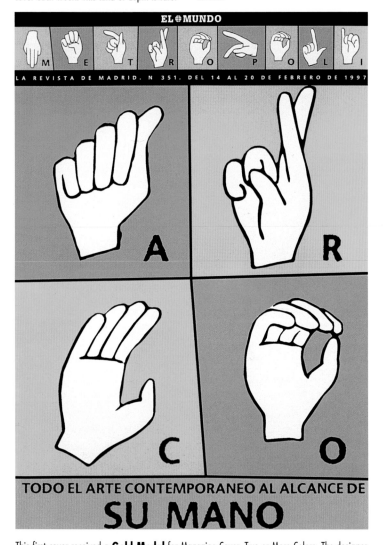

This first cover received a **Gold Medal** for Magazine Cover, Two or More Colors. The designer is unafraid of redesigning the publication each week. It's a good exercise in alternative conceptualization, and just a marvel.

• • • • •

Esta primera tapa recibió la Medalla de Oro a la Tapa de Revista de Dos o Más colores. El diseñador no teme re-diseñar la publicación todas las semanas. Es un buen ejercicio de concepción informativa, simplemente una maravilla.

These six covers received a **Gold Medal** for Magazine Portfolio.

• • • • •

Estas seis tapas recibieron la Medalla de Oro por Portafolio de Revista.

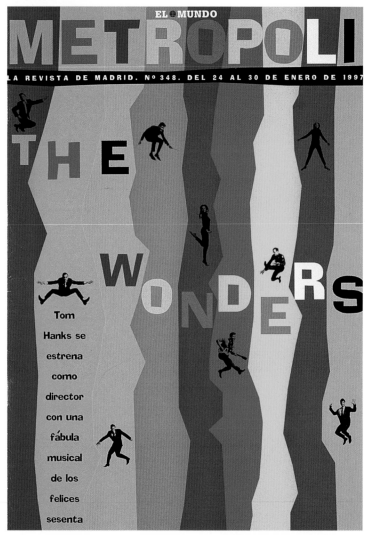

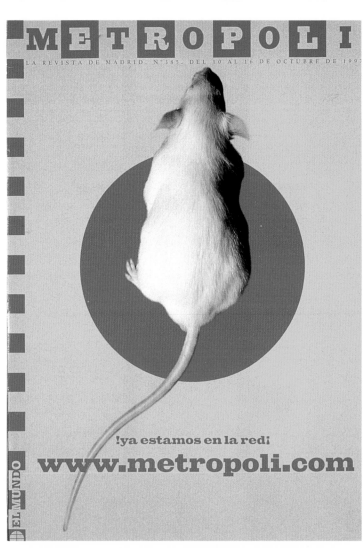

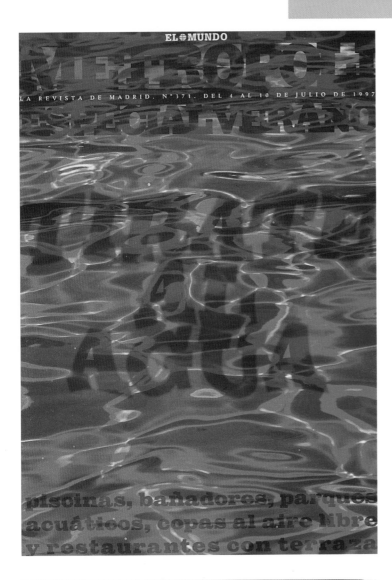

Awarded a **JSR** for the quality and depth of pure understanding in 36 weeks' covers out of 52. It blew us away. He deals with type exercises, period pieces and manipulation of iconographic images. It's incredible to see this amount of range in one person.

Ganador del premio JSR por la calidad y profundidad de comprensión pura en 36 tapas de 52 semanas. Nos dejó pasmados. Él realiza ejercicios de tipografía, piezas de época y manipulación de imágenes iconográficas. Es increíble el alcance que puede abarcar una sola persona.

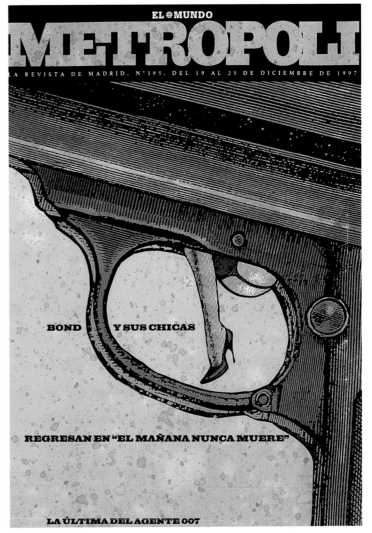

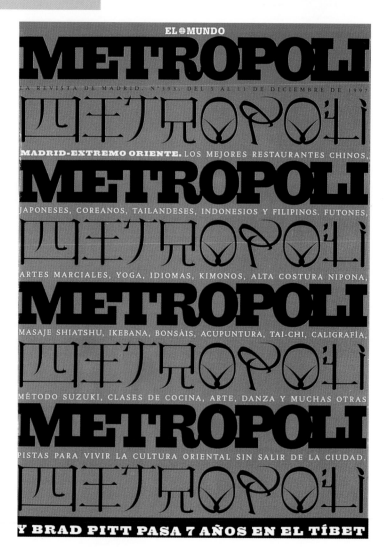

These three covers received a **Silver Medal** for Magazine Portfolio

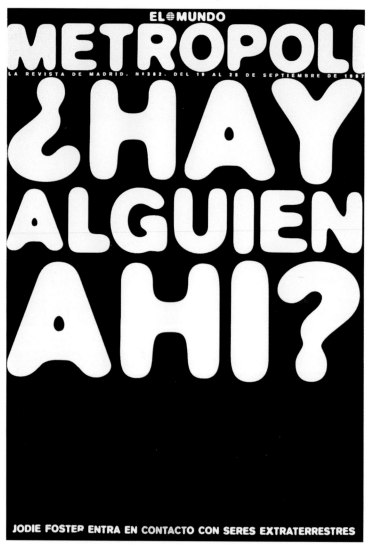

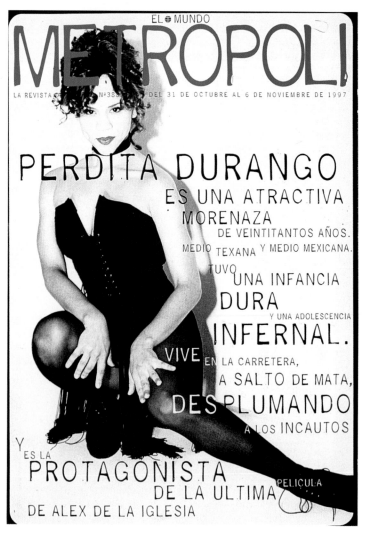

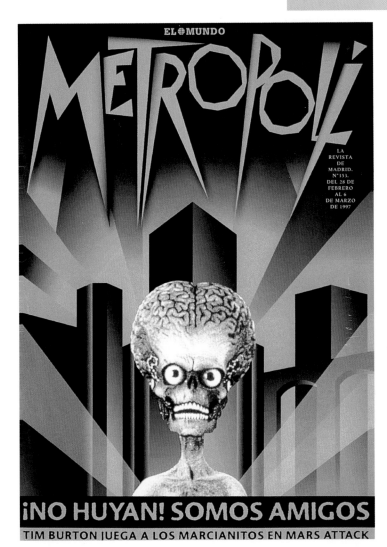

These three covers received a **Silver Medal** for Magazine Portfolio

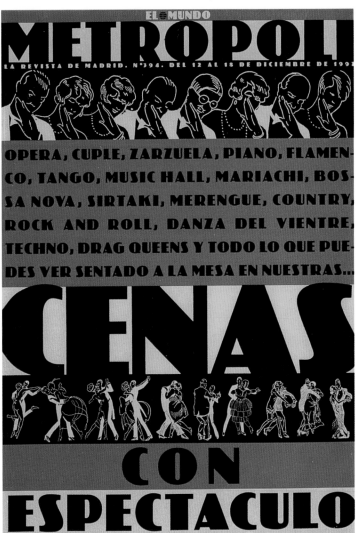

These two covers received an **Award of Excellence** for Magazine Portfolio

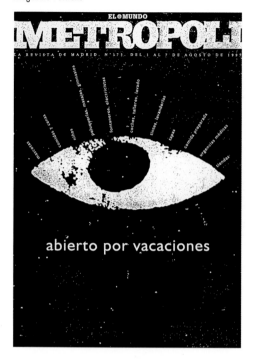

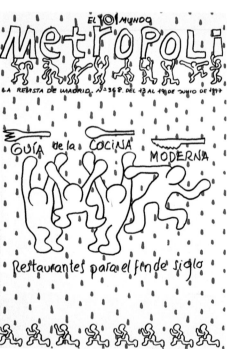

These two covers received an **Award of Excellence** for Magazine Portfolio

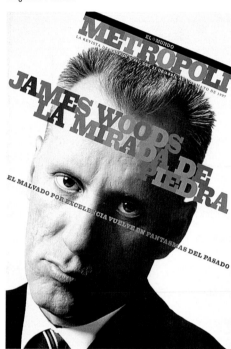

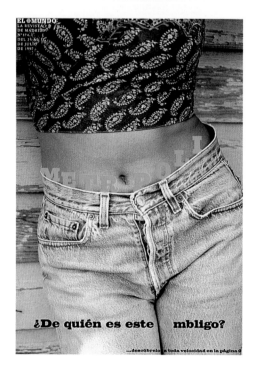

These two covers received an **Award of Excellence** for Magazine Portfolio

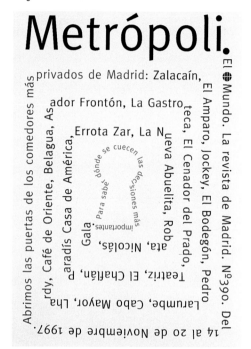

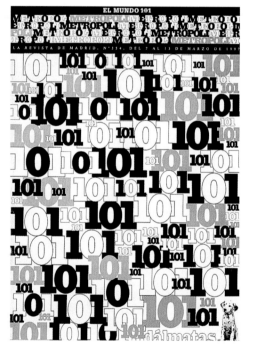

This page received a **Silver Medal** for Magazine Cover

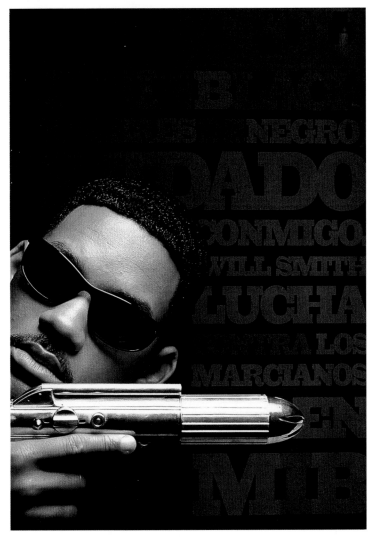

This page received a **Silver Medal** for Magazine Cover

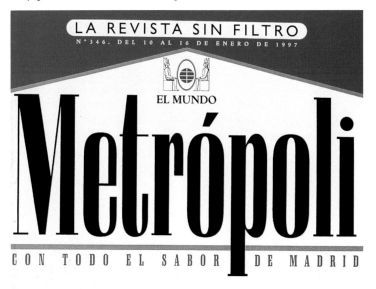

Gold & JSR
•for Feature page
DN. på stan
Stockholm, Sweden

Peter Alenas, Art Director & Designer; **Pompe Hedengren**, Art Director & Designer; **Lotten Ekman**, Designer

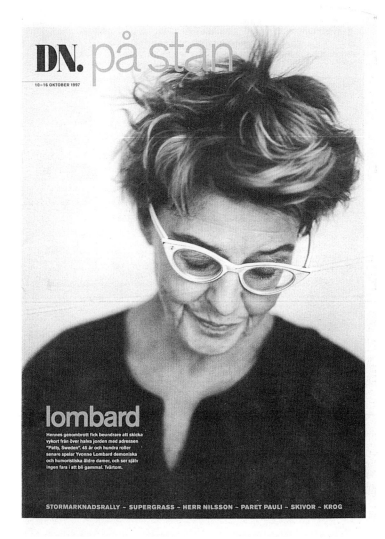

Awarded a **Gold Medal** for this section which is as good as it gets, we like the level of sensibility, the use of photos, illustration and typography. It's at a consistently high level. It has restraint without being boring. Nobody's doing this. We can't believe how psyched we got when we saw this.

Also awarded a **JSR** from the entire panel of judges for innovative design and for leading newspaper design in new directions. As designers, we are always searching for the next step. This publication is taking the next step. They're using classic typography in a modern way — it's understated but very bold. There's an excellence in the level of photography and illustration that we haven't seen anywhere else. There is a beautiful balance of proportion, type and illustration size. The designer is comfortable with the size of the page. The color palette is uniform from section to section. It has an enormous vitality and points to a future direction for us all.

Ganador de una Medalla de Oro por esta sección que mejor no puede ser. Nos gustó el nivel de sensibilidad, el uso de la fotografía, la ilustración y la tipografía. Todo de alto nivel. Tiene límites sin ser aburrido. Nadie hace esto. No podemos creer lo que nos anonadó ver esto.

Además ganó un JSR por el diseño innovador y por liderar el diseño de periódicos hacia nuevas direcciones. Como diseñadores, siempre estamos a la búsqueda del siguiente paso. Esta publicación está dando el siguiente paso. Usan la tipografía clásica de manera moderna — sutil pero audaz. Un nivel de fotografía e ilustración excelente que no hemos visto en ningún otro lado. Existe un exquisito equilibrio de proporción, tipografía y tamaño de la ilustración. El diseñador se siente cómodo en ese tamaño de página. La paleta de colores es uniforme de una sección a la otra. Posee una enorme vitalidad y nos indica el rumbo a seguir a todos los demás.

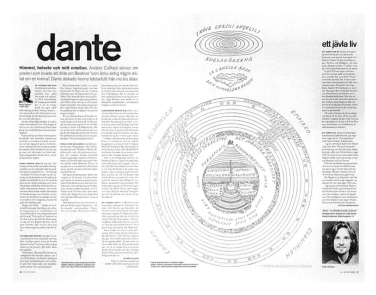

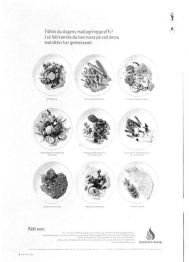

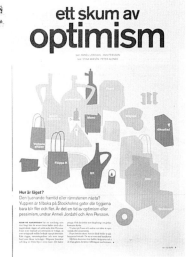

Awarded **JSR** for great use of art and information. So often you see gratuitous art — this art melds with the information and provides a focal point for the page.

Ganador del **JSR** por un excelente uso del arte y la información. Tan frecuentemente se ve el uso gratuito del arte, este arte se funde con la información y provee un punto focal a la página.

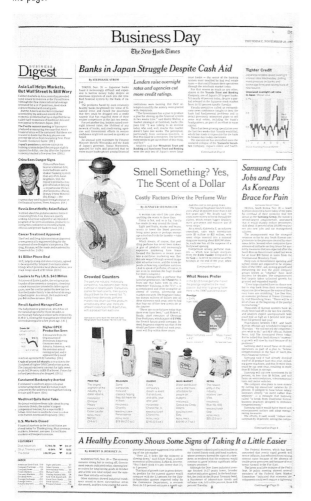

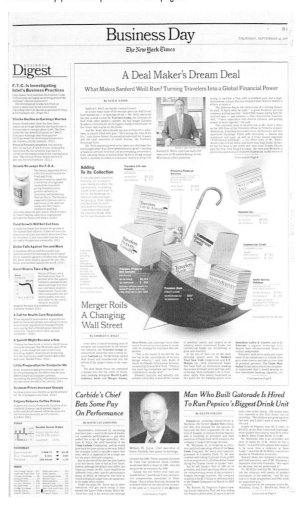

Silver & JSR
•for News Portfolio

The New York Times

New York, NY

Tim Oliver, Presentation Editor

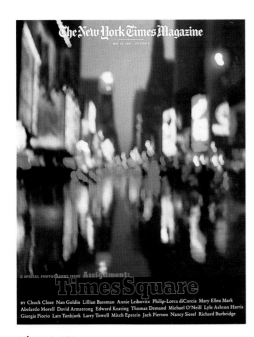

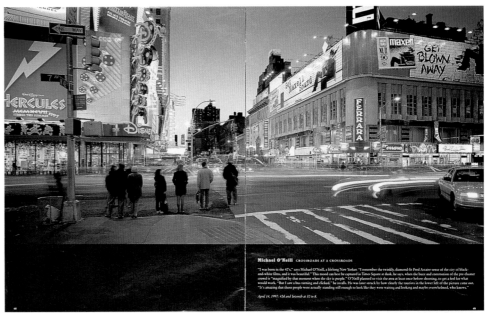

Silver & JSR
•for Magazine Special Section
•Also an **Award of Excellence** for Photo Series or Story

The New York Times Magazine

New York, NY

Janet Froelich, Art Director; Catherine Gilmore-Barnes, Designer;
Kathy Ryan, Photo Editor

Assignment Times Square was awarded a **JSR** for photo editing, sequencing and design. The judges were impressed with the restrained use of photo size. It was a visual rollercoaster. It takes the reader up and down but very smoothly.

Assignment Times Square recibió un JSR por la edición fotográfica, secuencia y diseño. Al jurado lo sorprendió el uso limitado del tamaño de las fotos. Fue un paseo visual pleno de altibajos. Lleva al lector hacia arriba y hacia abajo pero muy suavemente.

Awarded a **JSR** for acting with urgency to tell its readers an important story as quickly and completely as possible. The work demonstrates journalistic teamwork and determination of the highest level.

Ganador de un JSR por actuar con urgencia para contar a los lectores una historia importante lo más rápida y completamente posible. El trabajo demuestra lo que es el trabajo periodístico en equipo y la determinación del más alto nivel.

Award of Excellence & JSR
• for Breaking News

Scotland on Sunday
Edinburgh, Scotland
Staff

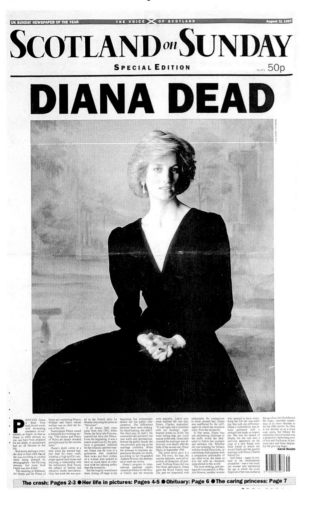

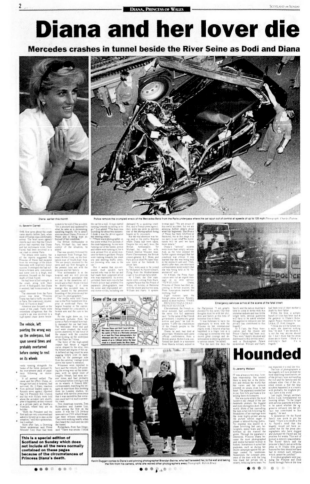

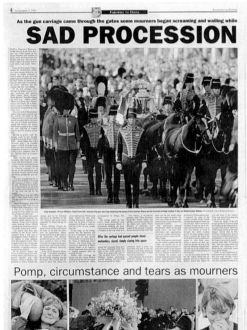

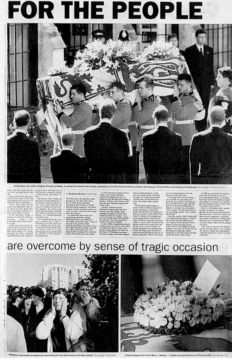

Pomp, circumstance and tears as mourners are overcome by sense of tragic occasion

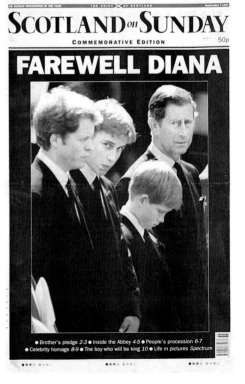

Silver & JSR
• for Breaking News

Scotland on Sunday
Edinburgh, Scotland
Staff

Awarded a **JSR** for acting with urgency to tell its readers an important story as quickly and completely as possible. The work demonstrates journalistic teamwork and determination of the highest level.

Ganador de un JSR por actuar con urgencia para contar a los lectores una historia importante lo más rápida y completamente posible. El trabajo demuestra lo que es el trabajo periodístico en equipo y la determinación del más alto nivel.

Chapter Three

NEWS

Continuing to pay tribute to the world's best newspaper designs, the 19th edition of The Best of Newspaper Design is a stunning collection of modern work. The included works were selected from more than 10,000 entries submitted by newspapers all over the world. This exceptional collection is an essential reference for anyone involved in print media, graphics, photography, design, journalism, or communications.

The competition, which is sponsored annually by the Society of News Design and the S.I. Newhouse School of Public Communications at Syracuse University, recognizes excellence in newspaper design and graphics. Awards include Best of Show, Gold, Silver, Award of Excellence, Special Recogni-tion, plus the honor of World's Best Designed Newspaper. Categories for judging include overall page design, portfolio, magazine cover design, art and illustration, photo journalism, and informational graphics.

This nineteenth edition presents the finest newspaper design in the field.

Selected by a panel of 21 judges of the Society for News Design, the award-winning pub-lications featured in this nineteenth edition were chosen for excellence in design.

The Best of Newspaper Design, 19th edition, features: Text in English and Spanish; 840 awards: World's Best-Designed Newspapers, Best of Show, Gold medals, Judges' Special Recognition, Silver medals, and Awards of Excel-lence. More than 12,100 entries were reviewed from hundreds of publications from around the world to select winners from 158 publications. Categories included: Overall design, news, features, portfolios, special coverage, special sections, magazines, art and illustration, photography, informational graphics and redesign.ign, art and illus

Continuing to pay tribute to the world's best newspaper designs, the 19th edition of The Best of Newspaper Design is a stunning collection of modern work. The included works were selected from more than 10,000 entries submitted by newspapers all over the world. This exceptional collection is an essential reference for anyone involved in print media, graphics, photography, design, journalism, or communications.

The competition, which is sponsored annually by the Society of News Design and the S.I. Newhouse School of Public Communications at Syracuse University, recognizes excellence in newspaper design and graphics. Awards include Best of Show, Gold, Silver, Award of Excellence, Special Recogni-tion,

Continuing to pay tribute to the world's best newspaper designs, the 19th edition of The Best of Newspaper Design is a stunning collection of modern work. The included works were selected from more than 10,000 entries submitted by newspapers all over the world. This exceptional collection is an essential reference for anyone involved in print media, graphics, photography, design, journalism, or communications.

The competition, which is sponsored annually by the Society of News Design and the S.I. Newhouse School of Public Communications at Syracuse University, recognizes excellence in newspaper design and graphics. Awards include Best of Show, Gold, Silver, Award of Excellence, Special Recogni-tion, plus the honor of World's Best Designed Newspaper. Categories for judging include overall page design, portfolio, magazine cover design, art and illustration, photo journalism, and informational graphics.

This nineteenth edition presents the finest newspaper design in the field.

Selected by a panel of 21 judges of the Society for News Design, the award-winning pub-lications featured in this nineteenth edition were chosen for excellence in design

The Best of Newspaper Design, 19th edition, features: all text in English and Spanish; more than five hundred awards: Best of Show, Judges' Special Recognition, Gold Medals, Sil-ver Medals, and Awards of Excellence; over five hundred newspapers from all around the world; categories such as overall page design, portfolio, magazine cover design, art and illustration, photo journalism, and informational graph-

Continuing to pay tribute to the world's best newspaper designs, the 19th edition of The Best of Newspaper Design is a stunning collection of modern work. The included works were selected from more than 10,000 entries submitted by newspapers all over the world. This exceptional collection is an essential reference for anyone involved in print media, graphics, photography, design, journalism, or communications.

The competition, which is sponsored annually by the Society of News Design and the S.I. Newhouse School of Public Communications at Syracuse University, recognizes excellence in newspaper design and graphics. Awards include Best of Show, Gold, Silver, Award of

Continuing to pay tribute to the world's best newspaper designs, the 19th edition of The Best of Newspaper Design is a stunning collection of modern work. This exceptional collection is an essential reference for anyone involved in print media, graphics, photography, design, journalism, or communications.

The competition, which is sponsored annually by the Society for News Design and the S.I. Newhouse School of Public Communications at Syracuse University, recognizes excellence in newspaper design and graphics. Awards include Best of Show, Gold, Silver, Award of Excellence, Special Recogni-tion, plus the honor of World's Best Designed Newspaper. Categories for judging include overall page design, portfolio, magazine cover design, art

NEWS SECTIONS
NEWS PAGES
BREAKING NEWS PAGES
SPECIAL NEWS TOPICS

sored annually by the Society for News Design and the S.I. Newhouse School of Public Communications at Syracuse University, recognizes excellence in newspaper design and graphics. Awards include Best of Show, Gold, Silver, Award of Excellence, Special Recogni-tion, plus the honor of World's Best Designed Newspaper. Categories for judging include overall page design, portfolio, magazine cover design, art and illustration, photo journalism, and informational graphics.

This nineteenth edition presents the finest newspaper design in the field.

Selected by a panel of judges of the Society of News Design, the award-winning newspapers featured in this nineteenth edition were cho-sen for excellence in design.

The Best of Newspaper Design, 19th edition, features: Text in English and Spanish; 840 awards: World's Best-Designed News-papers, Best of Show, Gold medals, Judges' Special Recognition, Silver medals, and Awards of Excel-lence. More than 12,100 entries were reviewed from hundreds of publica-tions from around the world to select winners from 158 publications. Categories included: Overall design, news, features, portfolios, special coverage, special sections, maga-

and illustration, photo journalism, and informational graphics.

This nineteenth edition presents the finest newspaper design in the field.

Selected by a panel of 21 judges of the Society for News Design, the award-winning pub-lications fea-tured in this nineteenth edition were chosen for excellence in design.

The Best of Newspaper Design, 19th edition, features: Text in English and Spanish; 840 awards: World's Best-Designed News-papers, Best of Show, Gold medals, Judges' Special Recognition, Silver medals, and Awards of Excel-lence. More than 12,100 entries were reviewed from hundreds of publica-tions from around the world to select winners from 158 publications. Categories included: Overall design, news, features, portfolios, special coverage, special sections, maga-zines, art and illustration, photogra-phy, informational graphics and redesigns. Selected by a panel of 21 Continuing to pay tribute to the world's best newspaper designs, the 19th edition of The Best of Newspaper Design is a stunning collection of modern work. The includ-ed works were selected from more than 10,000 entries submitted by newspapers all over the world. This exceptional collection is an essential reference for anyone involved in print media, graphics, photography, design, journalism, or communica-

The competition, which is spon-

mational graphics.

This nineteenth edition presents the finest newspaper design in the field.

Selected by a panel of 21 judges of the Society for News Design, the award-winning publications featured in this nineteenth edition were chosen for excellence in design.

The Best of Newspaper Design, 19th edition, features: Text in English and Spanish; 840 awards: World's Best-Designed Newspapers, Best of Show, Gold medals, Judges' Special Recognition, Silver medals, and Awards of Excel-lence. More than 12,100 entries were reviewed from hundreds of publications from around the world to select winners from 158 publications. Categories included: Continuing to pay tribute to the world's best newspaper designs, the 19th edition of The Best of Newspaper Design is a stunning collection of modern work. The included works were selected from more than 10,000 entries submitted by newspapers all over the world. This exceptional collection is an essential reference for anyone involved in print media, graphics, photography, design, journalism, or communica-

The competition, which is spon-

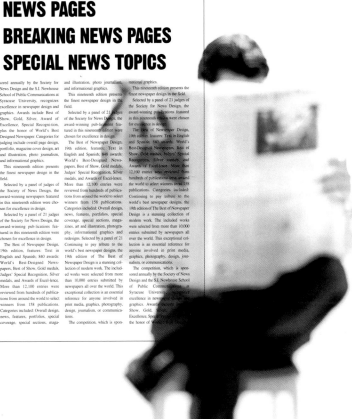

Award of Excellence
The Scotsman
Edinburgh, Scotland
Staff

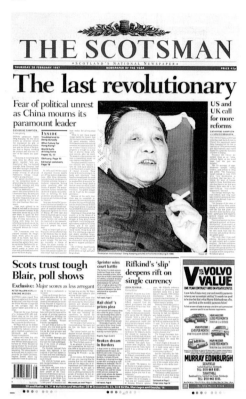

Award of Excellence
Missoulian
Missoula, MT
Tad Brooks, News Editor; **Jake Ellison,** Assistant News Editor

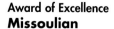
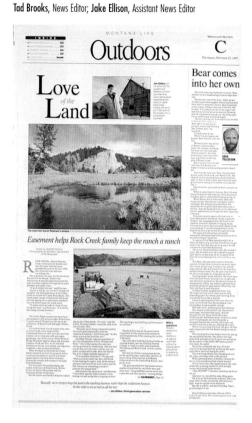

Award of Excellence
The Virginian-Pilot
Norfolk, VA
Staff

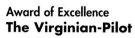
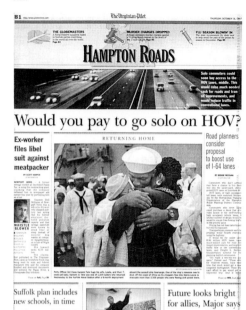

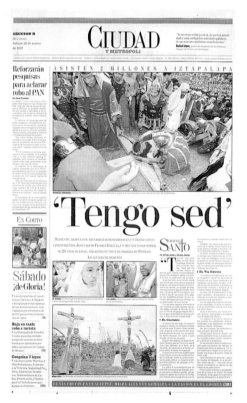

Award of Excellence
Reforma
México City, México
Daniel Esqueda Guadalajara, Graphics Coordinator; **Ignacio Guerrero,** Section Designer; **Oscar Yáñez,** Designer; **Oscar Santiago Méndez,** Designer; **María Luisa Díaz de León,** General Editor; **Adrián Rueda,** General Editor; **Jorge Andrés Gómez Pineda,** Editor; **Gustavo Hernández,** Editor; **Emilio Deheza,** Art Director; **Eduardo Danilo,** Design Consultant

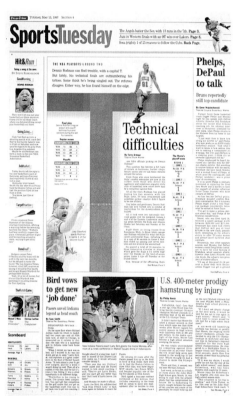

Award of Excellence
Chicago Tribune
Chicago, IL
Staff

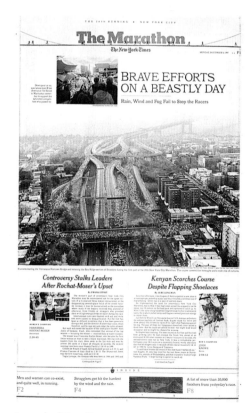

Award of Excellence
•Also an Award of Excellence for Breaking News
The New York Times
New York, NY
Wayne Kamidoi, Designer; **Lee Yarosh,** Designer; **Joe Ward,** Graphics Editor; **Bedel Saget,** Graphics Editor; **Stephen Jesselli,** Picture Editor; **Sarah Kass,** Picture Editor; **Barton Silverman,** Photographer; **Sports Staff**

Silver
The American
Westhampton Beach, NY

Joseph E. Baron, Art Director; Joanna K. Dounelis, Senior Design Associate; Tara Pastina, Design Associate

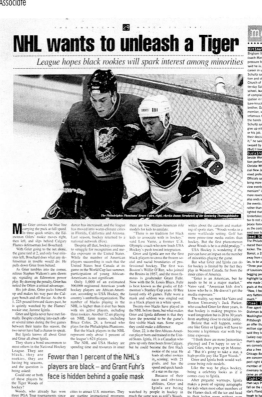

NHL wants to unleash a Tiger
League hopes black rookies will spark interest among minorities

Fewer than 1 percent of the NHL's players are black – and Grant Fuhr's face is hidden behind a goalie mask

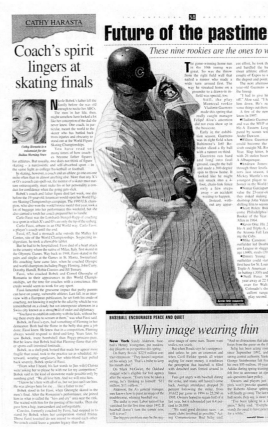

CATHY HARASTA

Coach's spirit lingers at skating finals

Future of the pastime
These nine rookies are the ones to watch

BASEBALL ENCOURAGES PEACE AND QUIET

Whiny image wearing thin

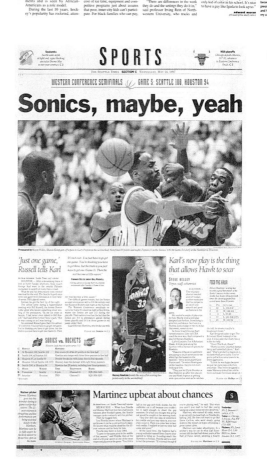

SPORTS

WESTERN CONFERENCE SEMIFINALS — GAME 5: SEATTLE 100, HOUSTON 94

Sonics, maybe, yeah

'Just one game,' Russell tells Karl

Karl's new play is the thing that allows Hawk to soar

STEVE KELLEY

SONICS vs. ROCKETS

Martinez upbeat about chances

Award of Excellence
The Seattle Times
Seattle, WA

Rick Lund, Designer; Michael Kellams, Designer; David Miller, Art Director; Jeff Bruce, Designer; Jeff King, Designer; Cathy Henkel, Sports Editor

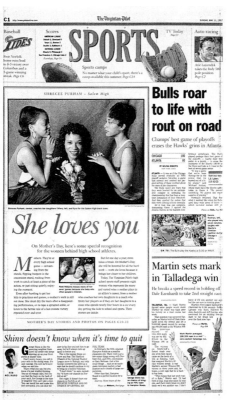

C1

The Virginian-Pilot

Baseball
SPORTS

TV Today

Auto racing

SHRECEE PURHAM – Salem High

Bulls roar to life with rout on road

Champs' best game of playoffs erases the Hawks' grins in Atlanta.

She loves you

On Mother's Day, here's some special recognition for the women behind high school athletes

Martin sets mark in Talladega win

Shinn doesn't know when it's time to quit

MOTHER'S DAY STORIES AND PHOTOS ON PAGES C10-C11

Award of Excellence
The Virginian-Pilot
Norfolk, VA

Staff

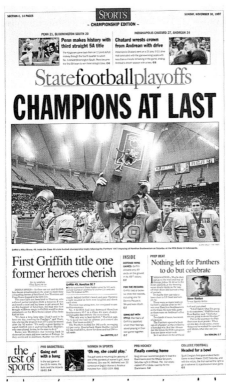

SECTION C, 14 PAGES

SPORTS
CHAMPIONSHIP EDITION

SUNDAY, NOVEMBER 30, 1997

Penn makes history with third straight 5A title

Chatard wrests crown from Andrean in OT

State football playoffs
CHAMPIONS AT LAST

First Griffith title one former heroes cherish

INSIDE

Nothing left for Panthers to do but celebrate

the rest of sports

PRO BASKETBALL

WOMEN IN SPORTS
'Oh my, she could play.'

PRO HOCKEY
Finally coming home

COLLEGE FOOTBALL
Headed for a bowl

Award of Excellence
•Also an Award of Excellence for Sports Page

The Times
Munster, IN

Dennis Varney, Designer; Matt Erickson, Designer; Orrin Schwarz, Asst. Sports Editor; Matt Mansfield, Deputy Managing Editor; David Campbell, Sports Editor

Silver
The Detroit News
Detroit, MI

Chris Kozlowski, A.M.E. Graphics/Design; David Kordalski, Graphics/Design Editor; Howard Lovy, Page Designer; Tim Summers, Graphic Artist; Satoshi Toyoshima, Graphic Artist; Chris Willis, Assistant Graphics Editor; James Borchuck, Photographer; Steve Fecht; Photo Director

Award of Excellence
Austin American-Statesman
Austin, TX

G.W. Babb, Design Director; Michelle Rice, News Editor; Zach Ryall, Director/Photography; Sandra Santos, Page One Editor; Staff

The Detroit News

FRIDAY, JANUARY 10, 1997

29 killed as plane dives into field near Monroe

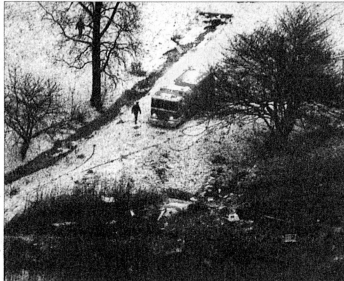

Inspectors and rescue workers had little to do after Delta-Comair Flight 3272 crashed in Monroe County on Thursday afternoon. Witnesses said the twin-engine turboprop went into a rolling nose-dive that ended in a volcanic eruption when the plane hit the ground just before 4 p.m.

James Borchuck / The Detroit News

FLIGHT FROM CINCINNATI WAS METRO-BOUND

* * *

Rescue workers find shattered bodies, silence

By Becky Beaupre, Joel J. Smith and James Tobin
The Detroit News

Perilous icing conditions prevailed across southern Michigan on Thursday when a Comair plane with an in-flight deicing failure in its past plunged into a Monroe County field, killing all 29 people aboard.

Official conclusions about the cause of the crash will likely take many months.

Investigators combed the crash site early today. Dick Rodriguez, investigator in charge for the National Transportation Safety Board (NTSB), said the wreckage and debris were spread over about 100 yards.

He also said they were unable to find the plane's "black box," which is a key resource in determining the cause of a crash.

But early speculation by experts and pilots centered on the icing that caused problems for many Metro Airport flights throughout the day — including flights scheduled to land within moments of the crash of Comair Flight 3272.

"Ice was building up on fuselages and wings all day long," Metro Airport spokesman Michael Conway said. "A significant percentage of our flights were affected."

As investigators converged on Detroit today from the NTSB, somber workers went about the grim work of identifying victims in the sparsely wooded field near Monroe where the plane fell from the sky.

The legless body of a woman clutching a child were among the discoveries made by Jerry Bartnik, head of the Monroe County Road Commission.

Please see PLANE, Page 4A

More inside
For more details on the crash, please see Pages 2A, 3A, 4A and 5A

The final moments

At about 3:50 p.m. Thursday, Comair commuter flight 3272 crashed near Ida. The flight, which originated in Cincinnati, was scheduled to land at Detroit Metro at 3:46 p.m. The cause of the crash has not been determined, but FAA investigators are on the scene. Here's what eyewitnesses saw:

1. The plane, an Embraer 120, was on approach to land at Detroit Metro Airport's runway 3R. The pilot gave no indication of trouble. Air Traffic Control handling was routine.

2. Witnesses report the plane went into a rolling nosedive, then crashed in a field.

3. The plane crashed near Ida, in Monroe County, about 18 miles southwest of Metro.

The weather

Light winds:
5 knots out of the northeast.
Visibility:
¾ mile; light snow and fog.
Clouds: Broken layers at 600 feet and 1,200 feet; overcast at 1,700 feet.
Temperature: 27°
Icing: Freezing rain reported earlier in the day

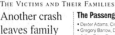

Flying on instruments

Even when visibility is zero, pilots can rely on a sophisticated navigation system called ILS that will precisely direct the aircraft to a safe landing. Flight 3272 followed an instrument approach to Detroit.

Sources: WeatherData (radar image), eyewitness reports, federal and local authorities.

Satoshi Toyoshima, Tim Summers, Chris Willis and David Kordalski / The Detroit News

THE VICTIMS AND THEIR FAMILIES

Another crash leaves family grieving

By Hawke Fracassa
The Detroit News

Adele Colagiovanni's nightmare keeps getting worse.

Two of the Washington Township mother's four children have perished in plane crashes in the past three weeks.

First, she found out while she was on vacation that her son, Brian Scully — a 36-year-old Spanish teacher and airline mechanic for Airborne Express — was killed in a Dec. 22 cargo plane crash in the mountains of Virginia.

Then on Thursday, one of Colagiovanni's daughters — a 37-year old Spanish teacher — died when Comair Flight 3272 crashed in Monroe County as she flying to attend services for her brother, Brian, in suburban Detroit.

Please see DEMARCO, Page 5A

Maureen DeMarco

The Passengers
- Dexter Adams, Cincinnati
- Gregory Barrow, Detroit
- Arthur Brice, Brookhaven, Miss.
- Roger Bransford, Atlanta
- Christine Brownlee, Helena, Mont.
- Scott Brownlee, Helena, Mont.
- Greg Douchard, Jackson, Miss.
- Geoffrey Davis, Detroit
- Maureen DeMarco, Denver
- Leo Feibau, Atlanta
- Mark Horman, Detroit
- Betty Jean Jones, Detroit
- Charles Jones, Detroit
- Steven McClain, Detroit
- Teri Muskovitz, Detroit
- Kim Passariello, Detroit
- Roy Raymond, Twin Falls, Idaho
- Vernamarie Raymond, Twin Falls, Idaho
- Jennifer Rosiak, Pensacola, Fla.
- Nicholas Rosiak, Pensacola, Fla.
- Richard Sharp, Detroit
- Keita Takenami, Colts Neck, N.J.
- Douglas A. Thomas, Detroit
- Charles Wansedel, Detroit
- Darlene Zagar, Danville, Ky.

The Crew
- Capt. Dixon Carlsen, Glencoe, Ky.
- 1st Officer Kenneth Reece, Cincinnati
- Flight Attendant Darinda Ogden, Lexington, Ky.

Calling The News

HOME DELIVERY: 800-395-3300
In the 313 area code: 222-6500
STORIES AND NEWS TIPS: 800-678-4115
ROBERT H. GILES, EDITOR & PUBLISHER
Office: 313-222-2588; Fax 313-223-4389

On the Internet

For the latest news and up-to-the-minute scores, check out our web site on the Internet: http://detnews.com

The Detroit News
A Gannett newspaper
123rd year No 141
Copyright, 1997
The Detroit News
Printed in the USA

VW will pay out $1.1 billion to settle GM lawsuit

The war between General Motors Corp. and Volkswagen AG is officially over.

VW agreed to pay GM $100 million in cash and buy $1 billion in parts over the next seven years to settle GM's industrial espionage civil case against VW and former purchasing chief J. Ignacio Lopez de Arriortua.

Under the deal, GM will drop its civil claims against VW, Lopez, Chairman Ferdinand Piech, supervisory board member Jens Neumann and all current and former VW employees named in the nine-month-old civil suits filed in Detroit federal court.

And it all happened under the noses of 5,000 journalists who were gathered in Detroit for the North American International Auto Show.

Intensive negotiations began Tuesday at a Washington law firm, where GM Chairman John F. Smith Jr. and other key GM executives were briefed between interviews with reporters.

Louis R. Hughes, president of GM's international operations, left reporters waiting 40 minutes Wednesday while getting an update on the talks.

■ Details, Page 1C

SPECIAL REPORT:
TRAGEDY IN TWISTERS' WAKE, A9-A13

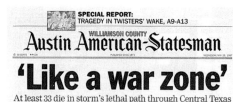

WILLIAMSON COUNTY
Austin American-Statesman

'Like a war zone'

At least 33 die in storm's lethal path through Central Texas

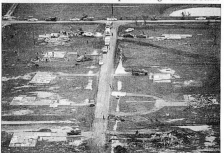

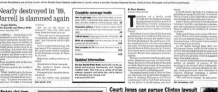

Nearly destroyed in '89, Jarrell is slammed again

By Clark Ostlin, Greg Castillo and Pamela Ward

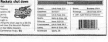

Court: Jones can pursue Clinton lawsuit

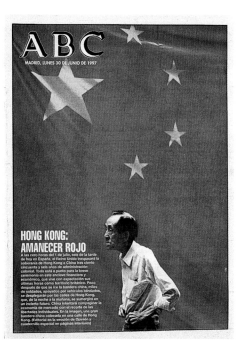

Award of Excellence
ABC
Madrid, Spain
Rosa María Rey, Designer's Chief; Miguel Angel Flores

Award of Excellence
The Charlotte Observer
Charlotte, NC

Crystal Dempsey, Page Designer; Monica Moses, Design Director; Susan Gilbert, Director/Photography; John Simmons, Photo Editor; Thé Pham, Photo Editor; Gary O'Brien, Photographer; Gayle Shomer, Photographer; Brian Melton; Page One Editor

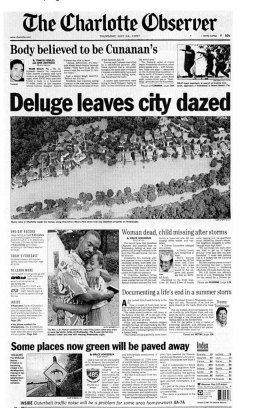

Award of Excellence
Detroit Free Press
Detroit, MI

David Dombrowski, Designer; Mary Schroeder, Photographer; Marty Westman, Graphic Artist; Hank Szerlag, Graphic Artist

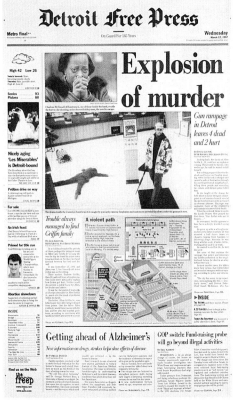

Award of Excellence
The Detroit News
Detroit, MI

Chris Kozlowski, A.M.E. Graphics/Design; David Kordalski, Graphics/Design Editor; Theresa Badovich, News Design Editor; Tim Summers, Graphic Artist; Satoshi Toyoshima, Graphic Artist; Joe Greco, Page Designer

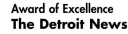

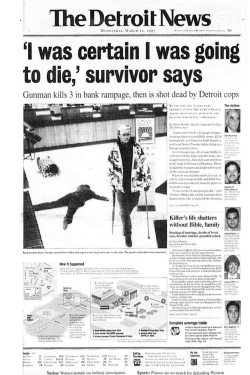

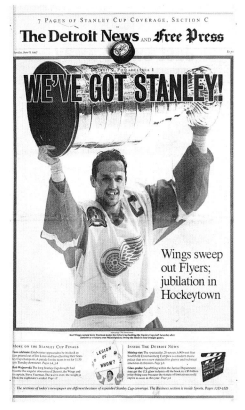

Award of Excellence
The Detroit News
Detroit, MI

Chris Kozlowski, A.M.E. Graphics/Design; Alan Lessig, Photographer; Steve Fecht, Photo Director; Michael Bown, Advanced Systems Editor

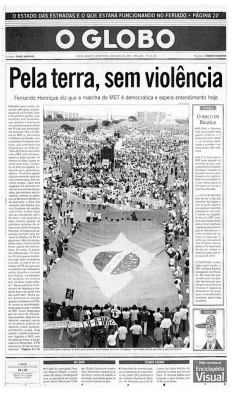

Award of Excellence
O Globo
Rio de Janeiro, Brazil

Rodolfo Fernandes, Deputy Chief Editor; Claudio Prudente, Designer; Fernando Maia, Photographer

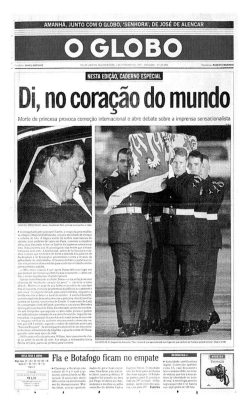

Award of Excellence
O Globo
Rio de Janeiro, Brazil

Agostinho Vieira, Editor; Léo Tavejnhansky, Art Editor

Award of Excellence
The Hartford Courant
Hartford, CT

Christian Potter Drury, Art Director; **Tom Wolfe**, Photo Editor; **Ingrid Muller**, Designer; **Richard Messina**, Photographer

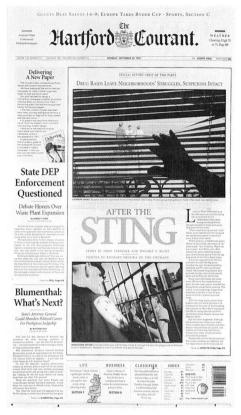

Award of Excellence
The Hartford Courant
Hartford, CT

Christian Potter Drury, Art Director; **Tom Wolfe**, Photo Editor; **Ingrid Muller**, Designer; **Jim Kuykendall**, Graphic Artist

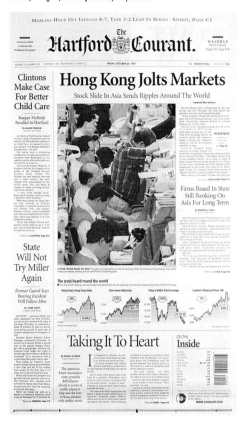

Award of Excellence
The Miami Herald
Miami, FL

Kris Strawser, Designer/Editor; **Mel Frishman**, Editor

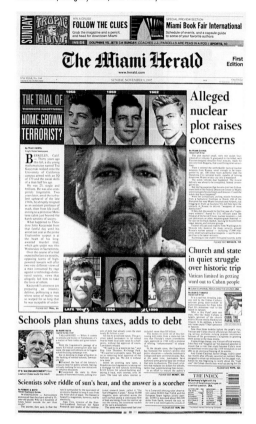

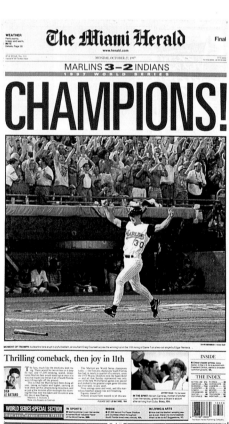

Award of Excellence
The Miami Herald
Miami, FL

Kris Strawser, Designer/Editor; **Mary Behne**, Editor

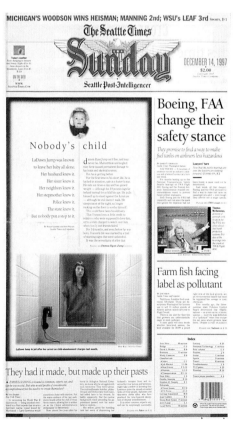

Award of Excellence
The Seattle Times
Seattle, WA

Michael Kellams, Designer; **Jacqui Banaszynski**, Series Editor; **Cathy McLain**, Sunday Editor; **David Miller**, Art Director

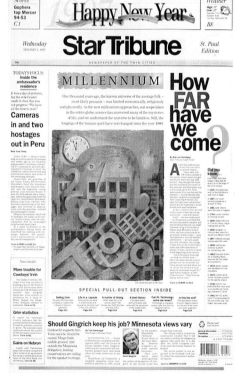

Award of Excellence
Star Tribune
Minneapolis, MN

Denise M. Reagan, Designer; **Graydon Royce**, Millenium Editor; **Hal Sanders**, Night 1A Editor; **Mike Reed**, Illustrator; **Billy Steve Clayton**, Graphic Artist

Award of Excellence
The Star-Ledger
Newark, NJ

Jane Hood, Designer; Pim Van Hemmen, Photo Editor; Charles Cooper, M.E./Production; John Lazarus, News Editor; George Frederick, A.M.E. Design; Richard Raska, Photographer

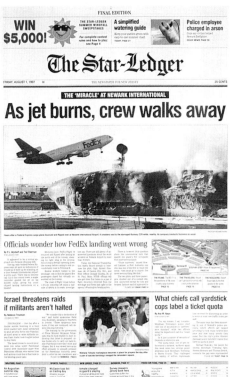

Award of Excellence
•Also an Award of Excellence for Breaking News
The Times-Picayune
New Orleans, LA

Stephen Wolgast, Designer; George Berke, Design Director; Doug Parker, Photo Editor; Angela Hill, Graphics Editor; Dan Shea, M.E.; Laura Jayne, News Editor

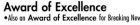

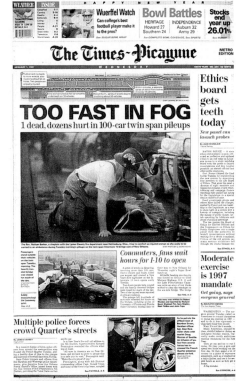

Award of Excellence
The Times-Picayune
New Orleans, LA

George Berke, Design Director; Betsy Carmody, Designer; Angela Hill, Graphics Editor; Dan Shea, M.E.; Laura Jayne, News Editor

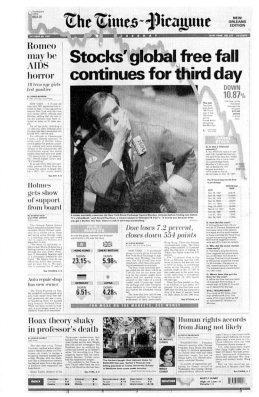

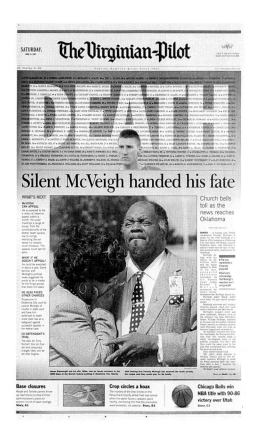

Award of Excellence
•Also an Award of Excellence for Breaking News
The Virginian-Pilot
Norfolk, VA

Lisa Cowan, Page Designer; Denis Finley, News Editor; Eric Seidman, Creative Director

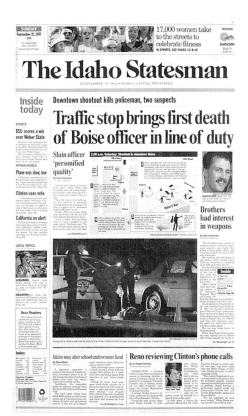

Award of Excellence
The Idaho Statesman
Boise, ID

Patrick Poyfair, Page Designer; Randy Wright, Page Designer; Gerry Melendez, Photographer; Patrick Davis, Graphic Artist

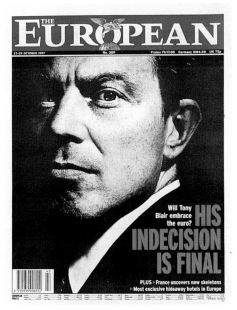

Award of Excellence
The European
London, England

John Belknap, Art Director

Award of Excellence
Providence Journal-Bulletin
Providence, RI

John Freidah, Photographer; **Thea Breite**, Asst. M.E./Visuals; **Lisa Newby**, Picture Editor/Designer

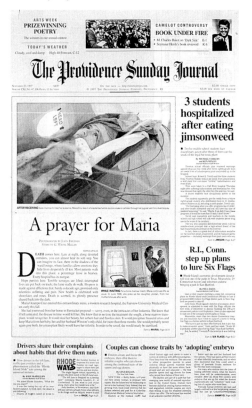

Award of Excellence
Savannah Morning News
Savannah, GA

Theresa Trenkamp, News Planner/Designer; **Brian D. Gross**, News Planner/Designer; **Drew Martin**, Graphic Artist

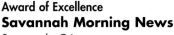
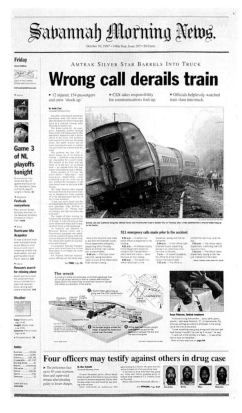

Award of Excellence
Savannah Morning News
Savannah, GA

Brian D. Gross, News Planner/Designer

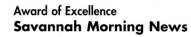
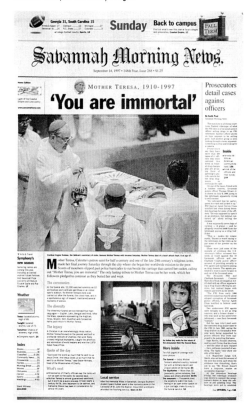

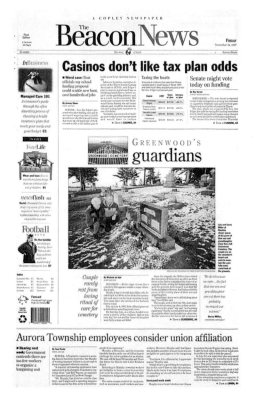

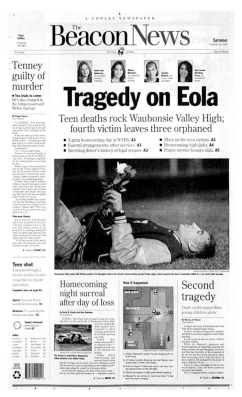

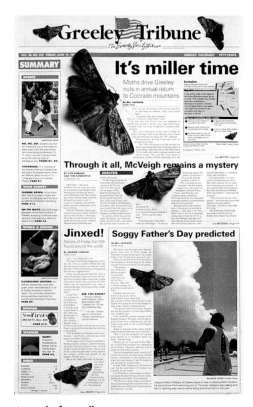

Award of Excellence
The Beacon News
Aurora, IL

Dan Ray, Designer; **James Denk**, Director/Graphics & Design; **Michelle Du Vair**, Photographer

Award of Excellence
The Beacon News
Aurora, IL

Jim King, Designer; **James Denk**, Director/Graphics & Design; **Brian Plonka**, Photographer; **Jamie Hollar**, Graphic Artist

Award of Excellence
Greeley Tribune
Greeley, CO

Mark French, Design Editor

Award of Excellence
Diario de Noticias

Huarte, Spain

Tita Lorenz, Designer; Javier Bergasa, Photographer; Patxi Cascante, Photographer

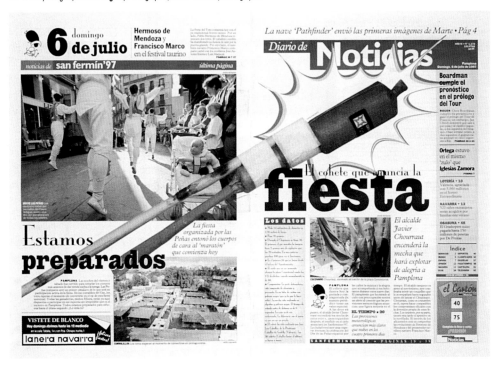

Award of Excellence
El Observador

Montevideo, Uruguay
Staff

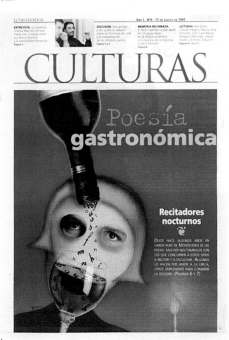

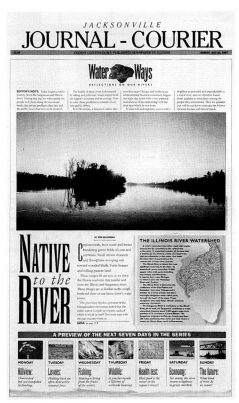

Award of Excellence
Jacksonville Journal-Courier

Jacksonville, IL

Mike Miner, Editor/Designer

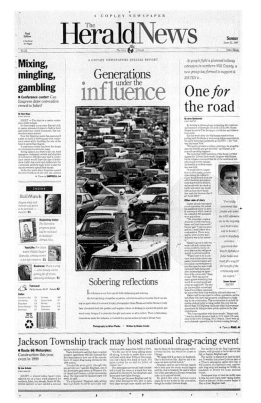

Award of Excellence
The Herald News

Aurora, IL

Karen Wolden, Designer; James Denk, Director/Graphics & Design; Brian Plonka, Photographer

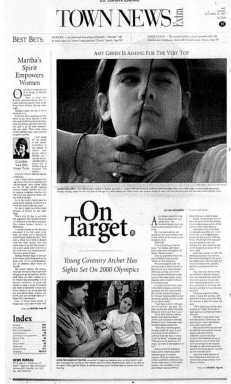

Award of Excellence
The Hartford Courant

Hartford, CT

Christian Potter Drury, Art Director; Rick Stewart, Designer; John Wolke, Photographer

Award of Excellence
Star Tribune
Minneapolis, MN

Jane Friedman, News Graphics Artist; Steve Brandt, Staff Writer; Joey McLeister, Photographer

Award of Excellence
The Times-Picayune
New Orleans, LA

George Berke, Design Director; James O'Byrne, News Editor; Angela Hill, Graphics Editor; Dan Swenson, Graphic Artist; Susan Koenig, Designer

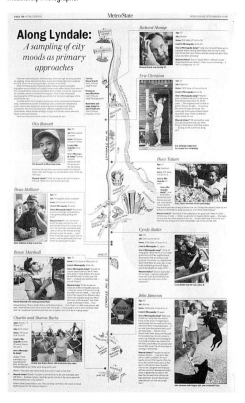

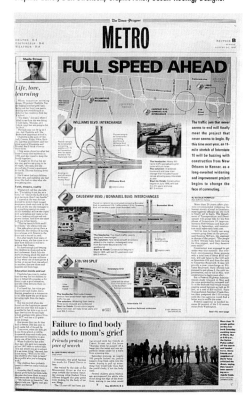

Silver
Folha de S.Paulo
São Paulo, Brazil

William Mariotto, Graphic Designer

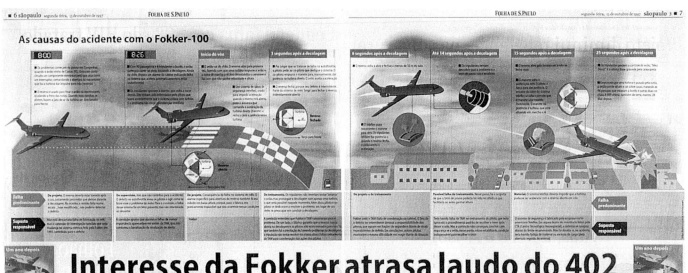

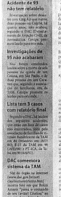

Award of Excellence
The Washington Post
Washington, DC

Cheney Gazzam Baltz, Assistant News Editor; **Michel duCille**, Photo Editor; **Nancy Andrews**, Photographer; **Robert Dorrell**, Graphic Artist

Silver
Reforma
México City, México

Ignacio Guerrero, Section Designer; **Daniel Esqueda Guadalajara**, Graphics Coordinator; **Juan Jesús Cortés**, Illustrator; **Emilio Deheza**, Art Director; **Eduardo Danilo**, Design Consultant; **Héctor Zamarrón**, Editor

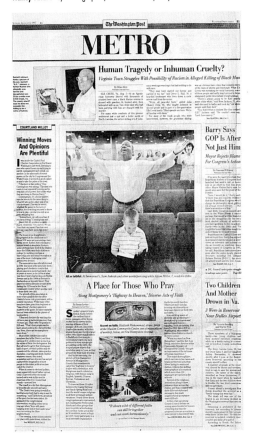

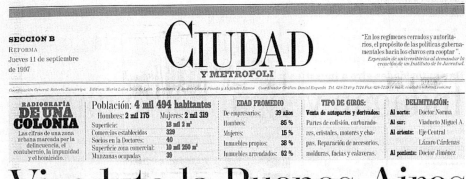

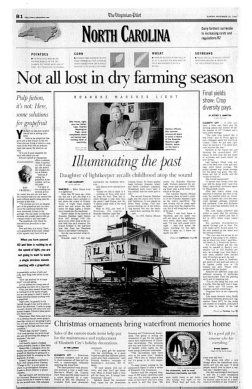

Award of Excellence
The Virginian-Pilot
Norfolk, VA

Harry Brandt, Page Designer; **Rob Morris**, News Editor

Award of Excellence
El Norte
Monterrey, México

Adrián Alvarez, Designer; **Jorge Obregón Garza**, Designer; **Reynaldo Márquez**, Section Editor; **Jorge Vidrio**, Graphics Editor; **Alexandro Medrano**, Graphics Editor; **Raúl Braulio Martinez**, Art Director; **Martha Treviño**, Editor Director; **Ramón Alberto Garza**; General Editor Director; **Edgar García**, Photo Artist

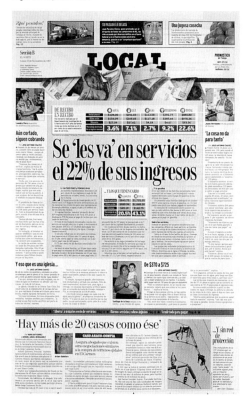

Award of Excellence
El Norte
Monterrey, México

Adrián Alvarez, Designer; **Isaac de Coss**, Illustrator; **Reynaldo Márquez**, Section Editor; **Jorge Vidrio**, Graphics Editor; **Alexandro Medrano**, Graphics Editor; **Raúl Braulio Martinez**, Art Director; **Martha Treviño**, Editor Director; **Ramón Alberto Garza**; General Editor Director

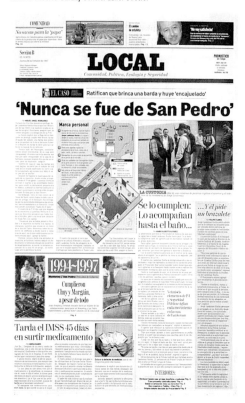

Award of Excellence
The News-Sentinel
Fort Wayne, IN

Derrick Barker, Page One Designer

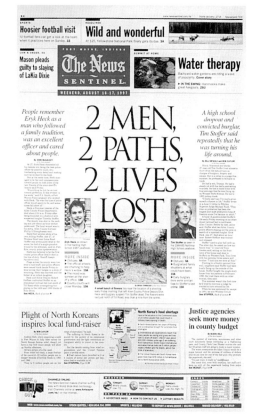

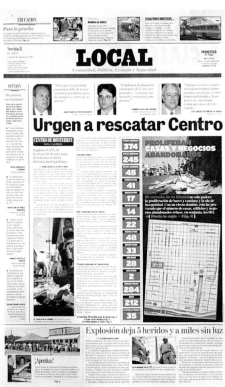

Award of Excellence
El Norte
Monterrey, México

Ramón Alberto Garza, General Editor Director; **Jorge Obregón Garza**, Designer; **Reynaldo Márquez**, Section Editor; **Jorge Vidrio**, Graphics Editor; **Alexandro Medrano**, Graphics Editor; **Raúl Braulio Martinez**, Art Director; **Martha Treviño**, Editor Director

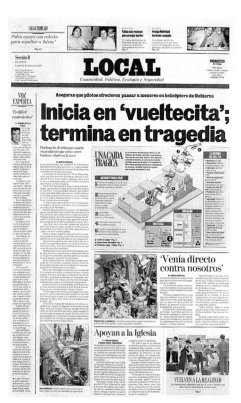

Award of Excellence
El Norte
Monterrey, México

Jorge Obregón Garza, Designer; **Eddie A. Macías**, Illustrator; **Reynaldo Márquez**, Section Editor; **Jorge Vidrio**, Graphics Editor; **Alexandro Medrano**, Graphics Editor; **Raúl Braulio Martinez**, Art Director; **Martha Treviño**, Editor Director; **Ramón Alberto Garza**; General Editor Director

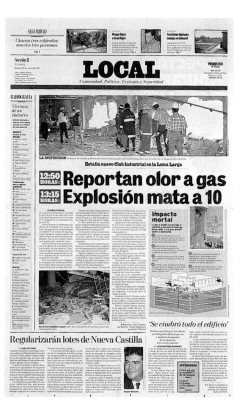

Award of Excellence
El Norte
Monterrey, México

Jorge Obregón Garza, Designer; **Luis Vazquez**, Illustrator; **Reynaldo Márquez**, Section Editor; **Jorge Vidrio**, Graphics Editor; **Alexandro Medrano**, Graphics Editor; **Raúl Braulio Martinez**, Art Director; **Martha Treviño**, Editor Director; **Ramón Alberto Garza**; General Editor Director

Award of Excellence
Reforma
México City, México

Oscar Yáñez, Designer; **Ignacio Guerrero**, Section Designer; **Daniel Esqueda Guadalajara**, Graphics Coordinator; **Adrián Rubio**, Illustrator; **Gustavo Hernández**, Editor; **Emilio Deheza**, Art Director; **Eduardo Danilo**, Design Consultant

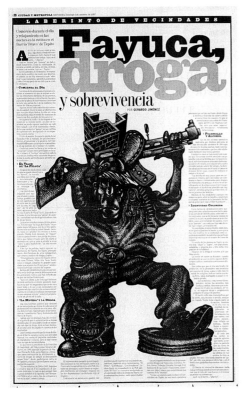

Award of Excellence
Reforma
México City, México

Daniel Esqueda Guadalajara, Designer/Photographer; **Carlos Almazán**, Editor; **Ignacio Guerrero**, Section Designer; **Emilio Deheza**, Art Director; **Eduardo Danilo**, Design Consultant

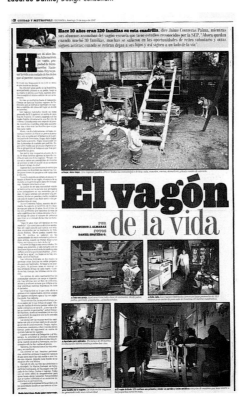

Award of Excellence
Reforma
México City, México

Daniel Esqueda Guadalajara, Graphic Coordinator; **Ignacio Guerrero**, Section Designer; **Juan Jesús Cortés**, Illustrator; **Jorge Andrés Gómez Pineda**, Editor; **Eduardo Danilo**, Design Consultant; **María Luisa Díaz de León**, Editor; **Emilio Deheza**, Art Director

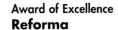
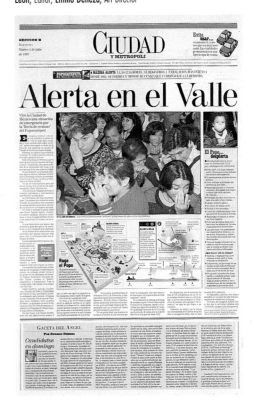

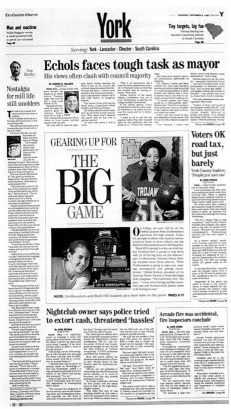

Award of Excellence
The Charlotte Observer
Charlotte, NC

Gina Davidson, Designer; **Bob Padgett**, Photographer; **Diedra Laird**, Photographer; **Monica Moses**, Design Director

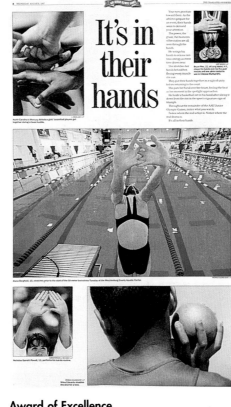

Award of Excellence
• Also an Award of Excellence for Photo Story
The Charlotte Observer
Charlotte, NC

Scott Goldman, Assistant Sports Editor/Designer; **Danielle Parks**, Designer; **John D. Simmons**, Photo Editor; **Laura Mueller**, Photographer; **Jeff Siner**, Photographer; **Patrick Schneider**, Photographer; **Christopher A. Record**, Photographer; **Gary O'Brien**, Photographer; **Monica Moses**, Design Director; **Susan Gilbert**, Director/Photography; **Gayle Shomer**, Photographer

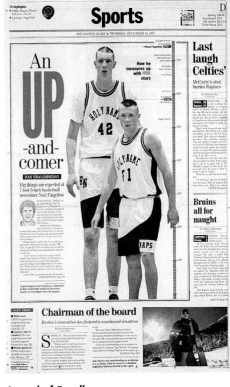

Award of Excellence
The Boston Globe
Boston, MA

Janet L. Michaud, Designer; **Sean McNaughton**, Graphic Artist; **Joe Sullivan**, Assistant Sports Editor; **Jim Davis**, Photographer

Award of Excellence
Göteborgs-Posten
Göteborg, Sweden

Thomas Andersson, Designer

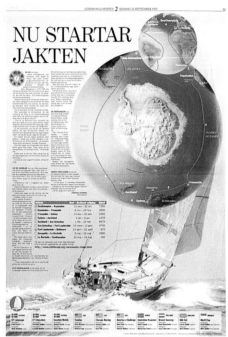

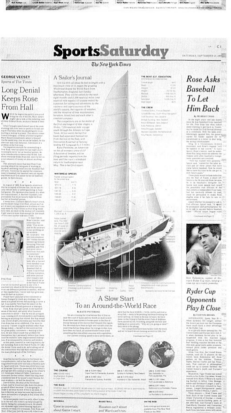

Award of Excellence
Marca
Madrid, Spain

César Galera, Graphic Artist and Designer; **José Juan Gámez**, Art Director

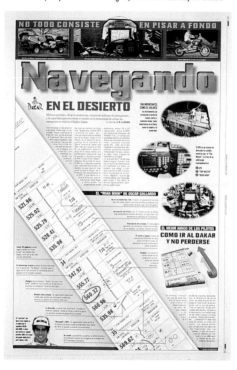

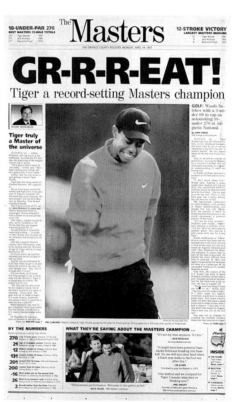

Award of Excellence
Chicago Tribune
Chicago, IL

Therese Shechter, Associate Graphics & Design Editor; **John Cherwa**, Sports Editor; **Joe Knowles**, Assistant Sports Editor; **Francisco Bernosconi**, Assistant Picture Editor; **Jim Prisching**, Photographer

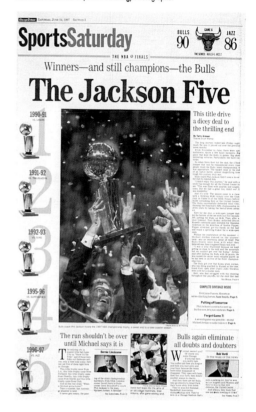

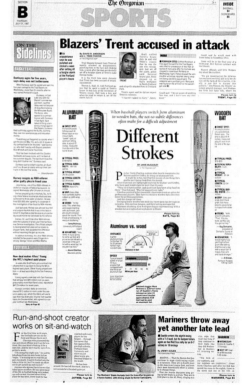

Award of Excellence
The New York Times
New York, NY

Wayne Kamidoi, Designer; **Juan Velasco**, Illustrator; **Joe Ward**, Graphics Editor

Award of Excellence
The Orange County Register
Santa Ana, CA

Kevin Byrne, Sports Design Team Leader; **Larry Nista**, Copy Editor; **Staff**

Award of Excellence
The Oregonian
Portland, OR

Chris Ralston, Designer

Award of Excellence
The Seattle Times
Seattle, WA

Rick Lund, Designer; Michael Kellams, Designer; David Miller, Art Director

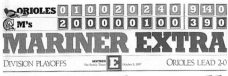

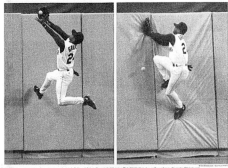

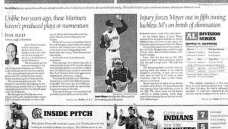

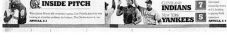

Award of Excellence
Star Tribune
Minneapolis, MN

Ray Grumney, Designer/News Graphics Director; Marlin Levison, Photographer; Doug Smith, Writer

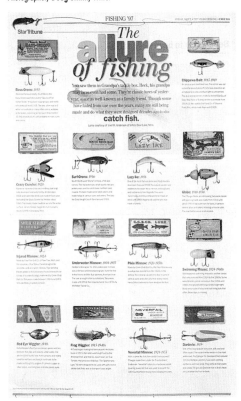

Award of Excellence
The Star-Ledger
Newark, NJ

Mark Morrissey, Designer; Noah Addis, Photographer; Kevin Whitmer, Sports Editor

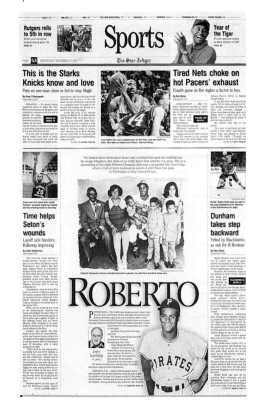

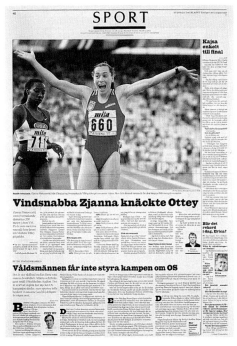

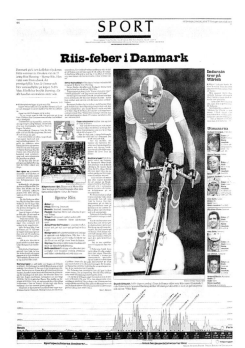

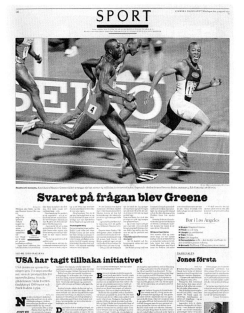

Award of Excellence
Svenska Dagbladet
Stockholm, Sweden
Staff

Award of Excellence
Svenska Dagbladet
Stockholm, Sweden
Staff

Award of Excellence
Svenska Dagbladet
Stockholm, Sweden
Staff

Award of Excellence
El Tiempo
Santa Fe de Bogota, Colombia

Beiman Pinilla, Graphics Editor; **Yesid Vargas**, Designer

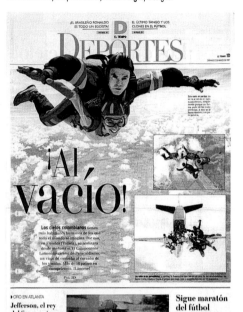

Award of Excellence
The Times-Picayune
New Orleans, LA

George Berke, Design Director; **Billy Turner**, Deputy Sports Editor; **Doug Parker**, Photo Editor; **Rusty Costanza**, Photographer; **Grant Staublin**, Designer

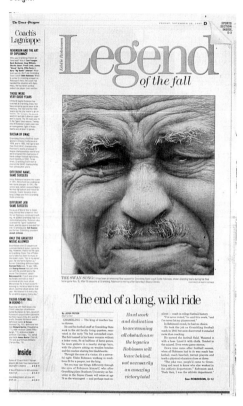

Award of Excellence
The Toronto Star
Toronto, Canada

Mark Atchison, Associate Sports Editor

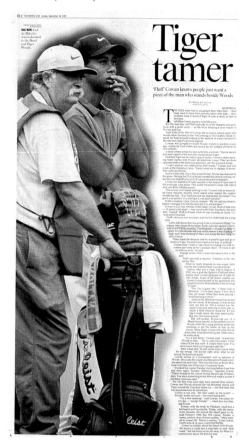

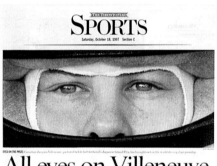

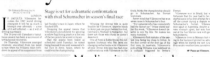

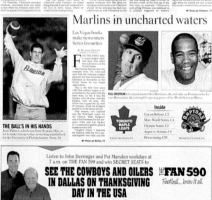

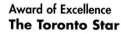

Award of Excellence
The Toronto Star
Toronto, Canada

Mark Atchison, Associate Sports Editor

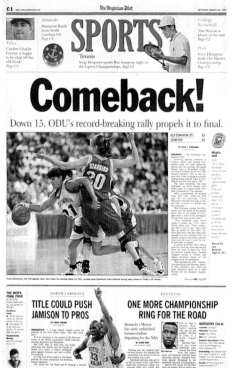

Award of Excellence
The Virginian-Pilot
Norfolk, VA

Latané Jones, Designer; **Bob Fleming**, Sports Editor; **Joe Garvey**, Sports Desk Team Leader

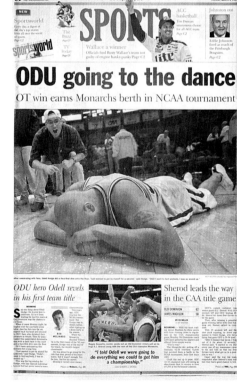

Award of Excellence
The Virginian-Pilot
Norfolk, VA

Latané Jones, Designer; **Bob Fleming**, Sports Editor; **Joe Garvey**, Sports Desk Team Leader; **Huy Nguyen**, Photographer

Silver
Lexington Herald-Leader
Lexington, KY

Willie Hiatt, Sports Copy Editor/Designer; **Steve Dorsey**, Presentation Director/Designer; **Greg Perry**, Photographer; **Mark Maloney**, Staff Writer; **Staff**

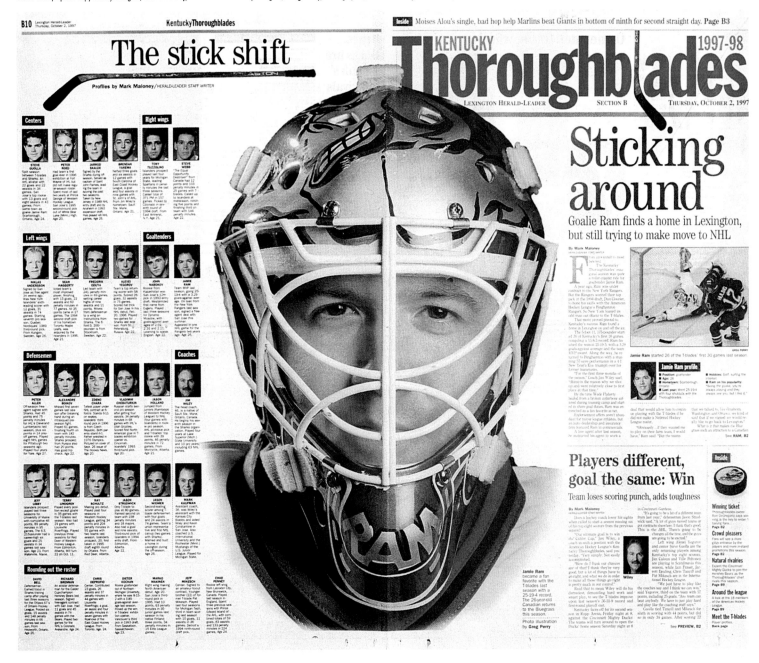

Award of Excellence
Asbury Park Press
Neptune, NJ

Annette J. Vázquez, Designer; **Harris G. Siegel**, M.E./Design & Photography; **Andrew Prendimano**, Art & Photo Director; **John Quinn**, M.E./Sports; **Pete Barzilai**, Sports Slot; **Greig Henderson**, Sports Slot; **Celeste LaBrosse**, Night Photo Editor; **Sports Staff**

Award of Excellence
Asbury Park Press
Neptune, NJ

Annette J. Vázquez, Designer; **Harris G. Siegel**, M.E./Design & Photography; **Andrew Prendimano**, Art & Photo Director; **John Quinn**, M.E./Sports; **Pete Barzilai**, Sports Slot; **Greig Henderson**, Sports Slot; **Celeste LaBrosse**, Night Photo Editor; **Sports Staff**

Award of Excellence
Asbury Park Press
Neptune, NJ

Christine A. Birch, Designer; **Harris G. Siegel**, M.E./Design & Photography; **Andrew Prendimano**, Art & Photo Director; **Ed Gabel**, Artist

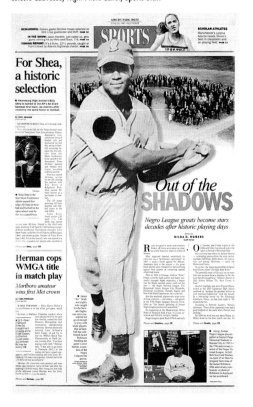

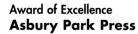
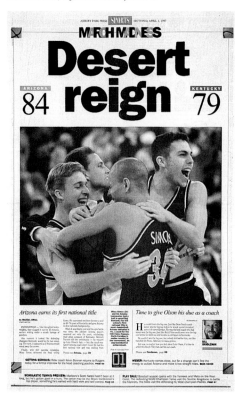

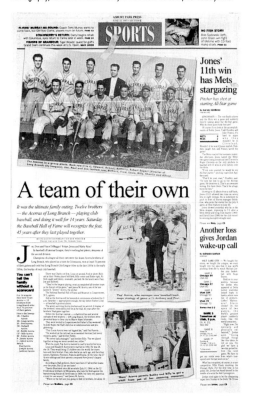

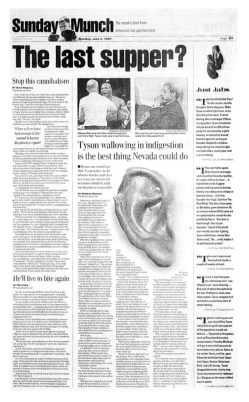

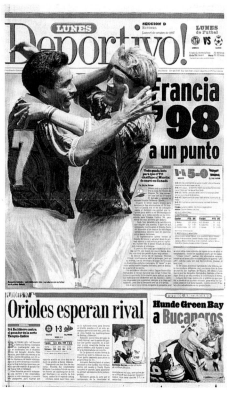

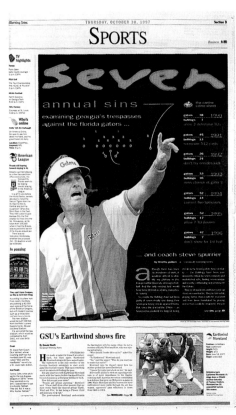

Award of Excellence
Post-Tribune
Gary, IN

Matt Dorney, Sports Editor; **Mark Thurman**, Graphic Artist; **Mark DeChant**, Presentation Editor

Award of Excellence
Reforma
México City, México

Emilio Deheza, Art Director; **Eduardo Danilo**, Design Consultant; **Roberto Gutiérrez Durán**, Section Designer; **Alejandro Gómez**, Editor; **Alberto Nava**, Photo Illustrator; **Guillermo Caballero**, Graphic Coordinator; **Luis Cortés**, Photographer

Award of Excellence
Savannah Morning News
Savannah, GA

Stephen D. Komives, Sports Planning Editor; **Timothy J. Guidera**, Sports Reporter

The Topeka Capital-Journal
Topeka, KS
Jeff Davis, Designer

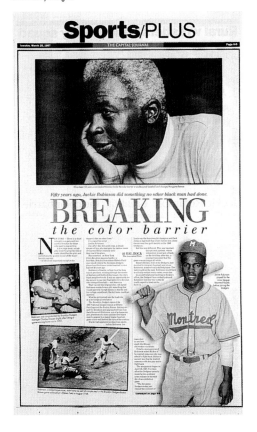

a.m. León
León, México
Gustavo Belman, Designer; **Beatriz Zambrano**, Art Director

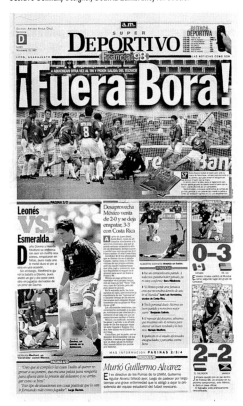

The Ball State Daily News
Muncie, IN
Chris Meighan, Designer

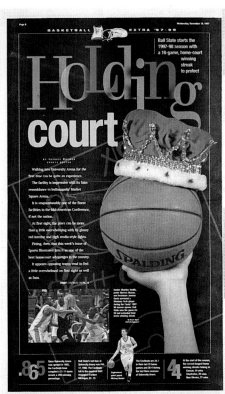

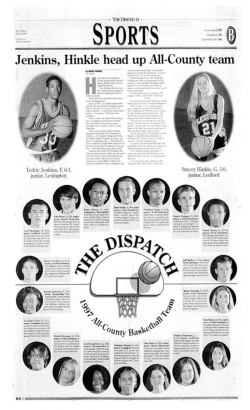

The Dispatch
Lexington, NC
Michelle Moore, Designer; **Donnie Roberts**, Photographer; **Bruce Wehrle**, Sports Writer/Editor; **Bryan Strickland**, Sports Writer/Editor

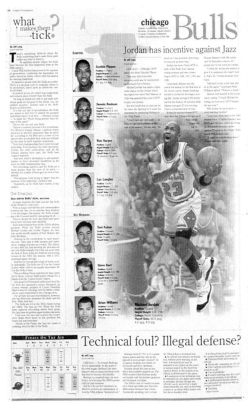
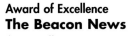

The Beacon News
Aurora, IL
Michael W. Whitley, Designer; **James Denk**, Director/Graphics & Design

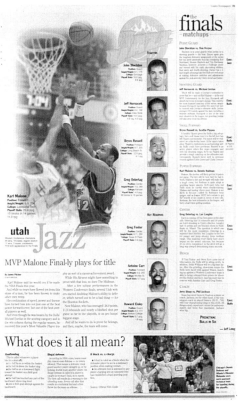

Award of Excellence
Diario de Noticias
Huarte, Spain
Silvia de Luis, Designer

Award of Excellence
Diario de Noticias
Huarte, Spain
Silvia de Luis, Designer

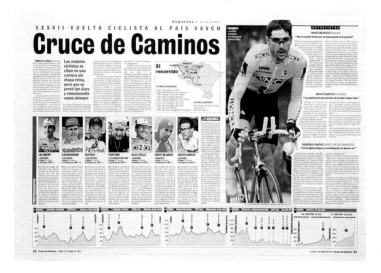

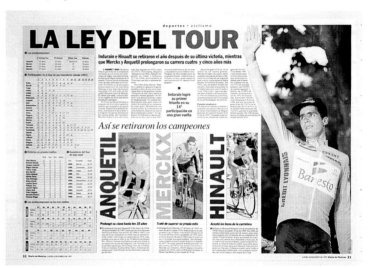

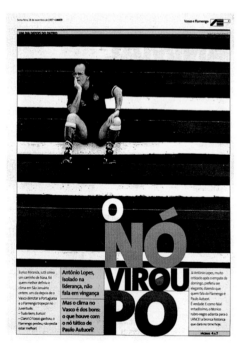

Award of Excellence
Lance!
Rio de Janeiro, Brazil
Neuza Tasca, Designer; **Sergio Rodrigues**, Executive Director; **Marco Antonio Rezende**, Photographer

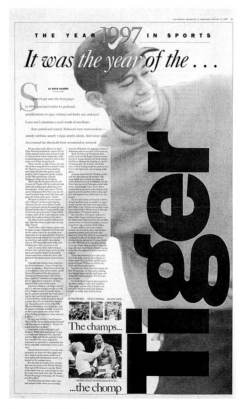

Award of Excellence
Jacksonville Journal-Courier
Jacksonville, IL
Mike Miner, Editor/Designer

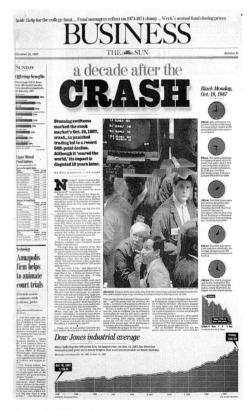

Award of Excellence
The Baltimore Sun
Baltimore, MD
Dan Clemens, News Designer; **Lauri Treston**, News Design Director; **Joseph Hutchinson**, A.M.E. Graphics/Design

Award of Excellence
The New York Times
New York, NY

John MacLeod, Art Director; **Carl Sharif**, Illustrator; **Dylan McClain**, Graphics Editor

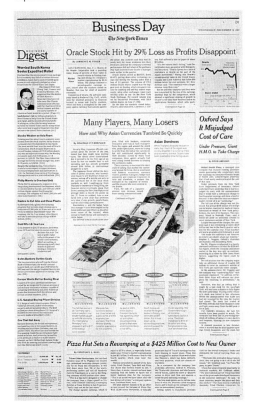

Award of Excellence
The New York Times
New York, NY

Tim Oliver, Presentation Editor; **Dylan McClain**, Graphics Editor; **Sarah Weissman**, Photo Editor; **Naum Kazhdan**, Photographer

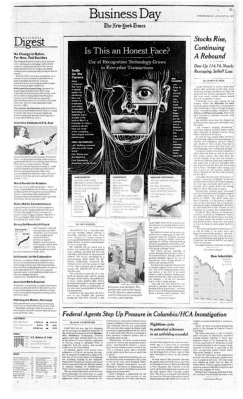

Award of Excellence
The Times-Picayune
New Orleans, LA

George Berke, Design Director; **Kenneth Harrison**, Illustrator; **Robert Scott**, Money Editor

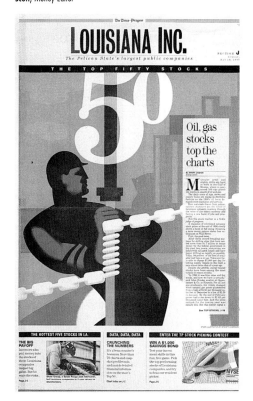

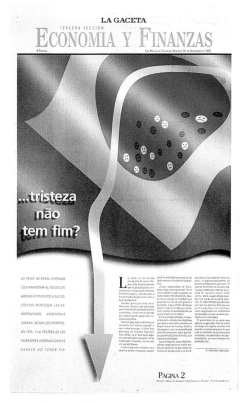

Award of Excellence
La Gaceta
San Miguel de Tucuman, Argentina

Sergio S. Fernandez, Art Director & Designer; **Daniel Fontanarrosa**, Illustrator; **Mario Garcia**, Design Consultant; **Antonio Arnedo**, Editor

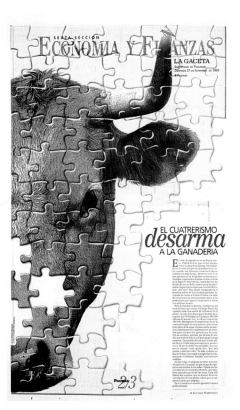

Award of Excellence
La Gaceta
San Miguel de Tucuman, Argentina

Sergio S. Fernandez, Art Director & Designer; **Daniel Fontanarrosa**, Illustrator; **Mario Garcia**, Design Consultant; **Gustavo Martinelli**, Editor

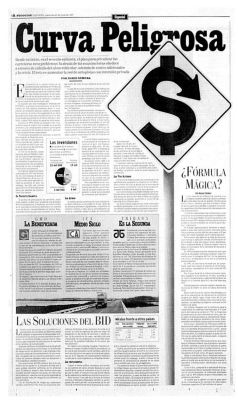

Award of Excellence
Reforma
México City, México

Emilio Deheza, Art Director; **Alberto Cervantes**, Illustrator; **Vicente Hernández**, Editor; **Eduardo Danilo**, Design Consultant; **Ricardo Peña**, Section Designer; **Ernesto Carrillo**, Design Editor; **Daniel Barbosa**, Designer

Award of Excellence
Reforma
México City, México

Emilio Deheza, Art Director; **Jorge Peñaloza**, Illustrator; **Alejandro Páez**, Editor; **Eduardo Danilo**, Design Consultant; **Ricardo Peña**, Section Designer; **Ernesto Carrillo**, Design Editor; **Raúl Espinosa de los Monteros**, Designer

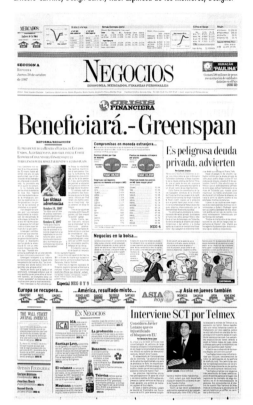

Award of Excellence
Reforma
México City, México

Emilio Deheza, Art Director; **Adrián Rubio**, Illustrator; **Martha Trejo**, Editor; **Eduardo Danilo**, Design Consultant; **Ricardo Peña**, Section Designer; **Ernesto Carrillo**, Design Editor; **Patricia Cárdenas**, Designer; **Vicente Hernández**, Editor

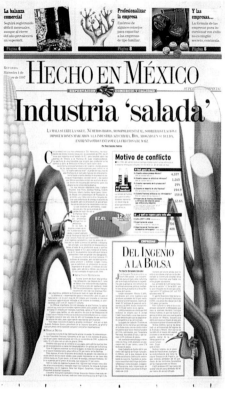

Award of Excellence
Reforma
México City, México

Emilio Deheza, Art Director; **Rodrigo Tovar**, Illustrator; **Alejandro Páez**, Editor; **Eduardo Danilo**, Design Consultant; **Ricardo Peña**, Section Designer; **Ernesto Carrillo**, Design Editor

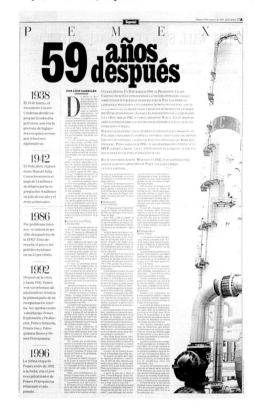

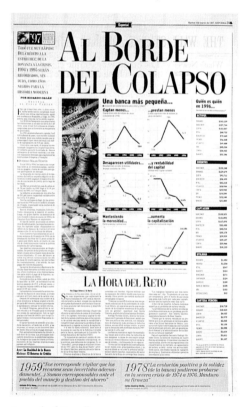

Award of Excellence
Reforma
México City, México

Ricardo Peña, Section Designer; **Alberto Cervantes**, Illustrator; **Martha Trejo**, Editor; **Ernesto Carrillo**, Design Editor; **Emilio Deheza**, Art Director; **Eduardo Danilo**, Design Consultant

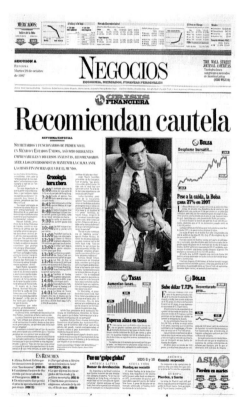

Award of Excellence
Reforma
México City, México

Ricardo Peña, Section Designer; **Alejandro Páez**, Editor; **Ernesto Carrillo**, Design Editor; **Emilio Deheza**, Art Director; **Eduardo Danilo**, Design Consultant

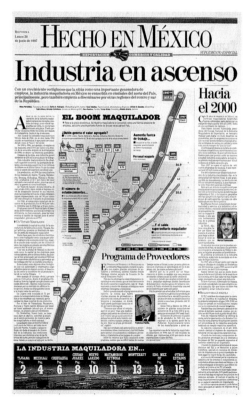

Award of Excellence
Reforma
México City, México

Ricardo Peña, Section Designer; **Ernesto Carrillo**, Design Editor; **Juan Jesús Cortés**, Illustrator; **Emilio Deheza**, Art Director; **Eduardo Danilo**, Design Consultant; **Martha Trejo**, Editor;

Silver
•Also **Silver** for News Portfolio
Expansión
Madrid, Spain

Pablo Ma Ramírez, Designer and Graphic Artist; **José Juan Gámez**, Art Director

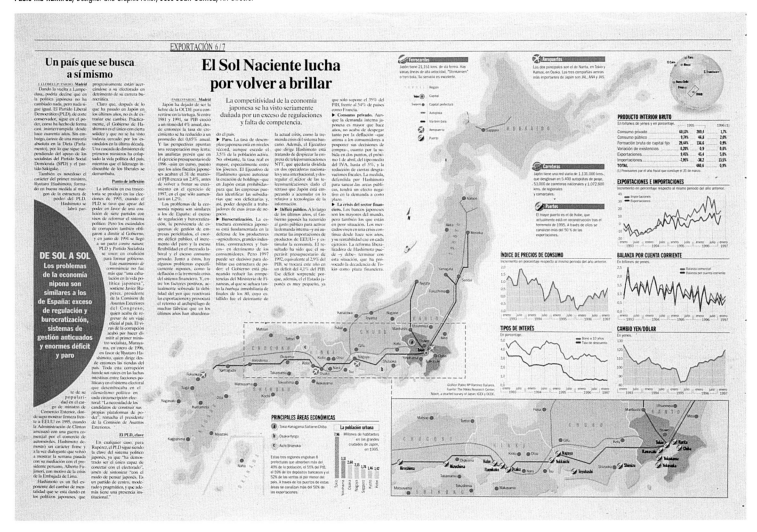

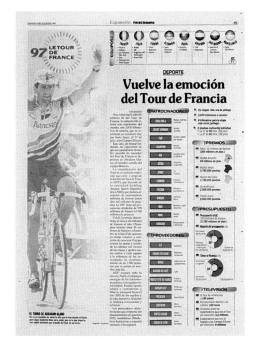

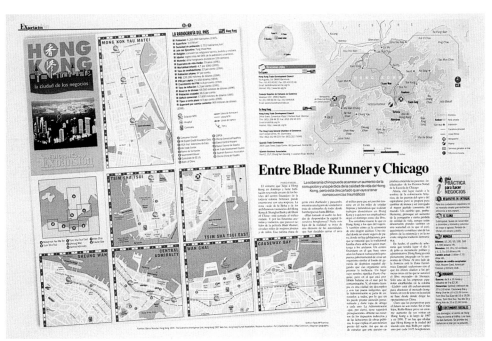

Award of Excellence
Expansión
Madrid, Spain

Diego Arambillet, Designer; **Mar Domingo**, Designer; **José Juan Gámez**, Art Director

Award of Excellence
Expansión
Madrid, Spain

Pablo Ma Ramírez, Designer and Graphic Artist; **José Juan Gámez**, Art Director

Award of Excellence
La Gaceta

San Miguel de Tucuman, Argentina

Daniel Fontanarrosa, Photo Illustrator; **Sergio S. Fernandez**, Art Director & Designer; **Mario Garcia**, Design Consultant; **Maria Ines Alvaro**, Editor

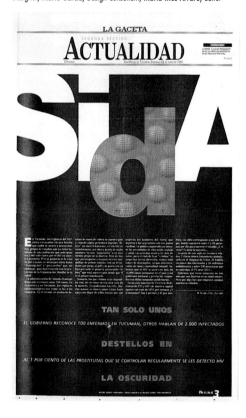

Award of Excellence
La Gaceta

San Miguel de Tucuman, Argentina

Sergio S. Fernandez, Art Director & Designer; **Daniel Fontanarrosa**, Photo Illustrator; **Mario Garcia**, Design Consultant; **Gustavo Rodriguez**, Editor; **Alvaro Aurane**, Editor; **Federico Abel**, Editor; **Federico Turpe**, Editor

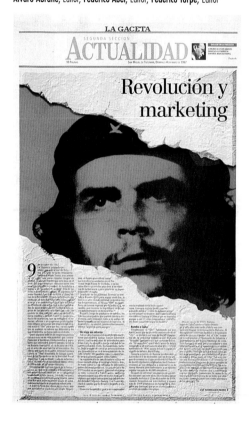

Award of Excellence
Pittsburgh Post-Gazette

Pittsburgh, PA

Kim Germovsek, Designer; **Christopher Pett-Ridge**, A.M.E. Graphics; **Bill Pliske**, Associate Editor/Graphics; **Anita Dufalla**, Art Director; **Andy Starnes**, Photographer

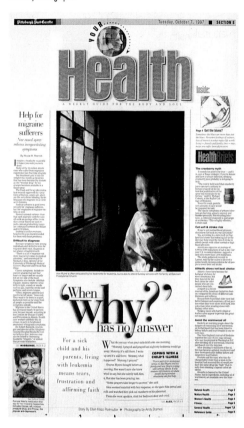

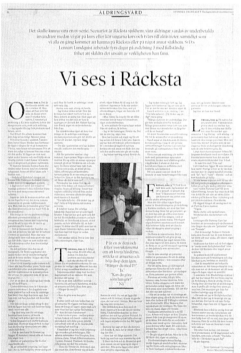

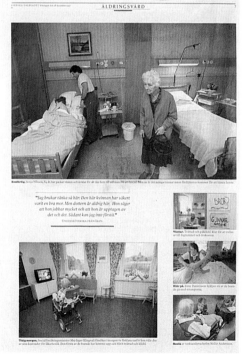

Award of Excellence
Svenska Dagbladet

Stockholm, Sweden

Staff

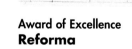

Award of Excellence
Reforma

México City, México

Xóchitl González, Section Designer; **Alejandro Banuet**, Graphics Editor; **Fabricio Vanden Broeck**, Artist; **Emilio Deheza**, Art Director; **Eduardo Danilo**, Design Consultant; **Luis Enrique López**, Editor

Award of Excellence
Asbury Park Press
Neptune, NJ

John Quinn, M.E./Sports; **Andrew Prendimano**, Art & Photo Director; **Harris G. Siegel**, M.E./Design & Photography, Designer; **Jacie Chun**, Illustrations

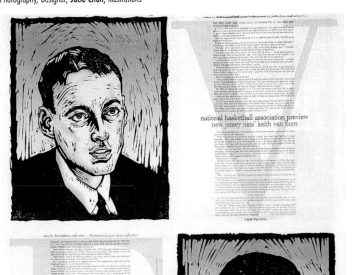

Award of Excellence
Svenska Dagbladet
Stockholm, Sweden

Staff

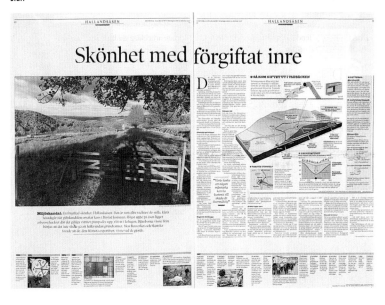

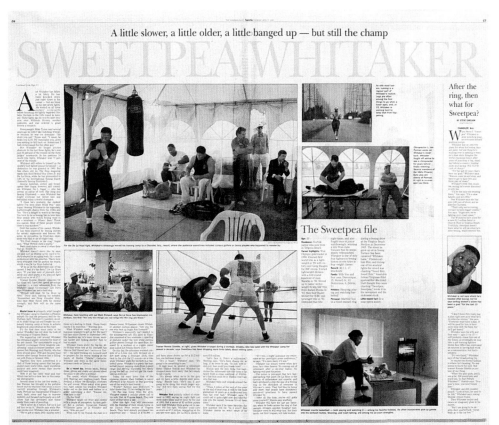

Award of Excellence
The Virginian-Pilot
Norfolk, VA

Courtney Murphy, Designer; **Carl Fincke**, Editor; **Beth Bergman**, Photographer; **Bill Kelly**, Photo Editor

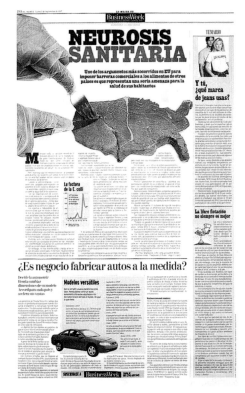

Award of Excellence
El Norte
Monterrey, México

Diego Carranza M. del C., Designer; **Gil Jesús Chavez**, Editor; **Mónica Patiño**, Photographer; **Jorge Vidrio**, Graphics Editor; **Karla García**, Electronic Photo; **Raúl Braulio Martinez**, Art Director; **Alejandro Medrano**, Graphics Editor

Award of Excellence
El Norte
Monterrey, México

Martín Alvarado L., Designer; **Antonio Puga**, Illustrator; **Jorge Vidrio**, Graphics Editor; **Alexandro Medrano**, Graphics Editor; **Raúl Braulio Martinez**, Art Director

Award of Excellence
Expansión
Madrid, Spain

María Jesús Rivera, Graphic Artist; **Pablo Ma Ramirez**, Designer; **José Juan Gámez**, Art Director

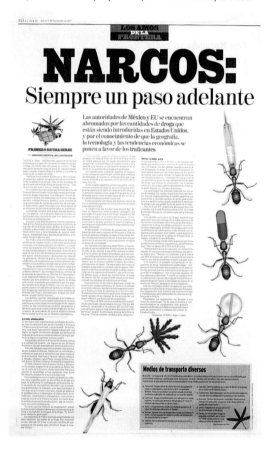

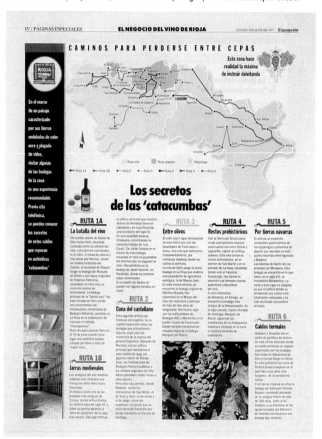

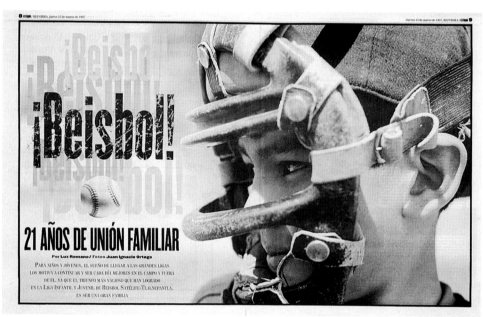

Award of Excellence
Reforma
México City, México

Daniel Esqueda Guadalajara, Graphic Coordinator/Designer; **Joseph Estavillo**, Section Designer; **Juan Ignacio Ortega**, Photographer; **Enrique Cárdenas**, Editor; **Ismael García**, Editor; **María Luisa Díaz de León**, General Editor; **Emilio Deheza**, Art Director; **Eduardo Danilo**, Design Consultant

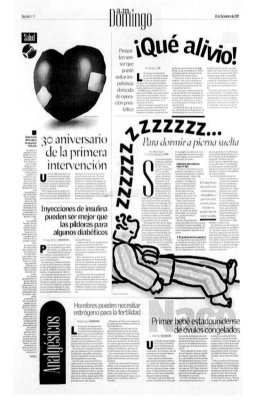

Award of Excellence
a.m. León
León, México

Gustavo Belman, Designer; **Beatriz Zambrano**, Art Director; **Alfonso Hurtado**, Editor

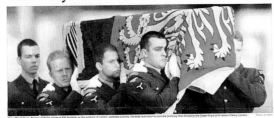

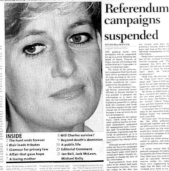

Silver
The Scotsman
Edinburgh, Scotland
Staff

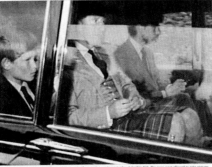

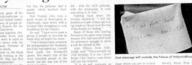

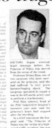

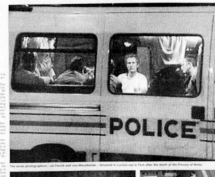

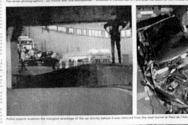

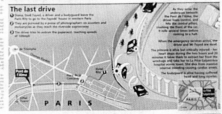

Silver
The Seattle Times
Seattle, WA
Michael Kellams, Designer; **Karen Klinkenberg**, Designer; **Cathy McLain**, Sunday Editor; **David Miller**, Art Director & Designer

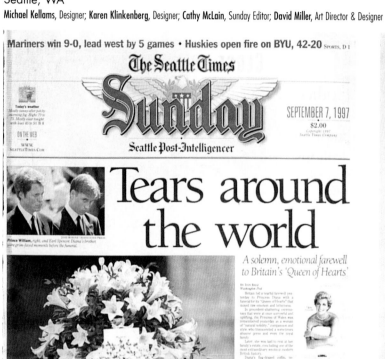

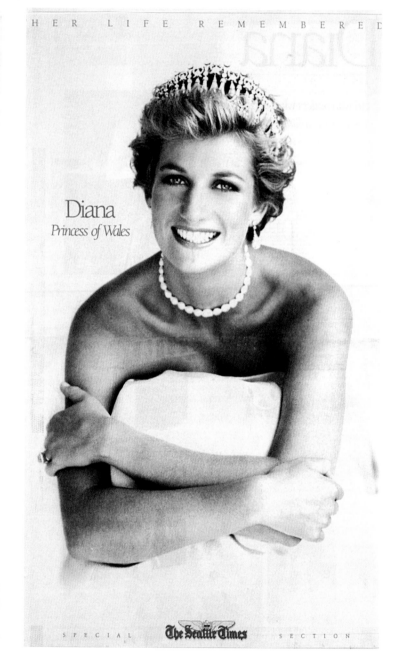

Mariners win 9-0, lead west by 5 games • Huskies open fire on BYU, 42-20 SPORTS, D 1

The Seattle Times

Sunday

Seattle Post-Intelligencer

SEPTEMBER 7, 1997
$2.00

Tears around the world

A solemn, emotional farewell to Britain's 'Queen of Hearts'

Prince William, right, and Earl Spencer, Diana's brother, wore grim-faced moments before the funeral.

Welsh Guards carry Princess Diana's casket from Westminster Abbey after the funeral service yesterday. The small wreath of white roses at the front was from Prince Harry, 12. His card said just "Mummy."

Brother delivers a tongue-lashing

Earl's eulogy skewers media and royals

Calcutta mourns Mother Teresa

HER LIFE REMEMBERED

Diana
Princess of Wales

Award of Excellence
The Honolulu Advertiser
Honolulu, HI

David F. Montesino, A.M.E. Design; Stephen Downes, Art Director; John Bender, Designer

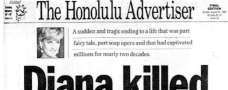

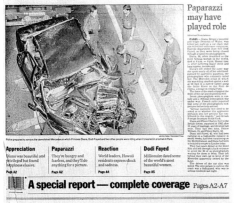

Award of Excellence
•Also an **Award of Excellence** for Special News Topics
The Daily Telegraph
London, England
Staff

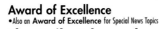

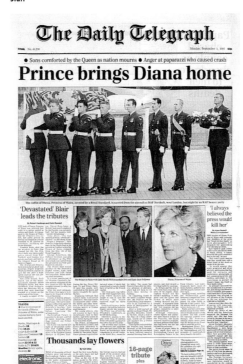

Award of Excellence
Folha de S.Paulo
São Paulo, Brazil

Paula Cesarino Costa, Special Section Editor; Jaime Spitzcovsky, International Editor; Jair de Oliveira, Page Designer; Arthur Fajardo, Deputy Art Editor; Luciana Vaz Guimarães, Page Designer; Adilson Secco, Graphic Designer; Mario Kanno, Graphic Designer; Marcelo Katsuki; Graphic Designer; Renata Letto, Graphic Designer

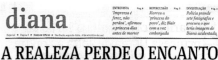

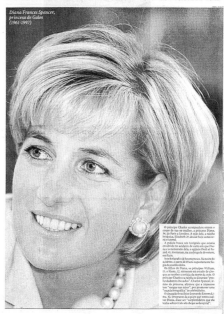

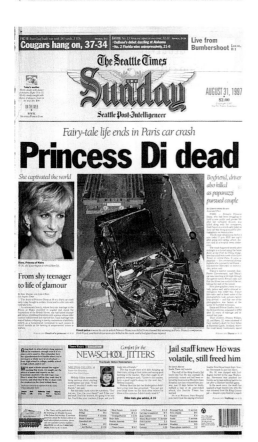

Award of Excellence
The Seattle Times
Seattle, WA

Michael Kellams, Designer; Karen Klinkenberg, Designer; Cathy McLain, Sunday Editor; David Miller, Art Director & Designer

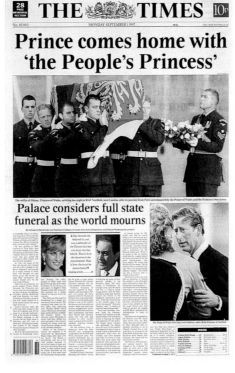

Award of Excellence
The Times
London, England
Staff

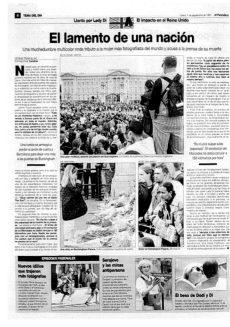

Award of Excellence
El Periodico de Catalunya
Barcelona, Spain

Olga Puig, Author; Ricard Sans, Design Editor; Dpto. Gente, Editor; Iosu de la Torre, Vice Editor

Silver
The Scotsman
Edinburgh, Scotland
Staff

THE SCOTSMAN
THE FUNERAL OF DIANA, PRINCESS OF WALES – SATURDAY, 6 SEPTEMBER 1997

Diana: A farewell

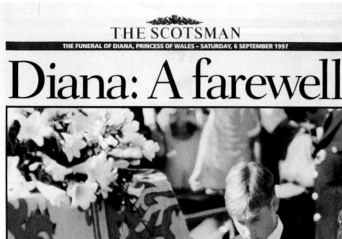

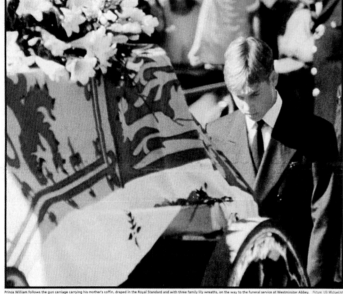

Prince William follows the gun carriage carrying his mother's coffin, draped in the Royal Standard and with three family lily wreaths, on the way to the funeral service at Westminster Abbey. Picture: Ulli Michael/AP

After a week of wailing, sermons, noise and news the defining moment was entirely silent

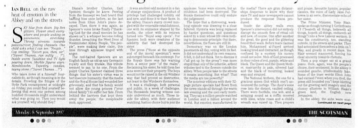

Monday, 8 September 1997

THE SCOTSMAN

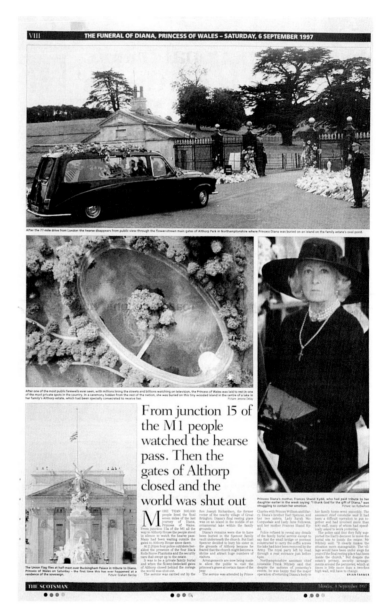

After the 77-mile drive from London the hearse disappears from public view through the flower-strewn main gates of Althorp Park in Northamptonshire where Princess Diana was buried on an island on the family estate's oval pond.

After one of the most public farewells ever seen, with millions lining the streets and billions watching on television, the Princess of Wales was laid to rest in one of the most private spots in the country. In a ceremony hidden from the rest of the nation, she was buried on this tiny wooded island in the centre of a lake in her family's Althorp estate, which had been specially consecrated to receive her. Picture: Jenine Delay

Princess Diana's mother, Frances Shand Kydd, who had paid tribute to her daughter earlier in the week saying: "I thank God for the gift of Diana," was struggling to contain her emotion. Picture: Ian Rutherford

The Union Flag flies at half-mast over Buckingham Palace in tribute to Diana, Princess of Wales on Saturday – the first time this has ever happened at a residence of the sovereign. Picture: Graham Barclay

From junction 15 of the M1 people watched the hearse pass. Then the gates of Althorp closed and the world was shut out

THE SCOTSMAN

Monday, 8 September 1997

Award of Excellence
The Detroit News
Detroit, MI

Chris Kozlowski, A.M.E. Graphics/Design; David Kordalski, Graphics/Design Editor; Theresa Badovich, News Design Editor; Mike Perkins, Designer; Diana Thomas, Designer; Roger Hensley, Designer; Joe Greco, Designer; Steve Fecht; Photo Director; Steve Haines, Asst. Photo Editor; Frank Lovinski, Deputy M.E.

Award of Excellence
The Hartford Courant
Hartford, CT

Christian Potter Drury, Art Director; Cecilia Prestamo, Photo Editor/Designer; Melanie Shaffer, Designer; Jim Kuykendal, Designer

Award of Excellence
Daily News
New York, NY

Bill St. Angelo, Sunday Design Director; Lou Parajos, Sunday News Editor; Brian Moss, News Editor; Bob Massi, News Editor; Nancy O'Brien, Assistant Sunday Editor

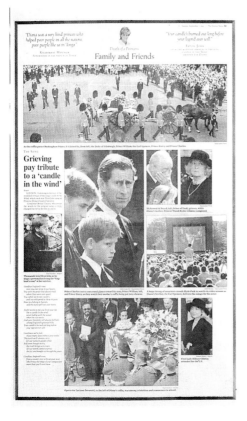

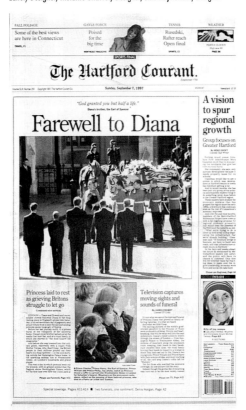

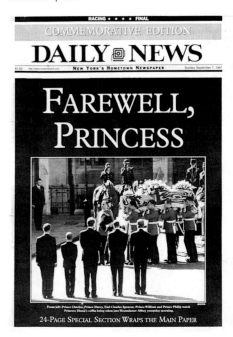

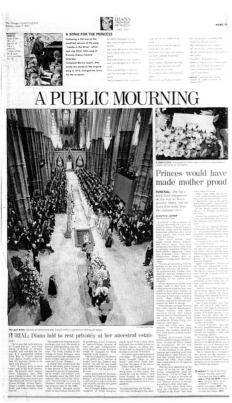

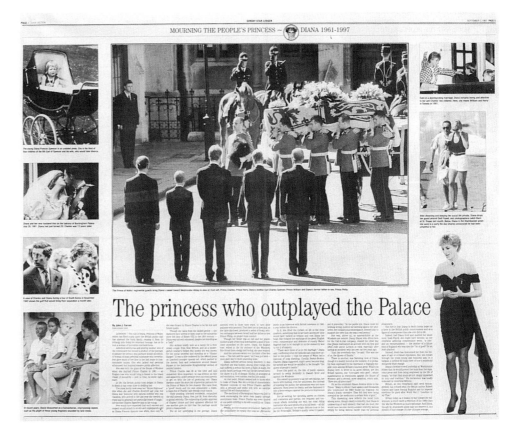

Award of Excellence
The Orange County Register
Santa Ana, CA
Staff

Award of Excellence
The Star-Ledger
Newark, NJ

Bob Bogert, Designer; Sharon Russell, Photo Editor; Charles Cooper, M.E./Production; Pablo Colon, Designer/Art Director; George Frederick, Designer/A.M.E. Design; Jane Hood, Designer; Fran Dauth, Editor; Susan Olds, Editor; Staff Reporters

Award of Excellence
The Times-Picayune
New Orleans, LA

George Berke, Design Director; **James O'Byrne**, Sunday Editor; **Susan Koenig**, Designer; **Doug Parker**, Photo Editor

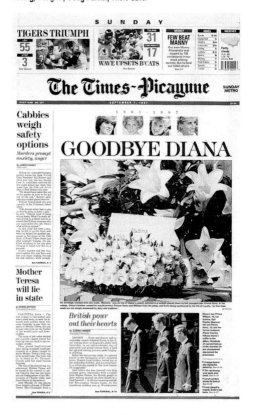

Award of Excellence
The Virginian-Pilot
Norfolk, VA

Lisa Cowan, Designer; **Denis Finley**, News Editor; **Andrea Smith**, Designer; **Courtney Murphy**, Designer/Art Director; **Eric Seidman**, Creative Director; **Paul Nelson**, Designer

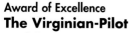

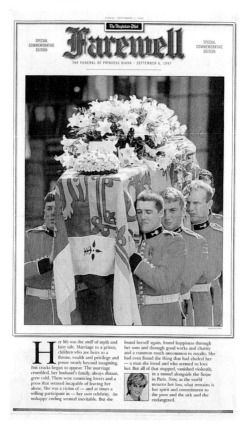

Award of Excellence
The Idaho Statesman
Boise, ID

Randy Wright, Designer; **Patrick Poyfair**, Designer; **Chris Hopfensperger**, Designer; **Jim Peak**, News Editor

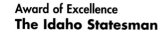

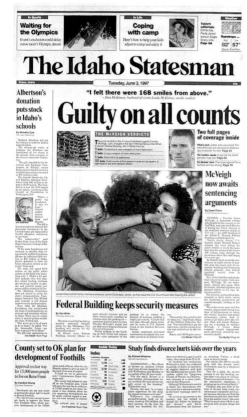

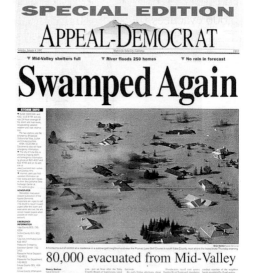

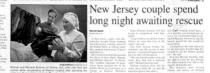

Award of Excellence
Appeal-Democrat
Marysville, CA

Julie Shirley, Editor

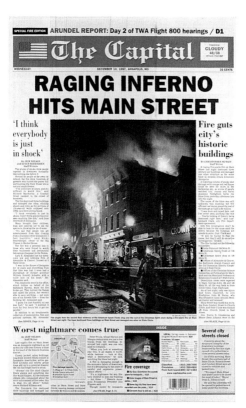

Award of Excellence
The Capital
Annapolis, MD

Scott Haring, Design Editor; **Loretta R. Haring**, News Editor

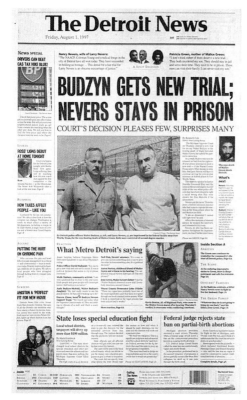

Award of Excellence
The Detroit News
Detroit, MI

Chris Kozlowski, A.M.E. Graphics/Design; **David Kordalski**, Graphics/Design Editor; **Theresa Badovich**, News Design Editor; **Tim Summers**, Graphic Artist; **Roger Hensley**, Page Designer; **Joe Greco**, Page Designer; **Howard Lovy**, Page Designer

Award of Excellence
The Detroit News
Detroit, MI

Chris Kozlowski, A.M.E. Graphics/Design; David Kordalski, Graphics/Design Editor; Theresa Badovich, News Design Editor; Tim Summers, Graphic Artist; Satoshi Toyoshima, Graphic Artist; Joe Greco, Page Designer; Roger Hensley, Page Designer; Howard Lovy; Page Designer

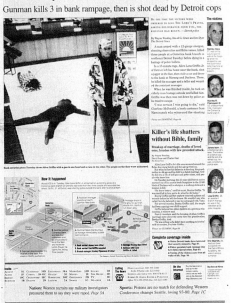

Award of Excellence
The Detroit News
Detroit, MI

Chris Kozlowski, A.M.E. Graphics/Design; David Kordalski, Graphics/Design Editor; Mike Perkins, Page Designer; Bill McMillan, News Editor; Luther Keith, AME/Sunday; Shanna Flowers, Deputy City Editor/Sunday; Cheryl Phillips, Assistant City Editor; Steve Fecht; Photo Director

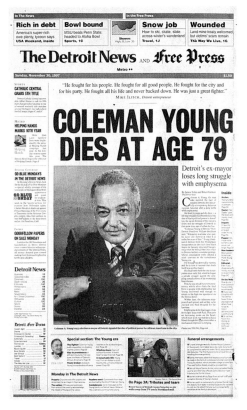

Award of Excellence
The Glendale News-Press
Tustin, CA

Geoff Bilau, News Editor

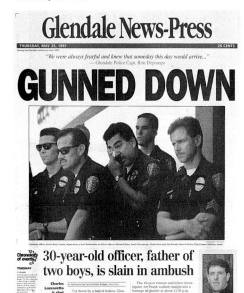

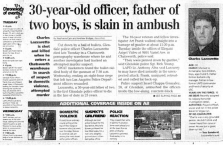

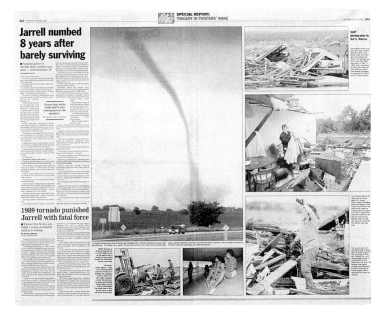

Award of Excellence
Austin American-Statesman
Austin, TX

G.W. Babb, Design Director; Michelle Rice, News Editor; Zach Ryall, Director/Photography; Sandra Santos, Page One Editor; Staff

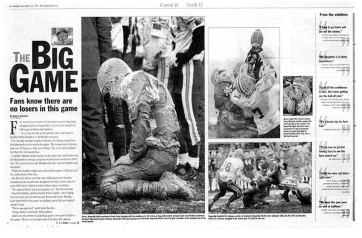

Award of Excellence
The Naperville Sun
Naperville, IL

Robb Montgomery, Design Editor; Brian Mohr, Designer; Darrell Goemaat, Photographer; Chris Stanford, Photographer; Roger Bartel, Regional Editor

Award of Excellence
Lexington Herald-Leader
Lexington, KY

Randy Medema, Designer; **Steve Dorsey,** Presentation Director/Designer; **Staff**

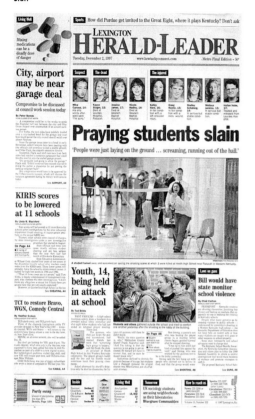

Award of Excellence
The Orange County Register
Santa Ana, CA

John Fabris, News Design Team Leader; **Bill Cunningham,** Focus Page Editor; **David Medzerian,** Design Team Leader; **Marcia Prouse,** Picture Editor; **Brenda Shoun,** Deputy Editor

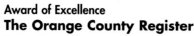
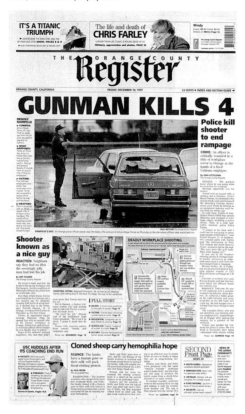

Award of Excellence
The Orange County Register
Santa Ana, CA

John Fabris, News Design Team Leader; **Maryanne Dell,** Senior Designer; **Patty Pitts,** Designer; **Marcia Prouse,** Picture Editor; **Brenda Shoun,** Deputy Editor; **Peter Nguyen,** Designer; **Michele Cardon,** Picture Editor

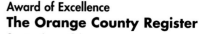
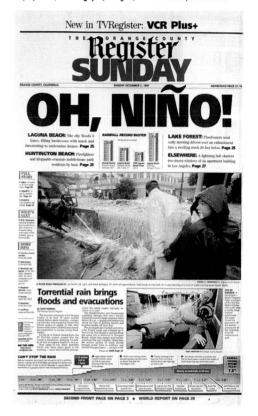

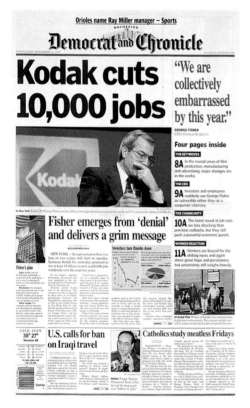

Award of Excellence
Rochester Democrat and Chronicle
Rochester, NY

Dennis R. Floss, A.M.E. Presentation/Designer; **Gary Piccirillo,** Asst. Presentation Editor/Designer; **Stan Wischnowski,** News Editor; **Steve Boerner,** Asst. Presentation Editor; **Annette Meade,** Asst. Graphics Editor; **Henry Howard,** Assistant News Editor; **Aimee Wiles,** Photographer; **Kevin M. Smith,** Artist; **Yvonne Lin,** Artist; **Kevin Rivoli,** Assistant Photo Editor

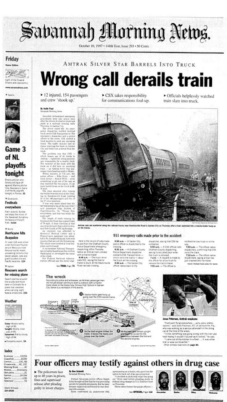

Award of Excellence
Savannah Morning News
Savannah, GA

Theresa Trenkamp, News Planner/Designer; **Brian D. Gross,** News Planner/Designer; **Drew Martin,** Graphic Artist

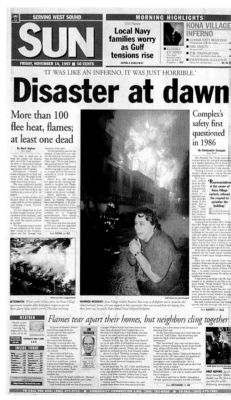

Award of Excellence
The Sun
Bremerton, WA

Staff

Award of Excellence
The Virginian-Pilot
Norfolk, VA

Lisa Cowan, Designer; Denis Finley, News Editor; Andrea Smith, Designer; Courtney Murphy, Designer; Eric Seidman, Creative Director; Mike Workman, Designer; Buddy Moore, Designer

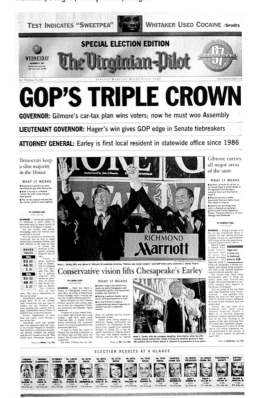

Award of Excellence
Clarin
Buenos Aires, Argentina

Iñaki Palacios, Art Director; Juan Elissetche, Design Editor; Vicente Dagnino, Design Editor; Federico Sosa, Graphic Designer; Carlos Vazquez, Graphic Designer; Maureen Holboll, Graphic Designer; Alberto Caputo, Graphic Designer; Osvaldo Estevao, Graphic Designer

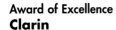

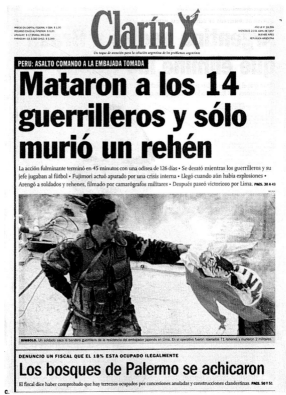

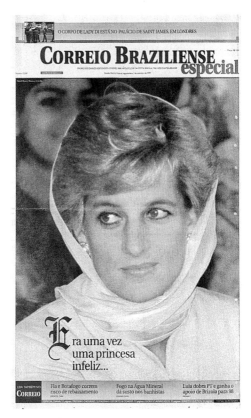

Award of Excellence
Correio Braziliense
Brasilia, Brazil

Versiani Versiani, Photo Editor; Ricardo Noblat, Editor; Chico Amaral, Art Editor; Russel Boyce, Photographer

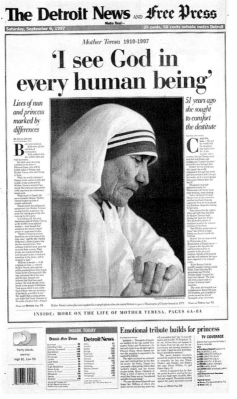

Award of Excellence
The Detroit News/Free Press
Detroit, MI

David Dombrowski, Designer; Jennifer George, Designer; Todd Winge, Photo Editor; Rick Nease, Graphics Artist

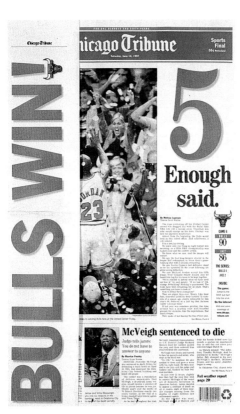

Award of Excellence
Chicago Tribune
Chicago, IL

Stacy Sweat, Graphics and Design Editor; Nuccio DiNuzzo, Photographer

Silver
•Also **Silver** for News Portfolio
The Detroit News
Detroit, MI

Chris Kozlowski, A.M.E. Graphics/Design; David Kordalski, Graphics/Design Editor; Tim Summers, Graphic Artist; Richard Epps, Page Designer; Daniel Janke, Page Designer; Satoshi Toyoshima, Graphic Artist; Darryl Swint, Graphic Artist; Rob Allstetter, Deputy Sports Editor

Award of Excellence
The Detroit News
Detroit, MI

Chris Kozlowski, A.M.E. Graphics/Design; David Kordalski, Graphics/Design Editor; Richard Epps, Designer; Daniel Janke, Designer; Rob Allstetter, Deputy Sports Editor; Tim Summers, Artist; Satoshi Toyoshima, Artist; Darryl Swint, Artist

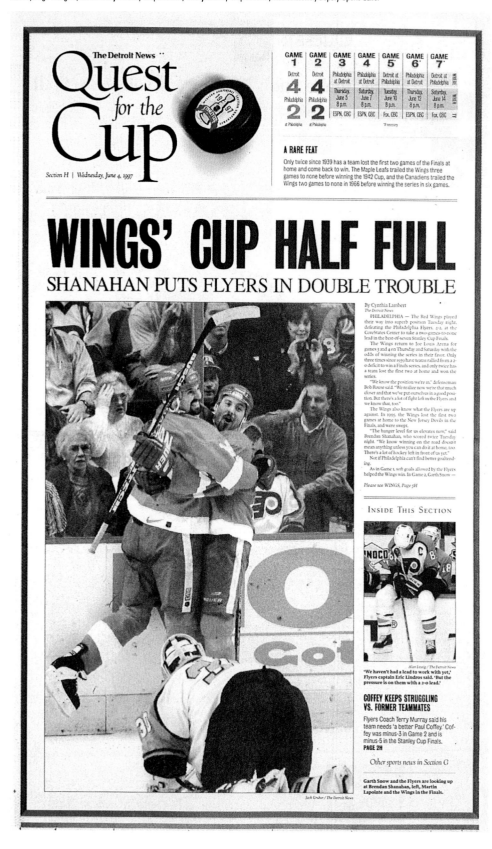

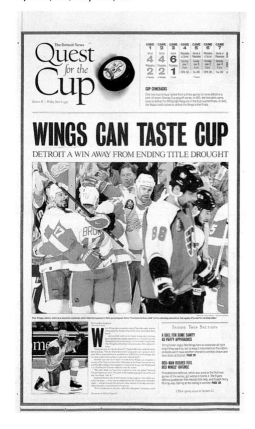

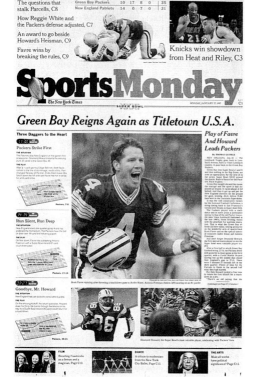

Award of Excellence
The New York Times
New York, NY

Wayne Kamidoi, Designer; Joe Ward, Graphics Editor; Stephen Jesselli, Picture Editor; Sarah Kass, Picture Editor

Silver
•Also an **Award of Excellence** for Sports Page

The Detroit News

Detroit, MI

Chris Kozlowski, A.M.E. Graphics/Design; **David Kordalski**, Graphics/Design Editor; **Tim Summers**, Graphic Artist; **Richard Epps**, Page Designer; **Daniel Janke**, Page Designer; **Satoshi Toyoshima**, Graphic Artist; **Darryl Swint**, Graphic Artist; **Daniel Mears**, Photographer

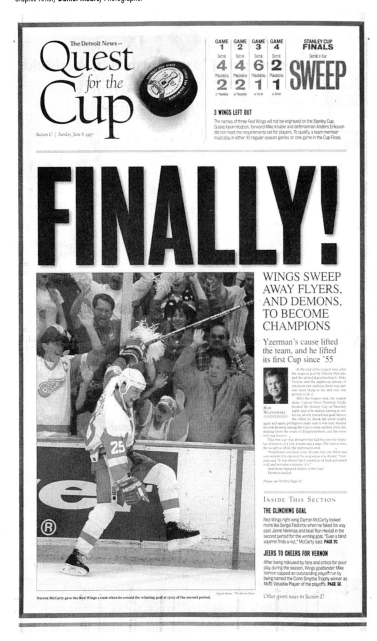

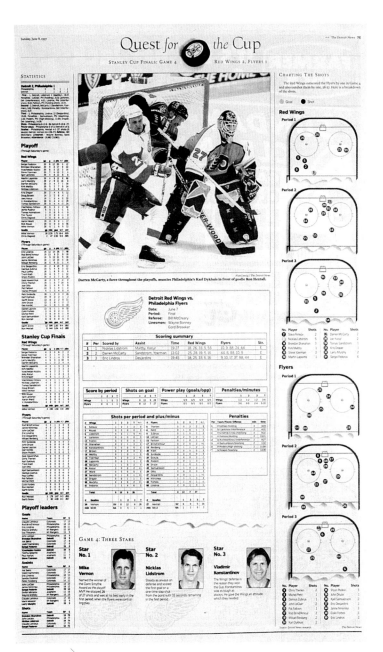

Award of Excellence
Star Tribune
Minneapolis, MN

Bobby Armstrong, Sports Layout Editor; Anders Ramberg, Design Director & Designer; Greg Branson, Graphic Designer; Marlin Levison, Photographer; Jeff Wheeler, Photographer; Vickie Kettlewell, Photo Editor; Tim Wheatley, Sports Section Coordinator; Mark Wolleman, Night Sports Section Coordinator

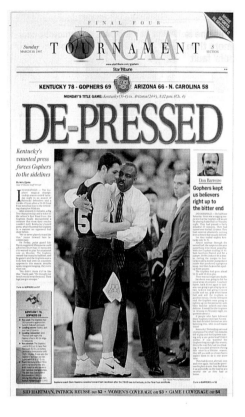

Award of Excellence
The Orange County Register
Santa Ana, CA

Staff

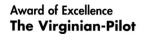
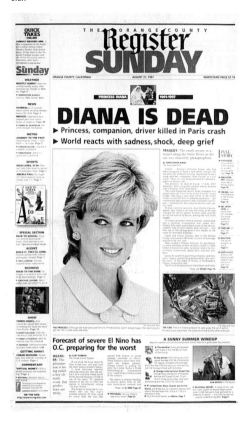

Award of Excellence
The Virginian-Pilot
Norfolk, VA

Buddy Moore, Designer; Andrea Smith, Designer; Sam Hundley, Designer; Lynette Holman, Designer; Hans Noel, Designer; Eric Seidman, Creative Director

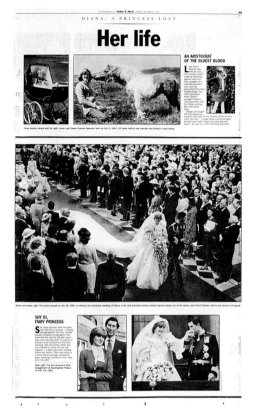

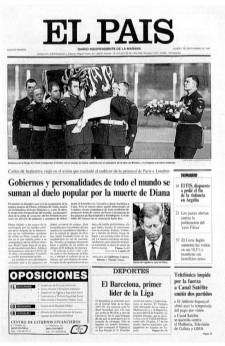

Award of Excellence
El Pais Semanal
Madrid, Spain

Javier López, Art Director; Techu Baragaño, Designer

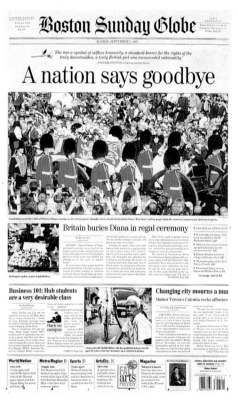

Award of Excellence
The Boston Globe
Boston, MA

Lucy Bartholomay, Art Director; Geoff Forester, Photo Editor; Regina Jones, Designer

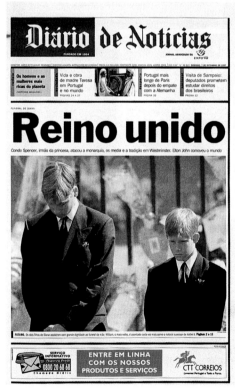

Award of Excellence
Diario de Noticias
Lisbon, Portugal

Mário B. Resendes, Editor-in-Chief; António Ribeiro Ferreira, Associate Editor-in-Chief; José Maria Ribeirinho, Art Director; Carlos Jorge, Designer; Machado, Designer; Sónia Matos, Designer

Award of Excellence
The San Diego Union-Tribune
San Diego, CA

Bill Gaspard, Designer; **Bill Dawson**, Designer; **Gordon Murray**, Designer; **Michael Franklin**, Photo Director

Award of Excellence
The Seattle Times
Seattle, WA

David Miller, Art Director & Designer; **Michael Kellams**, Designer; **Karen Klinkenberg**, Designer; **Mike Stanton**, Executive News Editor; **John B. Saul**, Deputy News Editor; **Cathy McLain**, Sunday Editor; **Fred Nelson**, Photo Editor; **Dean Rutz**, Photo Editor

Award of Excellence
The Charlotte Observer
Charlotte, NC

Steve Gunn, Project Editor; **Monica Moses**, Design Director/Designer; **Susan Gilbert**, Director/Photography; **Christopher A. Record**, Photographer; **Thé Pham**, Photo Editor; **Nancy Stancill**, Reporter; **Dwuan June**, Designer; **Danielle Parks**, Designer

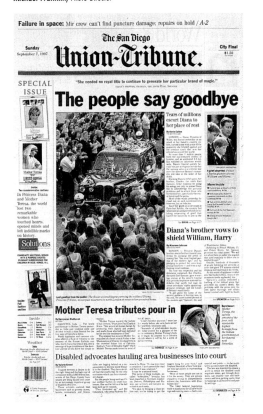

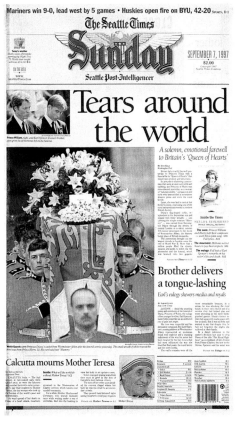

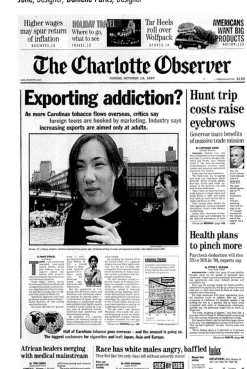

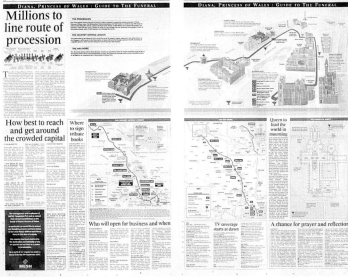

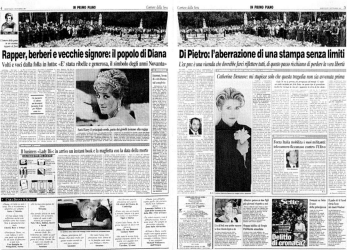

Award of Excellence
The Times
London, England
Staff

Award of Excellence
Corriere della Sera
Milan, Italy

Gianluigi Colin, Art Director; **Giovanni Angeli**, Page Designer/Infographics Consultant; **Sergio Pilone**, Sub-Art Editor; **Marco Gillo**, Page Designer; **Carlo Cardinale**, Page Designer; **Michele Peroglio**, Page Designer; **Stefano Salvia**, Page Designer; **Marcello Valoncini**, Graphic Designer

Silver
Jacksonville Journal-Courier
Jacksonville, IL

Mike Miner, Editor/Designer

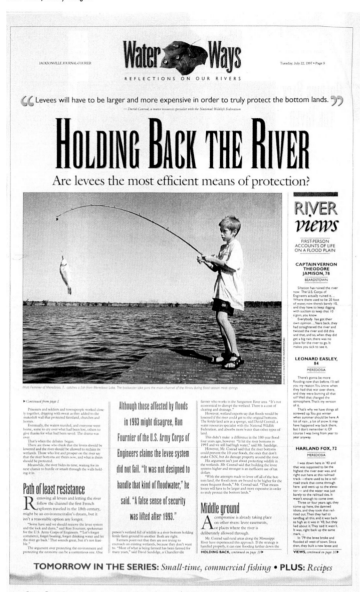

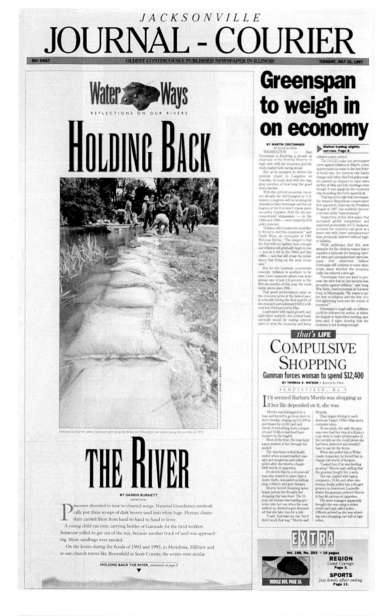

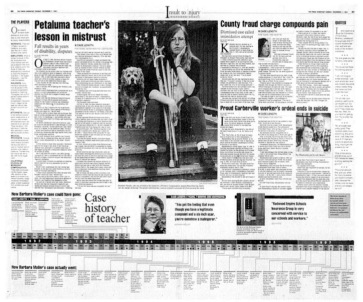

Award of Excellence
The Press Democrat
Santa Rosa, CA

Ken Heidel, Designer/Copy Editor; **Mark Aronoff**, Photographer; **Gary Newman**, Artist; **Mary Fricker**, Writer; **Brad Bollinger**, Business Editor; **Bob Norberg**, Staff Writer

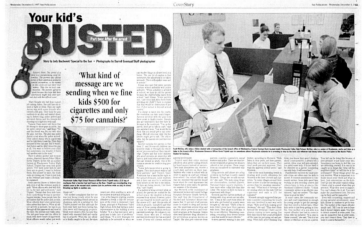

Award of Excellence
The Naperville Sun
Naperville, IL

Robb Montgomery, Design Editor; **Jim Kutina**, Photo Editor; **Darrell Goemaat**, Photographer; **William Burghardt**, Feature Editor

Award of Excellence
Los Angeles Times
Costa Mesa, CA

Chuck Nigash, Design Editor; **Clarence Williams**, Photographer

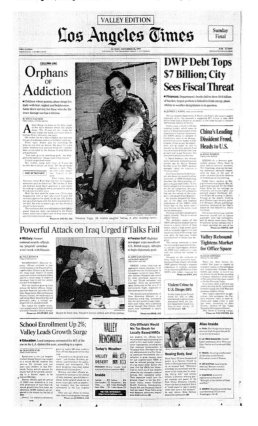

Award of Excellence
The San Diego Union-Tribune
San Diego, CA

Laurie Harker, Designer; **John Gibbins**, Photographer; **Michael Franklin**, Photo Director

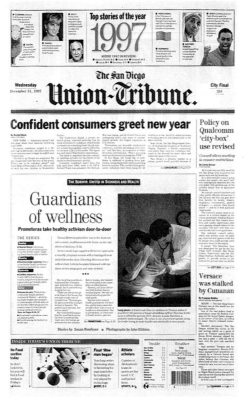

Award of Excellence
St. Paul Pioneer Press
St. Paul, MN

Staff

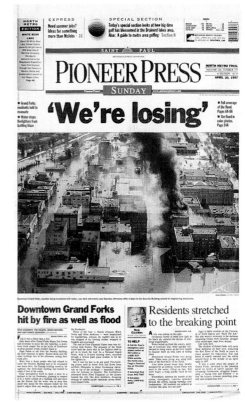

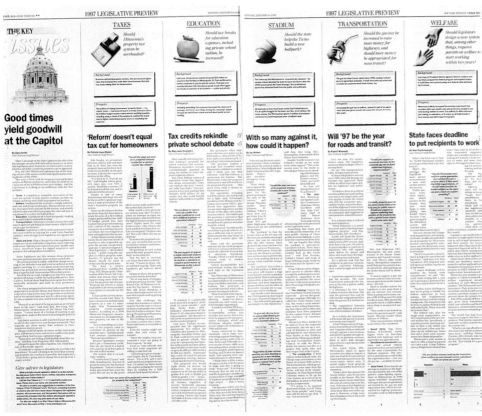

Award of Excellence
Star Tribune
Minneapolis, MN

Ray Grumney, Graphics Director; **Greg Branson**, Graphic Artist; **Dennis McGrath**, Politics/Govt. Team Leader; **John Stefany**, Copy Editor; **Anders Ramberg**, Design Director; **Bill Dunn**, Visual Content Editor

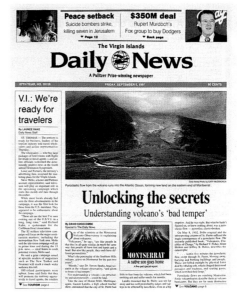

Award of Excellence
The Virgin Islands Daily News
St. Thomas, BVI

Steve Rockstein, Design Editor

Silver
El Pais Semanal
Madrid, Spain
Staff

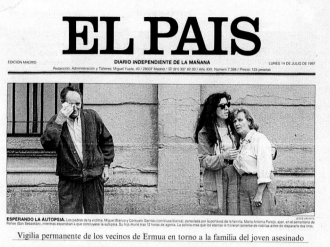

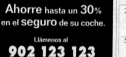

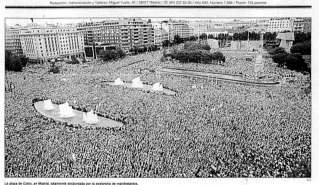

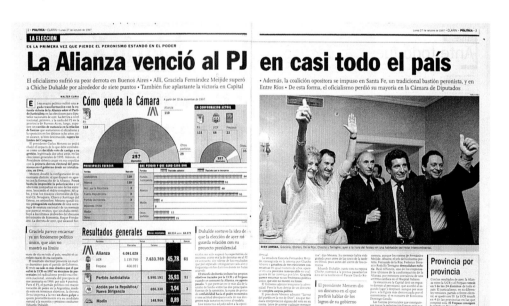

Award of Excellence
Clarin

Buenos Aires, Argentina

Iñaki Palacios, Art Director; Juan Elissetche, Design Editor; Vicente Dagnino, Design Editor; Federico Sosa, Graphic Designer; Carlos Vasquez, Graphic Designer; Maureen Holboll, Graphic Designer; Alberto Caputo, Graphic Designer; Osvaldo Estanao, Graphic Designer

Award of Excellence
Morgenavisen Jyllands-Posten

Viby J., Denmark

Anni Kristensen, Sub-Editor; Gert Gram, News Graphic Artist; Agnete Holk, News Graphic Artist; Rina Kjeldgaard, News Graphic Artist; Rasmus Sand Høyer, Illustrator; Lars Krabbe, Photographer; Hanne Loop, Photographer; Bo Svane; Photographer; Torben Stroyer, Photographer; Thomas Tolstrup, Photographer

Award of Excellence
The San Diego Union-Tribune
San Diego, CA

Michael Canepa, Designer; **Nelvin Cepeda**, Photographer; **Michael Franklin**, Photo Director

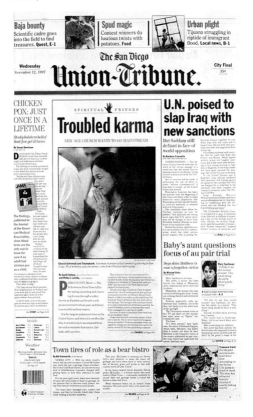

Award of Excellence
Star Tribune
Minneapolis, MN

Ray Grumney, News Graphics Director; **Greg Branson**, Graphic Designer; **Denise Reagan**, Designer; **Maria Lettman**, Public Safety Team Leader; **Anders Ramberg**, Design Director; **Bill Dunn**, Visual Content Editor; **Mark Boswell**, Graphic Designer; **A-1 Layout Team**; **A Section Layout Team**; **Public Safety Team Writers**

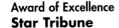
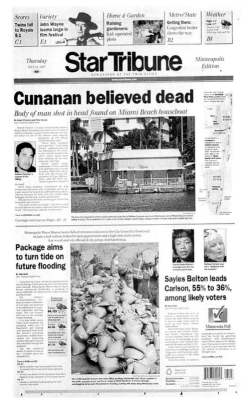

Award of Excellence
The Press Democrat
Santa Rosa, CA

Ron Makabe, Page Designer/Copy Editor; **Annie Wells**, Photographer; **Sharon Henry**, Artist

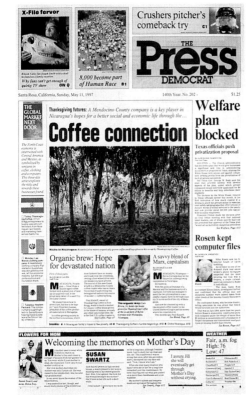

Award of Excellence
The Virginian-Pilot
Norfolk, VA

Lisa Cowan, Page Designer; **Denis Finley**, News Editor; **Latané Jones**, Designer; **Paul Nelson**, Designer

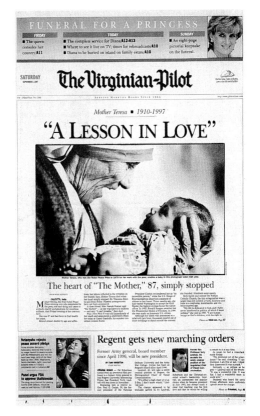

Award of Excellence
Asbury Park Press
Neptune, NJ

Christine A. Birch, Designer; **Harris G. Siegel**, M.E./Design & Photography; **Andrew Prendimano**, Art & Photo Director; **Rick Makin**, Editor; **Debra LaQuaglia**, Editor

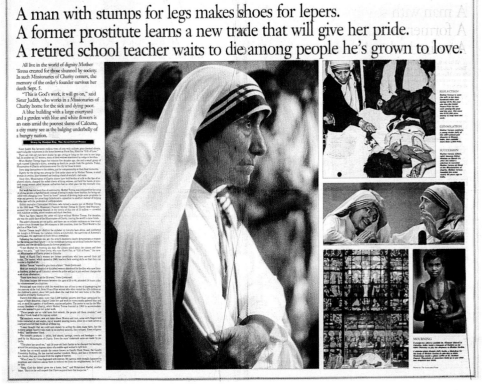

Gold
The Charlotte Observer

Charlotte, NC

Scott Goldman, Assistant Sports Editor/Designer; **Danielle Parks**, Designer; **Monica Moses**, Design Director; **Larry Davidson**, Designer;
Michael Persinger, Deputy Sports Editor ; **John D. Simmons**, Photo Editor; **Gary Schwab**, Executive Sports Editor; **Photo Staff**; **Sports Staff**

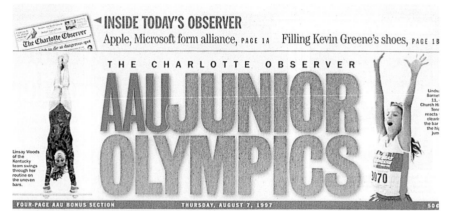

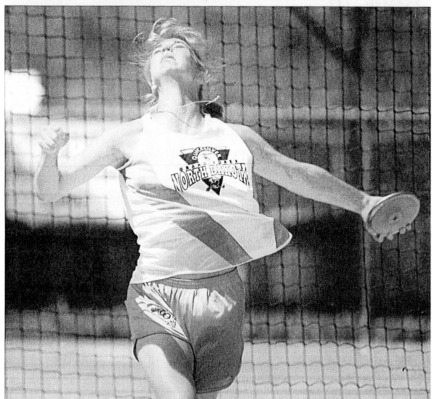

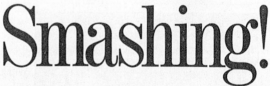

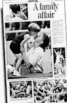

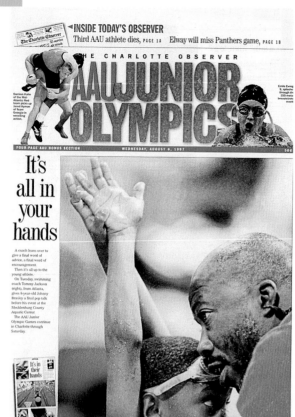

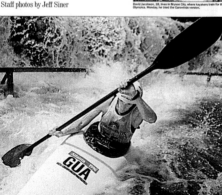

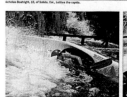

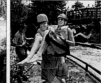

These **Gold Medal** pages are at the soul of sports: blood, sweat and tears.

• • • • •

Estas páginas ganadoras de medalla de oro son el alma de los deportes: sangre, sudor y lágrimas.

Silver
The Boston Globe
Boston, MA

Robin Romano, Assistant Sports Editor/Projects; **Janet L. Michaud**, Designer; **Richard Sanchez**, Graphic Artist; **Sports Staff**

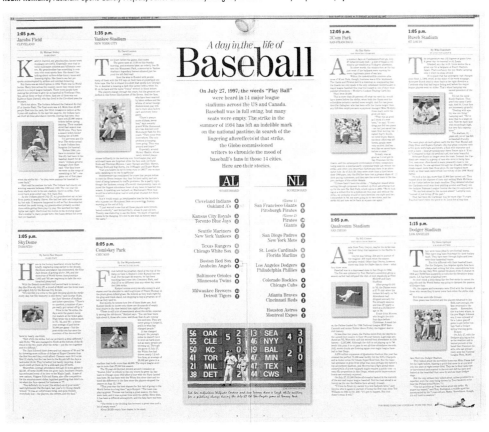

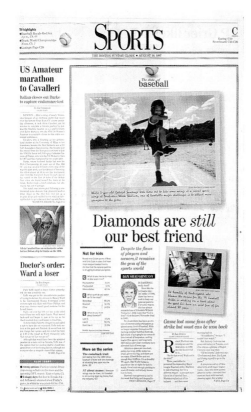

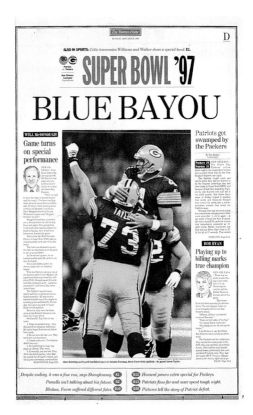

Award of Excellence
The Boston Globe
Boston, MA

Lucy Bartholomay, Page One Designer; **Janet L. Michaud**, Designer; **Richard Sanchez**, Graphic Artist

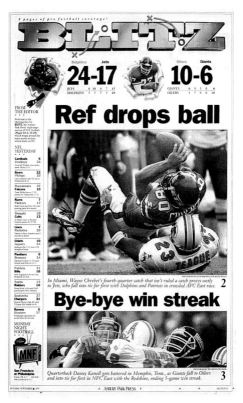

Award of Excellence
Asbury Park Press
Neptune, NJ

Christine A. Birch, Designer; **Harris G. Siegel**, M.E./Design & Photography; **Andrew Prendimano**, Art & Photo Director; **John Quinn**, M.E./Sports; **Craig Schmidt**, Designer; **Theresa Holmes-Stenson**, Photo Editor; **Gary Potosky**, Editor; **Jeff Paslay**; Designer; **Robert T. Collins**, President & Publisher

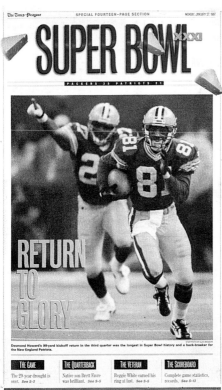

Award of Excellence
The Times-Picayune
New Orleans, LA
Staff

Silver
•Also an **Award of Excellence** for Breaking News
The Detroit News
Detroit, MI

Chris Kozlowski, A.M.E. Graphics/Design; David Kordalski, Graphics/Design Editor; Rob Allstetter, Deputy Sports Editor; Richard Epps, Page Designer; Dan Janke, Page Designer; Satoshi Toyoshima, Graphic Artist; Tim Summers, Graphic Artist; Darryl Swint, Graphic Artist; Steve Fecht; Photo Director; Steve Haines, Assistant Photo Editor; Michael Brown, Advanced Systems Editor

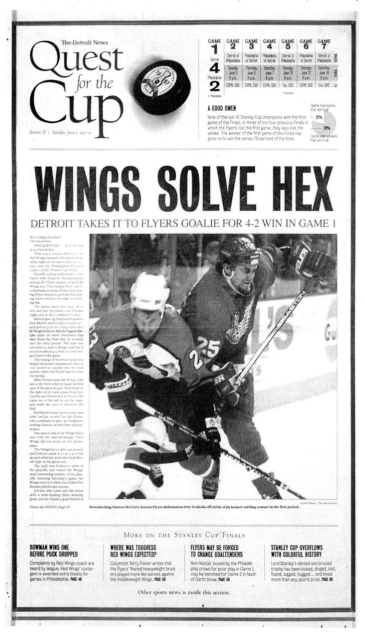

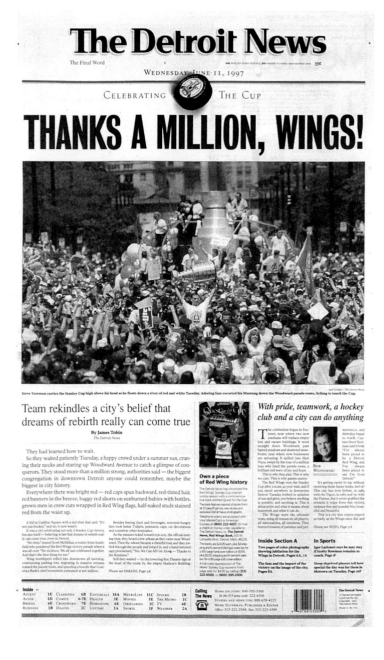

Chapter Four

FEATURES

Continuing to pay tribute to the world's best newspaper designs, the 19th edition of The Best of Newspaper Design is a stunning collection of modern work. The included works were selected from more than 10,000 entries submitted by newspapers all over the world. This exceptional collection is an essential reference for anyone involved in print media, graphics, photography, design, journalism, or communications.

The competition, which is sponsored annually by the Society of News Design and the S.I. Newhouse School of Public Communications at Syracuse University, recognizes excellence in newspaper design and graphics. Awards include Best of Show, Gold, Silver, Award of Excellence, Special Recognition, plus the honor of World's Best Designed Newspaper. Categories for

The competition, which is sponsored annually by the Society of News Design and the S.I. Newhouse School of Public Communications at Syracuse University, recognizes excellence in newspaper design and graphics. Awards include Best of Show, Gold, Silver, Award of Excellence, Special Recogni-tion, plus the honor of World's Best Designed Newspaper. Categories for judging include overall page design, portfolio, magazine cover design, art and illustration, photo journalism, and informational graphics.

Continuing to pay tribute to the world's best newspaper designs, the 19th edition of The Best of Newspaper Design is a stunning collection of modern work. The included works were selected from more than 10,000 entries submitted by newspapers all over the world. This exceptional collection is an essential refer-

Continuing to pay tribute to the world's best newspaper designs, the 19th edition of The Best of Newspaper Design is a stunning collection of modern work. The included works were selected from more than 10,000 entries submitted by newspapers all over the world. This exceptional collection is an essential reference for anyone involved in print media, graphics, photography, design, journalism, or communications.

The competition, which is sponsored annually by the Society for News Design and the S.I. Newhouse School of Public Communications at Syracuse University, recognizes excellence in newspaper design and graphics. Awards include Best of Show, Gold, Silver, Award of Excellence, Special Recogni-tion, plus the honor of World's Best Designed Newspaper. Categories for

The competition, which is sponsored annually by the Society of News Design and the S.I. Newhouse School of Public Communications at Syracuse University, recognizes excellence in newspaper design and graphics. Awards include Best of Show, Gold, Silver, Award of Excellence, Special Recogni-tion, plus the honor of World's Best Designed Newspaper. Categories for judging include overall page design, portfolio, magazine cover design, art and illustration, photo journalism, and informational graphics.

Continuing to pay tribute to the world's best newspaper designs, the 19th edition of The Best of Newspaper Design is a stunning collection of modern work. The included works were selected from more than 10,000 entries submitted by newspapers all over the world. This exceptional collection is an essential

Continuing to pay tribute to the world's best newspaper designs, the 19th edition of The Best of Newspaper Design is a stunning collection of modern work. The included works were selected from more than 10,000 entries submitted by newspapers all over the world. This exceptional collection is an essential reference for anyone involved in print media, graphics, photography, design, journalism, or communications.

The competition, which is sponsored annually by the Society for News Design and the S.I. Newhouse School of Public Communications at Syracuse University, recognizes excellence in newspaper design and graphics. Awards include Best of Show, Gold, Silver, Award of Excellence, Special Recogni-tion, plus the honor of World's Best Designed Newspaper. Categories for judging include overall page design, portfolio, magazine cover design, art and illustration, photo journalism, and informational graphics.

This nineteenth edition presents the finest newspaper design in the field.

Selected by a panel of 21 judges of the Society for News Design, the award-winning pub-lications featured in this nineteenth edition were chosen for excellence in design.

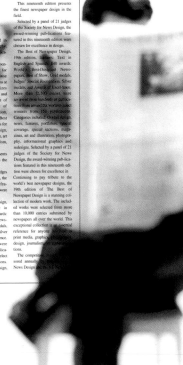

REGULARLY APPEARING SECTIONS

PAGE DESIGN

judging include overall page design, portfolio, magazine cover design, art and illustration, photo journalism, and informational graphics.

This nineteenth edition presents the finest newspaper design in the field.

Selected by a panel of 21 judges of the Society for News Design, the award-winning pub-lications featured in this nineteenth edition were chosen for excellence in design.

The Best of Newspaper Design, 19th edition, features: Text in English and Spanish; 840 awards: World's Best-Designed Newspapers, Best of Show, Gold medals, Judges' Special Recognition, Silver medals, and Awards of Excel-lence. More than 12,100 entries were reviewed from hundreds of publications from around the world to select winners from 158 publications. Categories included: Overall design, news, features, port-folios, special coverage, special sec-tions, magazines, art and illustration, photography, informational graphics

Continuing to pay tribute to the world's best newspaper designs, the 19th edition of The Best of Newspaper Design is a stunning collection of modern work. The included works were selected from more than 10,000 entries submitted by newspapers all over the world. This exceptional collection is an essential reference for anyone involved in print media, graphics, photography, design, journalism, or communications.

ence for anyone involved in print media, graphics, photography, design, journalism, or communica-tions.

The competition, which is sponsored annually by the Society of News Design and the S.I. Newhouse School of Public Communications at Syracuse University, recognizes excellence in newspaper design and graphics. Awards include Best of Show, Gold, Silver, Award of Excellence, Special Recogni-tion, plus the honor of World's Best Designed Newspaper. Categories for judging include overall page design, portfolio, magazine cover design, art and illustration, photo journalism, and informational graphics.

This nineteenth edition presents the finest newspaper design in the field.

Selected by a panel of judges of the Society for News Design, the award-winning newspapers featured in this nineteenth edition were chosen for excellence in design.

Selected by a panel of 21 judges of the Society for News Design, the award-winning pub-lications featured in this nineteenth edition were chosen for excellence in design.

The Best of Newspaper Design, 19th edition, features: all text in Continuing to pay tribute to the world's best newspaper designs, the 19th edition of The Best of Newspaper Design is a stunning collection of modern work. The included works were selected from more than

judging include overall page design, portfolio, magazine cover design, art and illustration, photo journalism, and informational graphics.

This nineteenth edition presents the finest newspaper design in the field.

Selected by a panel of judges of the Society of News Design, the award-winning newspapers featured in this nineteenth edition were cho-sen for excellence in design.

Selected by a panel of 21 judges of the Society for News Design, the award-winning pub-lications fea-tured in this nineteenth edition were chosen for excellence in design.

The Best of Newspaper Design, 19th edition, features: Text in English and Spanish; 840 awards: World's Best-Designed Newspapers, Best of Show, Gold medals, Judges' Special Recognition, Silver medals, and Awards of Excel-lence. More than 12,100 entries were reviewed from hundreds of publications from around the world to select winners from 158 publications. Categories included: Overall design, news, fea-tures, portfolios, special coverage, special sections, magazines, art and illustration, photography, informa-tional graphics and redesigns.

Continuing to pay tribute to the world's best newspaper designs, the 19th edition of The Best of Newspaper Design is a stunning col-lection of modern work. The includ-

reference for anyone involved in print media, graphics, photography, design, journalism, or communications.

The competition, which is sponsored annually by the Society for News Design and the S.I. Newhouse School of Public Communications at Syracuse University, recognizes excellence in newspaper design and graphics. Awards include Best of Show, Gold, Silver, Award of Excellence, Special Recogni-tion, plus the honor of World's Best Designed Newspaper. Categories for judging include overall page design, portfolio, magazine cover design, art and illustration, photo journalism, and informational graphics.

Selected by a panel of 21 judges of the Society for News Design, the award-winning pub-lications fea-tured in this nineteenth edition were chosen for excellence in design.

The Best of Newspaper Design, 19th edition, features: Text in English and Spanish; 840 awards: World's Best-Designed News-papers, Best of Show, Gold medals, Judges' Special Recognition, Silver medals, and Awards of Excel-lence. More than 12,100 entries were reviewed from hundreds of publica-tions from around the world to select winners from 158 publications. Categories included: Overall design,

Gold
El Pais
Madrid, Spain

Luis Galán, Designer;
Jesús Martinez, Designer;
Francisco Góhez, Designer

The Babelia section is awarded a **Gold Medal** for its seriousness and thoughtfulness. The basic format is exquisite. It has executed everything consistently well. The pacing is very good. El Pais is El Neato.

• • • • •

La sección Babelia recibió una Medalla de Oro por su seriedad y consideración. El formato básico es exquisito. Ha ejecutado todo uniformemente bien. El ritmo es muy bueno. El País es El Neato.

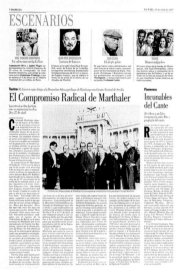

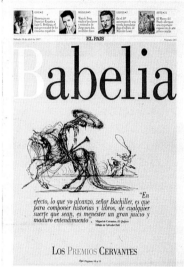

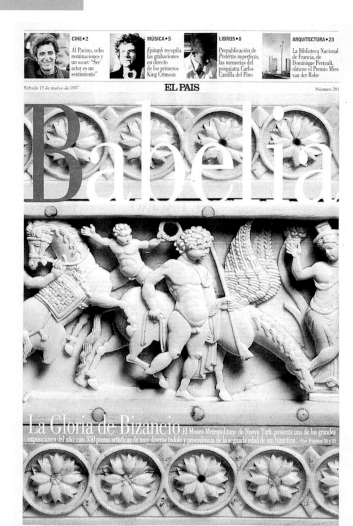

La Gloria de Bizancio El Museo Metropolitano de Nueva York presenta una de las grandes exposiciones del año: casi 350 piezas artísticas de muy diversa índole y procedencia de la segunda edad de oro bizantina.

ARTE

ANCIANOS

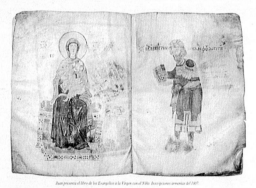

843-1261: LA GLORIA DE BIZANCIO

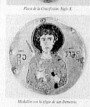

EL ORO Y LA PÚRPURA
CARLOS GARCÍA GUAL

UN ACONTECIMIENTO INTERNACIONAL

Award of Excellence
The Washington Post
Washington, DC

Bonnie Benwick, Layout/Graphics Editor; **Carol Porter,** Art Director; **Peter Alsberg,** Artist; **Steve Luxenberg,** Outlook Editor

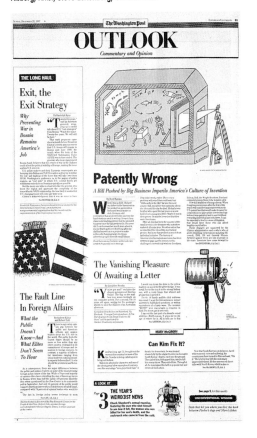

Award of Excellence
La Nacion
Buenos Aires, Argentina

Norberto Lema, Designer

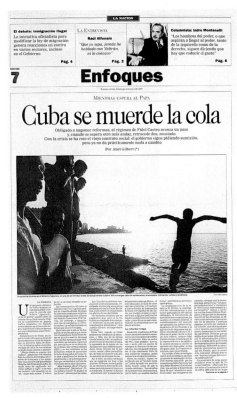

Award of Excellence
The News & Observer
Raleigh, NC

Nicole Werbeck, News Designer; **Keith Simmons,** Graphic Artist; **J. Damon Cain,** Director/News Design; **Van Denton,** Q Editor; **Burgetta Wheeler,** Q Assistant Editor

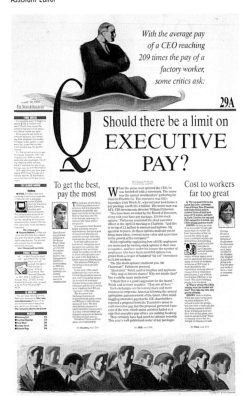

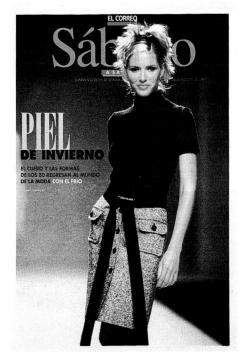

Award of Excellence
El Correo
Bilbao, Spain

Mikel Garica, Designer; **Mari Carmen Navarro,** Designer; **Pacho Igartua,** Designer; **Aurelio Garrote,** Design Editor; **Jesús Aycart,** Art Director; **Alberto Torregrosa,** Editorial Art & Design Consultant

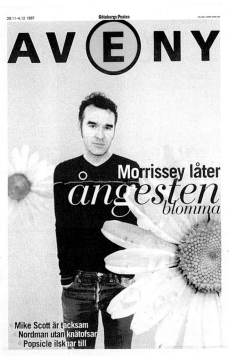

Award of Excellence
Goteborgs-Posten
Göteborg, Sweden

Henrik Strömberg, Designer; **Patrik Andersson,** Designer; **Rune Stenberg,** Designer; **Karina Hansson,** Designer

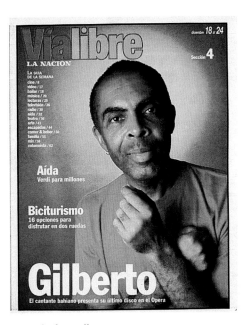

Award of Excellence
La Nacion
Buenos Aires, Argentina

Marina Rainis, Designer; **David Sisso,** Picture Editor

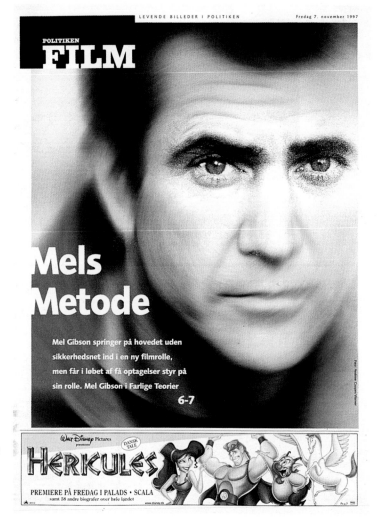

LEVENDE BILLEDER I POLITIKEN   Fredag 7. november 1997

POLITIKEN
FILM

Mels Metode

Mel Gibson springer på hovedet uden sikkerhedsnet ind i en ny filmrolle, men får i løbet af få optagelser styr på sin rolle. Mel Gibson i Farlige Teorier

6-7

Walt Disney Pictures   DANSK TALE
HERKULES
PREMIERE PÅ FREDAG I PALADS · SCALA
samt 58 andre biografer over hele landet   www.disney.dk

Silver
Politiken
Copenhagen,
Denmark

Charlotte Sejer, Editor; **Else Bjørn,**
Copy Editor; **Søren Nyeland,** Design
Editor; **Kristoffer Osterbye,**
Designer; **Tomas Ostergren,**
Designer; **Katinka Bukh,** Designer;
Elisabeth von Eyben, Designer;
Jeanne Olson, Designer

Award of Excellence
El Pais
Madrid, Spain

Luis Galán, Designer; **Jesús Martínez,** Designer; **Francisco Geohez,**
Designer

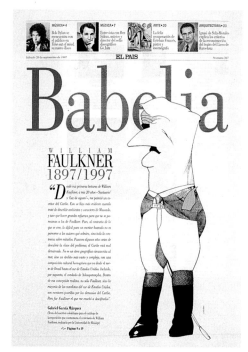

Babelia

WILLIAM
FAULKNER
1897/1997

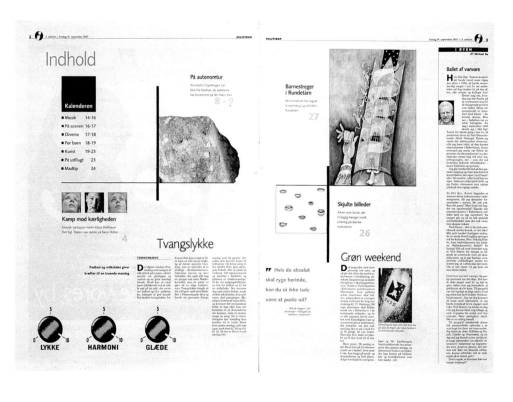

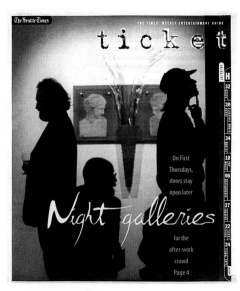

ticket

Night galleries

On First
Thursdays,
doors stay
open later

for the
after-work
crowd

Page 4

Award of Excellence
The Seattle Times
Seattle, WA

Jeff Neumann, Designer; **Tracy Porter,** Designer; **Marian Wachter,**
Designer; **David Miller,** Art Director

Award of Excellence
Le Soleil
Québec, Canada

Louise Pépin, Designer; **Richard Boisvert,** Designer; **Raymond Giroux,** A.M.E.

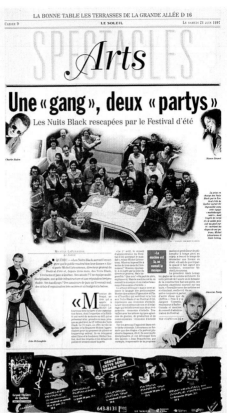

Award of Excellence
The Courier News
Aurora, IL

James Denk, Director/Graphics & Design; **Staff**

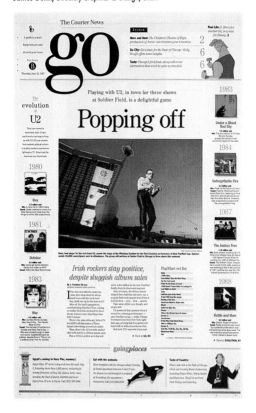

Award of Excellence
El Correo
Bilbao, Spain

Mikel García, Designer; **Mari Carmen Navarro,** Designer; **Jesús Aycart,** Art Director; **Alberto Torregrosa,** Editorial Art & Design Consultant; **Pacho Igartua,** Designer; **Aurelio Garrote,** Design Editor

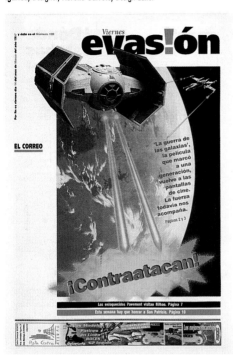

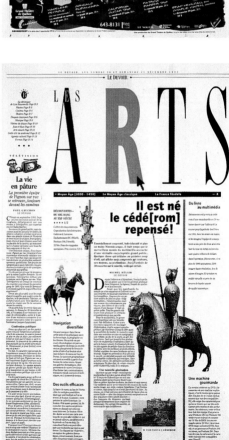

Award of Excellence
Le Devoir
Montreal, Canada

Lise Bissonnette, Publisher; **Bernard Descôteaux,** Editor-in-Chief; **Claude Beauregard,** News Director; **Roland-Yves Carignan,** Art Director & Designer; **Normand Thériault,** Arts Section Director; **Michel Bélair,** Copy Editor

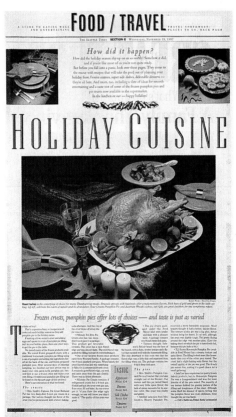

Award of Excellence
The Seattle Times
Seattle, WA

Carol Nakagawa, Designer; **Marian Wachter,** Designer; **David Miller,** Art Director

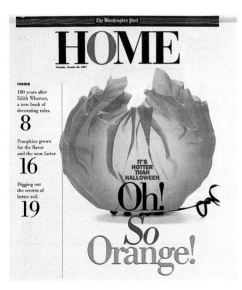

Award of Excellence
•Also an Award of Excellence for Home/ Real Estate Page
The Washington Post
Washington, DC

Alice Kresse, Art Director & Designer; **Kathy Legg,** Picture Editor

Award of Excellence
The Seattle Times
Seattle, WA

Carol Nakagawa, Designer; David Miller, Art Director

Award of Excellence
Clarin
Buenos Aires, Argentina

Iñaki Palacios, Art Director; Tea Alberti, Design Editor; Oscar Bejarano, Graphic Designer; Alejandro Lo Celso, Graphic Designer; Omar Olivella, Graphic Designer; Matilde Oliveros, Graphic Designer; Pablo Ruiz, Graphic Designer; Carolina Wainsztok, Graphic Designer

Award of Excellence
•Also an Award of Excellence for Other Page
NRC Handelsblad
Rotterdam, The Netherlands

Marinka Reuten, Design Editor; Wendy Panders, Design Editor; Maarten Boddaert, Graphic Artist; Pepijn Provily, Photographer; Bas Czerwinski, Photographer

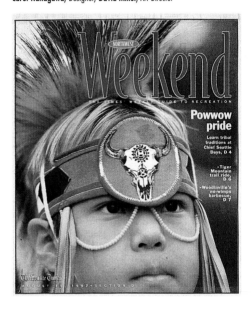

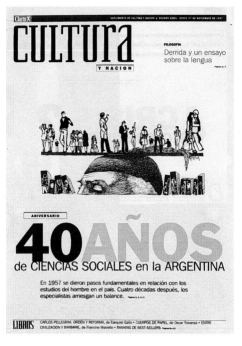

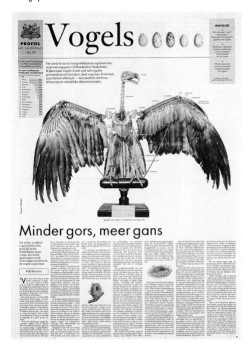

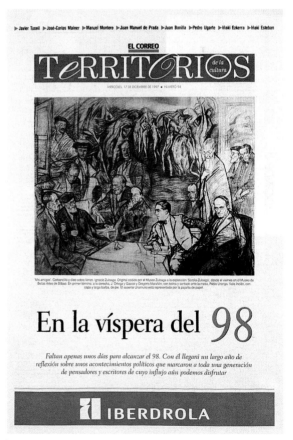

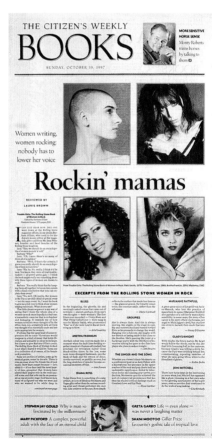

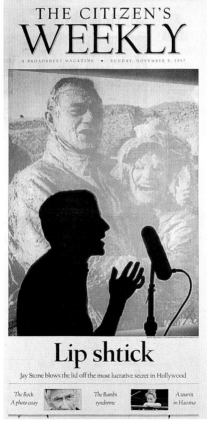

Award of Excellence
El Correo
Bilbao, Spain

Mikel García, Designer; Mari Carmen Navarro, Designer; Jesús Aycart, Art Director; Alberto Torregrosa, Editorial Art & Design Consultant ; Pacho Igartua, Designer; Aurelio Garrote, Design Editor

Award of Excellence
The Ottawa Citizen
Ottawa, Canada

Neil Reynolds, Editor; Jordan Juby, Designer; Carl Neustaedter, Design Director

Award of Excellence
The Ottawa Citizen
Ottawa, Canada

Neil Reynolds, Editor; Lynn McAuley, Editor of Weekly; Carl Neustaedter, Design Director; Kit Collins, Designer; Jordan Juby, Designer

Awarded a **Gold Medal** for its vibrancy and excitement; it has dignity. It's very fresh. Wonderful use of color.

• • • • •

Ganador de una Medalla de Oro por ser vibrante y emocionante; posee dignidad. Es fresco. Espléndido uso del color.

Gold
El Observador
Montevideo, Uruguay
Staff

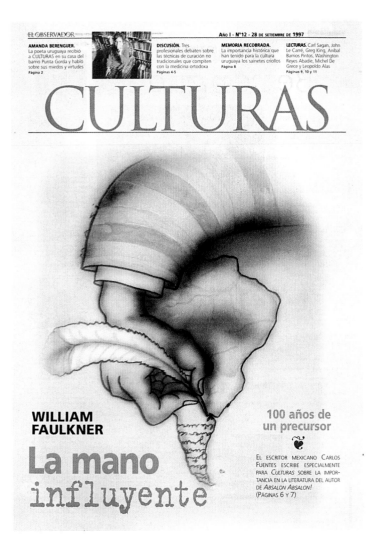

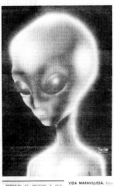

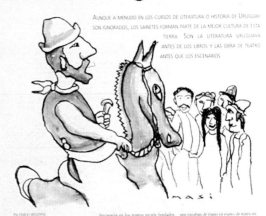

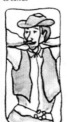

Award of Excellence
Chicago Tribune
Chicago, IL

Stephen Ravenscraft, Art Director; **Peter Gorner**, Perspective Editor; **Wendy Navratil**, Assistant Perspective Editor; **Kevin Pope**, Illustrator; **Katrina Wittkamp**, Assistant Picture Editor

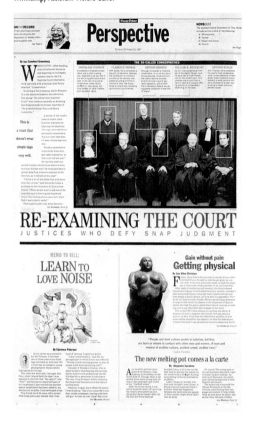

Award of Excellence
The Columbus Dispatch
Columbus, OH

Scott Minister, Art Director; **Todd Bayha**, Designer; **Tom Baker**, Infographics Artist

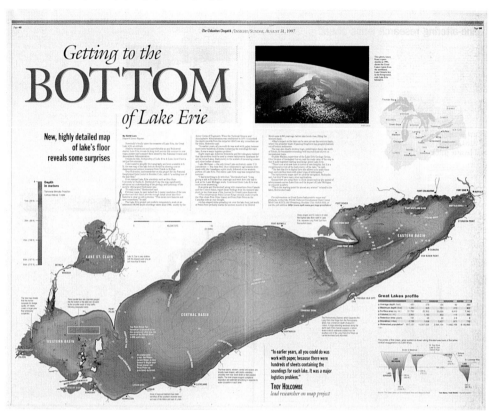

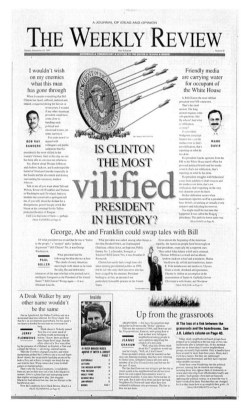

Award of Excellence
Fort Worth Star-Telegram
Fort Worth, TX

Bob Davis, Op-Ed/Sunday Editor

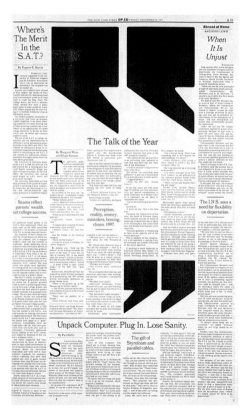

Award of Excellence
The New York Times
New York, NY

Nicholas Blechman, Art Director; **Paula Scher**, Illustrator

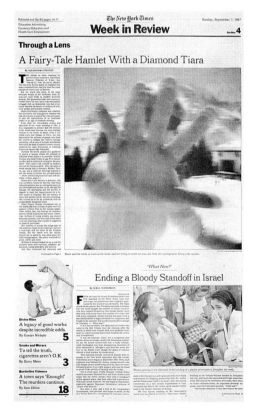

Award of Excellence
The New York Times
New York, NY

Greg Ryan, Art Director; **Rick Perry**, Photo Editor

Award of Excellence
The Washington Post
Washington, DC

Steve Luxenberg, Editor/Outlook; **Carol Porter-Esmailpour**, Art Director;
Randall Mays, Illustrator

Silver
Los Angeles Times/Orange County Edition
Costa Mesa, CA

Colin Crawford, Director/Photography; **Mark Boster**, Photographer; **Kirk Christ**, Designer; **Kris Onuigbo**, Art Director

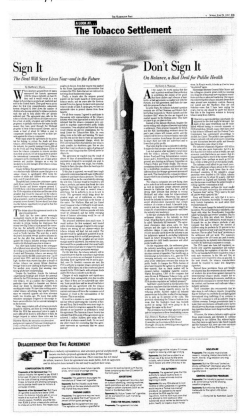

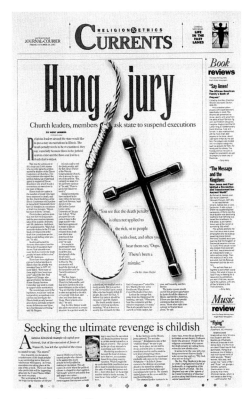

Award of Excellence
Jacksonville Journal-Courier
Jacksonville, IL

Mike Miner, Editor/Designer; **Guido Strotheide**, Editor/Designer

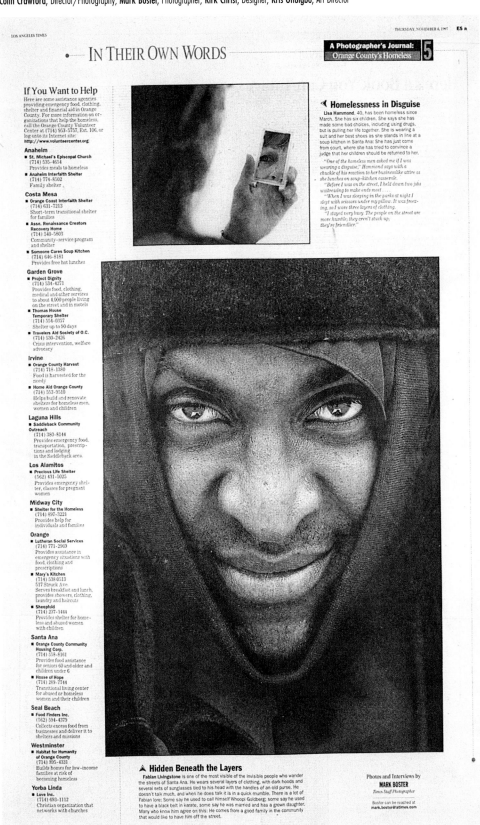

Award of Excellence
DN. på stan
Stockholm, Sweden

Peter Alenas, Art Director; **Pompe Hedengren**, Art Director & Designer; **Ulf Huett**, Photographer

Award of Excellence
The Commercial Appeal
Memphis, TN

Marc Riseling, Page Designer; **Robert Cohen**, Photographer; **Kevin Robbins**, Reporter

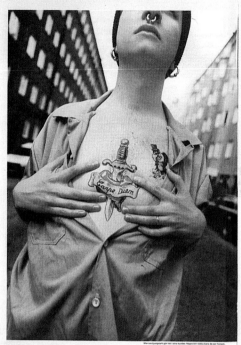

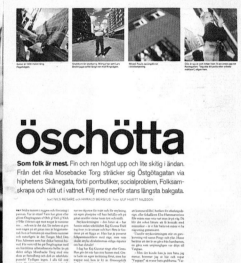

öschötta

Som folk är mest. Fin och ren högst upp och lite skitig i ändan. Från det rika Mosebacke Torg sträcker sig Östgötagatan via hiphetens Skånegata, förbi porrbutiker, socialproblem, Folksamskrapa och rätt ut i vattnet. Följ med nerför stans längsta bakgata.

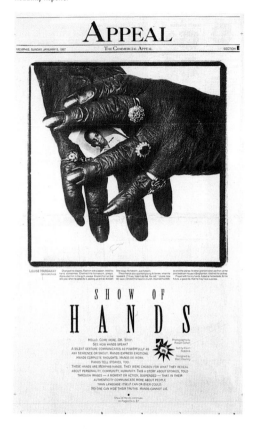

SHOW OF HANDS

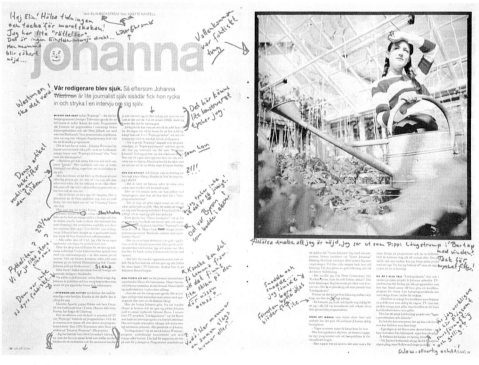

Award of Excellence
DN. på stan
Stockholm, Sweden

Peter Alenas, Art Director; **Pompe Hedengren**, Art Director & Designer; **Anette Nantell**, Photographer

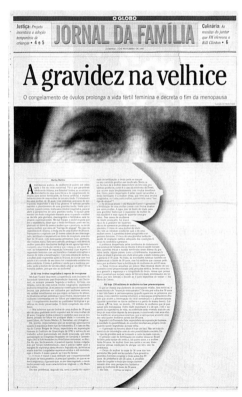

JORNAL DA FAMÍLIA

A gravidez na velhice
O congelamento de óvulos prolonga a vida fértil feminina e decreta o fim da menopausa

Award of Excellence
O Globo
Rio de Janeiro, Brazil

Marília Martins, Editor; **Leila Barbosa**, Designer; **Cláudio Duarte**, Illustrator

Award of Excellence
•Also an **Award of Excellence** fo Photo Story
DN. på stan
Stockholm, Sweden

Peter Alenas, Art Director & Designer; **Pompe Hedengren**, Art Director; **Anette Nantell**, Photographer

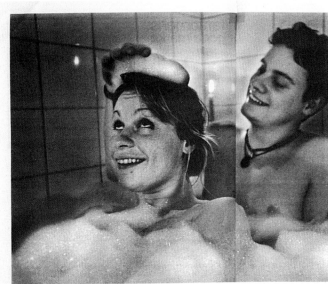

Award of Excellence
Morgenavisen Jyllands-Posten
Viby J., Denmark

Michael Lykke, Photographer; **Mette Holbæk Kristiansen**, Reporter; **Ole Gravesen**, Layout Editor

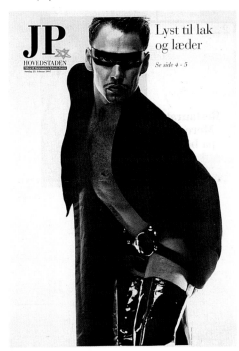

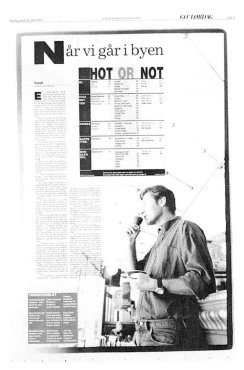

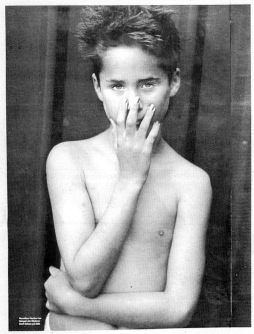

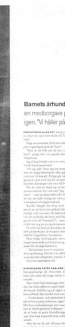

Award of Excellence
Morgenavisen Jyllands-Posten
Viby J., Denmark

Ingolf Graae-Michelsen, Subeditor; **Bodil Krogh**, Subeditor; **Anne Villemoes**, Reporter; **Rina Kjeldgaard**, Artist

Award of Excellence
DN. på stan
Stockholm, Sweden

Peter Alenas, Art Director & Designer; **Pompe Hedengren**, Art Director; **Karolina Henke**, Photographer

Silver
Die Woche
Hamburg, Germany

Manfred Bissinger, Editor-in-Chief; Kurt Breme, Executive Editor; Hans-Ulrich Joerges, Executive Editor; Dirk Linke, Art Director; Andreas Schomberg, Associate Art Director; Armin Ogris, Designer; Stefan Semrau, Designer; Jessica Winter, Designer; Florian Poehl, Designer/Informational Graphics; Reinhard Schulz-Schaeffer, Designer/Informational Graphics

Award of Excellence
St. Petersburg Times
St. Petersburg, FL

Greg Perez, Feature Designer

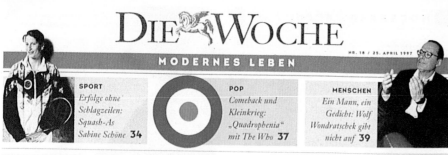

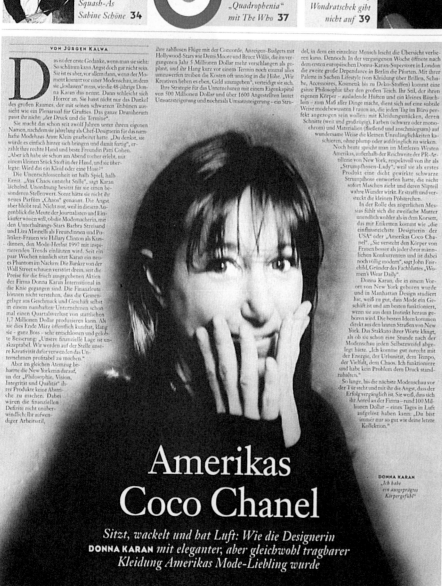

Amerikas Coco Chanel

Sitzt, wackelt und hat Luft: Wie die Designerin
DONNA KARAN *mit eleganter, aber gleichwohl tragbarer Kleidung Amerikas Mode-Liebling wurde*

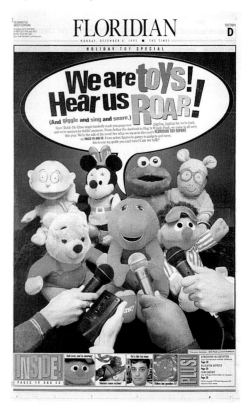

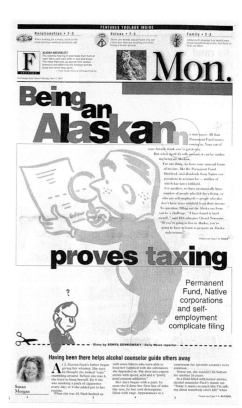

Award of Excellence
Anchorage Daily News
Anchorage, AK

Greg Epkes, Designer

Award of Excellence
Anchorage Daily News
Anchorage, AK
Pamela Dunlap-Shohl, Illustrator & Designer

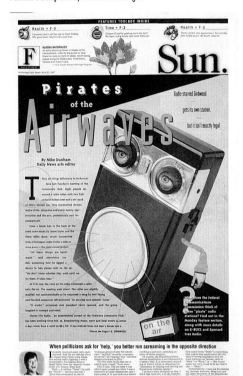

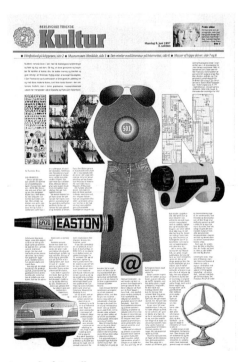

Award of Excellence
Berlingske Tidende
Copenhagen, Denmark
Gregers Jensen, Designer

Silver
La Voz del Interior
Córdoba, Argentina

Javier Candellero, Designer; **Miguel De Lorenzi**, Art Director; **Juan Carlos González**, Editor; **Luis Remonda**, Publisher; **Mario Garcia**, Design Consultant

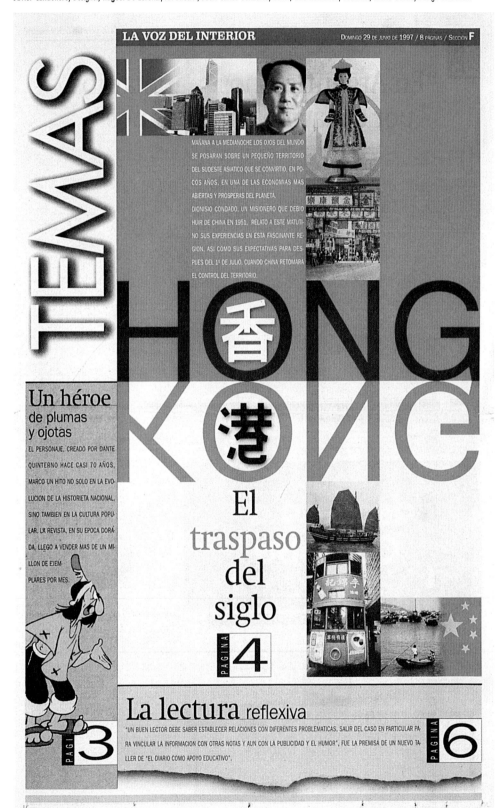

Award of Excellence
La Voz del Interior
Córdoba, Argentina

Javier Candellero, Art Director & Designer; **Juan Carlos González**, Editor;
Luis Remonda, Publisher; **Mario Garcia**, Design Consultant

Award of Excellence
La Voz del Interior
Córdoba, Argentina

Javier Candellero, Art Director, Designer & Illustrator; **Juan Carlos
González**, Editor; **Luis Remonda**, Publisher; **Mario Garcia**, Design
Consultant

Award of Excellence
La Voz del Interior
Córdoba, Argentina

Javier Candellero, Illustrator & Designer; **Miguel De Lorenzi**, Art Director;
Juan Carlos González, Editor; **Luis Remonda**, Publisher; **Mario Garcia**,
Design Consultant

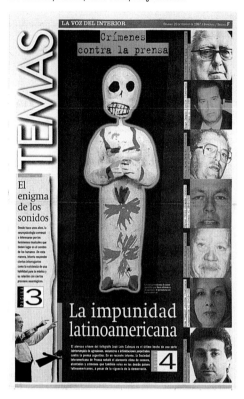

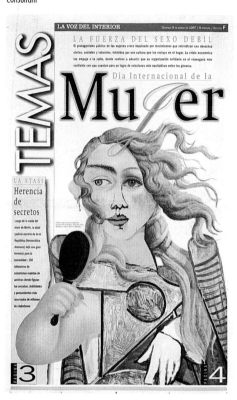

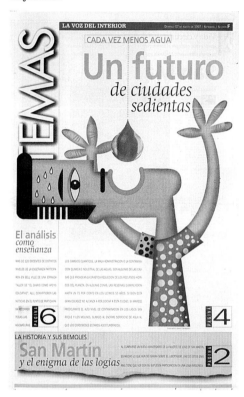

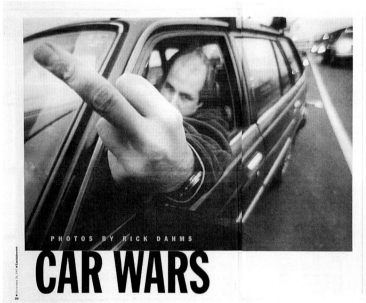

CAR WARS

Award of Excellence
Eastsideweek
Seattle, WA

Barbara Dow, Designer & Art Director; **Rick Dahms**, Photographer

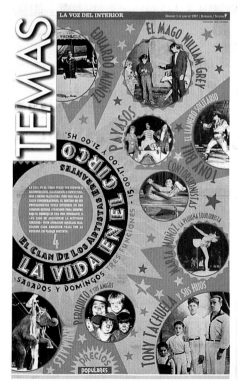

Award of Excellence
La Voz del Interior
Córdoba, Argentina

Javier Candellero, Illustrator & Designer; **Miguel De Lorenzi**, Art Director;
Juan Carlos González, Editor; **Luis Remonda**, Publisher; **Mario Garcia**,
Design Consultant

Award of Excellence
The Beacon News
Aurora, IL

Steve Hartley, Designer; **James Denk,** Director/Graphics & Design; **Steve Buyansky,** Photographer

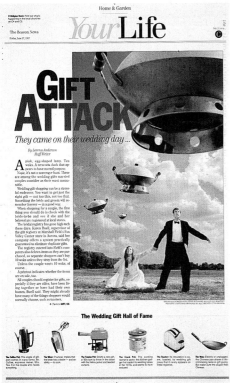

Award of Excellence
The Herald News
Aurora, IL

Paul Wallen Jr., Designer; **James Denk,** Director/Design & Graphics; **Dale Roe,** Artist

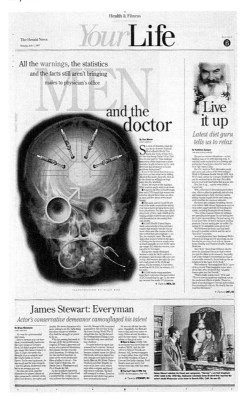

Award of Excellence
Jacksonville Journal-Courier
Jacksonville, IL

Mike Miner, Editor/Designer

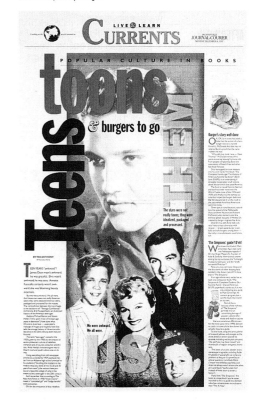

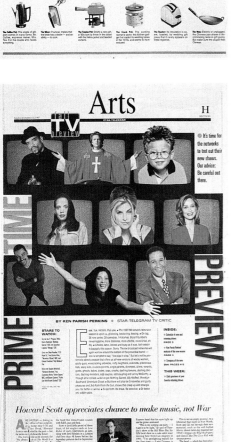

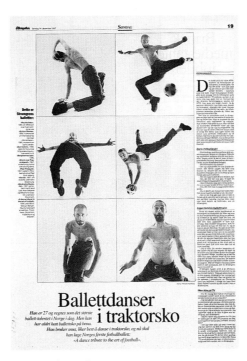

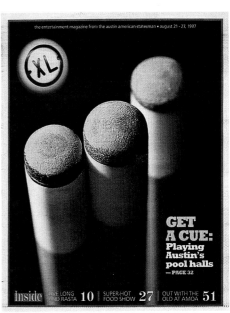

Award of Excellence
Fort Worth Star-Telegram
Fort Worth, TX

Carol Parker, Design Editor

Award of Excellence
Aftenposten
Oslo, Norway

Staff

Award of Excellence
Austin American-Statesman
Austin, TX

Mike Sutter, Art Director; **Sarah Glinsmann,** Designer

Award of Excellence
El Mundo
Madrid, Spain

Carmelo Caderot, Design Director; **Jose Carlos Saiz**, Designer

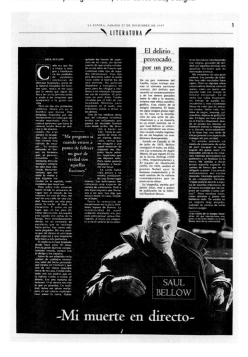

Award of Excellence
Goteborgs-Posten
Göteborg, Sweden

Henrik Strömberg, Designer; **Magnus Sundberg**, Photographer

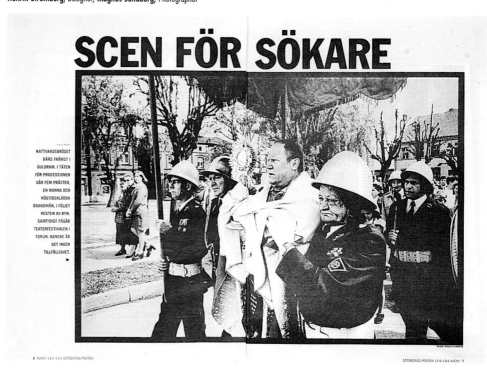

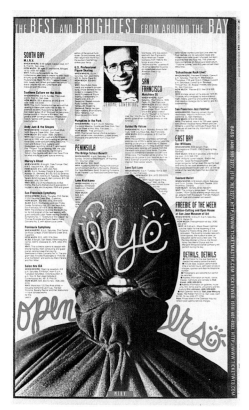

Award of Excellence
San Jose Mercury News
San Jose, CA

Jenny Anderson, Designer

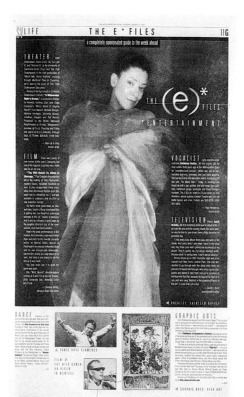

Award of Excellence
San Jose Mercury News
San Jose, CA

Rebecca Hall, Designer

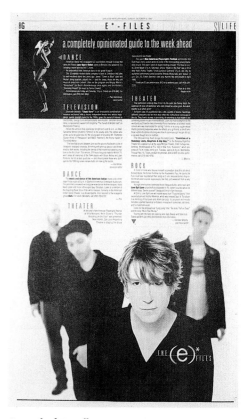

Award of Excellence
San Jose Mercury News
San Jose, CA

Rebecca Hall, Designer

Award of Excellence
The Toronto Star
Toronto, Canada
Jo-Ann Dodds, Designer; **Rob Salem**, Editor

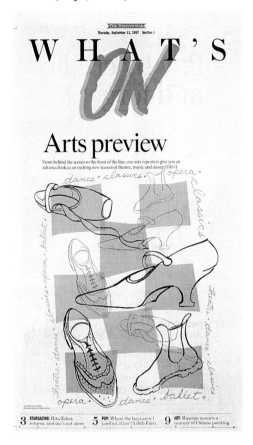

Award of Excellence
San Jose Mercury News
San Jose, CA
Jenny Anderson, Designer; **Nuri Ducassi**, Design Director

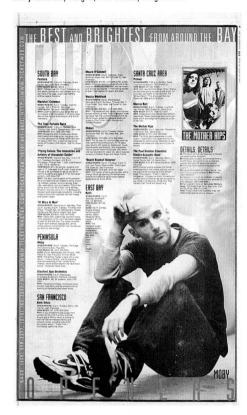

Award of Excellence
The Seattle Times
Seattle, WA
Tracy Porter, Designer; **David Miller**, Art Director

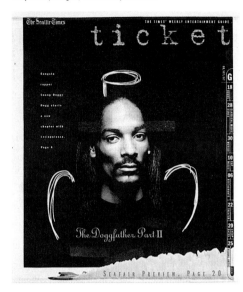

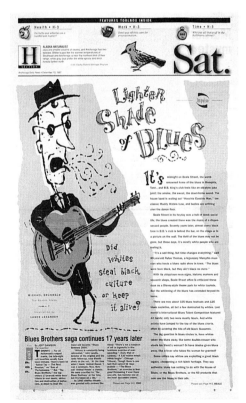

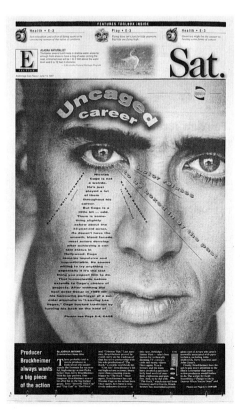

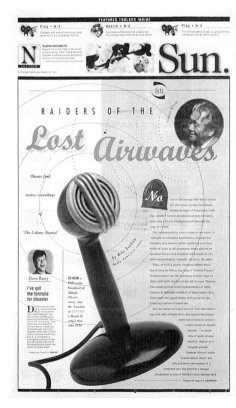

Award of Excellence
Anchorage Daily News
Anchorage, AK
Lance Lekander, Art Director, Designer & Illustrator

Award of Excellence
Anchorage Daily News
Anchorage, AK
Lance Lekander, Art Director & Designer; **Neil Davenport**, Photographer

Award of Excellence
Anchorage Daily News
Anchorage, AK
Pamela Dunlap-Shohl, Designer

Silver
Anchorage Daily News
Anchorage, AK
Lance Lekander, Art Director & Designer; Alaister Thain, Photographer

Award of Excellence
Dayton Daily News
Dayton, OH
Randy Palmer, Designer; James Lloyd, Section Editor; Lee Waigand, Art Director

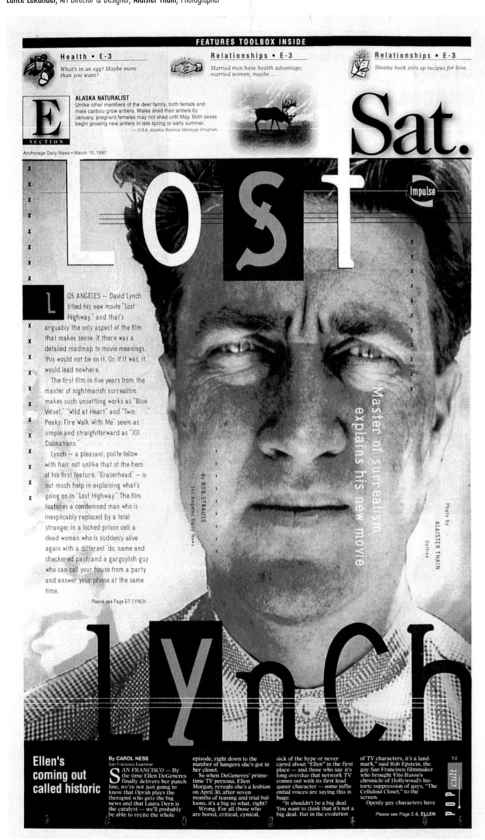

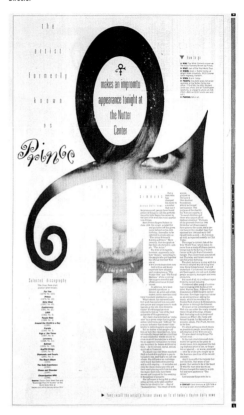

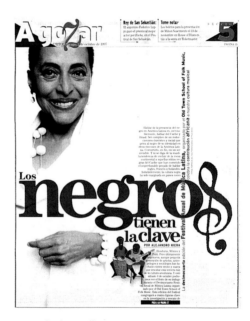

Award of Excellence
¡Exito!
Chicago, IL
Victor Sanchez, Designer; Old Town School, Photo; Alejandro Riera, Reporter; Arturo Jiménez, Art Director; Alejandro Escalona, Editor

Award of Excellence
La Gaceta
San Miguel de Tucuman, Argentina

Sebastian Rosso, Designer; **Sergio S. Fernandez**, Art Director; **Mario Garcia**, Design Consultant; **Raul Valverdi**, Photo Illustrator

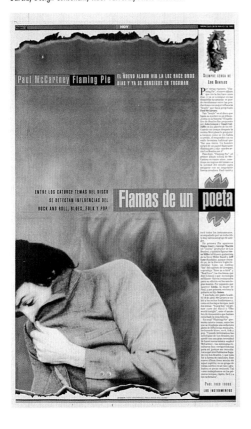

Award of Excellence
La Gaceta
San Miguel de Tucuman, Argentina

Sebastian Rosso, Designer; **Sergio S. Fernandez**, Art Director; **Mario Garcia**, Design Consultant; **Raul Valverdi**, Photo Illustrator

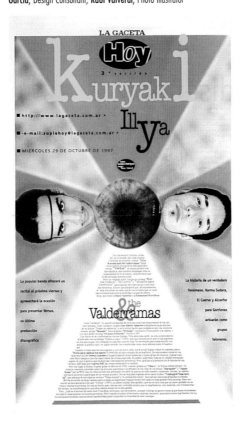

Award of Excellence
¡Exito!
Chicago, IL

Monica Lopez, Designer; **Huella Latina**, Photographer; **Alejandro Riera**, Reporter; **Arturo Jiménez**, Art Director; **Alejandro Escalona**, Editor; **Tony Majeri**, Senior Design Editor

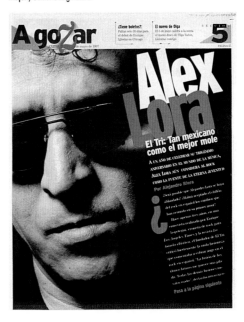

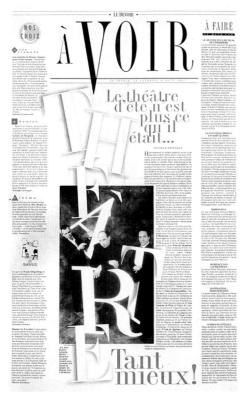

Award of Excellence
Le Devoir
Montreal, Canada

Lise Bissonnette, Publisher; **Bernard Descôteaux**, Editor; **Claude Beauregard**, News Editor; **Roland-Yves Carignan**, Art Director & Designer; **Normand Thériault**, Arts Section Director; **Michel Bélair**, Copy Editor

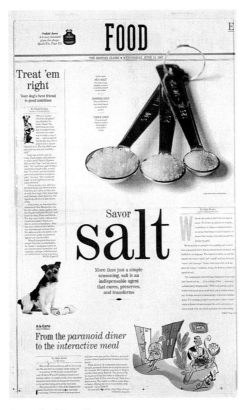

Award of Excellence
The Boston Globe
Boston, MA

Jacqueline Berthet, Art Director & Designer; **Steven Salerno**, Illustrator; **John Blanding**, Photographer; **Fiona Luis**, Editor

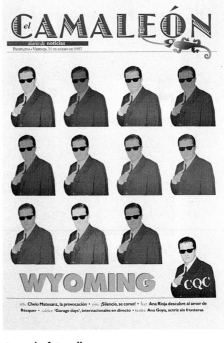

Award of Excellence
Diario de Noticias
Huarte, Spain

Juan Pablo Maset, Designer

Award of Excellence
The Boston Globe
Boston, MA

Jacqueline Berthet, Art Director/Designer; **John Blanding**, Photographer; **Tom Herde**, Photographer; **Fiona Luis**, Editor

Award of Excellence
The Boston Globe
Boston, MA

Jacqueline Berthet, Art Director & Designer; **John Blanding**, Photographer; **Fiona Luis**, Editor

Award of Excellence
Chicago Tribune
Chicago, IL

David Syrek, Art Director; **Bob Fila**, Photographer

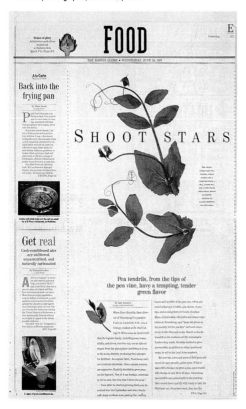

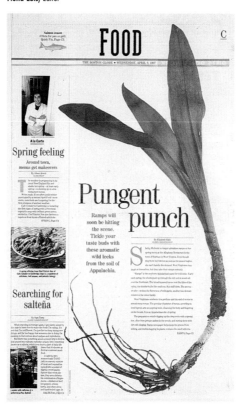

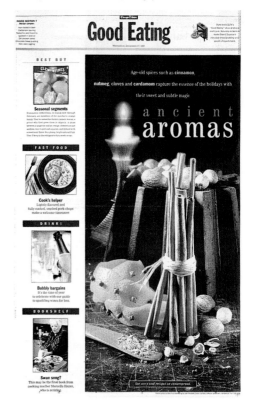

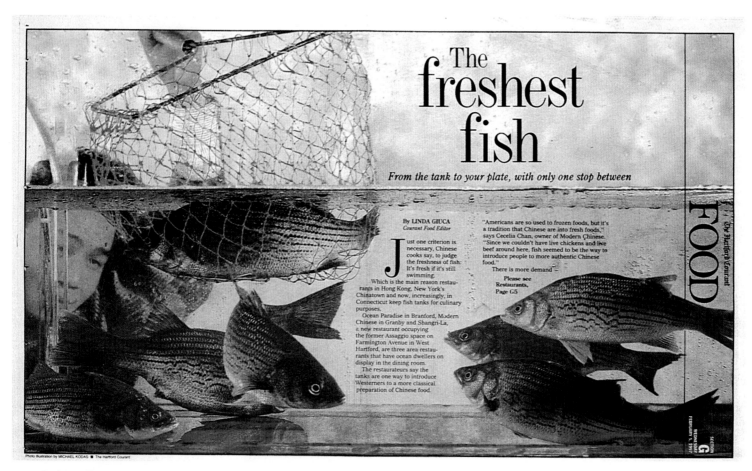

Award of Excellence
The Hartford Courant
Hartford, CT

Christian Potter Drury, Art Director; **Cecelia Prestamo**, Photo Editor; **Melanie Shaffer**, Designer; **Michael Kodas**, Photographer

Award of Excellence
The Seattle Times

Seattle, WA

Tracy Porter, Designer; David Miller, Art Director

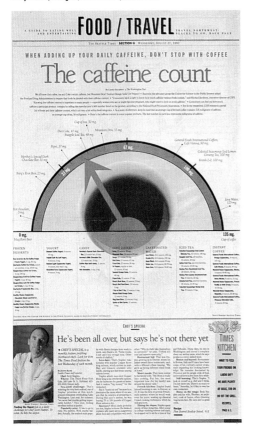

Award of Excellence
Milwaukee Journal Sentinel

Milwaukee, WI

Lonnie Turner, Feature Designer; **Kenneth Miller**, Feature Design Editor;
Geoffrey Blaesing, Senior Editor/Graphics & Design

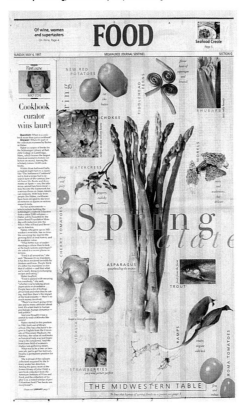

Award of Excellence
The New York Times

New York, NY

Richard Aloisio, Art Director; Kiyoshi Togashi, Photographer

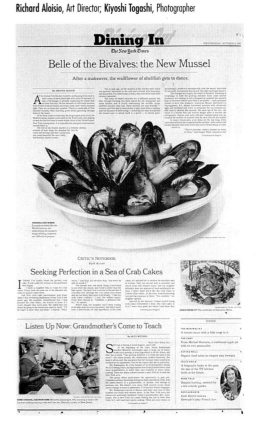

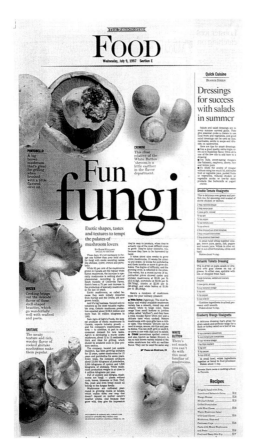

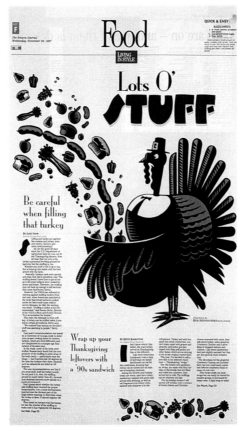

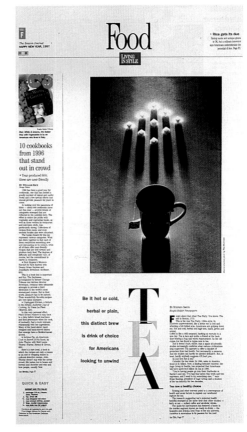

Award of Excellence
The Toronto Star

Toronto, Canada

Catherine Pike, Designer; Marion Kane, Editor; Sue Sampson, Copy
Editor; Bernard Weil, Photographer; Barb Holland, Reporter; Vivian
MacDonald, Editor

Award of Excellence
Akron Beacon Journal

Akron, OH

Rick Steinhauser, Staff Designer/Illustrator

Award of Excellence
Akron Beacon Journal

Akron, OH

Dennis Gordon, Designer; Phil Masturzo, Photographer

Award of Excellence
Anchorage Daily News
Anchorage, AK

Pamela Dunlap-Shohl, Designer; Silver Moon Graphics, Illustrator

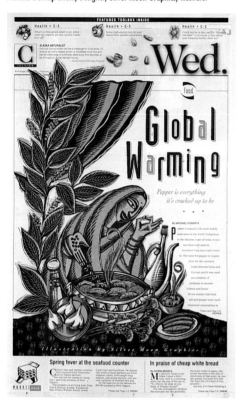

Award of Excellence
El Norte
Monterrey, México

Graciela Sánchez, Designer; Guillermo Castillo, Illustrator; Rosa Mária Castellanos, Electronic Photo; Andrés Reyes, Photographer; Altagracia Fuentes, Editor; Raúl Braulio Martinez, Art Director; Martha Treviño, Editor Director; Ramón A. Garza; General Editor Director; Carmen Escobedo, Graphics Editor

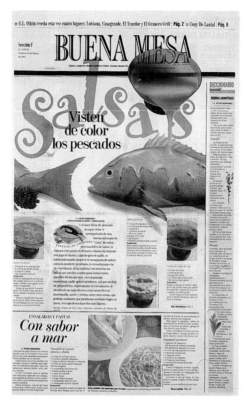

Award of Excellence
Reforma
México City, México

Mayte Amezcua, Designer; Adriana Woodward, Photo Artist; Aronatiuh S. Bracho, Photographer; Alejandro Banuet, Graphics Editor; Celia Marin, Editor; Eduardo Danilo, Design Consultant; Emilio Deheza, Art Director

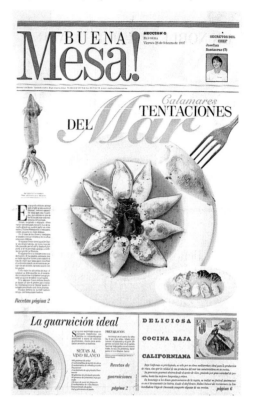

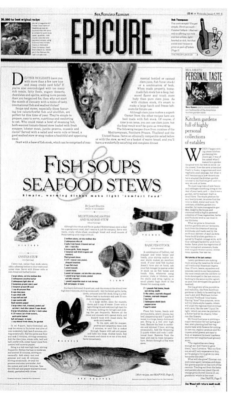

Award of Excellence
San Francisco Examiner
San Francisco, CA

Kelly Frankeny, A.M.E. Design; Richard Paoli, Director/Photography; Elizabeth Mangelsdorf, Photo Editor; Marge Rice, Graphics Editor; Jo Mancuso, Epicure Editor; Don McCartney, Senior Designer; Christina Koci Hernandez, Photographer

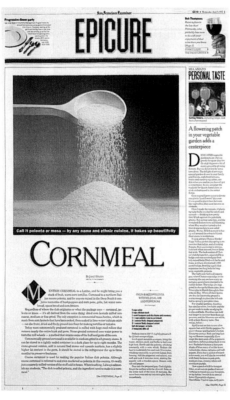

Award of Excellence
San Francisco Examiner
San Francisco, CA

Kelly Frankeny, A.M.E Design; Richard Paoli, Director/Photography; Elizabeth Mangelsdorf, Photo Editor; Marge Rice, Graphics Editor; Jo Mancuso, Epicure Editor; Don McCartney, Senior Designer; Chris Hardy, Photographer

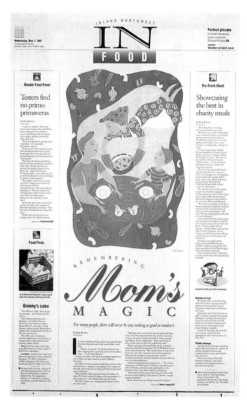

Award of Excellence
The Spokesman-Review
Spokane, WA

John K. Nelson, Design Editor

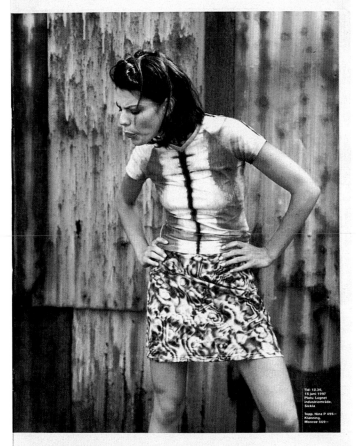

viktiga roller, har senare använts av irakiska, libyska och egyptiska styrkor i konflikter med Israel. Fast Egypten har sedan 1973 valt mer neutrala kamouflagemönster, det påstår Tim och Quentin Newark i "Brassey's Book of Camouflage", en illustrerad historia om kamouflagemönstrens märkliga väg från tankvagnar via hjälmar till gatumode.

I dag finns mer än 350 nationellt präglade, inbördes mycket olika kamouflagemönster. Varje ny nation skapar ett eget, det är en lika viktig del i den nationella identiteten som flaggans färger och nödvändigt för att skilja vän från fiende ute i bushen. Enligt författarna till boken var de brittiska styrkorna under kriget vid Persiska viken tvungna att snabbt ta fram nya kamouflagevarianter eftersom det klassiskt brittiska ökenkamouflagemönstret tidigare hade sålts till Irak. ▶

27 JUNI – 3 JULI 17

Gold
DN. på stan
Stockholm, Sweden

Peter Alenas, Art Director & Designer; **Pompe Hedengren**, Art Director; **Karolina Henke**, Photographer

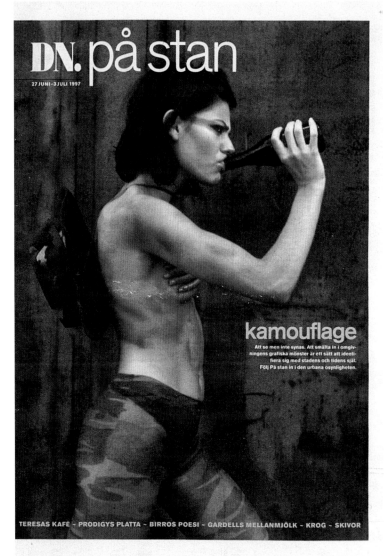

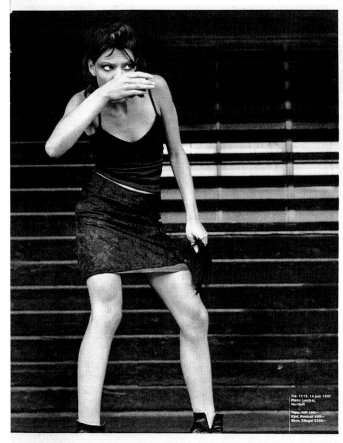

I städer är det fullt av skyltar och reklam, att klä sig i plagg med tryckt text och varumärken över hela kroppen är därför också en form av urbant kamouflage som knyter tillbaka till de schamanistiska föreställningar man tror fick förhistoriska jägare att klä sig som sitt byte i djurhudar och fjädrar. Ett sätt att identifiera sig med stadens och tidens själ helt enkelt, inte konstigare än att klä sig i frack på Nobelfesten och lika beige som kollegorna på kontoret.

A och O är att inte vara enfärgad och stå stilla när fienden tittar åt ditt håll.

SUSANNE PAGOLD

"Brassey's Book of Camouflage" är utgiven av det brittiska bokförlaget Brassey's 1996, och innehåller texter av militärhistorikern Tim Newark: grafiske formgivaren Quentin Newark och samlaren Dr J F Borsalino.

27 JUNI – 3 JULI 19

This **Gold Medal** was awarded for concepts that work and continue to the inside spreads. Grids work beautifully. Images and type are very understated in a classic grid and type use. The photographic images are on the cutting edge. Strong realism in the images shows the photographer and designers are aware of the content, not the models. The content speaks for itself. The backgrounds work for the photographs and make the images clear. The photographs and page design work with a strong visual presentation.

●●●●●

Esta Medalla de Oro fue otorgada por los conceptos que funcionan y continúan en las páginas interiores. Las grillas funcionan a las mil maravillas. Las imágenes y los tipos son muy sutiles en un uso clásico de las grillas y los tipos. Las imágenes fotográficas son de avanzada. El fuerte realismo de las imágenes demuestra que el fotógrafo y los diseñadores conocen el contenido, no los modelos. El contenido habla por sí mismo. Los fondos son adecuados para las fotografías y hacen que las imágenes sean claras. Las fotografías y el diseño logran una fuerte presentación visual.

Award of Excellence
Morgenavisen Jyllands-Posten
Viby J., Denmark

Bodil Krogh, Subeditor

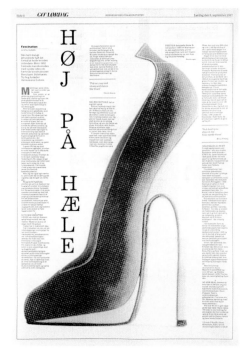

Award of Excellence
The Dallas Morning News
Dallas, TX

Laura Betts, Designer; **Tammy Theis,** Stylist; **William Snyder,** Photographer

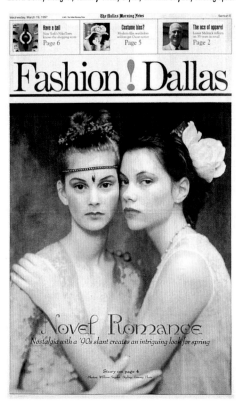

Award of Excellence
O Globo
Rio de Janeiro, Brazil

Mara Caballero, Editor; **Leonardo Drummond,** Designer

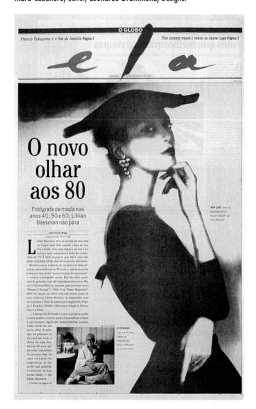

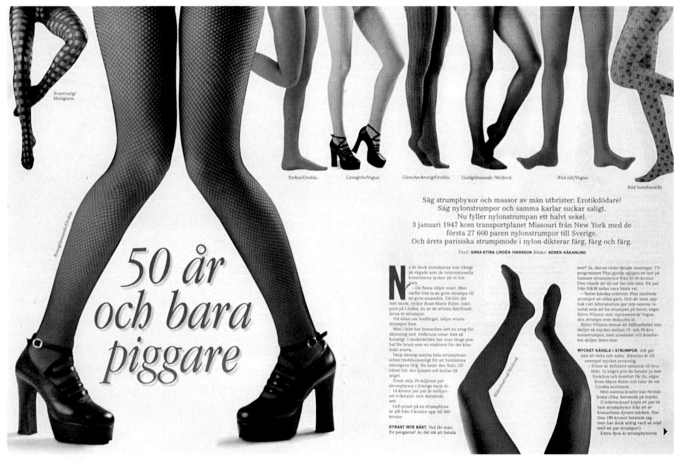

Award of Excellence
Goteborgs-Posten
Göteborg, Sweden

Gunilla Wernhamn, Designer; **Soren Håkanlind,** Photographer

Award of Excellence
The San Francisco Chronicle
San Francisco, CA

Hulda Nelson, Art Director; **Rico Mendez**, Designer

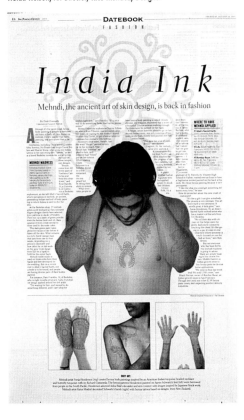

Award of Excellence
San Jose Mercury News
San Jose, CA

Rebecca Hall, Designer; **Nuri Ducassi**, Design Director

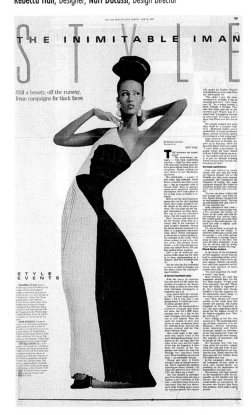

Award of Excellence
San Jose Mercury News
San Jose, CA

Rebecca Hall, Designer; **Brian Griffin**, Designer; **Sue Morrow**, Design Director

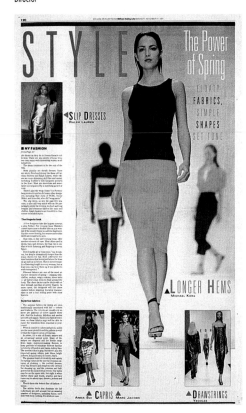

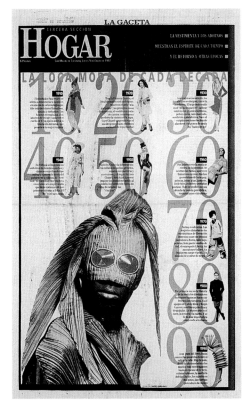

Award of Excellence
•Also an **Award of Excellence** for Features Portfolio
La Gaceta
San Miguel de Tucuman, Argentina

Ruben Falci, Designer; **Sergio S. Fernandez**, Art Director; **Mario Garcia**, Design Consultant

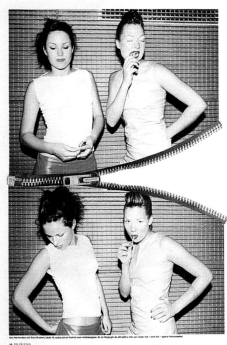

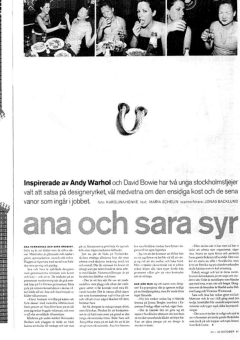

Award of Excellence
DN. på stan
Stockholm, Sweden

Peter Alenas, Art Director; **Pompe Hedengren**, Art Director & Designer; **Karolina Henke**, Photographer; **Jonas Backlund**, Electronic Manipulation

Award of Excellence
La Gaceta
San Miguel de Tucuman, Argentina

Ruben Falci, Designer; Sergio Fernandez, Art Director; Mario Garcia, Design Consultant; Raul Valverdi, Photo Illustrator

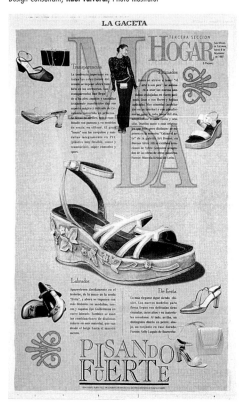

Award of Excellence
El Norte
Monterrey, México

Lourdes De la Rosa, Designer; Juan José Cerón, Photographer; Diana Marcos, Editor; Carmen Escobedo, Graphics Editor; Ramón A. Garza, General Editor Director; Raúl Braulio Martinez, Art Director; Martha Treviño, Editor Director

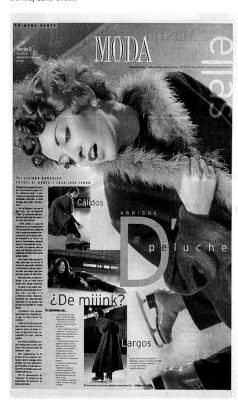

Award of Excellence
The Gazette
Montreal, Canada

Gayle Grin, Feature Design Editor & Designer; Ruben Toledo, Illustrator; Iona Monahan, Fashion Editor; Cecelia McGuire, Living Editor

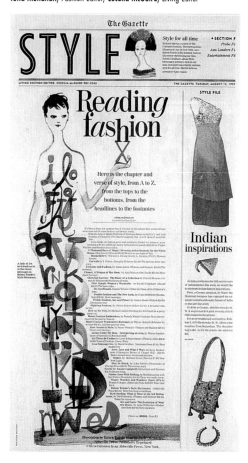

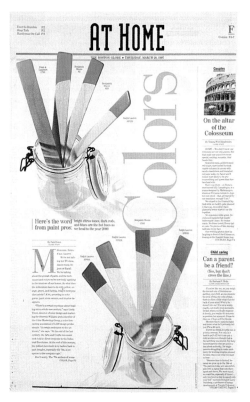

Award of Excellence
The Boston Globe
Boston, MA

Keith Webb, Art Director & Designer; Pam Berry, Photographer; Fiona Luis, Editor

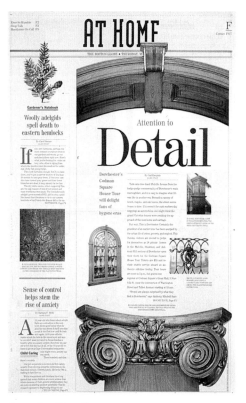

Award of Excellence
The Boston Globe
Boston, MA

Keith Webb, Art Director & Designer; Wendy Maeda, Photographer; Fiona Luis, Editor

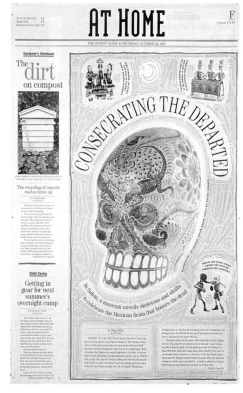

Award of Excellence
The Boston Globe
Boston, MA

Keith Webb, Art Director & Designer & Illustrator; Fiona Luis, Editor

Award of Excellence
The Boston Globe
Boston, MA

Keith Webb, Art Director & Designer; **Fiona Luis**, Editor; **Sally Gall**, Photographer

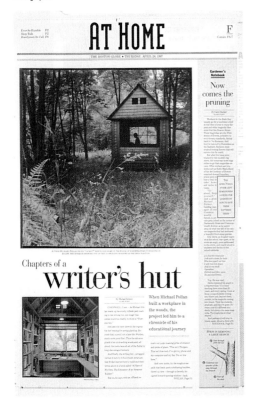

Silver
The Baltimore Sun
Baltimore, MD

Peter Yuill, Features Design Editor; **Victor Panichkul**, Features Design Director; **Joseph Hutchinson**, A.M.E. Graphics/Design

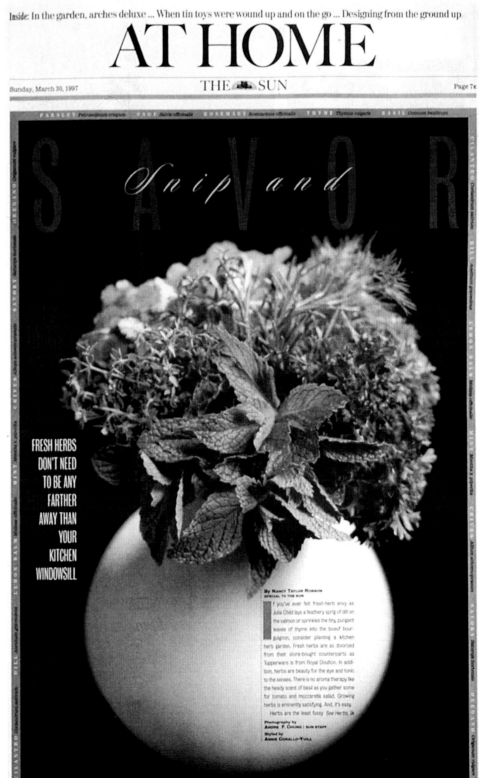

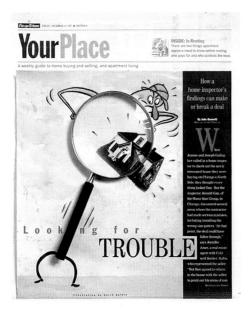

Award of Excellence
Chicago Tribune
Chicago, IL

David Syrek, Art Director; **David Goldin**, Illustrator

Award of Excellence
Chicago Tribune
Chicago, IL

Herman Vega, Art Director; **Elaine Matsushita**, Editor

Award of Excellence
Reforma
México City, México

Elba Debernardi, Designer; **Alejandro Banuet**, Graphics Editor; **Celia Marín**, Editor; **Emilio Deheza**, Art Director; **Eduardo Danilo**, Design Consultant

Award of Excellence
•Also an Award of Excellence for Features Portfolio
The Boston Globe
Boston, MA

Sue Dawson, Art Director; **Jerry Morris**, Editor; **Dick Carpenter**, Associate Editor

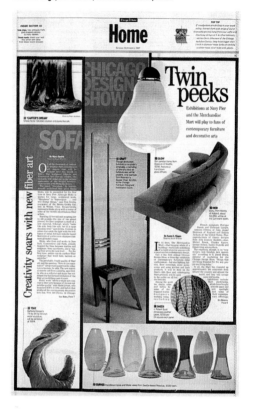

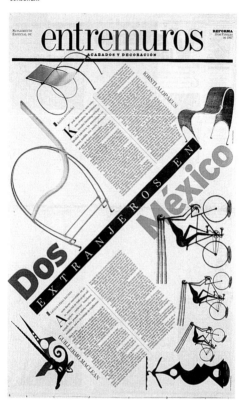

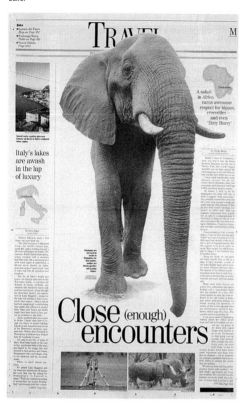

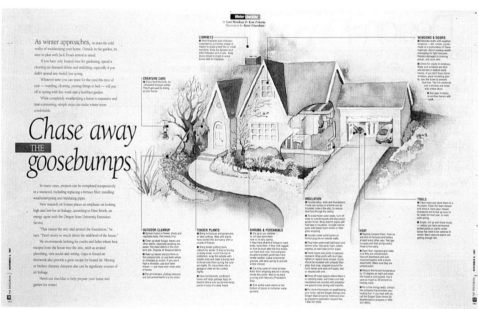

Award of Excellence
The Oregonian
Portland, OR

Joan Carlin, Visuals Editor

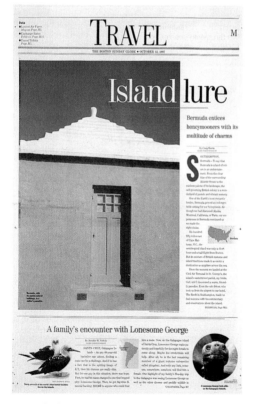

Award of Excellence
The Boston Globe
Boston, MA

Sue Dawson, Art Director; **Jerry Morris**, Editor; **Dick Carpenter**, Associate Editor

Award of Excellence
The Boston Globe
Boston, MA

Sue Dawson, Art Director; Jerry Morris, Editor; Dick Carpenter, Associate Editor

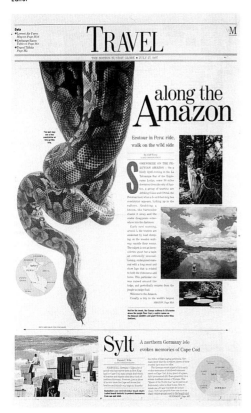

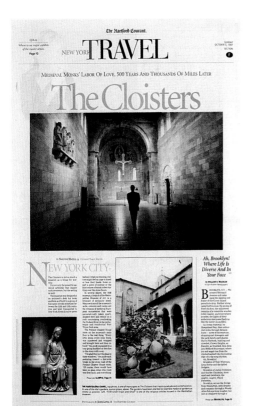

Award of Excellence
The Hartford Courant
Hartford, CT

Christian Potter Drury, Art Director; Cecilia Prestamo, Photo Editor/Designer

Silver
NRC Handelsblad
Rotterdam, The Netherlands

Kees Endenburg, Design Editor; Sieb Posthuma, Illustrator

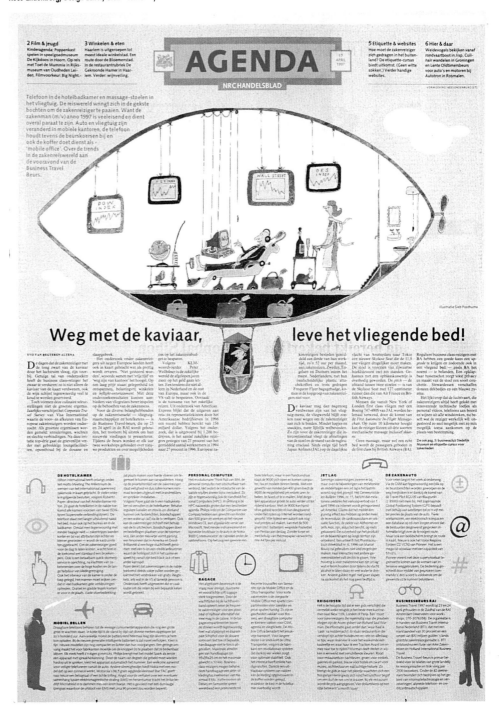

Award of Excellence
The Hartford Courant
Hartford, CT

Christian Potter Drury, Art Director; **Cecilia Prestamo**, Photo Editor/Designer

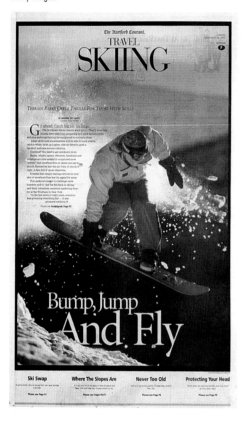

Award of Excellence
The New York Times
New York, NY

Nicki Kalish, Art Director; **David McLimans**, Illustrator

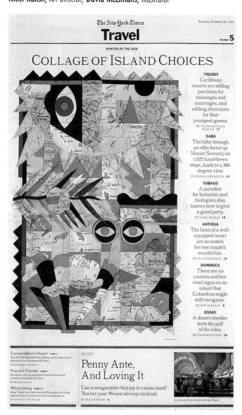

Award of Excellence
The Oregonian
Portland, OR

Nancy Casey, Designer; **Shawn Vitt**, Assistant Art Director

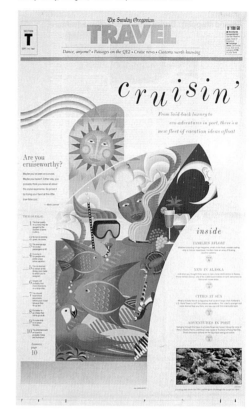

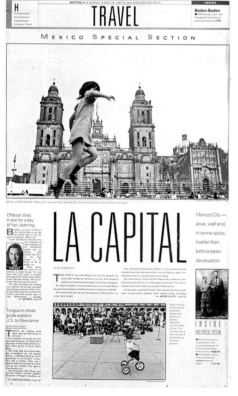

Award of Excellence
San Jose Mercury News
San Jose, CA

Jenny Anderson, Designer; **Nuri Ducassi**, Design Director; **Richard Koci Hernandez**, Photographer

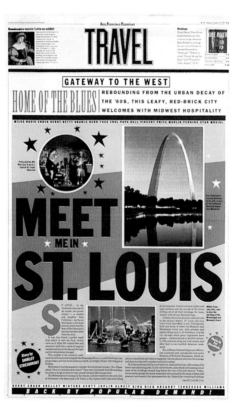

Award of Excellence
San Francisco Examiner
San Francisco, CA

Kelly Frankeny, A.M.E. Design; **Richard Paoli**, Director/Photography; **Elizabeth Mangelsdorf**, Photo Editor; **Marge Rice**, Graphics Editor; **John Flinn**, Travel Editor; **Don McCartney**, Senior Designer; **Andrew Skwish**, Designer

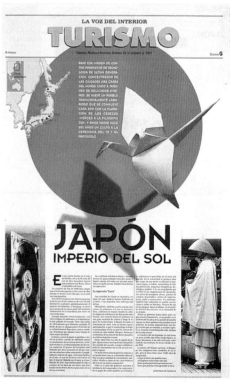

Award of Excellence
La Voz del Interior
Córdoba, Argentina

Julio Bariles, Designer; **Miguel De Lorenzi**, Art Director & Designer; **Graciela Remonda**, Editor; **Luis Remonda**, Publisher; **Mario Garcia**, Design Consultant

Award of Excellence
•Also an Award of Excellence for Photo Illustration
The Hartford Courant
Hartford, CT

Christian Potter Drury, Art Director; Cecilia Prestamo, Photo Editor; Melanie Shaffer, Designer; Richard Messina, Photographer

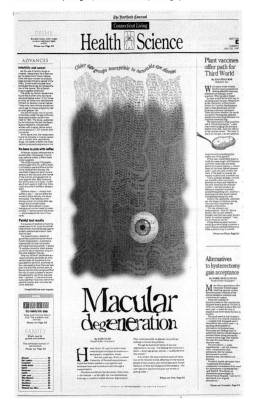

Award of Excellence
•Also an Award of Excellence for Illustration
The New York Times
New York, NY

Michael Valenti, Art Director; Michael Rothman, Illustrator

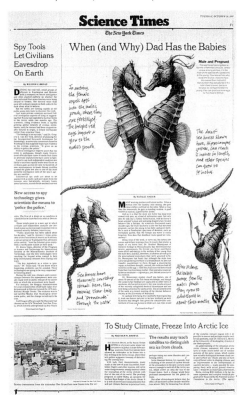

Award of Excellence
•Also an Award of Excellence for Informational Graphics
The New York Times
New York, NY

Michael Valenti, Art Director; Juan Velasco, Graphics Editor/Illustrator

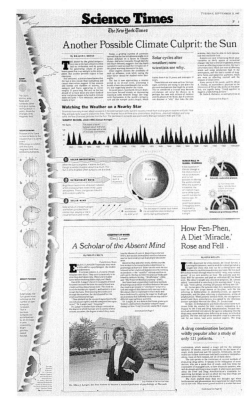

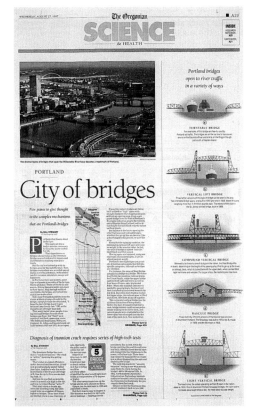

Award of Excellence
The Oregonian
Portland, OR

Michael Mode, Graphic Artist; Linda Shankweiler, Art Director & Designer

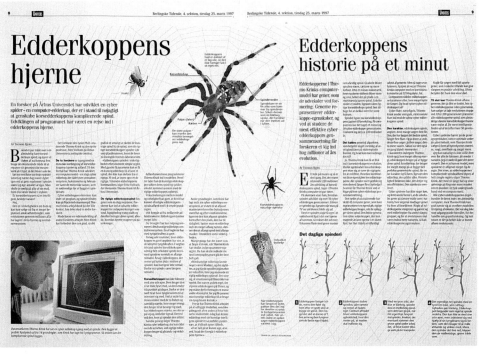

Award of Excellence
Berlingske Tidende
Copenhagen, Denmark

Ida Jerichow, Visualizer

Silver
•Also an **Award of Excellence** for
Photo Story

DN. på stan

Stockholm, Sweden

Peter Alenas, Art Director; **Pompe**
Hedengren, Art Director & Designer;
Frederik Sandin Carlson,
Photographer

på hotell

Fem våningar, 190 män. En av dem är Charles.
Dokumentärfotografen Fredrik Sandin Carlson har under ett par år
följt livet på Monumentet, det sista av Stockholms ungkarlshotell.

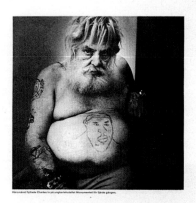

Här återvänt flyttade Charles in på ungkarlshotellet Monumentet för fjärde gången.

24 DN. PÅ STAN   28 NOVEMBER – 4 DECEMBER 25

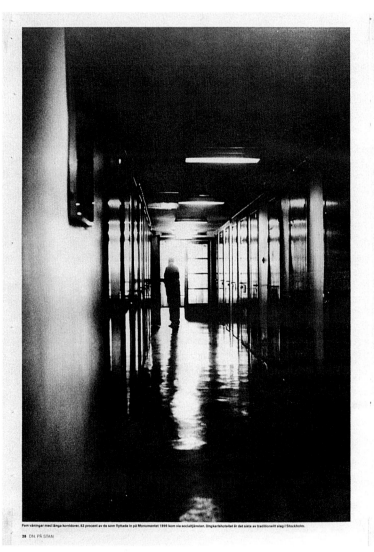

Fem våningar med långa korridorer. 63 procent av de som flyttade in på Monumentet 1996 kom via socialtjänsten. Ungkarlshotellet är det sista av traditionellt slag i Stockholm.

28 DN. PÅ STAN

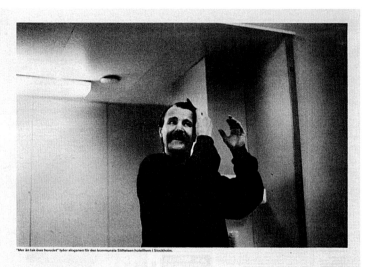

"Mer än tak över huvudet" lyder sloganen för den kommunala Stiftelsen hotellhem i Stockholm.

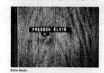

I textremsan: Gud utrustade mig med sinna egenskaper.

Elvis lever.

Julafton 1996.

monumentet

NÅGON GÅR ALLTID omkring i
arbetskläder, trots att han inte
har något arbete att gå till.
Han accepterar inte riktigt sin
situation, trots nästan tio år på
Monumentet. Kanske känns
det lättare när omgivningen
tror att allt är som det ska, han
ser ju ut som om han är på väg
till ett bygge eller en verkstad.
Kanske känns det lättare och
kanske känns det förflutna livet
närmare inpå – det förflutna livet med arbete, pengar, bostad
och trygghet.

Ett rum på ungkarlshotellet
Monumentet i södra änden av
Ostgötagatan är tio kvadrat-
meter stort. Någon sa att det
är som hytten på en finlands-
båt. Efter den senaste hyres-
höjningen kostar rummet nästan 2000 kronor i inkladen,
institutionsmöblerat. Fem våningar, långa korridorer, fyrtio
rum per våning, något färre på
bottenvåningen, tre toiletter
och två duschar per våning,
inga telefoner på rummen.

Av de 190 männen som bor
på Monumentet lever några ett
välordnat liv, de flesta ett mer
kaotiskt. Ungkarlshotellen

byggdes för att män från lands-
orten som fått arbete i staden
skulle ha någonstans att bo,
men bara en kort tid tills man
hittat något mer ordnat. För
en del var dock det sättet att
leva ideal och här finns någon
som bott större delen av sitt liv
på Monumentet.

"Mer än tak över huvudet"
lyder slogan för den kom-
munala Stiftelsen hotellhem i
Stockholm, SHIS, som driver
ungkarlshotell, hotellhem och
kommunens flyktingbostäder.
Monumentet är det sista av de
traditionella ungkarlshotellen,
som under 1996 fick 115 nya
hyresgäster varav 83 procent
placerades av socialtjänsten.
De senaste årens stora ned-
skärningar inom psykiatrin har
märkts tydligt. Efterfrågan på
rummen ökar, och "samtidigt
har gästernas sociala proble-
matik blivit fortsatt tyngre"
enligt årsrapporten för 1996.

FREDRIK SANDIN CARLSON

Fredrik Sandin Carlsons bilder
från ungkarlshotellet Monumentet ställs ut på Stockholms
stadsmuseum under 1998.

28 NOVEMBER – 4 DECEMBER 29

Award of Excellence
Asbury Park Press
Neptune, NJ

Mark Voger, Editor/Designer & Artist; **Ed Gabel**, Artist; **Kathy Voglesong**, Photographer; **Andrew Prendimano**, Art & Photo Director; **Harris G. Siegel**, M.E./Design & Photography

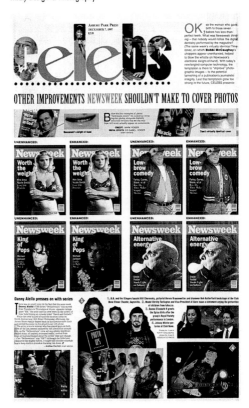

Award of Excellence
Asbury Park Press
Neptune, NJ

Mark Voger, Editor/Designer; **Andrew Prendimano**, Art & Photo Director; **Harris G. Siegel**, M.E./Design & Photography

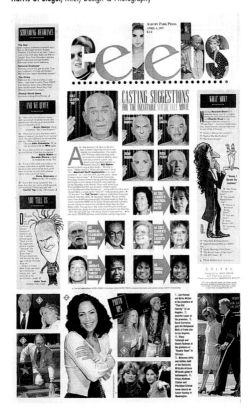

Award of Excellence
Clarin
Buenos Aires, Argentina

Iñaki Palacios, Art Director; **Tea Alberti**, Design Editor; **Oscar Bejarano**, Graphic Designer; **Omar Olivella**, Graphic Designer; **Matilde Oliveros**, Graphic Designer; **Pablo Ruiz**, Graphic Designer; **Carolina Wainsztok**, Graphic Designer; **Alejandro Lo Celso**, Graphic Designer

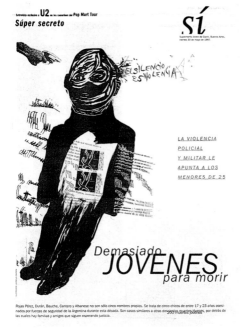

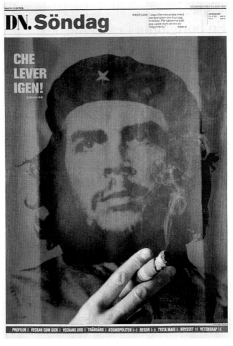

Award of Excellence
Dagens Nyheter
Stockholm, Sweden

Ulla Wingård, Design Director; **John Bark**, Creative Director/Designer; **Sam Stadener**, Photographer

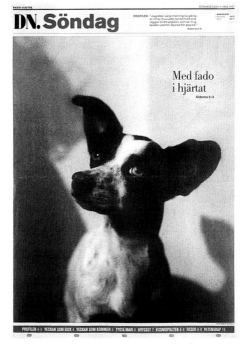

Award of Excellence
Dagens Nyheter
Stockholm, Sweden

Ulla Wingård, Design Director; **John Bark**, Creative Director; **Mats Odeen**, Art Director & Designer; **Robert Blombäck**, Photographer

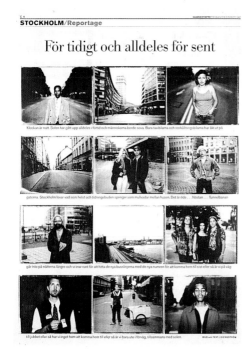

Award of Excellence
Dagens Nyheter
Stockholm, Sweden

Ulla Wingård, Design Director; **John Bark**, Creative Director; **Ina Blomster**, Designer; **F.H. Engström**, Photographer; **Benkt Eurenius**, Photo Editor

Award of Excellence
Dagens Nyheter
Stockholm, Sweden
Ulla Wingård, Design Director; **John Bark**, Creative Director; **Magnus Nilsson**, Designer; **Håkan Burell**, Designer

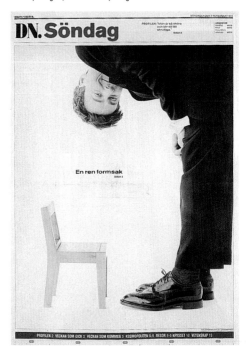

Award of Excellence
Dagens Nyheter
Stockholm, Sweden
Ulla Wingård, Design Director; **John Bark**, Creative Director; **Ylva Magnusson**, Designer; **Johan Furusjö**, Designer

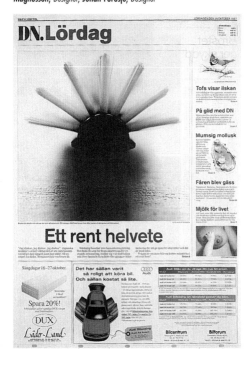

Award of Excellence
DN. på stan
Stockholm, Sweden
Peter Alenas, Art Director; **Pompe Hedengren**, Art Director; **Lotta Kühlhorn**, Art Director & Illustrator

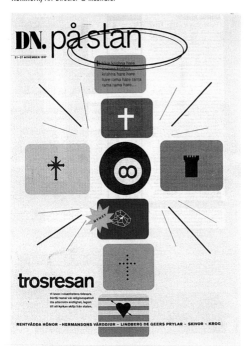

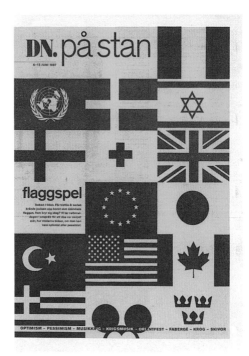

Award of Excellence
DN. på stan
Stockholm, Sweden
Peter Alenas, Art Director, Designer & Illustrator; **Pompe Hedengren**, Art Director

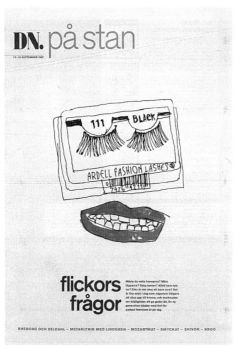

Award of Excellence
DN. på stan
Stockholm, Sweden
Peter Alenas, Art Director; **Pompe Hedengren**, Art Director & Designer; **Lovisa Burfitt**, Illustrator; **Beauusma Schyffert**, Illustrator

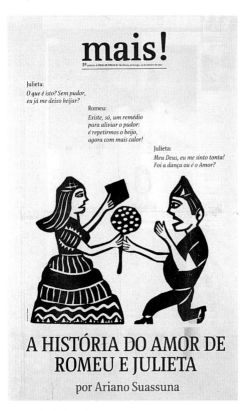

Award of Excellence
Folha de S.Paulo
São Paulo, Brazil
Alcino Leite Neto, Sunday Cultural Supplement; **Renata Buono**, Designer

Award of Excellence
The Hartford Courant
Hartford, CT

Christian Potter Drury, Art Director; **Cecilia Prestamo**, Photo Editor;
Christopher Moore, Designer

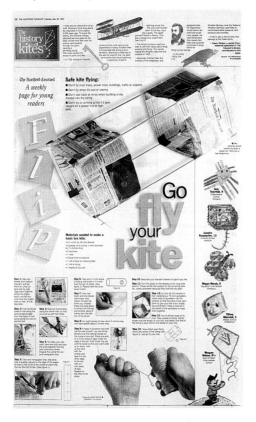

Award of Excellence
Goteborgs-Posten
Göteborg, Sweden

Karin Sandquist, Designer; **Cissi Håkansson**, Artist

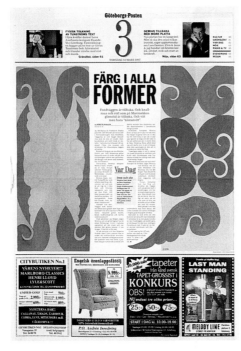

Award of Excellence
Morgenavisen Jyllands-Posten
Viby J., Denmark

Jens Kaiser, Editor; **Lars Pryds**, Designer

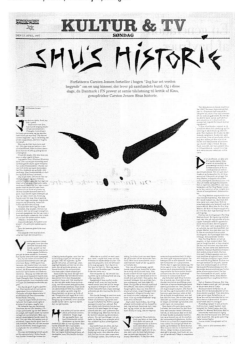

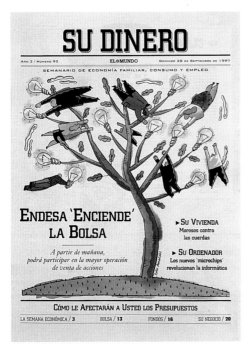

Award of Excellence
El Mundo
Madrid, Spain

Carmelo Caderot, Design Director; **Manuel de Miguel**, Assistant Art
Director; **Toño Benavides**, Illustrator; **Miguel Arzoz**, Designer

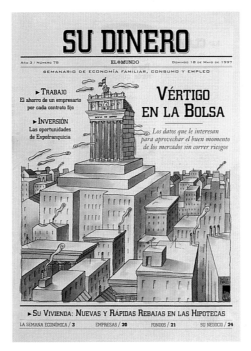

Award of Excellence
•Also an **Award of Excellence** for Illustration Portfolio
El Mundo
Madrid, Spain

Carmelo Caderot, Design Director; **Manuel de Miguel**, Assistant Art
Director; **Toño Benavides**, Illustrator; **Miguel Arzoz**, Designer

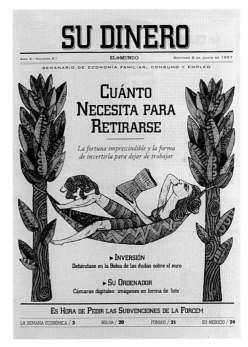

Award of Excellence
•Also an **Award of Excellence** for Illustration
El Mundo
Madrid, Spain

Carmelo Caderot, Design Director; **Manuel de Miguel**, Assistant Art
Director; **Victoria Martos**, Illustrator; **Miguel Arzoz**, Designer

Award of Excellence
Anchorage Daily News
Anchorage, AK

Lance Lekander, Designer & Art Director

Award of Excellence
Anchorage Daily News
Anchorage, AK

Lance Lekander, Designer, Art Director & Illustrator

Award of Excellence
•Also an Award of Excellence for Magazine Portfolio
Anchorage Daily News
Anchorage, AK

Lance Lekander, Designer, Art Director & Illustrator

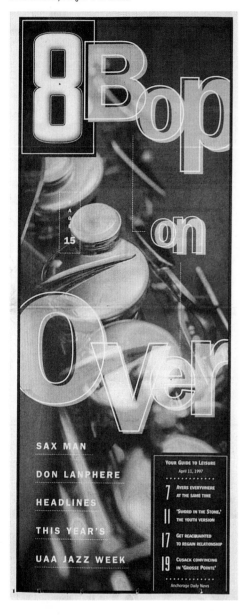

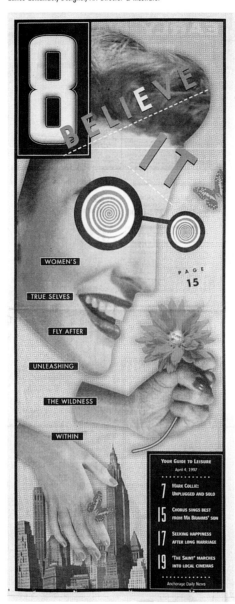

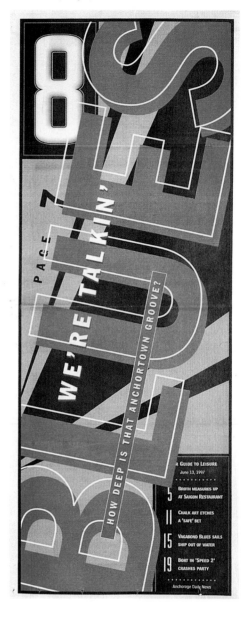

Award of Excellence
Asbury Park Press
Neptune, NJ

Jeff Paslay, Designer; Harris G. Siegel,
M.E./Design & Photography; Andrew Prendimano,
Art & Photo Director; Adriana Libreros, Illustrator

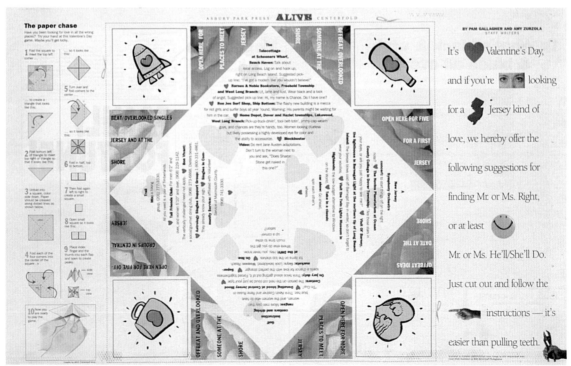

Award of Excellence
La Gaceta
San Miguel de Tucuman, Argentina

Hector Reinoso Gallo, Designer; **Sergio S. Fernandez**, Art Director; **Mario Garcia**, Design Consultant; **Daniel Fontanarrosa**, Photo Illustrator

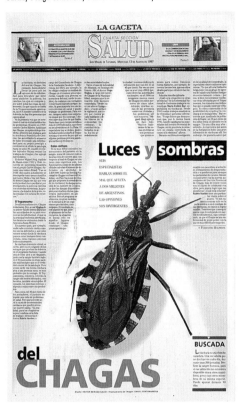

Silver
La Gaceta
San Miguel de Tucuman, Argentina

Sebastian Rosso, Designer; **Sergio S. Fernandez**, Art Director; **Mario Garcia**, Design Consultant; **Raul Valverdi**, Photo Illustrator

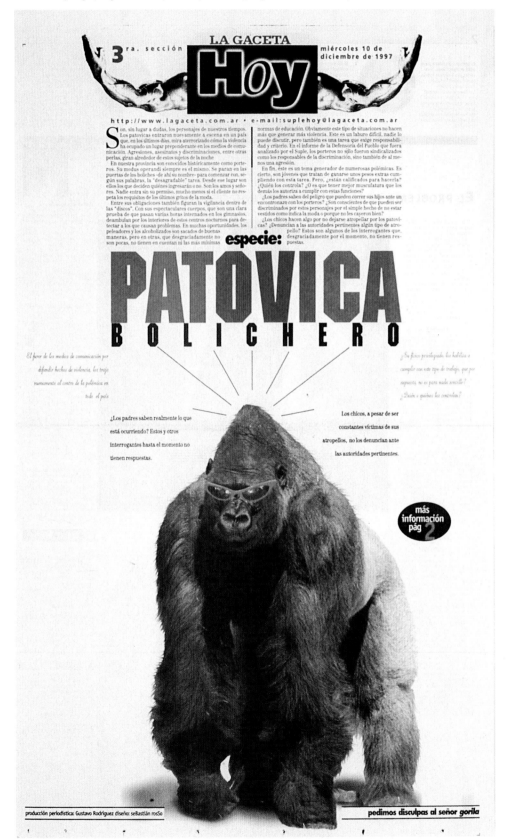

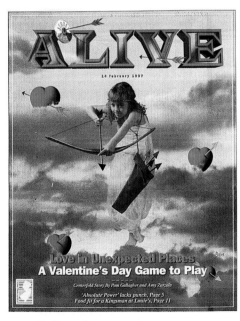

Award of Excellence
Asbury Park Press
Neptune, NJ

Kathy Dzielak, Editor; **Harris G. Siegel**, M.E./Design & Photography; **Andrew Prendimano**, Art & Photo Director; **Harry Ziegler**, M.E./Lifestyles; **Ed Gabel**, Graphic Artist; **Mark Kseniak**, Designer; **Bob Bielk**, Photo Illustration

Silver
La Gaceta
San Miguel de Tucuman, Argentina
Sebastian Rosso, Designer; **Sergio S. Fernandez**, Art Director; **Mario Garcia**, Design Consultant

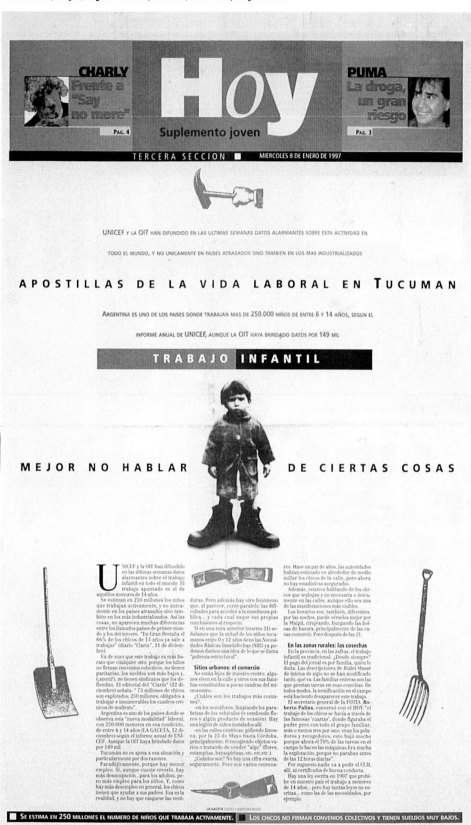

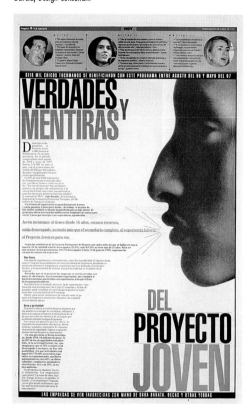

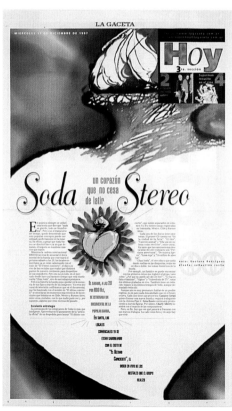

Award of Excellence
La Gaceta
San Miguel de Tucuman, Argentina

Sebastian Rosso, Designer; **Sergio S. Fernandez**, Art Director; **Mario García**, Design Consultant

Silver
Reforma
México City, México

Mayte Amezcua, Designer; **Alejandro Banuet**, Graphics Editor; **Beatriz de León**, Editor; **Emilio Deheza**, Art Director; **Eduardo Danilo**, Design Consultant; **Barry Domínguez**, Photographer

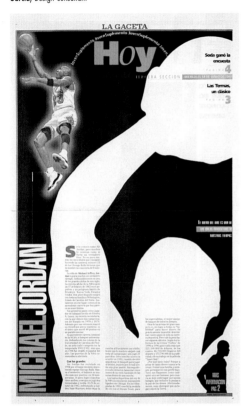

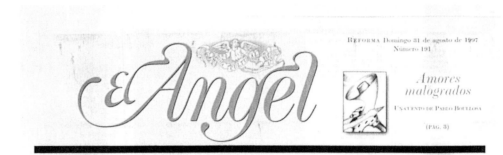

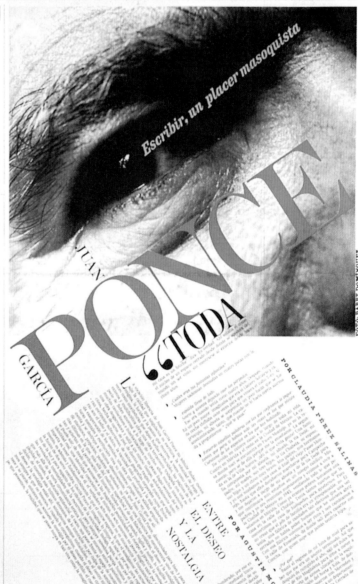

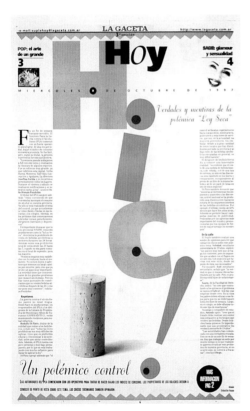

Award of Excellence
La Gaceta
San Miguel de Tucuman, Argentina

Sebastian Rosso, Designer; **Sergio S. Fernandez**, Art Director; **Mario García**, Design Consultant

Award of Excellence
El Norte
Monterrey, México

Graciela Sánchez, Designer; **Guillermo Castillo**, Photo Illustrator; **Juan José Cerón**, Photographer; **Amaro Campos**, Editor; **Carmen Escobedo**, Graphics Editor; **Raúl Braulio Martinez**, Art Director; **Martha Treviño**, Editor Director; **Ramón A. Garza**, General Editor Director

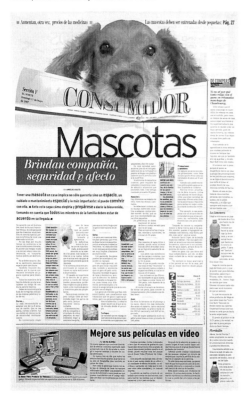

Award of Excellence
Reforma
México City, México

Daniel Esqueda Guadalajara, Designer; **Xóchitl González**, Section Designer; **Dinorah Basáñez**, Editor; **Emilio Deheza**, Art Director; **Ana Lorena Ochoa**, Photographer; **Eduardo Danilo**, Design Consultant

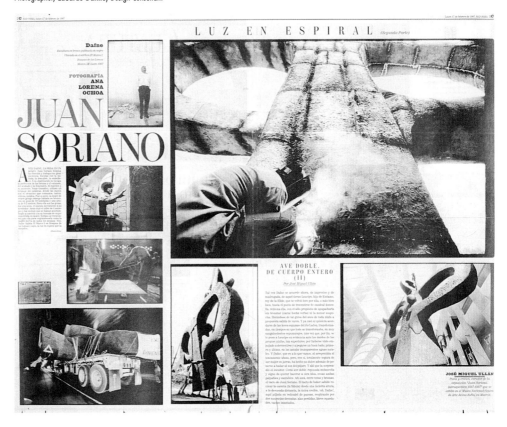

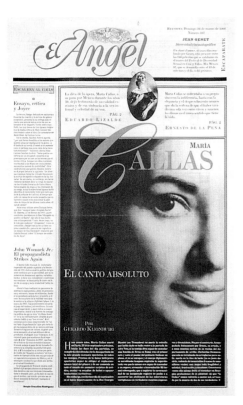

Award of Excellence
Reforma
México City, México

Mayte Amezcua, Designer; **Alejandro Banuet**, Graphics Editor; **Beatriz de León**, Editor; **Emilio Deheza**, Art Director; **Eduardo Danilo**, Design Consultant

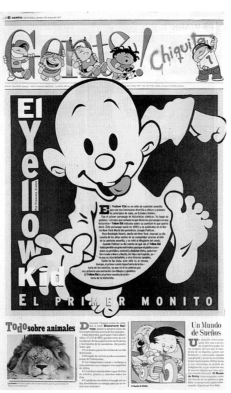

Award of Excellence
Reforma
México City, México

Regina Landa, Designer; **Ana Isabel Aguayo**, Editor; **Erika Sosa**, Graphics Coordinator; **Alejandro Banuet**, Graphics Editor; **Emilio Deheza**, Art Director; **Eduardo Danilo**, Design Consultant

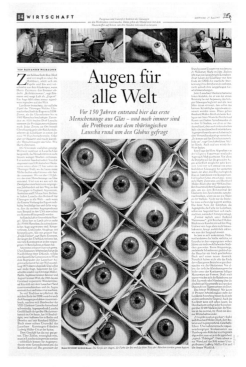

Award of Excellence
Die Woche
Hamburg, Germany

Manfred Bissinger, Editor-in-Chief; **Kurt Breme**, Executive Editor; **Hans-Ulrich Joerges**, Executive Editor; **Dirk Linke**, Art Director; **Andreas Schomberg**, Associate Art Director; **Armin Ogris**, Designer; **Stefan Semrau**, Designer; **Jessica Winter**; Designer; **Florian Poehl**, Designer/Informational Graphics; **Reinhard Schulz-Schaeffer**, Designer/Informational Graphics

Award of Excellence
The Ball State Daily News
Muncie, IN
Bill Webster, Designer

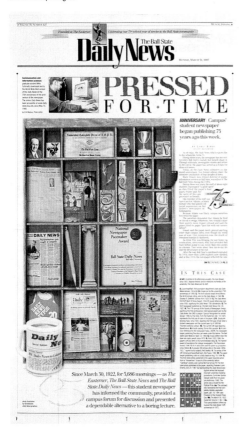

Award of Excellence
Jacksonville Journal-Courier
Jacksonville, IL
Mike Miner, Editor/Designer

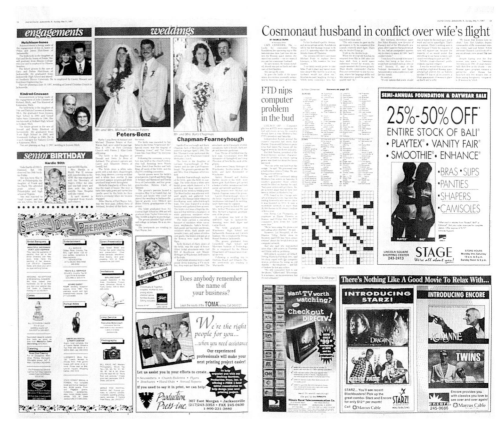

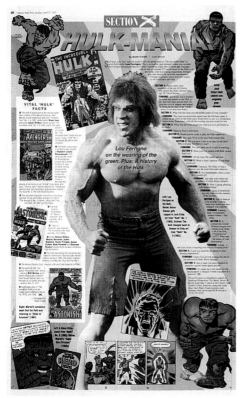

Award of Excellence
Asbury Park Press
Neptune, NJ
Mark Voger, Designer & Editor; **Harris G. Siegel**, M.E./Design & Photography; **Andrew Prendimano**, Art & Photo Director

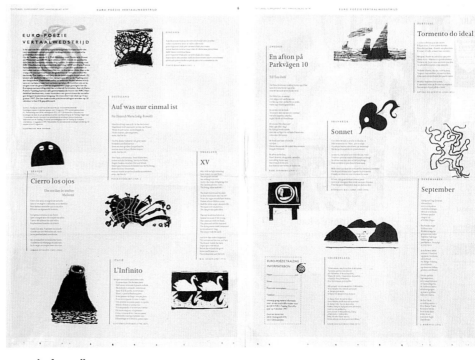

Award of Excellence
NRC Handelsblad
Rotterdam, The Netherlands
Nancy Lemmers, Design Editor; **Wim Hofman**, Illustrator

Award of Excellence
The Oregonian
Portland, OR

Joan Carlin, Visuals Editor, Homes & Gardens

Award of Excellence
NRC Handelsblad
Rotterdam, The Netherlands

Nancy Lemmers, Design Editor

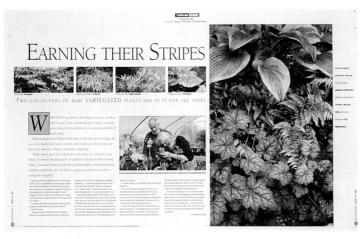

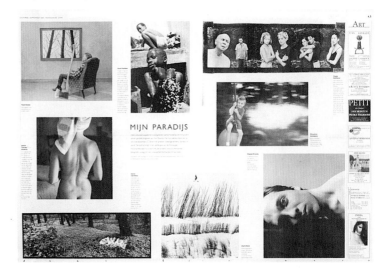

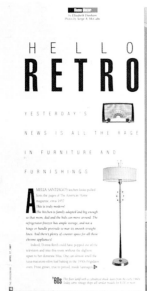

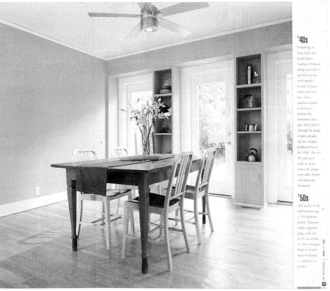

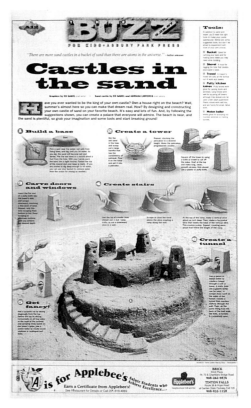

Award of Excellence
The Oregonian
Portland, OR

Joan Carlin, Visuals Editor, Homes & Gardens

Award of Excellence
Asbury Park Press
Neptune, NJ

Debra LaQuaglia, Editor; **Harris G. Siegel**, M.E./Design & Photography;
Andrew Prendimano, Art & Photo Director; **Adriana Libreros**, Design; **Ed
Gabel**, Graphic Artist

Silver
Asbury Park Press
Neptune, NJ

Daryl Stone, Photographer; **Harris G. Siegel**, M.E./Design & Photography, Designer; **Andrew Prendimano**, Art & Photo Director; **James J. Connolly**, Photographer; **Ed Gabel**, Graphic Artist; **John Quinn**, M.E./Sports; **Denis Brodeur**, Photographer

ASBURY PARK PRESS
OCTOBER 2, 1997

NHL PREVIEW 1997-1998 | NEW YORK RANGERS

MESSIER GRETZKY

A STORY BY CHRIS BALDWIN, STAFF WRITER

WAYNE GRETZKY'S EYES KEEP WANDERING TO THE EMPTY LOCKER ACROSS THE ROOM. IT IS THE TEAM SUPERSTAR'S LOCKER. THE BIGGEST LOCKER. THE ONE THAT PLAYERS WOULD JOSTLE TO CLAIM, UNDER ORDINARY CIRCUMSTANCES. ¶ BUT GRETZKY DOESN'T WANT IT. NONE OF THE RANGERS FEEL RIGHT ABOUT TAKING IT. NOT GRETZKY, THE SUPERSTAR'S SUPERSTAR. NOT BRIAN LEETCH, THE ALL-STAR DEFENSEMAN WHO SEEMS TO HAVE LEADER WRITTEN ALL OVER HIM. NOT MIKE RICHTER, THE CASTLE-WALL OF A GOALIE WHO MAKES THE RANGER MAGIC IN MAY. ¶ IT IS MARK MESSIER'S LOCKER. YOU

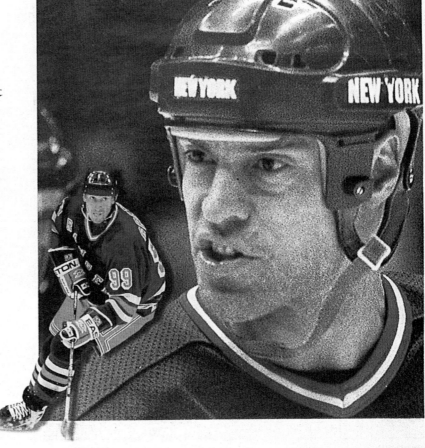

MESSIER PHOTO BY DARYL STONE, STAFF PHOTOGRAPHER
GRETZKY PHOTO BY JAMES J. CONNOLLY, STAFF PHOTOGRAPHER

[SEE RANGERS, PAGE C9]

ASBURY PARK PRESS
OCTOBER 2, 1997

NHL PREVIEW 1997-1998 | NEW JERSEY DEVILS

LEMAIRE GILMOUR

A STORY BY KISHA CIABATTARI, STAFF WRITER

ALTHOUGH YOU'D LIKELY DIE TRYING TO GET JACQUES LEMAIRE OR LOU LAMORIELLO TO ADMIT IT, THE DEVILS HAVE PRIVATELY HAD A CHANGE OF HEART. ¶ THE BUSINESS OF SCORING — WHICH HAS ALWAYS TAKEN A BACK SEAT TO THE FRANCHISE PHILOSOPHY STRESSING GOALTENDING AND DEFENSE — CAN NO LONGER BE RELEGATED TO THAT CROSSED-FINGERS, GOALS-WILL-COME LEAP OF OFFENSIVE FAITH. ¶ THE TRANSITION GAME SUPPOSED TO BE THE REWARD AND NATURAL CONSE-QUENCE OF BEING A DEVOUT LITTLE BACKCHECKER HASN'T BEEN THERE SINCE CLAUDE LEMIEUX GOT

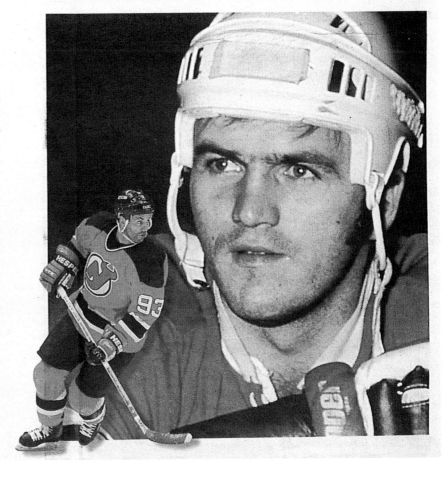

GILMOUR PHOTO BY DARYL STONE, STAFF PHOTOGRAPHER
LEMAIRE PHOTO BY DENIS BRODEUR, MONTREAL CANADIENS PHOTOGRAPHER

[SEE DEVILS, PAGE C9]

Award of Excellence
Asbury Park Press
Neptune, NJ

Kathy Dzielak, Editor; **Harris G. Siegel**, M.E./Design &
Photography; **Andrew Prendimano**, Art & Photo Director;
Adriana Libreros, Design; **Mary Iuvone**, Photographer

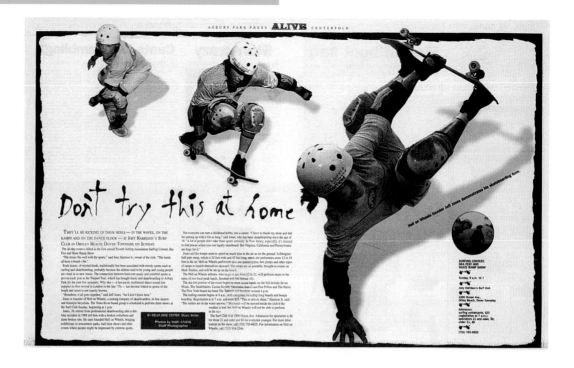

Award of Excellence
The Herald-Sun
Durham, NC

Pete Corson, Feature Designer

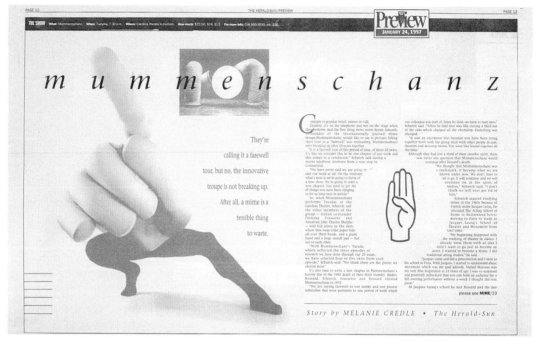

Award of Excellence
Home News & Tribune
East Brunswick, NJ

Andrew Phillips, Designer; **Tom Peyton**, Art Director; **Harris G.
Siegel**, M.E. Design & Photography; **Tammy Paolino**, On the Go
Editor; **Marc Ascher**, Photo Editor

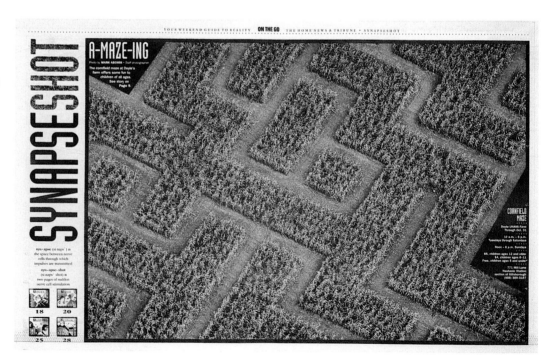

Chapter Five

MAGAZINES

Continuing to pay tribute to the world's best newspaper designs, the 19th edition of The Best of Newspaper Design is a stunning collection of modern work. The included works were selected from more than 10,000 entries submitted by newspapers all over the world. This exceptional collection is an essential reference for anyone involved in print media, graphics, photography, design, journalism, or communications.

The competition, which is sponsored annually by the Society of News Design and the S.I. Newhouse School of Public Communications at Syracuse University, recognizes excellence in newspaper design and graphics. Awards include Best of Show, Gold, Silver, Award of Excellence, Special Recogni-tion, plus the honor of World's Best Designed Newspaper. Categories for judging include overall page design, portfolio, magazine cover design, art and illustration, photo journalism, and informational graphics.

This nineteenth edition presents the finest newspaper design in the field.

Selected by a panel of 21 judges of the Society for News Design, the award-winning pub-lications featured in this nineteenth edition were chosen for excellence in design.

The Best of Newspaper Design, 19th edition, features: Text in English and Spanish; 840 awards: World's Best-Designed Newspapers, Best of Show, Gold medals, Judges' Special Recognition, Silver medals, and Awards of Excel-lence. More than 12,100 entries were reviewed from hundreds of publications from around the world to select winners from 158 publications. Categories included: Overall design, news, features, portfolios, special coverage, special sections, magazines, art and illustration, photography, informational graphics Continuing to pay tribute to the world's best newspaper designs, the 19th edition of The Best of Newspaper Design is a stunning collection of modern work. The included works were selected from more than 10,000 entries submitted by newspapers all over the world. This exceptional collection is an essential reference for anyone involved in print media, graphics, photography, design, journalism, or communications.

The competition, which is sponsored annually by the Society of News Design and the S.I. Newhouse School of Public Communications at Syracuse University, recognizes excellence in newspaper design and graphics. Awards include Best of Show, Gold, Silver, Award of Excellence, Special Recogni-tion, plus the honor of World's Best Designed Newspaper. Categories for judging include overall page design,

The competition, which is sponsored annually by the Society of News Design and the S.I. Newhouse School of Public Communications at Syracuse University, recognizes excellence in newspaper design and graphics. Awards include Best of Show, Gold, Silver, Award of Excellence, Special Recogni-tion, plus the honor of World's Best Designed Newspaper. Categories for judging include overall page design, portfolio, magazine cover design, art and illustration, photo journalism, and informational graphics. The competition, which is sponsored annually by the Society of News Design and the S.I. Newhouse School of Public Communications at Syracuse University, recognizes excellence in newspaper design and graphics. Awards include Best of Show, Gold, Silver, Award of Excellence, Special Recogni-tion, plus the honor of World's Best Designed Newspaper. Categories for judging include overall page design, portfolio, magazine cover design, art and illustration, photo journalism, and informational graphics.

This nineteenth edition presents the finest newspaper design in the field.

Selected by a panel of judges of the Society of News Design, the award-winning newspapers featured in this nineteenth edition were chosen for excellence in design.

Selected by a panel of 21 judges of the Society for News Design, the award-winning newspapers featured in this nineteenth edition were chosen for excellence in design.

The Best of Newspaper Design, 19th edition, features: all text in English and Spanish; more than five hundred awards: Best of Show, Judges' Special Recognition, Gold Medals, Sil-ver Medals, and Awards of Excellence; over five hundred newspapers from all around the world; categories such as overall page design, portfolio, magazine cover design, art and illustration, photo journalism, and informational graphics Continuing to pay tribute to the world's best newspaper designs, the 19th edition of The Best of Newspaper Design is a stunning collection of modern work. The included works were selected from more than 10,000 entries submitted by newspapers all over the world. This exceptional collection is an essential reference for anyone involved in print media, graphics, photography, design, journalism, or communications.

The competition, which is sponsored annually by the Society of News Design and the S.I. Newhouse School of Public Communications at Syracuse University, recognizes excellence in newspaper design and graphics. Awards include Best of

Continuing to pay tribute to the world's best newspaper designs, the 19th edition of The Best of Newspaper Design is a stunning collection of modern work. The included works were selected from more than 10,000 entries submitted by newspapers all over the world. This exceptional collection is an essential reference for anyone involved in print media, graphics, photography, design, journalism, or communications.

The competition, which is sponsored annually by the Society for

OVERALL DESIGN

SPECIAL SECTIONS

News Design and the S.I. Newhouse School of Public Communications at Syracuse University, recognizes excellence in newspaper design and graphics. Awards include Best of Show, Gold, Silver, Award of Excellence, Special Recogni-tion, plus the honor of World's Best Designed Newspaper. Categories for judging include overall page design, portfolio, magazine cover design, art and illustration, photo journalism, and informational graphics.

This nineteenth edition presents the finest newspaper design in the field.

Selected by a panel of judges of the Society of News Design, the award-winning newspapers featured in this nineteenth edition were chosen for excellence in design.

Selected by a panel of 21 judges of the Society for News Design, the award-winning pub-lications featured in this nineteenth edition were chosen for excellence in design.

The Best of Newspaper Design, 19th edition, features: Text in English and Spanish; 840 awards: World's Best-Designed News-papers, Best of Show, Gold medals, Judges' Special Recognition, Silver medals, and Awards of Excel-lence. More than 12,100 entries were reviewed from hundreds of publica-tions from around the world to select winners from 158 publications. Categories included: Overall design, Continuing to pay tribute to the world's best newspaper designs, the 19th edition of The Best of Newspaper Design is a stunning collection of modern work. The included works were selected from more than 10,000 entries submitted by newspapers all over the world. This exceptional collection is an essential reference for anyone involved in print media, graphics, photography, design, journalism, or communica-

competition, which is sponsored annually by the Society for News Design and the S.I. Newhouse School of Public Communications at Syracuse University, recognizes excellence in newspaper design and graphics. Awards include Best of Show, Gold, Silver, Award of Excellence, Special Recogni-tion, plus the honor of World's Best Designed Newspaper. Categories for judging include overall page design, portfolio, magazine cover design, art and illustration, photo journalism, and informational graphics.

This nineteenth edition presents the finest newspaper design to the field.

Selected by a panel of 21 judges of the Society for News Design, the award-winning newspapers featured in this nineteenth edition were chosen for excellence in design.

The Best of Newspaper Design, 19th edition, features: Text in English and Spanish; 840 awards: World's Best-Designed News-papers, Best of Show, Gold medals, Judges' Special Recognition, Silver medals, and Awards of Excel-lence. More than 12,100 entries were reviewed from hundreds of publica-tions from around the world to select winners from 158 publications. Categories included: Overall design, news, features, portfolios, special coverage, special sections, maga-zines, art and illustration, photogra-phy, informational graphics and redesigns. Selected by a panel of 21 judges of the Society for News Design, the award-winning pub-lications Continuing to pay tribute to the world's best newspaper designs, the 19th edition of The Best of Newspaper Design is a stunning col-lection of modern work. The includ-ed works were selected from more than 10,000 entries submitted by newspapers all over the world. This exceptional collection is an essential reference for anyone involved in print media, graphics, photography, design, journalism, or communica-

News Design and the S.I. Newhouse School of Public Communications at Syracuse University, recognizes excellence in newspaper design and graphics. Awards include Best of Show, Gold, Silver, Award of Excellence, Special Recogni-tion, plus the honor of World's Best Designed Newspaper. Categories for judging include overall page design, portfolio, magazine cover design, art and illustration, photo journalism, and informational graphics.

This nineteenth edition presents the finest newspaper design in the field.

Selected by a panel of 21 judges of the Society for News Design, the award-winning pub-lications fea-tured in this nineteenth edition were chosen for excellence in design.

The Best of Newspaper Design, 19th edition, features: Text in English and Spanish; 840 awards: World's Best-Designed News-papers, Best of Show, Gold medals, Judges' Special Recognition, Silver medals, and Awards of Excel-lence. More than 12,100 entries were reviewed from hundreds of publica-tions from around the world to select winners from 158 publications. Categories included: Overall design, Continuing to pay tribute to the world's best newspaper designs, the 19th edition of The Best of Newspaper Design is a stunning col-lection of modern work. This exceptional collection is an essential reference for anyone involved in print media, graphics, photography, design, journalism, or communica-tions.

The competition, which is spon-sored annually by the Society for News Design and the S.I. Newhouse School of Public Communications at

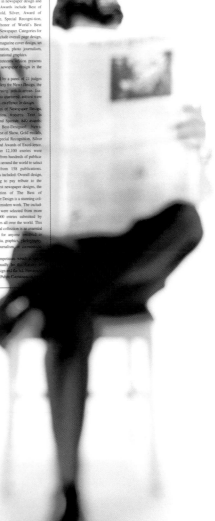

Award of Excellence
Diario de Noticias
Lisbon, Portugal

Mário B. Resendes, Editor-in-Chief; **António Ribeiro Ferreira,** Associate Editor-in-Chief; **José Maria Ribeirinho,** Art Director; **Pedro Rolo Duarte,** Editor; **Luís Silva Dias,** Design Editor; **Miguel Pedroso,** Designer

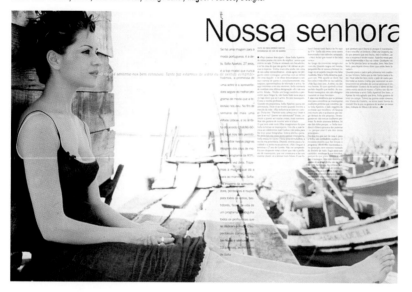

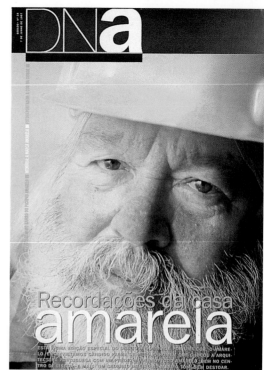

Award of Excellence
El Pais de las Tentaciones
Madrid, Spain

David Garcia, Art Director; **Nuria Muiña,** Art Editor; **Tori Alimbau,** Art Editor; **Fernando Gutierrez,** Graphic Designer; **Cesar Paredes,** Art Dept.; **Guillermo Trigo,** Art Dept.; **José Guillermo Abad,** Art Dept.; **Julian Arroyo,** Art Dept.

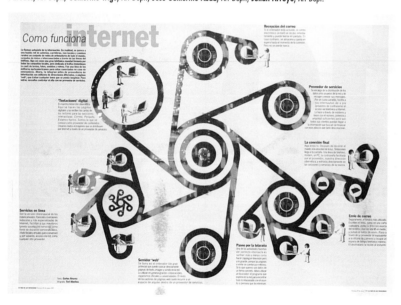

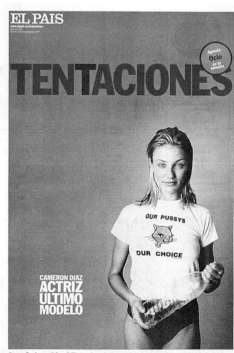

San Sebastián 97: todas las películas en la capital del cine

Award of Excellence
The Sunday Age
Melbourne, Australia

Sally Robinson, Editor; **Angus Holland,** Deputy Editor; **Robin Cowcher,** Art Director; **Troy Dunkley,** Designer; **John McDonald,** Production Editor; **Kathryn McNess,** Sub-Editor; **Sophie Douez,** Editorial Assistant

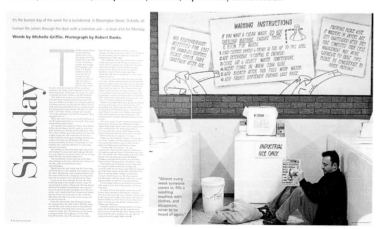

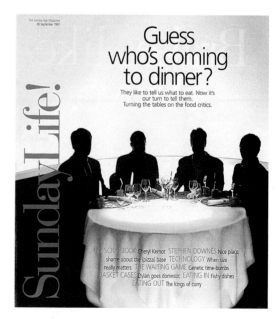

Award of Excellence
El Pais Semanal
Madrid, Spain

David García, Art Director; Eugenio González, Design Director; Maripaz Domingo, Designer; Gustavo Sánchez, Designer; Alex M. Roig, Editor-in-Chief; Jose Manuel Navia, Photographer

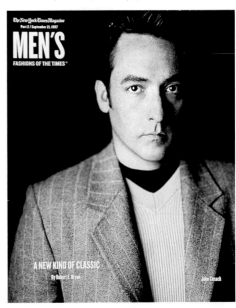

Award of Excellence
The New York Times
New York, NY

Michael Valenti, Art Director; Robert Bryan, Editor

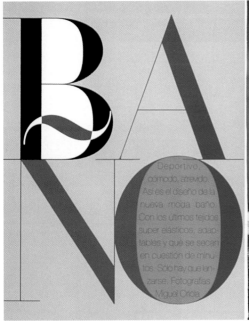

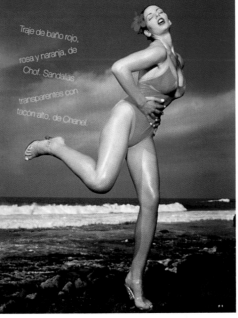

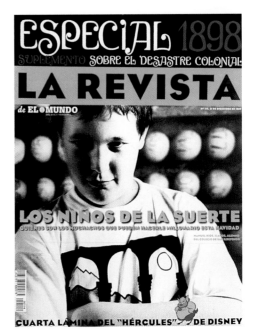

Award of Excellence
El Mundo/La Revista
Madrid, Spain

Rondrigo Sanchez, Art Director; Maria Gonzalez, Designer; Amparo Redondo, Designer; Carmelo Caderot, Design Director

Award of Excellence
El Mundo/La Revista
Madrid, Spain

Rodrigo Sanchez, Art Director; Maria Gonzalez, Designer; Amparo Redondo, Designer; Carmelo Caderot, Design Director

Gold
El Mundo Metropoli
Madrid, Spain
Carmelo Caderot, Design Director; **Maria Gonzalez**, Designer; **Rodrigo Sanchez**, Art Director/Designer

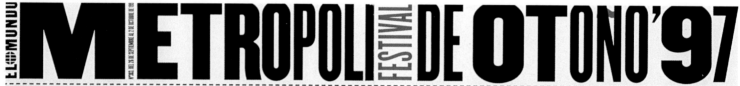

EL MUNDO **METROPOLI** FESTIVAL **DE OTOÑO'97**

TEATRO

ELSINOR LA TEMPESTAD
MEASURE FOR MEASURE
DE WILLIAM SHAKESPEARE

DIRECCION CALIXTO BIEITO
MAQUINA HAMLET DE HEINER MULLER

TORITO BRAVO, DE AITOR MAZO. A CIEGAS, DE JESUS CAMPOS. ZIGURAT, CON TEXTOS DE MANUEL VICENT. LA DANSE DES POULES, DE ABEL Y GORDON. EL REY DE LOS ANIMALES ES IDIOTA, DE CARLOS MARQUERIE. FLESH, DE FRANTIC ASSEMBLY. MATEO, DE ARMANDO DISCEPOLO. MEDEA MIX, COMPAÑIA METADONES. LA MAS FUERTE, DE AUGUST STRINDBERG. EL HOMBRE DE LA FLOR EN LA BOCA, DE PIRANDELLO. CON EL AMOR NO SE JUEGA, DE MUSSET. SI LA JOCONDE AVAIT DES JAMBES, DEL THEATRE DU MOUVEMENT. STOP CALLING ME VERNON, POR THE RIGHT SIZE. LOBAS Y ZORRAS, DE FRANCISCO NIEVA

EL AVARO DE MOLIERE LA DAMA BOBA

ARTE, DE YASMINA REZA
ORACULOS DE E. VARGAS
BUST OF JANGO DE JANGO EDWARDS
EL CANTARO ROTO DE HEINRICH VON KLEIST FAUSTO DE GOETHE
DE LOPE

TEATRO MUSICAL

CARMEN

HANNA SCHYGULLA CANTA
THE GRAND SCENA OPERA COMPANY
SWEENEY TODD
EL BARBERO DIABOLICO DE LA CALLE FLEET
CON CONSTANTINO ROMERO
DIRECCION: MARIO GAS

OPERA ANDALUZA DE CORNETAS Y TAMBORES, DE SALVADOR TAVORA

DANZA

ANDE YO CALIENTE..., COMPAÑIA ARRIERITOS. EL PEZ DE LA TORRE NADA EN EL ASFALTO Y SOLOS, COMPAÑIA DANZABIERTA. BUENOS AIRES TANGO, COMPAÑIA ARGENTINA ANIBAL PANNUNZIO Y MAGUI DANNI. PILOBOLUS TOO, PILOBOLUS THEATRE

BARYSHNIKOV TEATRO ALBENIZ DEL 29 DE OCTUBRE AL 1 DE NOVIEMBRE

LES BALLETS TROCKADERO DE MONTE CARLO

SALOME DE OSCAR WILDE
HADAS... LE ROYAUME DU MILIEU, COMPAÑIA LA LICORNE
BERNARDA GUERNICA, ANTONIO CANALES
THARP COMPAÑIA TWYLA THARP
L'ATELIER EN PIECES, DE MATHILDE MONNIER
ESPEJOS DE VIENTO DE MARCO BERRIEL

MUSICA

DESPEDIDA DE LOS ESCENARIOS DE
CHAVELA VARGAS

A CORAZON ABIERTO
CON REMEDIOS AMAYA LA YERBABUENA ENRIQUE MORENTE JOSE MERCE JOSE MENESE ESPERANZA FERNANDEZ

POESIA DE LA ESCUCHA, CARMEN LINARES CANTA POESIAS DE J.A. VALENTE Y MUSICA DE MAURICIO SOTELO. MUSICA EN MADRID, RECITAL DE PIANO DE HUMBERTO QUAGLIATA. ESCENAS DE LA VIDA COTIDIANA, OPERA DE MINUSCULO FORMATO
EL AMOR BRUJO DE FALLA
SCHUBERT EN EL ALMA ASTOR PIAZZOLLA, TANGO ORQUESTA DE CAMBRA DEL TEATRE LLIURE
INSPIRATION THE HARLEM GOSPEL SINGERS

POESIA DE LA GENERACION **DEL 27**
EXPOSICIONES
ESTAMPA
ARTE ESPAÑOL CONTEMPORANEO
FOTOGRAFIAS DE AUGUST STRINDBERG
KEATONIANA, UN SUEÑO DE BUSTER KEATON

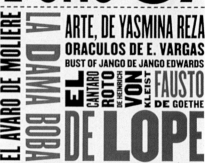

Awarded a **Gold Medal** for its balance within each unit and as a whole, this cover has complete balance. An intuitive mastery of type. The weights work well and have perfect hierarchy.

• • • • •

Ganadora de una Medalla de Oro por su equilibrio dentro de cada unidad y como un todo, esta tapa posee un equilibrio completo. Una maestría intuitiva de la tipografía. Los pesos se contraponen bien y poseen una jerarquía perfecta.

Silver
El Mundo Metropoli
Madrid, Spain
Carmelo Caderot, Design Director; Maria Gonzalez, Designer; Rodrigo Sanchez, Art Director/Designer

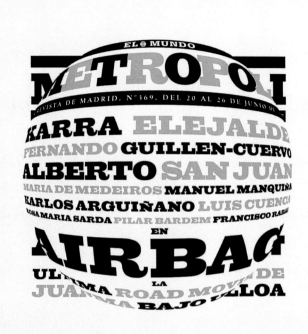

Silver
El Mundo/La Revista
Madrid, Spain
Rondrigo Sanchez, Art Director; Maria Gonzalez, Designer; Amparo Redondo, Designer; Carmelo Caderot, Design Director; Dodot, Illustrator

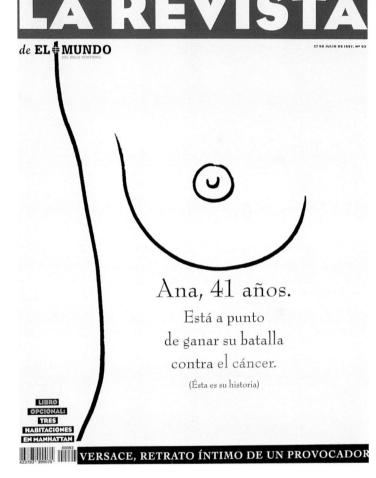

Silver
El Mundo Metropoli
Madrid, Spain
Carmelo Caderot, Design Director; Maria Gonzalez, Designer; Rodrigo Sanchez, Art Director/Designer

Award of Excellence
El Mundo Metropoli
Madrid, Spain

Carmelo Caderot, Design Director; **Maria Gonzalez**, Designer; **Rodrigo Sanchez**, Art Director/Designer

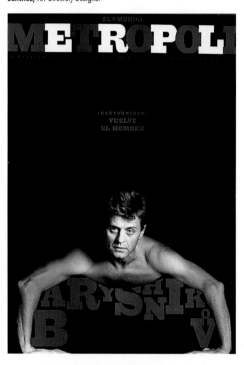

Award of Excellence
El Mundo Metropoli
Madrid, Spain

Carmelo Caderot, Design Director; **Maria Gonzalez**, Designer; **Rodrigo Sanchez**, Art Director/Designer

Award of Excellence
El Mundo Metropoli
Madrid, Spain

Carmelo Caderot, Design Director; **Maria Gonzalez**, Designer; **Rodrigo Sanchez**, Art Director/Designer

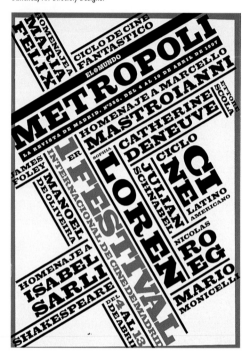

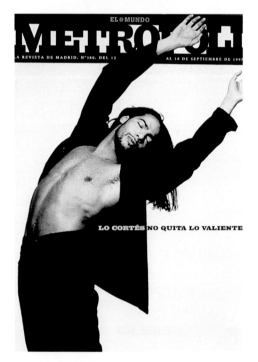

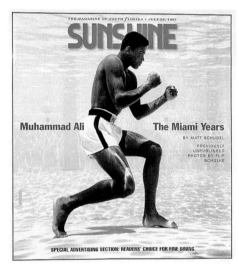

Award of Excellence
Sun-Sentinel/Sunshine Magazine
Ft. Lauderdale, FL

Greg Carannante, Associate Editor/Design Director; **Flip Schulke**, Photographer

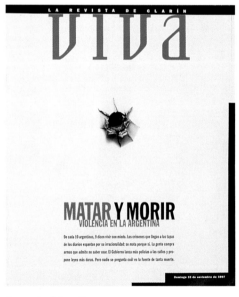

Award of Excellence
Clarin/VIVA
Buenos Aires, Argentina

Iñaki Palacios, Design Director; **Gustavo Lo Valvo**, Art Director; **Rodolfo Luna**, Designer; **Isabel Beruti**, Designer; **Adriana Di Pietro**, Designer; **Hugo Vasiliev**, Designer; **María Marta Parodi**, Designer; **Sergio Juan**, Designer

Award of Excellence
El Mundo Metropoli
Madrid, Spain

Carmelo Caderot, Design Director; **Maria Gonzalez**, Designer; **Rodrigo Sanchez**, Art Director/Designer

Silver
Diario de Noticias

Lisbon, Portugal

Mário B. Resendes, Editor-in-Chief; António Ribeiro Ferreira, Associate Editor-in-Chief; José Maria Ribeirinho, Art Director; Pedro Rolo Duarte, Editor; Luís Silva Dias, Design Editor; Miguel Pedroso, Designer

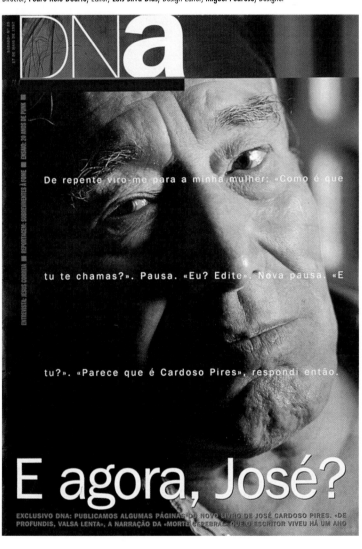

Silver
El Pais de las Tentaciones

Madrid, Spain

David Garcia, Art Director; Nuria Muiña, Art Editor; Tori Alimbau, Art Editor; Fernando Gutierrez, Graphic Designer; Cesar Paredes, Art Dept.; Guillermo Trigo, Art Dept.; José Guillermo Abad, Art Dept.; Julian Arroyo, Art Dept.

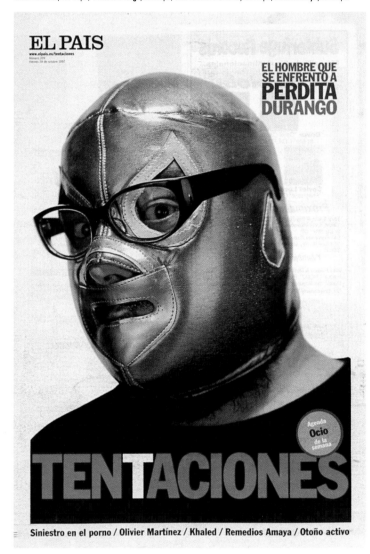

Award of Excellence
The Financial Times
London, England
Tomaso Capuano, Art Editor

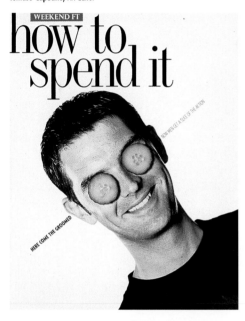

Award of Excellence
Diario de Noticias
Lisbon, Portugal
Mário B. Resendes, Editor-in-Chief; António Ribeiro Ferreira, Associate
Editor-in-Chief; José Maria Ribeirinho, Art Director; Pedro Rolo Duarte,
Editor; Luís Silva Dias, Design Editor; Miguel Pedroso, Designer

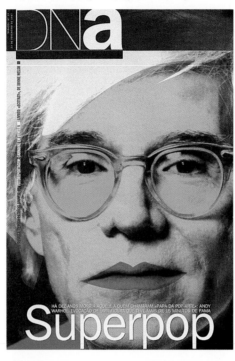

Award of Excellence
El Mundo Metropoli
Madrid, Spain
Carmelo Caderot, Design Director; Maria Gonzalez, Designer; Rodrigo
Sanchez, Art Director/Designer

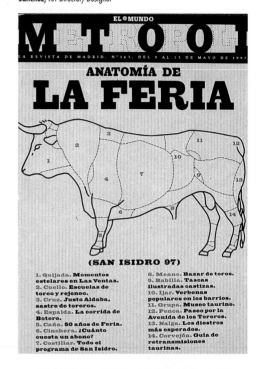

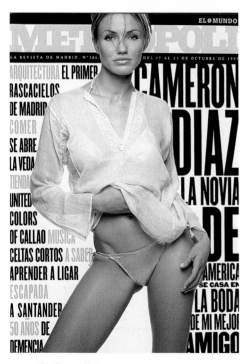

Award of Excellence
El Mundo Metropoli
Madrid, Spain
Carmelo Caderot, Design Director; Maria Gonzalez, Designer; Rodrigo
Sanchez, Art Director/Designer

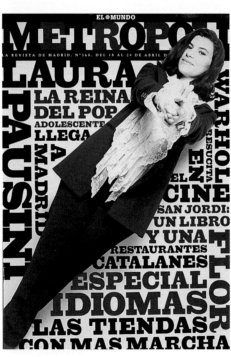

Award of Excellence
El Mundo Metropoli
Madrid, Spain
Carmelo Caderot, Design Director; Maria Gonzalez, Designer; Rodrigo
Sanchez, Art Director/Designer

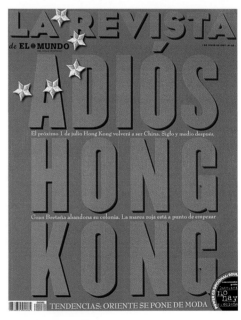

Award of Excellence
El Mundo/La Revista
Madrid, Spain
Rodrigo Sanchez, Art Director; Maria Gonzalez, Designer; Amparo
Redondo, Designer; Carmelo Caderot, Design Director

Award of Excellence
The New York Times Magazine
New York, NY

Janet Froelich, Art Director; Lisa Naftolin, Designer; Kathy Ryan, Photo Editor; Sally Gail, Photographer

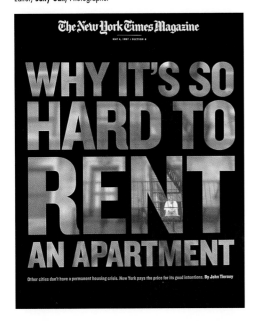

Award of Excellence
The New York Times Magazine
New York, NY

Linda Brewer, Art Director; Michael Moran, Photographer

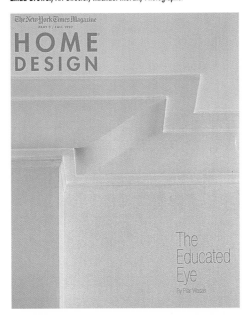

Award of Excellence
The New York Times Magazine
New York, NY

Janet Froelich, Art Director; Catherine Gilmore-Barnes, Designer; Barbara Nessim, Illustrator

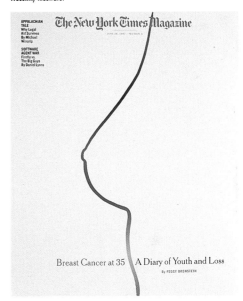

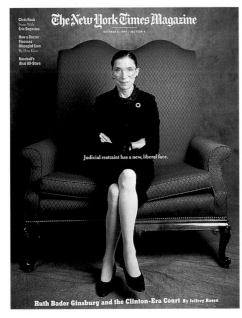

Award of Excellence
The New York Times Magazine
New York, NY

Janet Froelich, Art Director & Designer; Kathy Ryan, Photo Editor; Timothy Greenfield-Sanders, Photographer

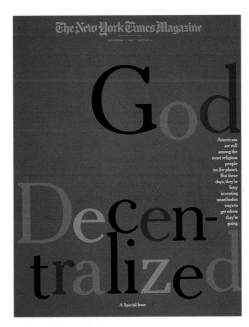

Award of Excellence
The New York Times Magazine
New York, NY

Janet Froelich, Art Director & Designer

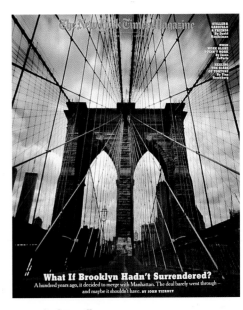

Award of Excellence
The New York Times Magazine
New York, NY

Janet Froelich, Art Director; Joel Cuyler, Designer; Kathy Ryan, Photo Editor; Tom Baril, Photographer

Award of Excellence
El Pais de las Tentaciones
Madrid, Spain

David Garcia, Art Director; Nuria Muiña, Art Editor; Tori Alimbau, Art Editor; Fernando Gutierrez, Graphic Designer; Cesar Paredes, Art Dept.; Guillermo Trigo, Art Dept.; José Guillermo Abad, Art Dept.; Julian Arroyo, Art Dept.

Award of Excellence
El Pais de las Tentaciones
Madrid, Spain

David Garcia, Art Director; Nuria Muiña, Art Editor; Tori Alimbau, Art Editor; Fernando Gutierrez, Graphic Designer; Cesar Paredes, Art Dept.; Guillermo Trigo, Art Dept.; José Guillermo Abad, Art Dept.; Julian Arroyo, Art Dept.

Award of Excellence
The New York Times Magazine
New York, NY

Janet Froelich, Art Director; Joel Cuyler, Designer

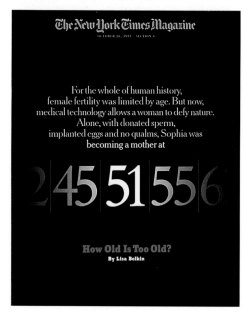

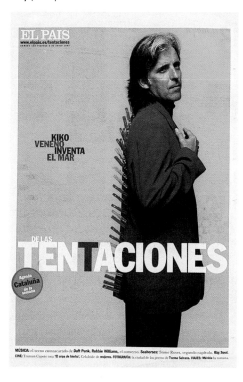

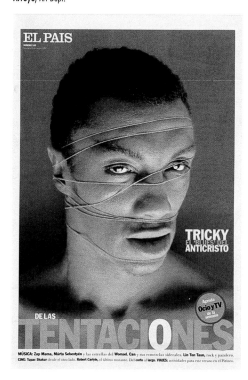

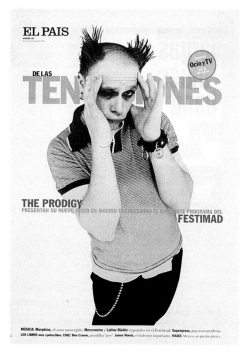

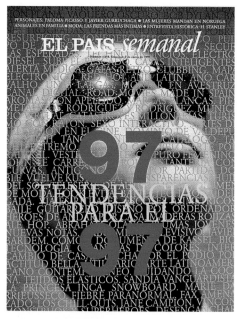

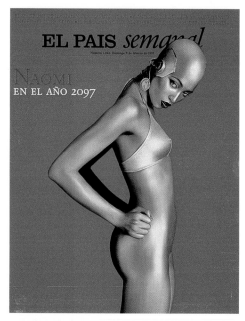

Award of Excellence
El Pais de las Tentaciones
Madrid, Spain

David Garcia, Art Director; Nuria Muiña, Art Editor; Tori Alimbau, Art Editor; Fernando Gutierrez, Graphic Designer; Cesar Paredes, Art Dept.; Guillermo Trigo, Art Dept.; José Guillermo Abad, Art Dept.; Julian Arroyo, Art Dept.

Award of Excellence
El Pais Semanal
Madrid, Spain

David García, Art Director; Eugenio González, Design Director; Maripaz Domingo, Designer; Gustavo Sánchez, Designer; Alex M. Roig, Editor-in-Chief; R. Seagraves, Photographer

Award of Excellence
El Pais Semanal
Madrid, Spain

David García, Art Director; Eugenio González, Design Director; Maripaz Domingo, Designer; Gustavo Sánchez, Designer; Alex M. Roig, Editor-in-Chief; Seb Janiak, Photographer

Award of Excellence
El Pais Semanal
Madrid, Spain

David García, Art Director; **Eugenio González**, Design Director; **Maripaz Domingo**, Designer; **Gustavo Sánchez**, Designer; **Alex M. Roig**, Editor-in-Chief

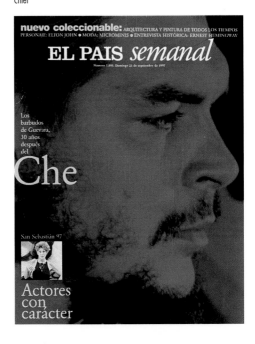

Award of Excellence
El Pais Semanal
Madrid, Spain

David García, Art Director; **Eugenio González**, Design Director; **Maripaz Domingo**, Designer; **Gustavo Sánchez**, Designer; **Alex M. Roig**, Editor-in-Chief; **José Manuel Navia**, Photographer

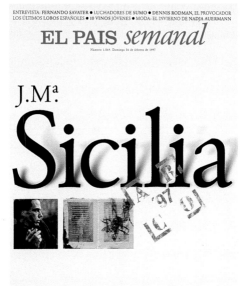

Award of Excellence
El Pais Semanal
Madrid, Spain

David García, Art Director; **Eugenio González**, Design Director; **Maripaz Domingo**, Designer; **Gustavo Sánchez**, Designer; **Alex M. Roig**, Editor-in-Chief; **Javier Mariscal**, Illustrator

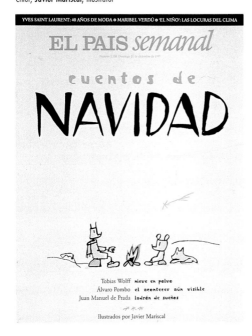

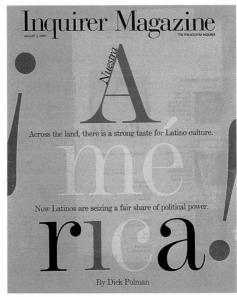

Award of Excellence
Philadelphia Inquirer Magazine
Philadelphia, PA

Christine Dunleavy, Art Director & Designer; **Susan Syrnick**, Assistant Art Director

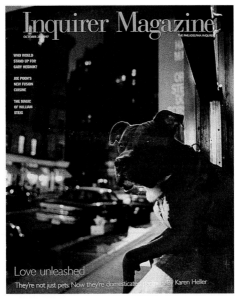

Award of Excellence
Philadelphia Inquirer Magazine
Philadelphia, PA

Christine Dunleavy, Art Director & Designer; **Susan Syrnick**, Assistant Art Director; **Andrea Mohin**, Photographer

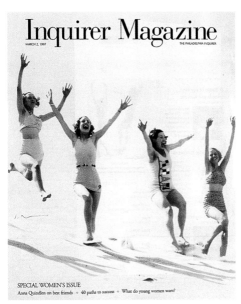

Award of Excellence
Philadelphia Inquirer Magazine
Philadelphia, PA

Christine Dunleavy, Art Director; **Susan Syrnick**, Assistant Art Director/ Designer

Award of Excellence
Reforma
México City, México

Emilio Deheza, Art Director; **Regina Landa**, Designer; **Erika Sosa**, Designer; **Eduardo Danilo**, Design Consultant; **Carlos Arias**, Editor; **Alejandro Banuet**, Graphics Editor; **Efraín Foglia**, Photo Artist

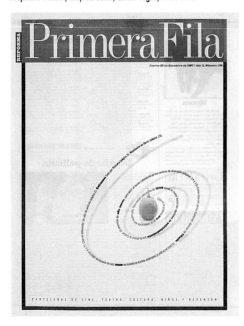

Award of Excellence
The Sunday Age
Melbourne, Australia

Sally Robinson, Editor; **Angus Holland**, Deputy Editor; **Robin Cowcher**, Art Director; **Troy Dunkley**, Designer; **John McDonald**, Production Editor; **Kathryn McNess**, Sub-Editor; **Sophie Douez**, Editorial Assistant

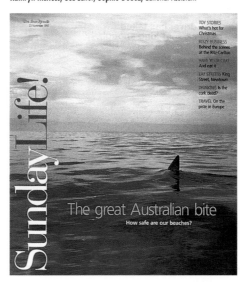

Award of Excellence
The Sunday Age
Melbourne, Australia

Sally Robinson, Editor; **Angus Holland**, Deputy Editor; **Robin Cowcher**, Art Director; **Troy Dunkley**, Designer; **John McDonald**, Production Editor; **Kathryn McNess**, Sub-Editor; **Sophie Douez**, Editorial Assistant

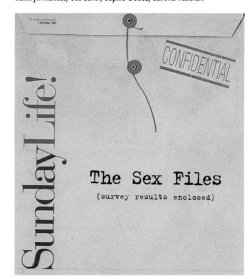

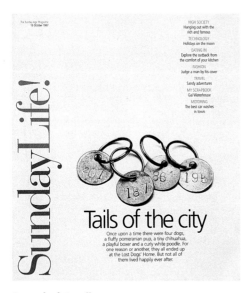

Award of Excellence
The Sunday Age
Melbourne, Australia

Sally Robinson, Editor; **Angus Holland**, Deputy Editor; **Robin Cowcher**, Art Director; **Troy Dunkley**, Designer; **John McDonald**, Production Editor; **Kathryn McNess**, Sub-Editor; **Sophie Douez**, Editorial Assistant

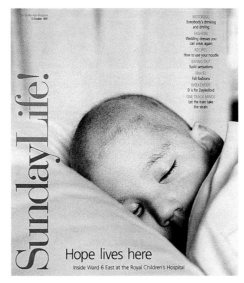

Award of Excellence
The Sunday Age
Melbourne, Australia

Sally Robinson, Editor; **Angus Holland**, Deputy Editor; **Robin Cowcher**, Art Director; **Troy Dunkley**, Designer; **John McDonald**, Production Editor; **Kathryn McNess**, Sub-Editor; **Sophie Douez**, Editorial Assistant

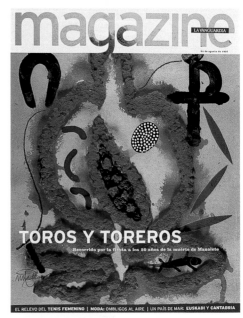

Award of Excellence
La Vanguardia
Barcelona, Spain

Carlos Pérez de Rozas Arribas, Art Director; **Rosa Mundet Poch**, Graphics Editor; **Ma José Oriol**, Designer; **Mònica Caparrós**, Designer; **Antonio Soto**, Design Director; **Joan Pere Viladecans**, Printer

Silver
The New York Times Magazine
New York, NY

Janet Froelich, Art Director; **Catherine Gilmore-Barnes**, Designer; **Maria Robledo**, Photographer

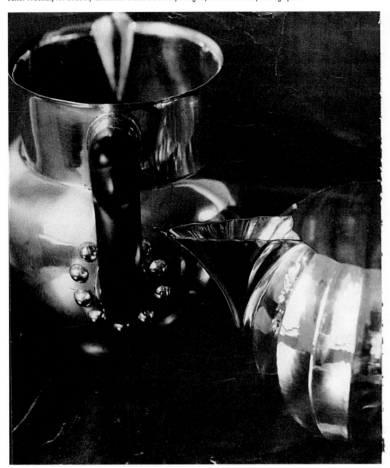

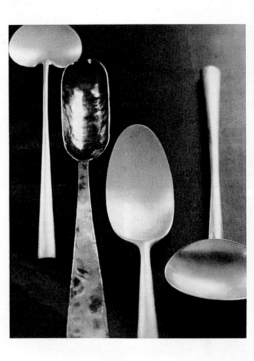

Silver Streak Like tinsel, silver adds shimmer to the season.
Photographs by Maria Robledo Styled by Suzanne Shaker

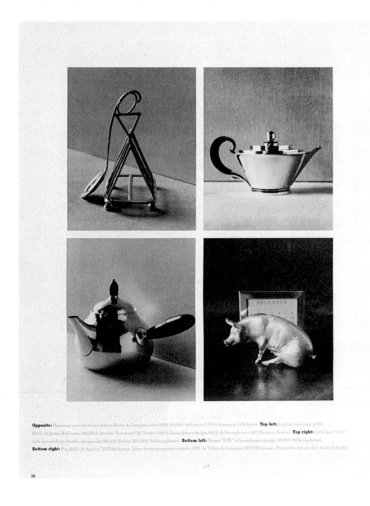

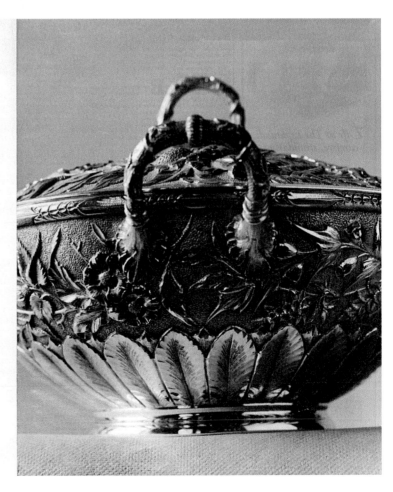

Award of Excellence
Clarin/VIVA
Buenos Aires, Argentina

Iñaki Palacios, Design Director; Gustavo Lo Valvo, Art Director; Rodolfo Luna, Designer; Isabel Beruti, Designer; Adriana Di Pietro, Designer; Hugo Vasiliev, Designer; María Marta Parodi, Designer; Sergio Juan, Designer

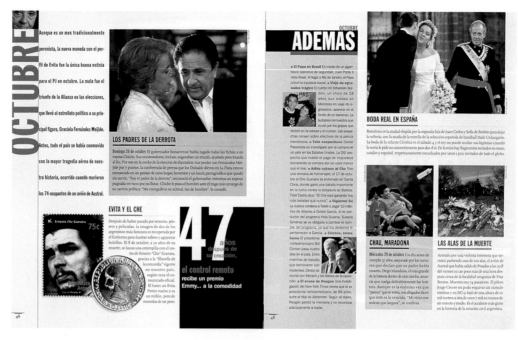

Award of Excellence
El Mundo/La Revista
Madrid, Spain

Rodrigo Sanchez, Art Director; Maria Gonzalez, Designer; Amparo Redondo, Designer; Carmelo Caderot, Design Director; Claudio Elinger, Photographer

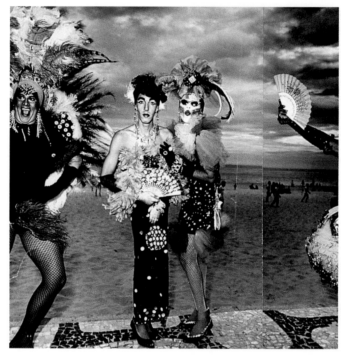
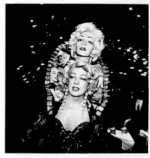

Award of Excellence
El Mundo/La Revista
Madrid, Spain

Rondrigo Sanchez, Art Director; Maria Gonzalez, Designer; Amparo Redondo, Designer; Carmelo Caderot, Design Director; Carma Casula, Photographer

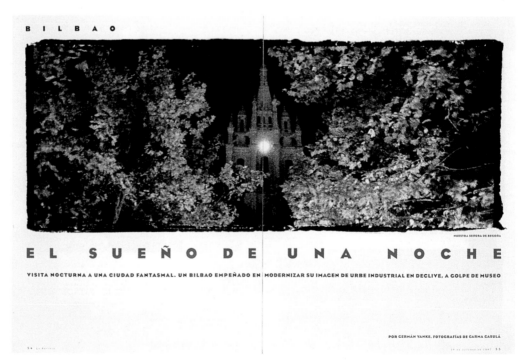

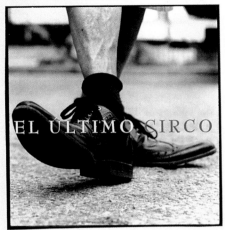

EL DE LOS HERMANOS RALUY ES LA ESENCIA MISMA DEL CIRCO, RESCATA EL

CIRCO PURO QUE LA TELEVISIÓN DEGRADÓ Y REGRESA A ESPAÑA TRAS QUINCE

AÑOS DE AUSENCIA, DE GIRA, DE ITINERANCIA POR EL MUNDO. EN SU REGRESO.

EL ÚLTIMO CIRCO

EL ÚLTIMO CIRCO EXPEDICIONARIO ESPAÑOL TRAE PRENDIDO EL PREMIO

NACIONAL DEL CIRCO, EL TRIUNFO DE LA ESTÉTICA FRENTE AL ESPECTÁCULO.

POR RAFAEL TORRES. FOTOGRAFÍAS DE ALBERTO GARCÍA ALIX

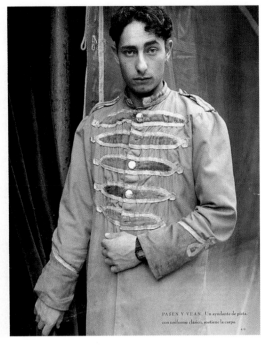

PASEN Y VEAN. Un ayudante de pista, con uniforme clásico, sostiene la carpa.

Award of Excellence
El Mundo/La Revista
Madrid, Spain

Rodrigo Sanchez, Art Director; Maria Gonzalez, Designer; Amparo Redondo, Designer; Carmelo Caderot, Design Director; Garcia Alix, Photographer

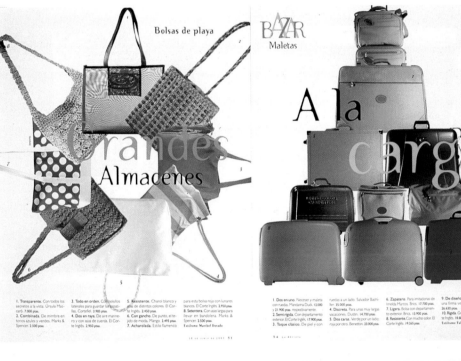

Bolsas de playa

Grandes Almacenes

BAZAR Maletas

A la carga

Award of Excellence
El Mundo/La Revista
Madrid, Spain

Rondrigo Sanchez, Art Director; Maria Gonzalez, Designer; Amparo Redondo, Designer; Carmelo Caderot, Design Director; Pimentel, Photographer

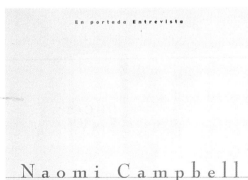

En portada **Entrevista**

Naomi Campbell

Tiene fama de caprichosa y de insoportable, requisitos indispensables para ejercer de auténtica diva. Por algo es una de las diez modelos mejor pagadas del mundo, musa de diseñadores y fotógrafos. Los novios y los zapatos son su debilidad y por sus brazos han pasado celebridades como Mike Tyson, Robert De Niro, Silvester Stallone o el bajista de U2, Adam Clayton. Pero, voluble como una "prima donna", sus amorios pueden durar un suspiro. En Navidades aseguraba que había encontrado al hombre de su vida en un millonario italiano mientras echaba el ojo a Joaquín Cortés. Desde hace cuatro meses, el bailarín y la modelo forman la pareja del año.
Por SVEN MICHAEL y STEFANIE ROSENKRANZ. Fotografías de KARL LAGERFELD

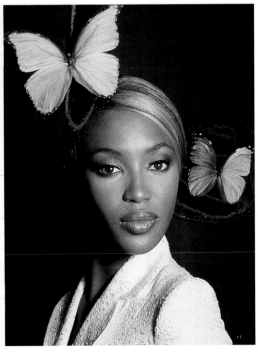

Award of Excellence
El Mundo/La Revista
Madrid, Spain

Rondrigo Sanchez, Art Director; Maria Gonzalez, Designer; Amparo Redondo, Designer; Carmelo Caderot, Design Director

Award of Excellence
El Pais de las Tentaciones
Madrid, Spain

David Garcia, Art Director; **Nuria Muiña**, Art Editor; **Tori Alimbau**, Art Editor; **Fernando Gutierrez**, Graphic Designer; **Cesar Paredes**, Art Dept.; **Guillermo Trigo**, Art Dept.; **José Guillermo Abad**, Art Dept.; **Julian Arroyo**, Art Dept.

Award of Excellence
El Pais de las Tentaciones
Madrid, Spain

David Garcia, Art Director; **Nuria Muiña**, Art Editor; **Tori Alimbau**, Art Editor; **Fernando Gutierrez**, Graphic Designer; **Cesar Paredes**, Art Dept.; **Guillermo Trigo**, Art Dept.; **José Guillermo Abad**, Art Dept.; **Julian Arroyo**, Art Dept.

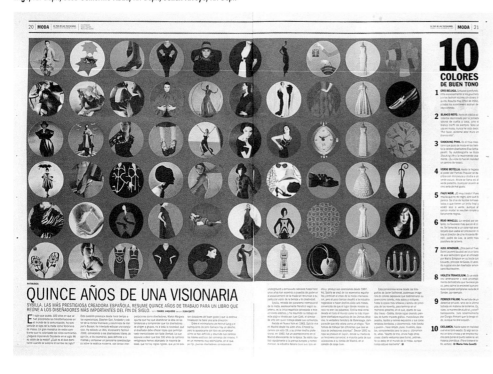

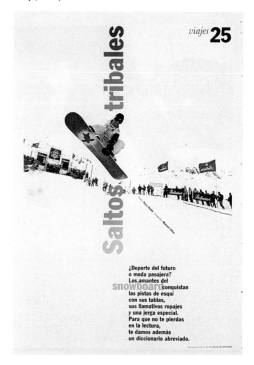

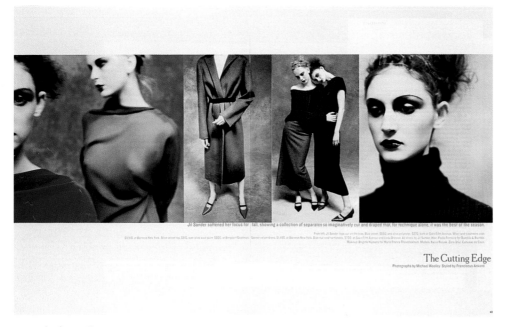

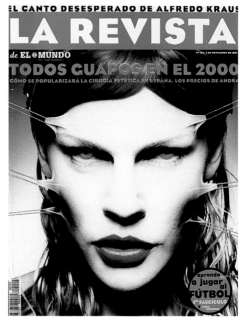

Award of Excellence
The New York Times Magazine
New York, NY

Janet Froelich, Art Director; **Lisa Naftolin**, Designer; **Michael Woolley**, Photographer; **Franciscus Ankoné**, Stylist

Award of Excellence
El Mundo/La Revista
Madrid, Spain

Rondrigo Sanchez, Art Director; **Maria Gonzalez**, Designer; **Amparo Redondo**, Designer; **Carmelo Caderot**, Design Director

Gian Paolo Barbieri nació en Milán en 1938. Consiguió renombre internacional en los años sesenta con sus fotografías de moda para la edición italiana de Vogue. En 1978 la publicación alemana Stern

lo reconoció como uno de los 14 mejores fotógrafos de moda. Sus trabajos se han expuesto en el Museo Victoria & Albert, en Londres, y en el Wiener Kunstforum, en Viena. Para realizar este trabajo sobre Madagascar Barbieri recorrió la isla en toda su extensión durante los meses de julio a agosto de 1994, y puso

especial interés en los pueblos, mercados y personajes. Asegura haber utilizado en blanco y negro "como un símbolo, ya que acumula grandes gamas de color" y le permite "hurgar estéticamente en la vida de Madagascar".

La luz envuelve en **Madagascar** paisajes de extrañas vegetaciones y refleja en la piel de los nativos el alma de la isla de Nossi

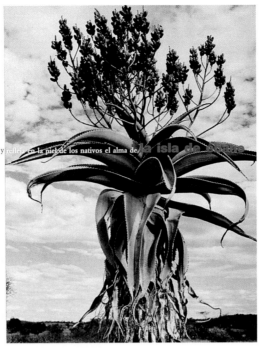

En uno de mis sueños de infancia Sandokán resultó seriamente herido luego de enfrentarse a unos negreros holandeses, y el muy leal Yáñez, luego de atender a su amigo, ordenó navegar a todo trapo rumbo a Madagascar. Treinta años más tarde, desde Punta da Barra, al norte de Inhambane, en Mozambique, subí a bordo de una embarcación de pescadores y navegué siguiendo la línea del Trópico de Capricornio hacia el este.

Unas 600 millas mide el canal de Mozambique, que separa África de Madagascar, la cuarta isla más grande del mundo, y a mitad de camino, entre peligrosos bancos de arena, se puede ver la desolada isla Europa, de soberanía francesa y habitada por miles de aves marinas que no graznan en francés. Por fin, tras dos días de navegación atracamos en Tuléar, una bella ciudad rodeada de manglares que abre las puertas de la enorme isla.

Una buena carretera permite recorrer los 1.600 kilómetros de longitud de la isla, desde Fort Dauphin por el sur hasta Diego Suárez por el norte, pero el que quiera conocer la isla de los sueños debe viajar por los estrechos senderos de la parte oeste y detenerse en las poblaciones de Maniá, Morondava, Bejo, Maintirano y Maronsay.

Entre la exuberante selva de ébano, palo de rosa, palisandro y rafia, aparecen de pronto las plantaciones de azúcar, de tabaco y los cultivos de los árboles de especias. El viejo ferrocarril que une Maintirano con Tananarive cruza una región en donde el aire húmedo impregna al viajero de los aromas del clavo de olor, la canela, pimienta y nuez moscada.

Las mujeres malgaches parecen sacadas de una novela de Salgari. Son bellas, altivas y enigmáticas, tal vez para dar argumentos a los hombres, que son afables y buenos conversadores. Según las guías de viaje, en Madagascar se habla francés y malgache, pero la proximidad con Mozambique hace que sea posible comunicarse en portugués sin problemas.

Una noche en cualquier taberna de Tamatave, mirando las olas del Índico cuya brisa no consigue paliar el calor pegajoso, impone beber ron de la isla y fumar los cigarros que las mujeres soban en sus muslos generosos. Entonces, el viajero debe unirse al rítmico tamborileo de las manos sobre las mesas y dejarse transportar por las historias que hablan de días muy lejanos, de una libertad arrebatada por los negreros franceses que los trajeron desde la Polinesia, de islas a las que regresan cada noche, en la nave alucinada del tabaco y el ron, en la barca infinita de los sueños.

TEXTO: LUIS SEPÚLVEDA / FOTOGRAFÍA: GIAN PAOLO BARBIERI

Award of Excellence
El Pais Semanal
Madrid, Spain

David García, Art Director; **Eugenio González**, Design Director; **Maripaz Domingo**, Designer; **Gustavo Sánchez**, Designer; **Alex M. Roig**, Editor-in-Chief

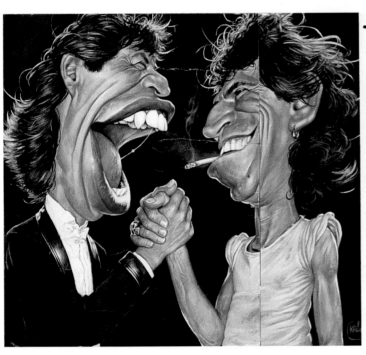

THE ROLLING STONES

NI LAS CANAS, NI LAS ARRUGAS, NI LOS ACHAQUES DE LA EDAD HAN LOGRADO APARTAR A ESTOS CINCUENTONES DE LOS ESCENARIOS. LOS ABUELOS DEL ROCK SE HAN EMBARCADO EN UNA NUEVA GIRA MUNDIAL PARA PRESENTAR SU ÚLTIMO DISCO "BRIDGES TO BABYLON". ESTÁN DISPUESTOS A SEGUIR DANDO GUERRA, Y ASÍ LO HARÁN A PARTIR DEL PRÓXIMO MARTES. POR LO MENOS MIENTRAS EL CUERPO AGUANTE.

TEXTO: ALBERT GUASCH
ILUSTRACIONES: SEBASTIAN KRÜGER

Award of Excellence
El Periodico de Catalunya/ El Dominical
Barcelona, Spain

Ferran Sendra, Designer; **Núria Miquel**, Designer; **Kim Salomon**, Designer; **Gerardo Della Santa**, Designer; **Ricardo Feriche**, Design Consultant; **Alejandro Yofre**, Photo Editor; **Albert Bertran**, Photo Editor; **Héctor Chimirri**, News Editor; **Josep Maria Ràfols**, Vice-Editor; **Sebastian Krüger**, Illustrator

What the museums aren't showing you.

Hidden Treasures
Photography by Michael S. Wirtz

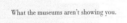

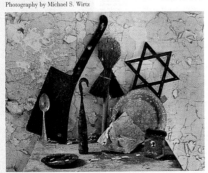

EASTERN STATE PENITENTIARY: (clockwise from bottom left) baluster, spoon, cleaver found in prison kitchen, book possibly used for opening skylights, brush, four of David Teva the escape pipes that now Cellblock 7, bowl, cigarette tin, and knife from an inmate's cachet.

The march of time leaves a rich trail of legend and progress, but mostly stuff. Lots and lots of stuff. Our attics or basements (or most likely both) are full of stuff, meaningful stuff, and so are the catacombs and garrets of our museums. Which, come to think of it, are frequently stocked from our personal treasure troves. There's a reason why the Smithsonian is dubbed "the

continued on facing page

continued from facing page

nation's attic."

Our area museums also have more than they can mount within their galleries. Inquirer staff photographer Michael S. Wirtz, in his search for buried treasure, did what many of us dream of doing: He took a long look at what hides behind many a shuttered portal.

What he discovered was an embarrassment of riches. At the Franklin Institute, there is a dull fragment of wrought iron that Benjamin Franklin happened to craft into a lightning rod for the Wister family. Three gold pendants from Colombia's Tolima region, a millennium and a half old, shine at Penn's University Museum. The Academy of Natural Sciences may hold the local waterhouse record, with 21 million species.

continued on Page 17

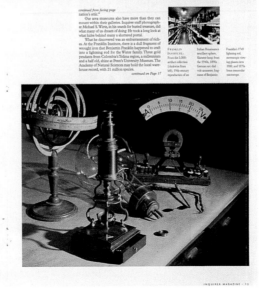

FRANKLIN INSTITUTE: From the 1,000-artifact collection (clockwise from left), 18th-century reproduction of an

Italian Renaissance auxiliary sphere, filament lamp from the 1940s, 1890s German see-thru toy, 19th-century reproduction of an

Franklin's 1749 lightning rod, microscope viewing glasses circa 1930, and 1870s brass telescope microscope.

Award of Excellence
Philadelphia Inquirer Magazine
Philadelphia, PA

Christine Dunleavy, Art Director; **Susan Syrnick**, Assistant Art Director & Designer; **Michael S. Wirtz**, Photographer

Award of Excellence
Philadelphia Inquirer Magazine
Philadelphia, PA

Christine Dunleavy, Art Director; **Susan Syrnick**, Assistant Art Director;
Andrea Mohin, Photographer; **Brian Grigsby**, Photographer; **Michel
Vanden Eeckhoudt**, Photographer; **Rebecca Barger**, Photographer; **Eric
Mencher**, Photographer

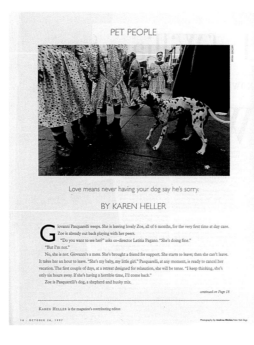

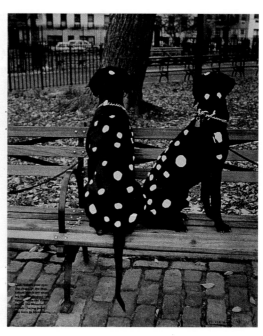

Award of Excellence
Philadelphia Inquirer Magazine
Philadelphia, PA

Christine Dunleavy, Art Director; **Susan Syrnick**, Assistant Art Director
& Designer; **Lisa Nilsson**, Illustrator; **Erin Jenson**, Illustrator; **Joe
Sorren**, Illustrator; **John S. Dykes**, Illustrator

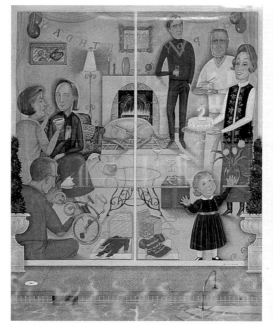

Award of Excellence
Philadelphia Inquirer Magazine
Philadelphia, PA

Christine Dunleavy, Art Director & Designer; **Susan Syrnick**, Assistant
Art Director; **Ron Tarver**, Photographer

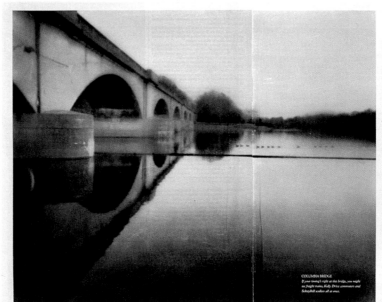

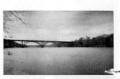

Chapter Six

SPECIAL SECTIONS

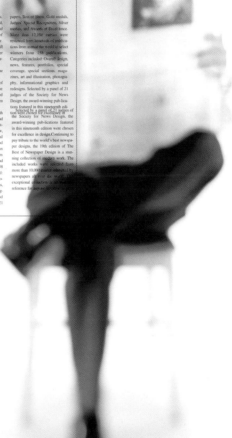

Continuing to pay tribute to the world's best newspaper designs, the 19th edition of The Best of Newspaper Design is a stunning collection of modern work. The included works were selected from more than 10,000 entries submitted by newspapers all over the world. This exceptional collection is an essential reference for anyone involved in

Continuing to pay tribute to the world's best newspaper designs, the 19th edition of The Best of Newspaper Design is a stunning collection of modern work. The included works were selected from more than 10,000 entries submitted by newspapers all over the world. This exceptional collection is an essential reference for anyone involved in print media, graphics, photography, design, journalism, or communications.

The competition, which is sponsored annually by the Society of News Design and the S.I. Newhouse School of Public Communications at Syracuse University, recognizes excellence in newspaper design and graphics. Awards include Best of Show, Gold, Silver, Award of Excellence, Special Recogni-tion, plus the honor of World's Best Designed Newspaper. Categories for judging include overall page design, portfolio, magazine cover design, art and illustration, photo journalism, and informational graphics.

This nineteenth edition presents the finest newspaper design in the field.

Selected by a panel of judges of the Society for News Design, the award-winning newspapers featured in this nineteenth edition were chosen for excellence in design.

The Best of Newspaper Design, 19th edition, features: Text in English and Spanish; 840 awards: World's Best-Designed Newspapers, Best of Show, Gold medals, Judges' Special Recognition, Silver medals, and Awards of Excel-lence. More than 12,100 entries were reviewed from hundreds of publications from around the world to select winners from 158 publications. Categories included: Overall design, news, features, portfolios, special coverage, special sections, magazines, art and illustration, photography, informational graphics and redesigns.ign, art and illus

Continuing to pay tribute to the world's best newspaper designs, the 19th edition of The Best of Newspaper Design is a stunning collection of modern work. The included works were selected from more than 10,000 entries submitted by newspapers all over the world. This exceptional collection is an essential reference for anyone involved in print media, graphics, photography,

The competition, which is sponsored annually by the Society of News Design and the S.I. Newhouse School of Public Communications at Syracuse University, recognizes excellence in newspaper design and graphics. Awards include Best of Show, Gold, Silver, Award of Excellence, Special Recogni-tion, plus the honor of World's Best Designed Newspaper. Categories for judging include overall page design, portfolio, magazine cover design, art and illustration, photo journalism, and informational graphics.

This nineteenth edition presents the finest newspaper design in the field.

Selected by a panel of judges of the Society for News Design, the award-winning newspapers featured in this nineteenth edition were chosen for excellence in design.

Selected by a panel of 21 judges of the Society for News Design, the award-winning pub-lications featured in this nineteenth edition were chosen for excellence in design.

The Best of Newspaper Design, 19th edition, features: all text in English and Spanish; more than five hundred awards: Best of Show, Judges' Special Recognition, Gold Medals, Sil-ver Medals, and Awards of Excellence; over five hundred newspapers from all around the world; categories such as overall page design, portfolio, magazine cover design, art and illustration, photo journalism, and informational graphicContinuing to pay tribute to the world's best newspaper designs, the 19th edition of The Best of Newspaper Design is a stunning col-lection of modern work. The included works were selected from more than 10,000 entries submitted by newspapers all over the world. This excep-tional collection is an essential refer-ence for anyone involved in print media, graphics, photography, design, journalism, or communica-tions.

Continuing to pay tribute to the world's best newspaper designs, the 19th edition of The Best of Newspaper Design is a stunning col-lection of modern work. The includ-ed works were selected from more than 10,000 entries submitted by newspapers all over the world. This exceptional collection is an essential reference for anyone involved in

Continuing to pay tribute to the world's best newspaper designs, the 19th edi-tion of The Best of Newspaper Design is a stunning collection of modern work. The included works were select-ed from more than 10,000 entries sub-mitted by newspapers all over the world. This exceptional collection is an essential reference for anyone involved in print media, graphics, photography, design, journalism, or communications.

The competition, which is sponsored annually by the Society for News Design and the S.I. Newhouse School of Public Communications at Syracuse University, recognizes excellence in

SINGLE-SUBJECT SERIES
COVER PAGE
INSIDE PAGES

newspaper design and graphics. Awards include Best of Show, Gold, Silver, Award of Excellence, Special Recogni-tion, plus the honor of World's Best Designed Newspaper. Categories for judging include overall page design, portfolio, magazine cover design, art and illustration, photo jour-nalism, and informational graphics.

This nineteenth edition presents the finest newspaper design in the field.

Selected by a panel of judges of the Society for News Design, the award-winning newspapers featured in this nineteenth edition were chosen for excellence in design.

Selected by a panel of 21 judges of the Society for News Design, the award-winning pub-lications featured in this nineteenth edition were chosen for excellence in design.

The Best of Newspaper Design, 19th edition, features: Text in English and Spanish; 840 awards: World's Best-Designed Newspapers, Best of Show, Gold medals, Judges' Special Recognition, Silver medals, and Awards of Excel-lence. More than 12,100 entries were reviewed from hundreds of publications from around the world to select winners from 158 publications. Categories included: Overall design, news, features, portfo-lios, special coverage, special sections, magazines, art and illustration, photog-raphy, informational graphics and redesigns. Selected by a panel of 21

Continuing to pay tribute to the world's best newspaper designs, the 19th edi-tion of The Best of Newspaper Design is a stunning collection of modern work. The included works were select-ed from more than 10,000 entries sub-mitted by newspapers all over the world. This exceptional collection is an essential reference for anyone involved in print media, graphics, photography, design, journalism, or communications.

The competition, which is sponsored annually by the Society for News Design and the S.I. Newhouse School of Public Communications at Syracuse University, recognizes excellence in

newspaper design and graphics. Awards include Best of Show, Gold, Silver, Award of Excellence. Special Recogni-tion, plus the honor of World's Best Designed Newspaper. Categories for judging include overall page design, portfolio, magazine cover design, art and illustration, photo jour-nalism, and informational graphics.

This nineteenth edition presents the finest newspaper design in the field.

Selected by a panel of 21 judges of the Society for News Design, the award-winning pub-lications featured in this nineteenth edition were chosen for excellence in design.

The Best of Newspaper Design, 19th edition, features: Text in English and Spanish; 840 awards: World's Best-Designed Newspapers, Best of Show, Gold medals, Judges' Special Recognition, Silver medals, and Awards of Excel-lence. More than 12,100 entries were reviewed from hundreds of publications from around the world to select winners from 158 publications. Categories included: Overall design, news, features, portfolios, special coverage, special sections, magazines, art and illustration, photog-raphy, informational graphics and redesigns. Selected by a panel of 21

Continuing to pay tribute to the world's best newspaper designs, the 19th edition of The Best of Newspaper Design is a stunning collection of modern work. The included works were select-ed from more than 10,000 entries sub-mitted by newspapers all over the world. This exceptional collection is an essential reference for anyone involved in print media, graphics, photography, design, journalism, or communications.

The competition, which is sponsored annually by the Society for News Design and the S.I. Newhouse School of Public Communications at Syracuse University, recognizes excellence in judging include overall page design, portfolio, magazine cover design, art and illustration, photo journalism, and informational graphics.

This nineteenth edition presents the finest newspaper design in the field.

Selected by a panel of 21 judges of the Society for News Design, the award-winning pub-lications fea-tured in this nineteenth edition were chosen for excellence in design.

The Best of Newspaper Design, 19th edition, features: Text in English and Spanish; 840 awards: World's Best-Designed News-papers, Best of Show, Gold medals, Judges' Special Recognitions, Silver medals, and Awards of Excel-lence. More than 12,100 entries were reviewed from hundreds of publica-tions from around the world to select winners from 158 publications. Categories included: Overall design, news, features, portfolios, special coverage, special sections, maga-zines, art and illustration, photogra-phy, informational graphics and redesigns. Selected by a panel of 21 judges of the Society for News Design, the award-winning pub-lica-tions featured in this nineteenth edi-Selected by a panel of 21 judges of the Society for News Design, the award-winning pub-lications featured in this nineteenth edition were chosen for excellence in design.Continuing to pay tribute to the world's best newspa-per designs, the 19th edition of The Best of Newspaper Design is a stun-ning collection of modern work. The included works were selected from more than 10,000 entries submitted by newspapers all over the world. This exceptional collection is an essential reference for anyone involved in

Gold
Chicago Tribune
Chicago, IL

Kristin Fitzpatrick, Art Director; **Robert Cross**, Photographer; **Randy Curwen**, Travel Editor; **Charles Apple**, Graphic Artist; **Therese Shechter**, Associate Graphics & Design Editor; **Dave Jahntz**, Graphic Artist; **Steve Duenes**, Graphic Artist; **Rick Tuma**, Graphic Artist; **Kevin Hand**, Graphic Artist; **Phil Geib**, Graphic Artist

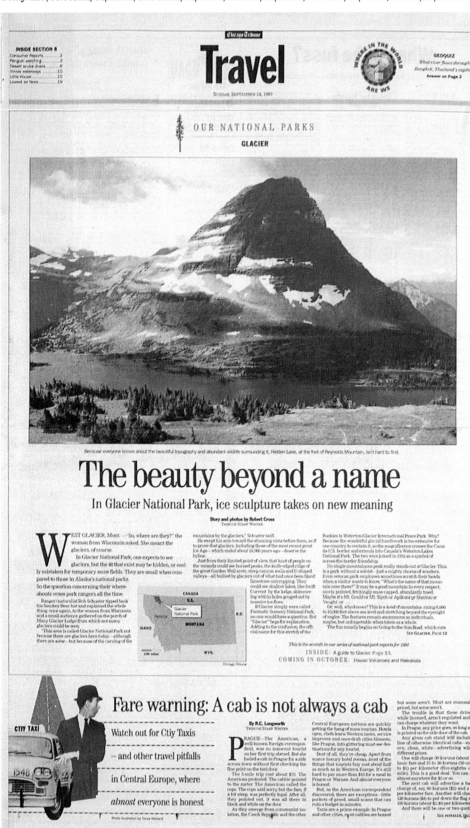

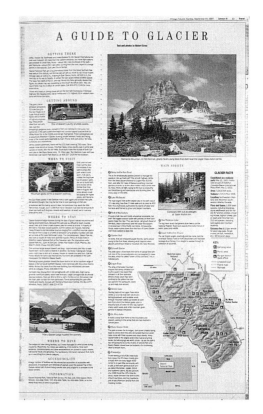

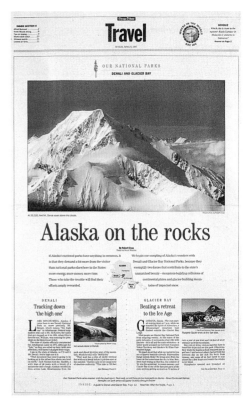

• Also an **Award of Excellence** for Travel Page

A **Gold Medal** was presented for its open layout, clean and crisp like the subject. Color palette and photos blend throughout the section. Understated typography showcases photos and graphics.

• • • • •

Se otorgó Medalla de Oro por su diagramación abierta, limpia y fresca como el sujeto. La paleta de colores y las fotografías se integran a la sección. La tipografía sutil destaca las fotos y los gráficos

Silver
Philadelphia Inquirer Magazine
Philadelphia, PA
Christine Dunleavy, Art Director & Designer; **Susan Syrnick**, Assistant Art Director; **Wiktor Sadowsky**, Illustrator; **Tom Curry**, Illustrator; **Greg Christie**, Illustrator; **Juliette Borda**, Illustrator; **Tim Bower**, Illustrator

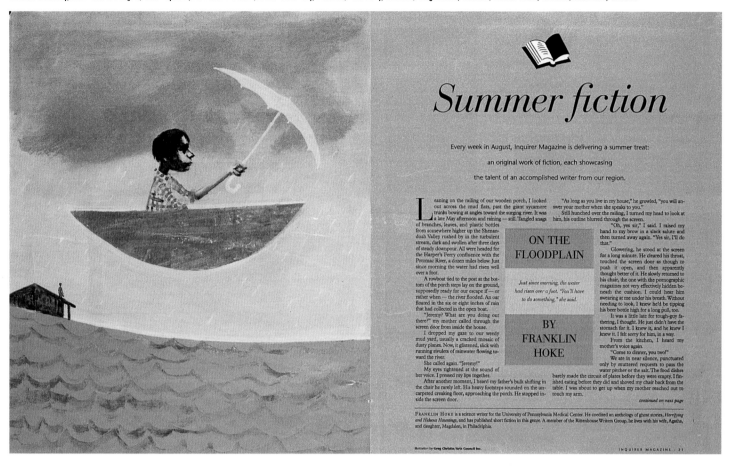

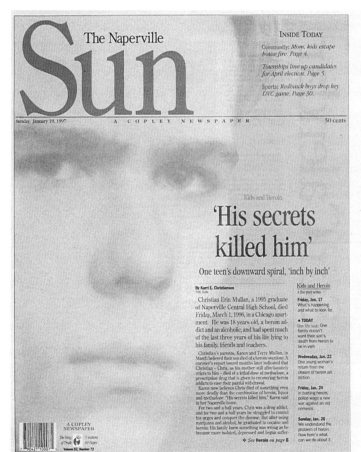

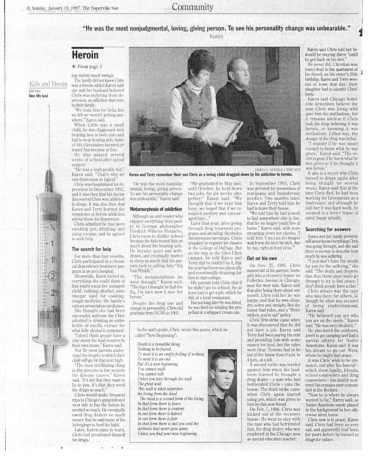

Silver
The Naperville Sun
Naperville, IL
Robb Montgomery, Design Editor; **Jim Kutina**, Photo Editor; **Bob Vavra**, City Editor; **Tim West**, Senior M.E.; **James C. Svehla**, Photographer; **Paul Klatt**, Photographer

Award of Excellence
Chicago Tribune
Chicago, IL

Joe Darrow, Art Director; Tim Bannon, Arts Editor

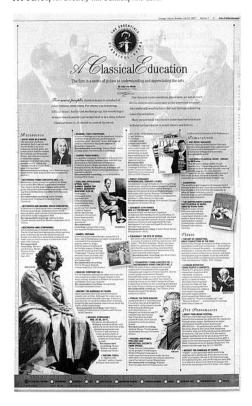

Award of Excellence
Chicago Tribune
Chicago, IL

Staff

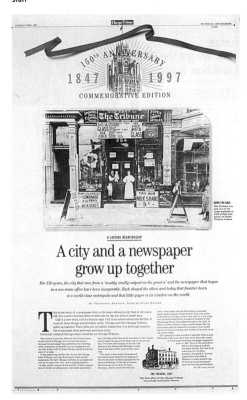

Award of Excellence
Philadelphia Daily News
Philadelphia, PA

John Sherlock, Graphics Editor; Anne Rae Massimiano, Designer; Michael Mercanti, Photo Editor

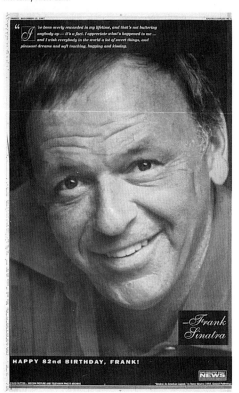

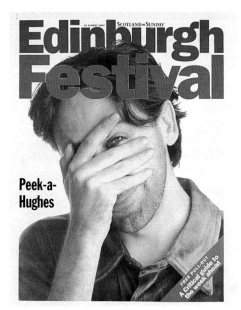

Award of Excellence
Scotland on Sunday
Edinburgh, Scotland

Neil Braidwood, Design Editor; Michael Gill, Deputy Design Editor

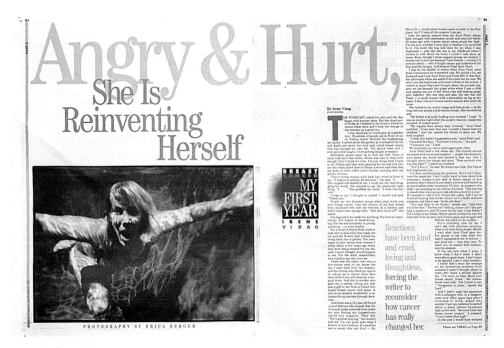

Award of Excellence
Newsday
Melville, NY

Miriam Smith, Art Director/Designer; Erica Berger, Photographer; Phyllis Singer, Editor; Renee Murawski, Copy Editor; Jim Dooley, Photo Editor

Award of Excellence
The Seattle Times

Seattle, WA

David Miller, Art Director; Michael Kellams, Designer; Mark Harrison, Photographer; Steve Ringman, Photographer; Jimi Lott, Photographer; Cathy Henkel, Sports Editor; Tom Reese, Photographer; Greg Gilbert; Photographer; Audrey Lee, Photographer

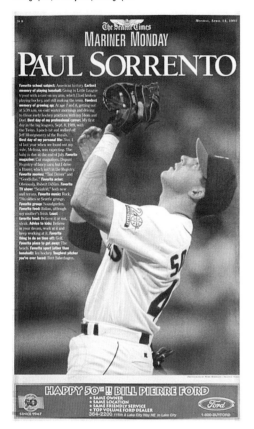

Award of Excellence
St. Petersburg Times

St. Petersburg, FL

Patty Cox, Designer; Neville Green, M.E.; Cherie Diez, Photographer; Sonya Doctorian, A.M.E./Photography; Don Morris, Art Director

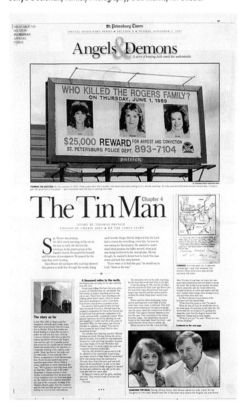

Award of Excellence
The Dallas Morning News

Dallas, TX

Lesley Becker, Designer; Jeff Goertzen, Illustrator

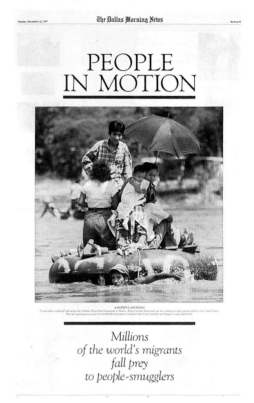

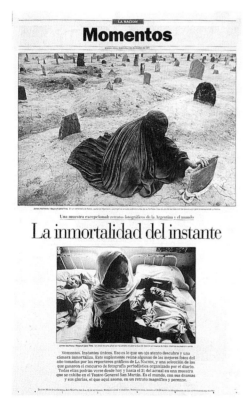

Award of Excellence
La Nacion

Buenos Aires, Argentina

Carmen Piaggio, Art Director; Don Rypka, Picture Editor; Carlos Guyot, Designer

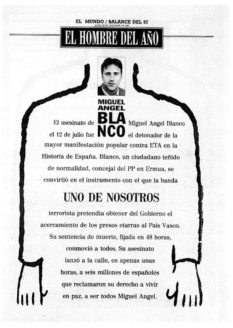

Award of Excellence
El Mundo

Madrid, Spain

Carmelo Caderot, Designer/Design Director

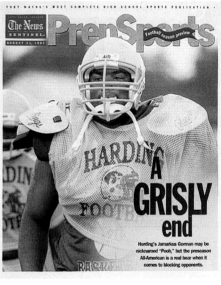

Award of Excellence
The News-Sentinel

Fort Wayne, IN

Brian Hayes, Designer & Graphic Artist; Erik Pupillo, PrepSports Editor; Casey O'Boyle, PrepSports Writer; Elbert Starks, Copy Editor; Steve Linsenmayer, Photographer; Mark Thompson-Kolar, Presentation Chief

Gold
Die Woche
Hamburg, Germany

Manfred Bissinger, Editor-in-Chief; Kurt Breme, Executive Editor; Hans-Ulrich Joerges, Executive Editor; Dirk Linke, Art Director; Andreas Schomberg, Associate Art Director; Armin Ogris, Designer; Stefan Semrau, Designer; Jessica Winter; Designer; Florian Poehl, Designer/Informational Graphics; Reinhard Schulz-Schaeffer, Designer/Informational Graphics

Awarded a **Gold Medal** for its fantastic cover — simple but strong interior display. Use of color and typography is wonderful. The design has a clean line throughout. It doesn't shout.

● ● ● ● ●

Ganador de la Medalla de Oro por su fantástica tapa — presentación interior simple y fuerte a la vez. Magnífico uso del color y la tipografía. El diseño posee una línea limpia. No aturde.

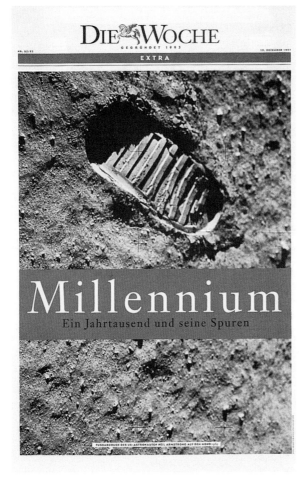

DIE WOCHE
GEGRÜNDET 1993
EXTRA

Millennium
Ein Jahrtausend und seine Spuren

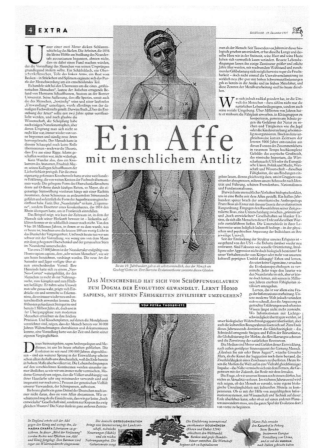

4 EXTRA

Ein Affe
mit menschlichem Antlitz

DAS MENSCHENBILD HAT SICH VOM SCHÖPFUNGSGLAUBEN ZUM DOGMA DER EVOLUTION GEWANDELT. LERNT HOMO SAPIENS, MIT SEINEN FÄHIGKEITEN ZIVILISIERT UMZUGEHEN?

VON PETRA THORBRIETZ

1215   1250   1252   1275

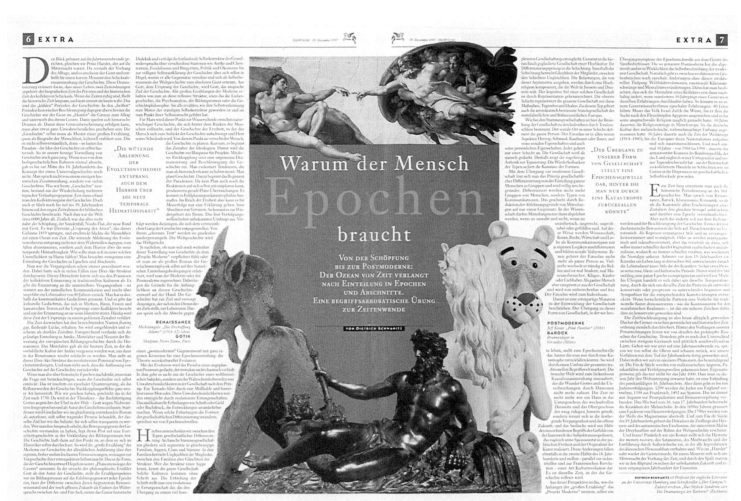

6 EXTRA

Warum der Mensch
Epochen
braucht

VON DER SCHÖPFUNG BIS ZUR POSTMODERNE: DER OZEAN VON ZEIT VERLANGT NACH EINTEILUNG IN EPOCHEN UND ABSCHNITTE. EINE BEGRIFFSAKROBATISCHE ÜBUNG ZUR ZEITENWENDE

VON DIETRICH SCHWANITZ

EXTRA 7

RENAISSANCE
GOTIK
POSTMODERNE
BAROCK

1358   1407   1412   1413   1445   1450   1453   1469   1492

Silver
Dagens Nyheter
Stockholm, Sweden
Ulla Wingård, Design Director; **John Bark**, Creative Director; **Pontus Hedengren**, Art Director

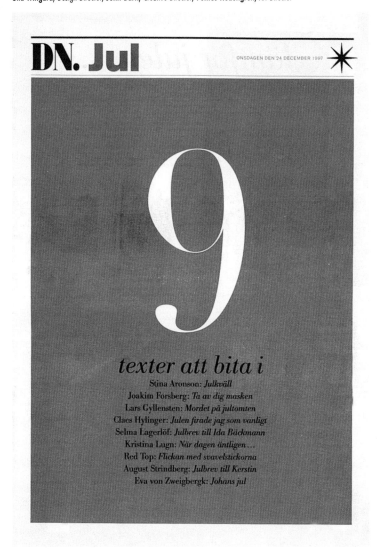

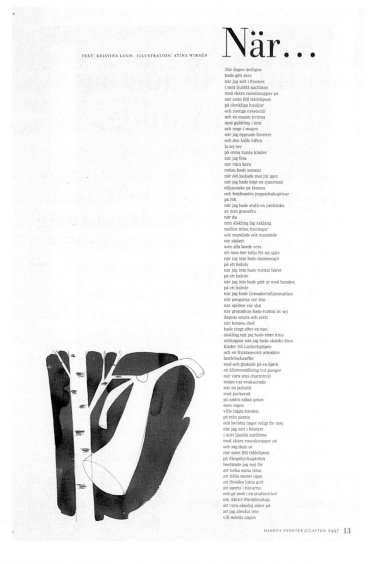

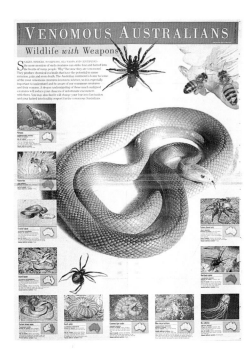

Award of Excellence
The Sunday Age
Melbourne, Australia

Garry Linnell, Editor; **Andrew Wolf**, Designer; **Kerrie Aulsebrook**, Coordinator

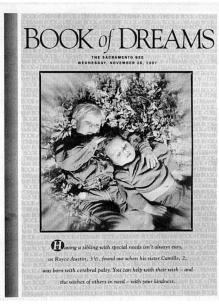

Award of Excellence
The Sacramento Bee
Sacramento, CA

Lisa Roberts Hahn, Photo Editor/Designer; **Randy Pench**, Photographer

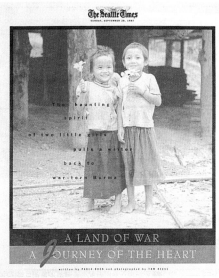

Award of Excellence
The Seattle Times
Seattle, WA

Tracy Porter, Designer; **David Miller**, Art Director; **Dave Boardman**, Editor; **Tom Reese**, Photographer; **Paula Bock**, Reporter; **Fred Nelson**, Photo Editor; **Liz McClure**, Art Director

Silver
Folha de S.Paulo
São Paulo, Brazil

Paula Cesarino Costa, Special Section Editor; **Didiana Prata**, Art Editor;
Jair de Oliveira, Page Designer; **Sebastião Salgado**, Photographer

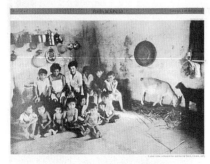

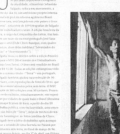

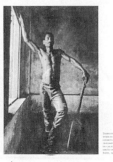

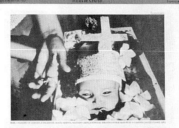

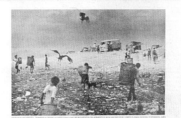

JOSÉ SARAMAGO

Silver
Jacksonville Journal-Courier
Jacksonville, IL

Mike Miner, Editor/Designer;
Steve Copper, Editor/Designer

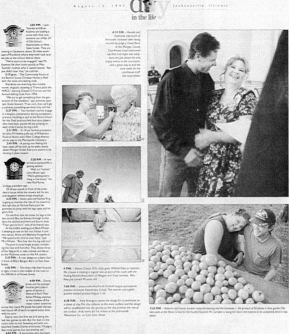

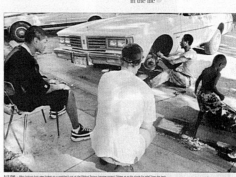

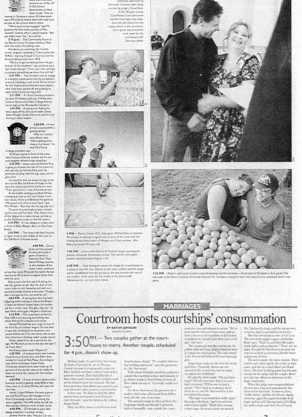

MARRIAGES
Courtroom hosts courtships' consummation

ON PATROL
All in a night's work: Tedium, good deeds, danger

Silver
El Mundo
Madrid, Spain
Carmelo Caderot, Design Director & Designer; **Carlos Garcia**, Photographer; **Mitxi**, Photographer

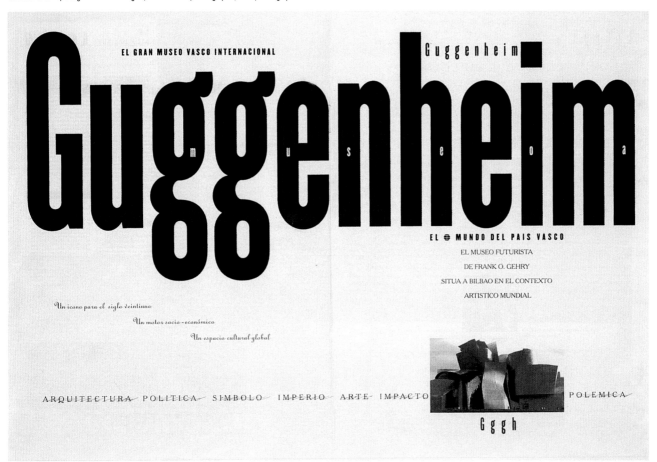

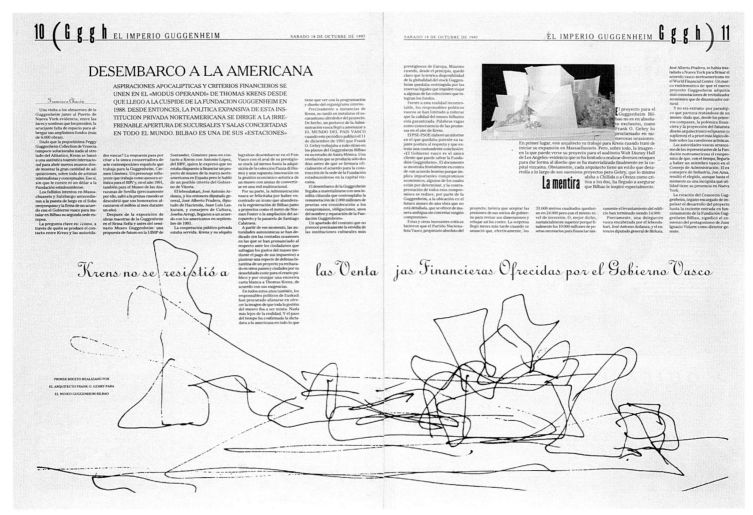

Silver
Diario de Noticias
Lisbon, Portugal

Mário B. Resendes, Editor-in-Chief; **Francisco Azevedo e Silva**, Associate Editor-in-Chief; **José Maria Ribeirinho**, Art Director; **Carlos Jorge**, Designer; **Luís Tenreiro**, Designer; **Júlio Gonçalves**, Designer

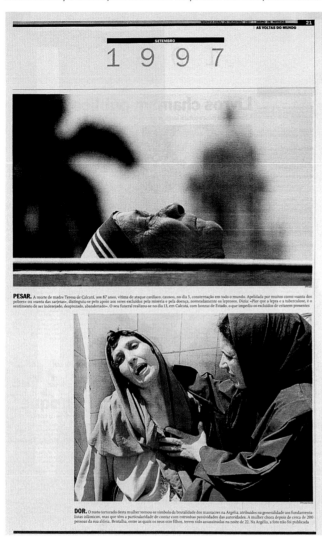

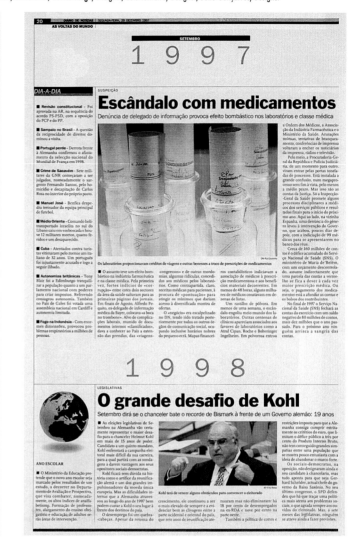

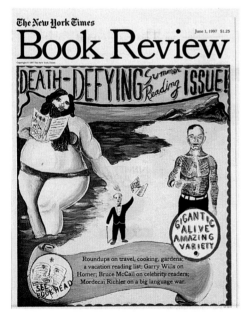

Award of Excellence
The New York Times
New York, NY

Steven Heller, Art Director; **Kit Keith**, Illustrator

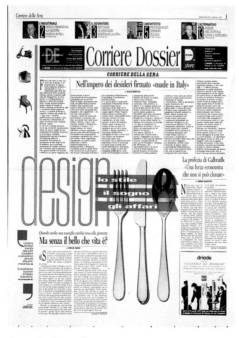

Award of Excellence
Corriere della Sera
Milan, Italy

Gianluigi Colin, Art Director; **Giovanni Angeli**, Page Designer; **Massimo Bernardi**, Graphic Artist; **Marco Vaglieri**, Graphic Artist

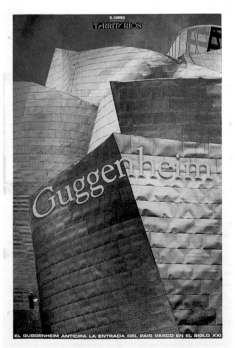

Award of Excellence
• Also an Award of Excellence for Cover Page
El Correo
Bilbao, Spain

Mari Carmen Navarro, Designer; **Alberto Torregrosa**, Editorial Art & Design Consultant; **Jesús Aycart**, Art Director; **José Luis Nocito**, Photographer; **Juan Ignacio Fernández**, Photo Editor

Award of Excellence
Middlesex News
Framingham, MA
Pat Capobianco, Design Director; Patrick McBride, Associate Design Director; Anne Parker, Designer; Andrea Haynes, Editor; Rus Lodi, M.E.; Joe Dwinell, Project Editor; Jason Levine, Assistant Project Editor; Michael Healy, Layout Coordinator

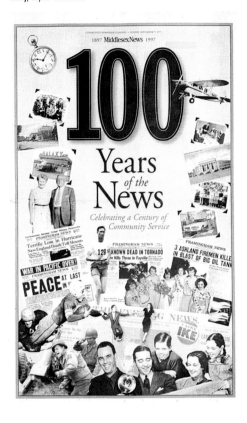

Award of Excellence
La Vanguardia
Barcelona, Spain
Carlos Pérez de Rozas Arribas, Art Director; Rosa Mundet Poch, Graphics Editor; Staff

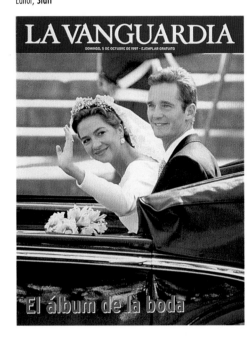

Award of Excellence
Philadelphia Daily News
Philadelphia, PA
John Sherlock, Designer; Jon Snyder, Designer; Jeff Samuels, Editor

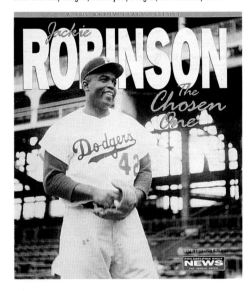

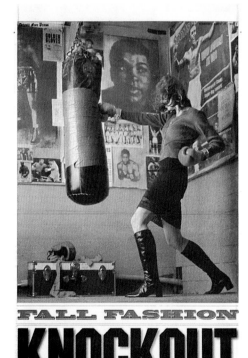

Award of Excellence
Detroit Free Press
Detroit, MI
Bryan Erickson, Designer; J. Kyle Keener, Photographer

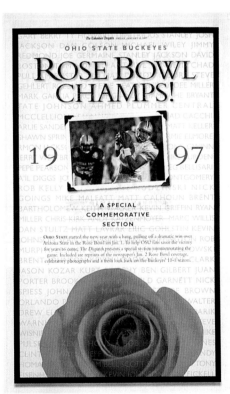

Award of Excellence
The Columbus Dispatch
Columbus, OH
Scott Minister, Art Director/Designer; Doug Miller, Artist

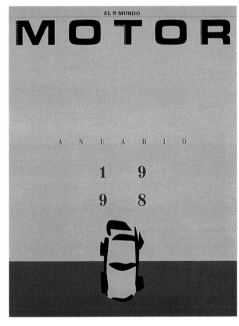

Award of Excellence
El Mundo
Madrid, Spain
Carmelo Caderot, Designer/Design Director; Manuel de Miguel, Assistant Art Director

Award of Excellence
Seattle Post-Intelligencer
Seattle, WA
Duane Hoffmann, Artist/Designer

Award of Excellence
El Mundo
Madrid, Spain
Carmelo Caderot, Designer/Design Director; **Manuel de Miguel**, Assistant Art Director; **Raul Arias**, Illustrator

Award of Excellence
The News & Observer
Raleigh, NC
Teresa Kriegsman, News Designer; **Roger Winstead**, Photographer

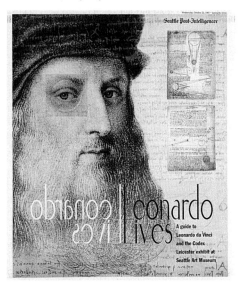

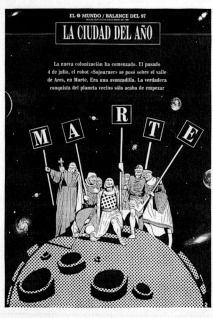

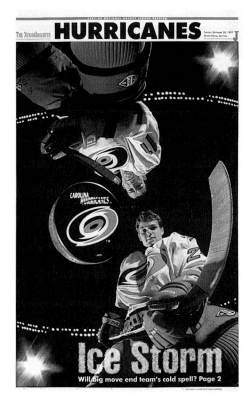

Award of Excellence
The Seattle Times
Seattle, WA
Jeff Neumann, Illustrator & Designer; **David Miller**, Art Director

Award of Excellence
The Wall Street Journal
New York, NY
James Condon, Graphics Director; **Marco Herrera**, Art Director & Designer; **Kristin McLallen**, Deputy Graphics Director

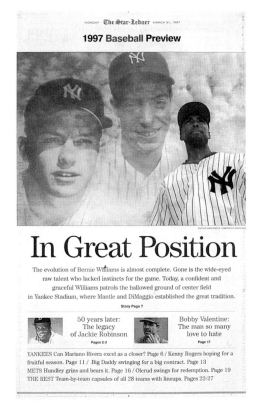

Award of Excellence
The Star-Ledger
Newark, NJ
George Frederick, Designer; **Andre Malok**, Illustrator; **Kevin Whitmer**, Sports Editor; **John O'Boyle**, Photographer

Award of Excellence
•Also an Award of Excellence for Features Portfolio
The Wall Street Journal Reports
New York, NY

Greg Leeds, Design Director & Designer; **Scott Baldwin,** Illustrator

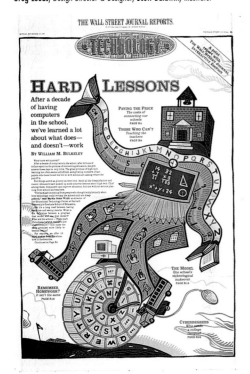

Award of Excellence
Dayton Daily News
Dayton, OH

M.B. Hopkins, Designer/Artist; **Lee Waigand,** Art Director; **Key Metts,** Designer; **Steve Spencer,** Artist; **John Hancock,** Artist

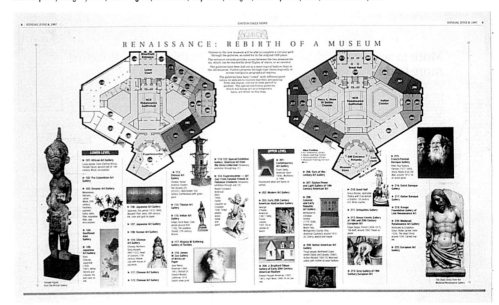

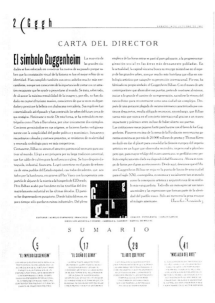

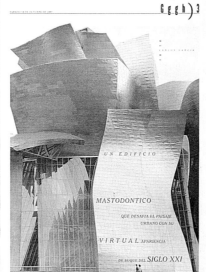

Award of Excellence
El Mundo
Madrid, Spain

Carmelo Caderot, Designer/Design Director; **Manuel de Miguel,** Assistant Art Director; **Aurelio Fernandez,** Deputy Editor; **Francisco Chacon,** Deputy Editor; **Carlos Garcia,** Photographer

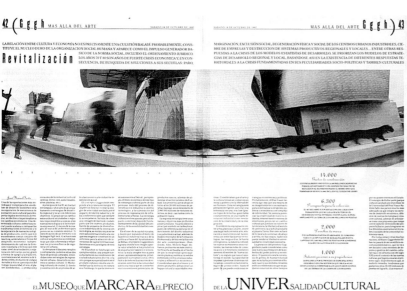

Award of Excellence
El Mundo
Madrid, Spain

Carmelo Caderot, Designer/Design Director; **Manuel de Miguel,** Assistant Art Director; **Aurelio Fernandez,** Deputy Editor; **Francisco Chacon,** Deputy Editor; **Carlos Garcia,** Photographer

Award of Excellence
The New York Times
New York, NY
Bernadette Dashiell, Art Director

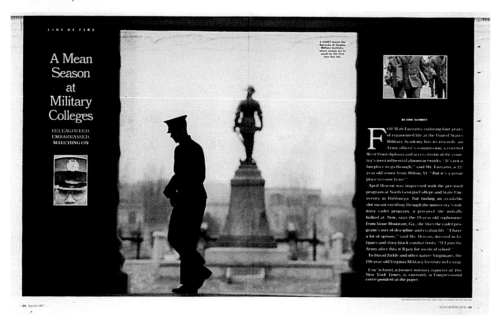

Award of Excellence
The Wall Street Journal
New York, NY
James Condon, Graphics Director; **Marco Herrera**, Art Director/Designer;
Kristin McLallen, Deputy Graphics Director

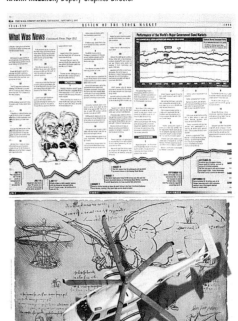

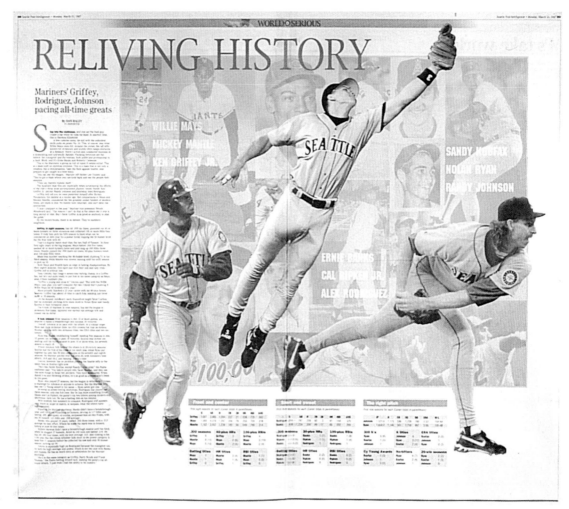

Award of Excellence
Seattle Post-Intelligencer
Seattle, WA
Duane Hoffmann, Artist/Designer; **Dwight Perry**, Editor

Chapter Seven

DESIGN PORTFOLIO

The competition, which is sponsored annually by the Society for News Design and the S.I. Newhouse School of Public Communications at Syracuse University, recognizes excellence in newspaper design and graphics. Awards include Best of Show, Gold, Silver, Award of Excellence, Special Recogni-tion, plus the honor of World's Best

judging include overall page design, portfolio, magazine cover design, art and illustration, photo journalism, and informational graphics. This nineteenth edition presents the finest newspaper design in the field.

Selected by a panel of 21 judges of the Society for News Design, the award-winning pub-lications featured in this nineteenth edition were

Continuing to pay tribute to the world's best newspaper designs, the 19th edition of The Best of Newspaper Design is a stunning collection of modern work. The included works were selected from more than 10,000 entries submitted by newspapers all over the world. This exceptional collection is an essential reference for anyone involved in print media, graphics, photography, design, journalism, or communications.

The competition, which is sponsored annually by the Society of News Design and the S.I. Newhouse School of Public Communications at Syracuse University, recognizes excellence in newspaper design and graphics. Awards include Best of Show, Gold, Silver, Award of Excellence, Special Recogni-tion, plus the honor of World's Best Designed Newspaper. Categories for judging include overall page design, portfolio, magazine cover design, art and illustration, photo journalism, and informational graphics.

This nineteenth edition presents the finest newspaper design in the field.

Selected by a panel of judges of the Society for News Design, the award-winning newspapers featured in this nineteenth edition were chosen for excellence in design.

The Best of Newspaper Design, 19th edition, features: Text in English and Spanish; 840 awards: World's Best-Designed Newspapers, Best of Show, Gold medals, Judges' Special Recognition, Silver medals, and Awards of Excel-lence. More than 12,100 entries were reviewed from hundreds of publications from around the world to select winners from 158 publications. Categories included: Overall design, news, features, portfolios, special coverage, special sections, magazines, art and illustration, photography, informational graphics and redesigns.ign, art and illustration.

Continuing to pay tribute to the world's best newspaper designs, the 19th edition of The Best of Newspaper Design is a stunning collection of modern work. The included works were selected from more than 10,000 entries submitted by newspapers all over the world. This exceptional collection is an essential reference for anyone involved in print

The competition, which is sponsored annually by the Society of News Design and the S.I. Newhouse School of Public Communications at Syracuse University, recognizes excellence in newspaper design and graphics. Awards include Best of Show, Gold, Silver, Award of Excellence, Special Recogni-tion, plus the honor of World's Best Designed Newspaper. Categories for judging include overall page design, portfolio, magazine cover design, art and illustration, photo journalism, and informational graphics.

This nineteenth edition presents the finest newspaper design in the field.

Selected by a panel of judges of the Society of News Design, the award-winning newspapers featured in this nineteenth edition were chosen for excellence in design.

Selected by a panel of 21 judges of the Society for News Design, the award-winning pub-lications featured in this nineteenth edition were chosen for excellence in design.

The Best of Newspaper Design, 19th edition, features: all text in English and Spanish; more than five hundred awards: Best of Show, Judges' Special Recognition, Gold Medals, Sil-ver Medals, and Awards of Excellence: over five hundred newspapers from all around the world; categories such as overall page design, portfolio, magazine cover design, art and illustration, photo journalism, and informational graphs Continuing to pay tribute to the world's best newspaper designs, the 19th edition of The Best of Newspaper Design is a stunning collection of modern work. The included works were selected from more than 10,000 entries submitted by newspapers all over the world. This exceptional collection is an essential reference for anyone involved in print media, graphics, photography, design, journalism, or communications.

The competition, which is sponsored annually by the Society for News Design and the S.I. Newhouse School of Public Communications at Syracuse University, recognizes

Continuing to pay tribute to the world's best newspaper designs, the 19th edition of The Best of Newspaper Design is a stunning collection of modern work. The included works were selected from more than 10,000 entries submitted by newspapers all over the world. This exceptional collection is an essential reference for anyone involved in print media, graphics, photography, design, journalism, or communications.

The competition, which is sponsored annually by the Society for News Design and the S.I. Newhouse School of Public Communications at Syracuse University, recognizes excellence in newspaper design and graphics. Awards include Best of Show, Gold, Silver, Award of Excellence, Special Recogni-tion, plus the honor of World's Best Designed Newspaper. Categories for judging include overall page design, portfolio, magazine cover design, art and illustration, photo journalism, and informational graphics.

This nineteenth edition presents the finest newspaper design in the field.

Selected by a panel of 21 judges of the Society for News Design, the award-winning newspapers featured in this nineteenth edition were chosen for excellence in design.

The Best of Newspaper Design, 19th edition, features: Text in English and Spanish; 840 awards: Continuing to pay tribute to the world's best newspaper designs, the 19th edition of The Best of Newspaper Design is a stunning collection of modern work. The included works were selected from more than 10,000 entries submitted by newspapers all over the world. This exceptional collection is an essential reference for anyone involved in print media, graphics, photography, design, journalism, or communications.

The competition, which is sponsored annually by the Society for News Design and the S.I. Newhouse School of Public Communications at Syracuse University, recognizes

The competition, which is sponsored annually by the Society for News Design and the S.I. Newhouse School of Public Communications at Syracuse University, recognizes excellence in newspaper design and graphics. Awards include Best of Show, Gold, Silver, Award of Excellence, Special Recogni-tion, plus the honor of World's Best Designed Newspaper. Categories for judging include overall page design, portfolio, magazine cover design, art and illustration, photo journalism, and informational graphics.

This nineteenth edition presents the finest newspaper design in the field.

Selected by a panel of 21 judges of the Society for News Design, the award-winning pub-lications featured in this nineteenth edition were chosen for excellence in design.

The Best of Newspaper Design, 19th edition, features: Text in English and Spanish; 840 awards: World's Best-Designed News-papers, Best of Show, Gold medals, Judges' Special Recognition, Silver medals, and Awards of Excel-lence.

NEWS
FEATURE
MAGAZINE
COMBINATION

More than 12,100 entries were reviewed from hundreds of publications from around the world to select winners from 158 publications. Categories included: Overall design, news, features, portfolios, special coverage, special sections, magazines, art and illustration, photography, informational graphics and redesigns. Selected by a panel of 21 judges of the Society for News Design, the award-winning pub-lications Continuing to pay tribute to the world's best newspaper designs, the

The Best of Newspaper Design, 19th edition, features: Text in English and Spanish; 840 awards: World's Best-Designed News-papers, Best of Show, Gold medals, Judges' Special Recognition, Silver medals, and Awards of Excel-lence. More than 12,100 entries were reviewed from hundreds of publications from around the world to select winners from 158 publications. Categories included: Overall design, news, features, portfolios, special coverage, special sections, magazines, art and illustration, photography, informational graphics and redesigns. Selected by a panel of 21 judges of the Society for News Design, the award-winning pub-lications featured in this nineteenth edition were chosen for excellence in The competition, which is sponsored annually by the Society of News Design and the S.I. Newhouse School of Public Communications at Syracuse University, recognizes excellence in newspaper design and graphics. Awards include Best of Show, Gold, Silver, Award of Excellence, Special Recogni-tion, plus the honor of World's Best

Designed Newspaper. Categories for judging include overall page design, portfolio, magazine cover design, art and illustration, photo journalism, and informational graphics.

This nineteenth edition presents the finest newspaper design in the field.

Selected by a panel of judges of the Society of News Design, the award-winning newspapers featured in this nineteenth edition were chosen for excellence in design.

Selected by a panel of 21 judges the Society for News Design

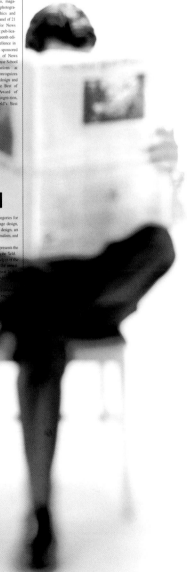

Silver
Asbury Park Press
Neptune, NJ

Harris G. Siegel, Designer

•Also an **Award of Excellence** for Inside News page

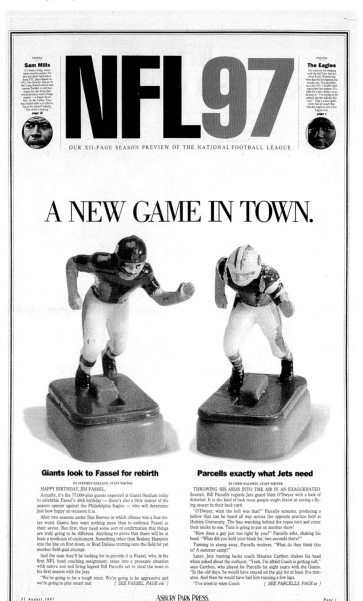

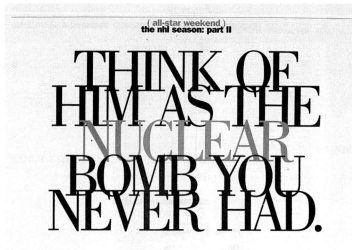

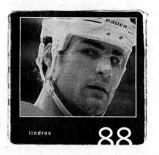

Silver
Pittsburgh Post-Gazette
Pittsburgh, PA
Christopher Pett-Ridge, A.M.E. Graphics

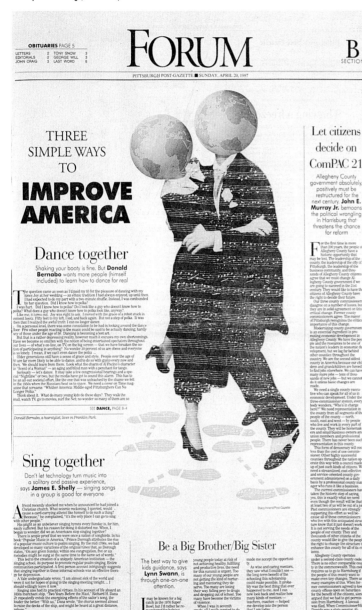

FORUM
B SECTION

PITTSBURGH POST-GAZETTE ■ SUNDAY, APRIL 20, 1997

OBITUARIES PAGE 5

LETTERS	2	TONY SNOW	3
EDITORIALS	2	GEORGE WILL	3
JOHN CRAIG	3	LAST WORD	6

THREE SIMPLE WAYS TO
IMPROVE AMERICA

Dance together

Shaking your booty is fun. But **Donald Bernabo** wants more people (himself included) to learn how to dance for real

Donald Bernabo, a hairstylist, lives in Franklin Park.

SEE DANCE, PAGE B-4

Sing together

Don't let technology turn music into a solitary and passive experience, says **James E. Shelly** — singing songs in a group is good for everyone

James E. Shelly is an archivist for the Herb Society of America, a historical consultant and a free-lance writer in Cleveland Heights.

SEE SING, PAGE B-4

Be a Big Brother/Big Sister

The best way to give kids guidance, says **Lynn Swann**, is through one-on-one attention.

Lynn Swann, a former wide receiver for the Pittsburgh Steelers, is on the board of Big Brothers/Big Sisters of America.

SEE SWANN, PAGE B-4

Let citizens decide on ComPAC 21

Allegheny County government absolutely, positively must be restructured for the next century. **John E. Murray Jr.** bemoans the political wrangling in Harrisburg that threatens the chance for reform

John E. Murray Jr., the president of Duquesne University, is chairman of ComPAC 21.

SEE COMPAC, PAGE B-4

FORUM
B SECTION

PITTSBURGH POST-GAZETTE ■ SUNDAY, DECEMBER 21, 1997

OBITUARIES PAGE 6

EDITORIAL	2	ELLEN GOODMAN	3
LETTERS	2	GEORGE F WILL	3
JOHN CRAIG	3	LAST WORD	10

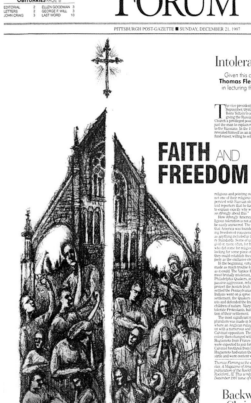

FAITH AND FREEDOM

Intolerance, American-style

Given this country's history of religious animosities, **Thomas Fleming** writes, Al Gore is on shaky ground in lecturing the Russians about the joys of ecumenism

Thomas Fleming is the editor of Chronicles: A Magazine of American Culture, a publication of the Rockford Institute in Rockford, Ill. This is reprinted from the December 1997 issue of Chronicles.

SEE INTOLERANCE, PAGE B-4

Backward, Christian soldiers

Liberal Christians in America are turning their backs on their persecuted co-religionists around the world, complains **Mark Tooley**

WASHINGTON

Mark Tooley is research associate for the Institute on Religion & Democracy in Washington, D.C.

SEE CHRISTIANS, PAGE B-4

Four ways of looking at the holiday season

Peter Kountz reflects on the qualities that make Christmas more than just a date on the calendar

Peter Kountz is president of Shady Side Academy.

SEE HOLIDAY, PAGE B-4

Award of Excellence

Award of Excellence
The Boston Globe
Boston, MA

Janet L. Michaud, Designer

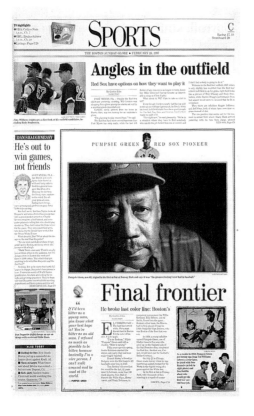

Award of Excellence
The Boston Globe
Boston, MA

Anthony J. Schultz, Art Director

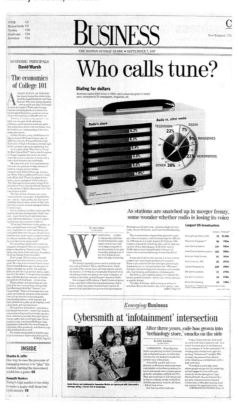

Award of Excellence
•Also an **Award of Excellence** for Business Page
The Charlotte Observer
Charlotte, NC

Barry Kolar, Designer; Monica Moses, Design Director; Jon Talton, Section Editor; George Breisacher, Artist

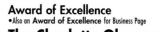
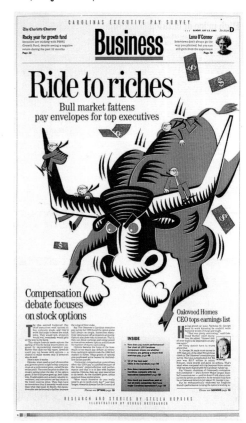

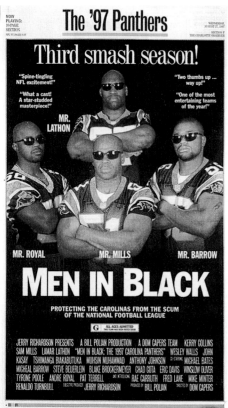

Award of Excellence
The Charlotte Observer
Charlotte, NC

Scott Goldman, Assistant Sports Editor

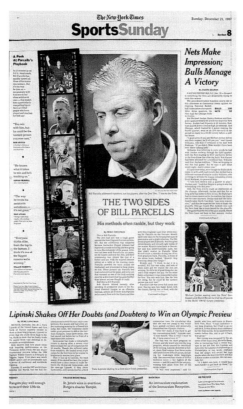

Award of Excellence
The New York Times
New York, NY

Lee Yarosh, Presentation Editor

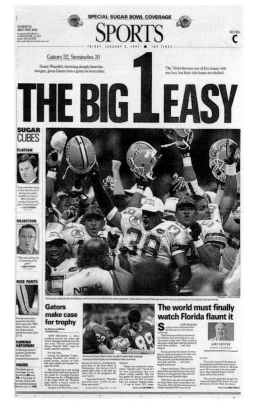

Award of Excellence
St. Petersburg Times
St. Petersburg, FL

Jim Melvin, Sunday Sports Editor

Award of Excellence
Sun-Sentinel/South Florida
Ft. Lauderdale, FL
Chris Kirkman, Graphic Reporter

Award of Excellence
The Virginian-Pilot
Norfolk, VA
Paul Nelson, Page Designer

Award of Excellence
The Washington Times
Washington, DC
Virginia Tinker Brace, Art Director

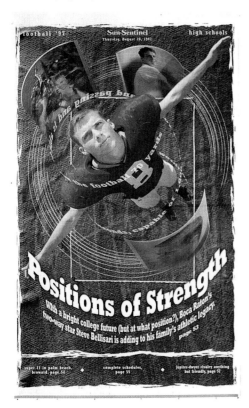

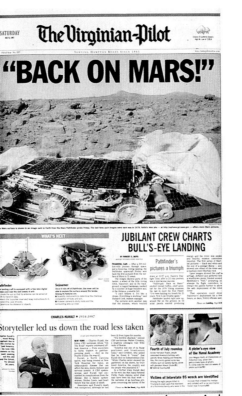

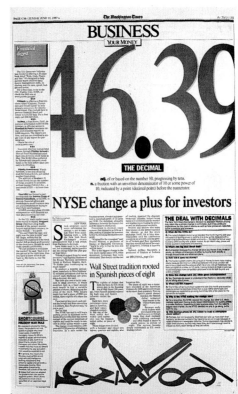

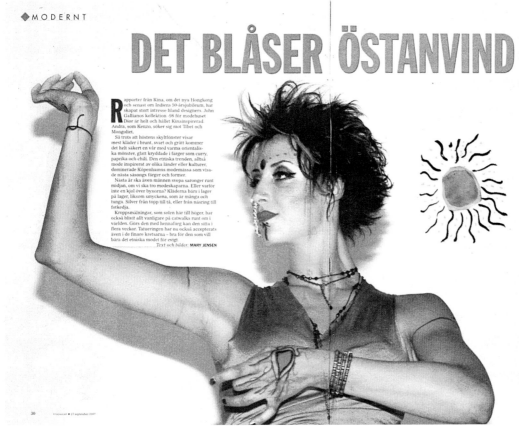

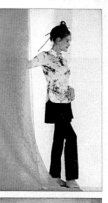

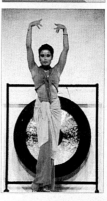

Award of Excellence
Goteborgs-Posten/TVÅ Dagar
Göteborg, Sweden
Gunilla Wernhamn, Designer

Gold
Expansión
Madrid, Spain

Pablo Ma Ramírez, Designer & Graphic Artist

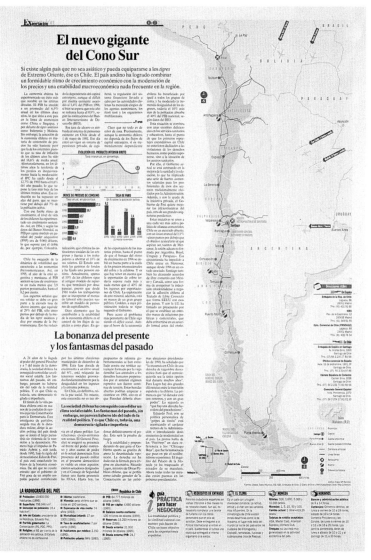

Awarded a **Gold Medal**, this designer has a very clear line. He works with a contrast between big and small. There is great attention to detail. The color palette is wonderful, especially on the peach paper.

•••••

Ganador de una Medalla de Oro, este diseñador posee una línea muy clara. Trabaja con un contraste entre lo grande y lo pequeño. Gran detalle. La paleta de colores es maravillosa, especialmente sobre papel color salmón.

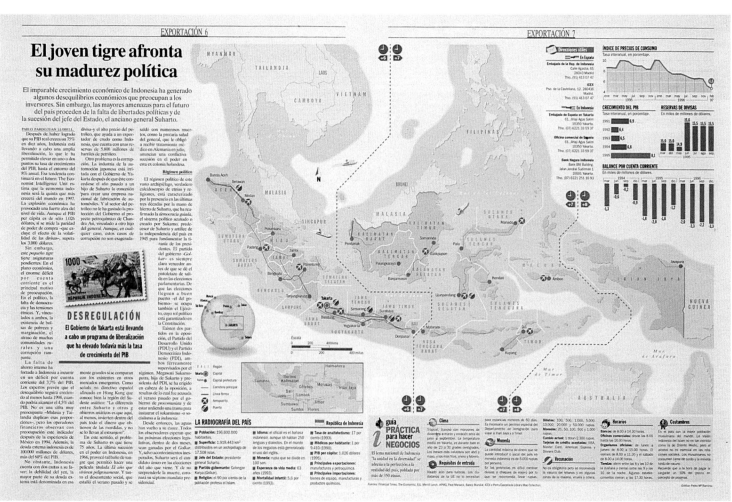

Award of Excellence
The Boston Globe
Boston, MA

Jacqueline Berthet, Art Director & Designer

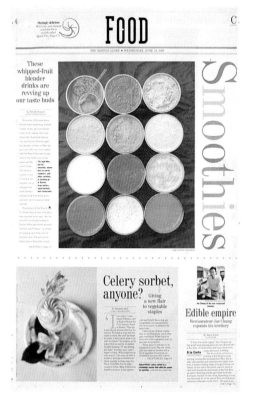

Award of Excellence
The New York Times
New York, NY

Linda Brewer, Art Director & Designer

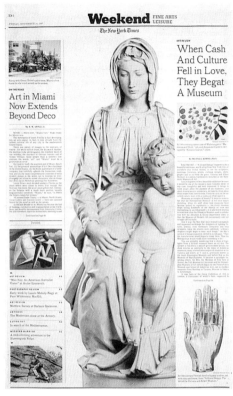

Award of Excellence
Anchorage Daily News
Anchorage, AK

Lance Lekander, Art Director & Designer

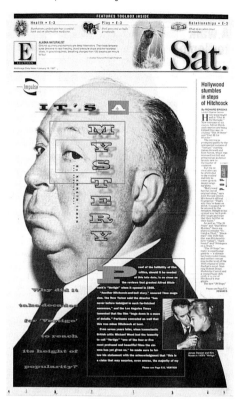

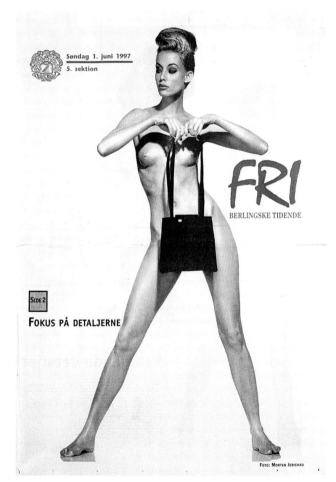

Award of Excellence
Berlingske Tidende
Copenhagen, Denmark

Bettina Kofmann, Illustrator & Designer

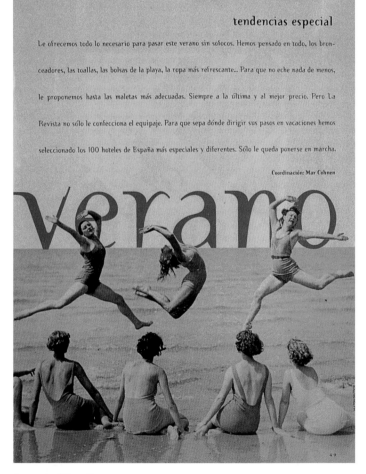

Award of Excellence
El Mundo/La Revista
Madrid, Spain

Maria Gonzalez, Designer

Award of Excellence
The Beacon News
Hammond, IN

Steven Hartley, Designer

Award of Excellence
The Beacon News
Norfolk, VA

Paul Wallen Jr., Design Editor

Award of Excellence
Le Devoir
Montreal, QC, Canada

Roland-Yves Carignan, Art Director & Designer

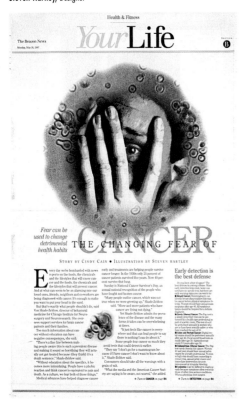

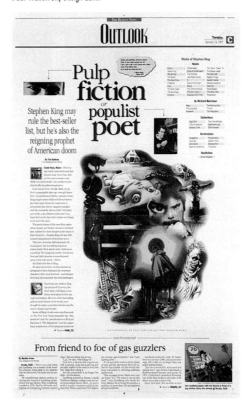

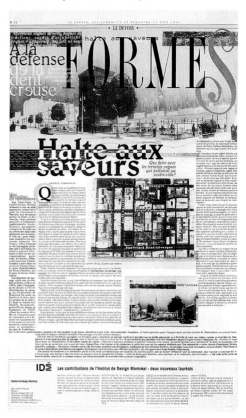

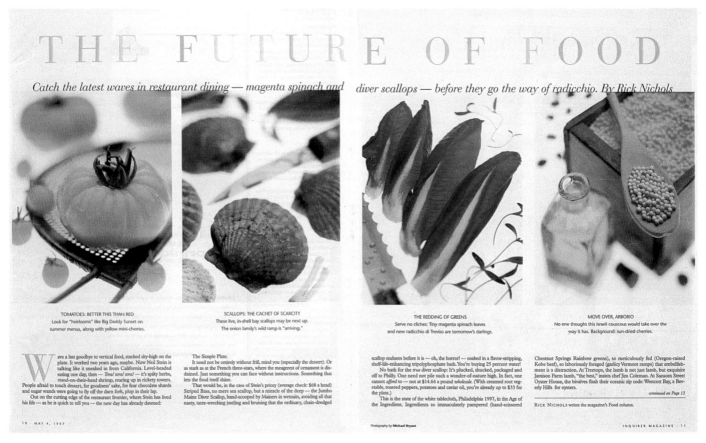

THE FUTURE OF FOOD

Catch the latest waves in restaurant dining — magenta spinach and diver scallops — before they go the way of radicchio. By Rick Nichols

TOMATOES: BETTER THIS THAN RED
Look for "heirlooms" like Big Daddy Sunset on
summer menus, along with yellow mini-cherries.

SCALLOPS: THE CACHET OF SCARCITY
These live, in-shell bay scallops may be next up.
The onion family's wild ramp is "arriving."

THE REDDING OF GREENS
Serve no cliches: Tiny magenta spinach leaves
and new radicchio di Treviso are tomorrow's darlings.

MOVE OVER, ARBORIO
No one thought this Israeli couscous would take over the
way it has. Background: sun-dried cherries.

Award of Excellence
Philadelphia Inquirer Magazine
Philadelphia, PA

Christine Dunleavy, Art Director

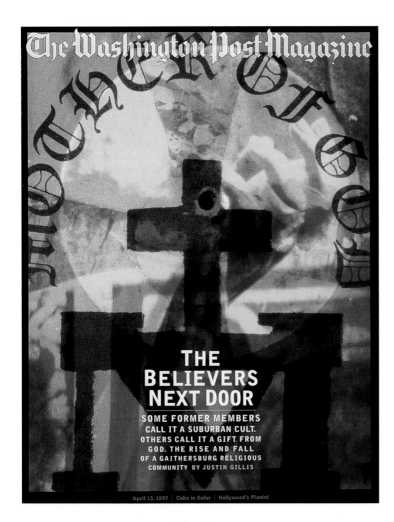

Award of Excellence
The Washington Post Magazine
Washington, DC
Kelly Doe, Art Director & Designer

Award of Excellence
El Mundo/La Revista
Madrid, Spain
Maria Gonzalez, Designer

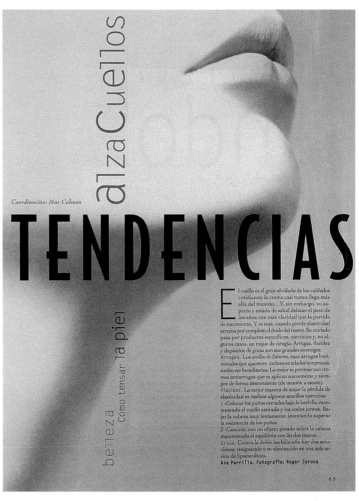

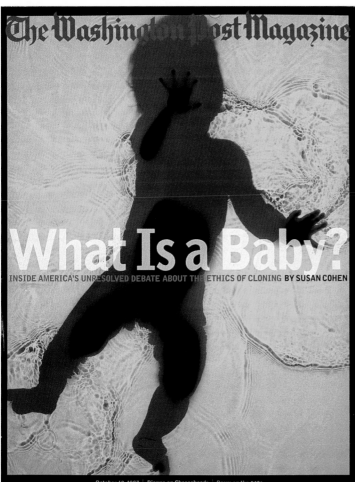

Award of Excellence
The Washington Post Magazine
Washington, DC
Kelly Doe, Art Director & Designer

Award of Excellence
The Sun
Mesa, AZ
Randy Mishler, Page Designer

Award of Excellence
The State
Columbia, SC
Nikki Life, Designer/Design Coordinator

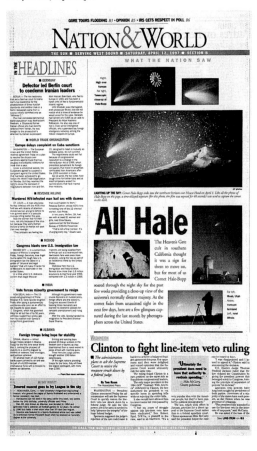

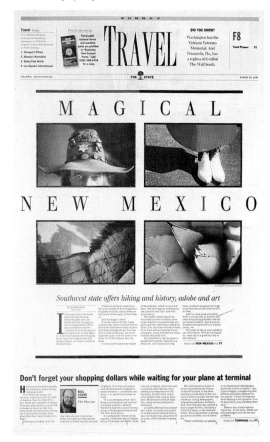

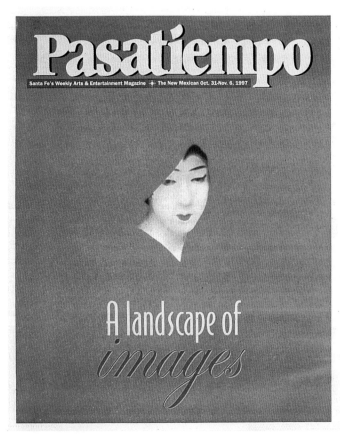

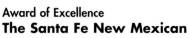

Award of Excellence
The Santa Fe New Mexican
Santa Fe, NM
Marcella Sandoval, Designer

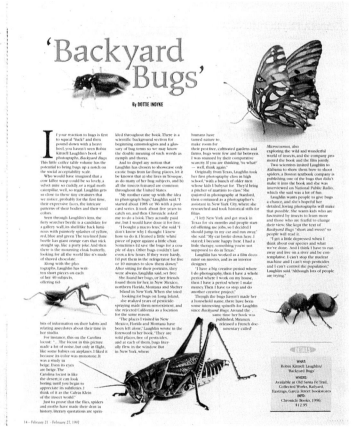

Chapter Eight

ILLUS-TRATION

Continuing to pay tribute to the world's best newspaper designs, the 19th edition of The Best of Newspaper Design is a stunning collection of modern work. The included works were selected from more than 10,000 entries submitted by newspapers all over the world. This exceptional collection is an essential reference for anyone involved in print media, graphics, photography, design, journalism, or communications.

The competition, which is sponsored annually by the Society of News Design and the S.I. Newhouse School of Public Communications at Syracuse University, recognizes excellence in newspaper design and graphics. Awards include Best of Show, Gold, Silver, Award of Excellence, Special Recogni-tion, plus the honor of World's Best Designed Newspaper. Categories for judging include overall page design, portfolio, magazine cover design, art and illustration, photo jour-nalism, and informational graphics.

This nineteenth edition presents the finest newspaper design in the field.

Selected by a panel of 21 judges of the Society for News Design, the award-winning pub-lications featured in this nineteenth edition were chosen for excellence in design.

The Best of Newspaper Design, 19th edition, features: Text in English and Spanish; 840 awards: World's Best-Designed Newspapers, Best of Show, Gold medals, Judges' Special Recognition, Silver medals, and Awards of Excel-lence. More than 12,100 entries were reviewed from hundreds of publications from around the world to select winners from 158 publications. Categories included: Overall design, news, features, portfo-lios, special coverage, special sections, magazines, art and illustration, photog-raphy, informational graphics and

Selected by a panel of 21 judges of the Society for News Design, the award-winning pub-lications featured in this nineteenth edition were chosen for excellence in design.Continuing to pay tribute to the world's best newspa-per designs, the 19th edition of The Best of Newspaper Design is a stun-ning collection of modern work. The included works were selected from more than 10,000 entries submitted by newspapers all over the world. This exceptional collection is an essential reference for anyone involved in print media, graphics, photography, design, journalism, or communications.

The competition, which is sponsored annually by the Society of News Design and the S.I. Newhouse School of Public Communications at Syracuse University, recognizes excellence in newspaper design and graphics. Awards include Best of Show, Gold, Silver, Award of Excellence, Special Recogni-tion, plus the honor of World's Best Designed Newspaper. Categories for judging include overall page design, portfolio, magazine cover design, art and illustration, photo jour-nalism, and informational graphics.

This nineteenth edition presents the finest newspaper design in the field.

Selected by a panel of judges of

Continuing to pay tribute to the world's best newspaper designs, the 19th edition of The Best of Newspaper Design is a stunning collection of mod-ern work. The included works were selected from more than 10,000 entries submitted by newspapers all over the world. This exceptional collection is an essential reference for anyone involved in print media, graphics, photography, design, journalism, or communica-tions.

The competition, which is sponsored annually by the Society for News Design and the S.I. Newhouse School of Public Communications at Syracuse University, recognizes excellence in newspaper design and graphics. Awards include Best of Show, Gold, Silver, Award of Excellence, Special Recogni-tion, plus the honor of World's Best Designed Newspaper. Categories for judging include overall page design, portfolio, magazine cover design, art and illustration, photo jour-nalism, and informational graphics.

This nineteenth edition presents the finest newspaper design in the field.

Selected by a panel of judges of the Society of News Design, the award-winning newspapers featured in this nineteenth edition were chosen for excellence in design.

Selected by a panel of 21 judges of the Society for News Design, the award-winning pub-lications featured in this nineteenth edition were chosen for excellence in design.Continuing to pay tribute to the world's best newspa-per designs, the 19th edition of The Best of Newspaper Design is a stun-ning collection of modern work. The included works were selected from more than 10,000 entries submitted by newspapers all over the world. This exceptional collection is an essential reference for anyone involved in print media, graphics, photography, design, journalism, or communications.

The competition, which is sponsored annually by the Society for News Design and the S.I. Newhouse School of Public Communications at Syracuse University, recognizes excellence in newspaper design and graphics. Awards include Best of Show, Gold, Silver, Award of Excellence, Special Recogni-tion, plus the honor of World's Best Designed Newspaper. Categories for judging include overall page design, portfolio, magazine cover design, art and illustration, photo jour-nalism, and informational graphics.

This nineteenth edition presents the finest newspaper design in the field.

Selected by a panel of 21 judges of

Continuing to pay tribute to the world's best newspaper designs, the 19th edition of The Best of Newspaper Design is a stunning collec-tion of modern work. The included works were selected from more than 10,000 entries submitted by newspa-pers all over the world. This excep-tional collection is an essential refer-ence for anyone involved in print media, graphics, photography, design, journalism, or communica-tions.

The competition, which is spon-sored annually by the Society for News Design and the S.I. Newhouse School of Public Communications at Syracuse University, recognizes excellence in newspaper design and graphics. Awards include Best of Show, Gold, Silver, Award of Excellence, Special Recogni-tion, plus the honor of World's Best Designed Newspaper. Categories for judging include overall page design, portfolio, magazine cover design, art and illustration, photo journalism, and informational graphics.

This nineteenth edition presents the finest newspaper design in the field.

Selected by a panel of 21 judges of the Society for News Design, the award-winning pub-lications featured in this nineteenth edition were chosen for excellence in design.

The Best of Newspaper Design, 19th edition, features: Text in English and Spanish; 840 awards: World's Best-Designed Newspapers, Best of Show, Gold medals, Judges' Special Recognition, Silver medals, and Awards of Excel-lence. More than 12,100 entries were reviewed from hundreds of publications from around the world to select winners from 158 publications. Categories included: Overall design, news, features, port-folios, special coverage, special sec-tions, magazines, art and illustration, photography, informational graphics and redesign. Selected by a panel of 21 judges of the Society for News Design, the award-winning pub-lica-tions featured in this nineteenth edi-tion were chosen for excellence in design.

BLACK & WHITE AND/OR ONE COLOR
TWO OR MORE COLORS
PORTFOLIO BY ONE ARTIST
PORTFOLIO BY MORE THAN ONE ARTIST

Society of News Design, the award-winning newspapers featured in this nineteenth edition were chosen for excellence in design.

Selected by a panel of 21 judges of the Society for News Design, the award-winning pub-lications featured in this nineteenth edition were chosen for excellence in design.

The Best of Newspaper Design, 19th edition, features: all text in

Selected by a panel of 21 judges of the Society for News Design, the award-winning pub-lications featured in this nineteenth edition were chosen for excellence in design.

The Best of Newspaper Design, 19th edition, features: Text in English and Spanish; 840 awards: World's Best-Designed Newspapers, Best of Show, Gold medals, Judges' Special Recognition, Silver medals, and

the Society for News Design, the award-winning pub-lications featured in this nineteenth edition were chosen for excellence in design.

The Best of Newspaper Design, 19th edition, features: Text in English and Spanish; 840 awards: World's Best-Designed Newspapers, Best of Show, Gold medals, Judges' Special Recognition, Silver medals, and Awards of Excel-lence. More than

Continuing to pay tribute to the world's best newspaper designs, the 19th edition of The Best of Newspaper Design is a stunning col-lection of modern work. The included works were selected from more than 10,000 entries submitted by newspa-pers all over the world. This excep-tional collection is an essential refer-ence for anyone involved in print media, graphics, photography, design,

Silver
**Dagens
Nyheter**
Stockholm,
Sweden
Stina Wirsén, Illustration
Director/Artist

Silver
Dagens Nyheter
Stockholm, Sweden
Stina Wirsén, Illustration Director/Artist

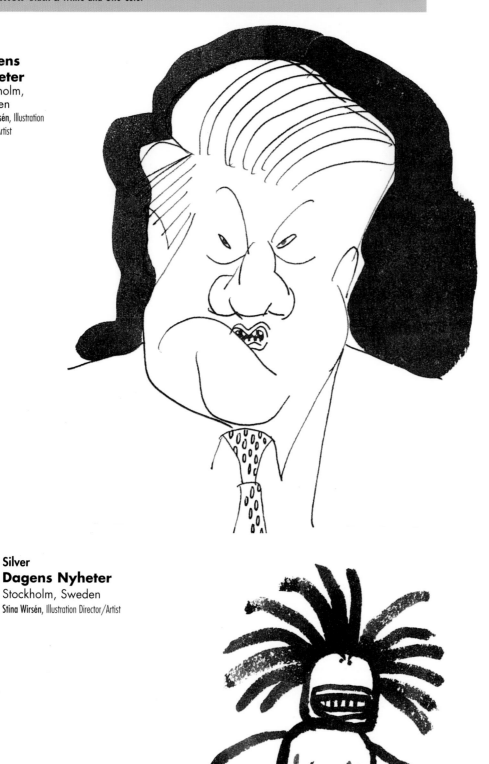

Silver
Dagens Nyheter
Stockholm, Sweden
Stina Wirsén, Illustration Director/Artist

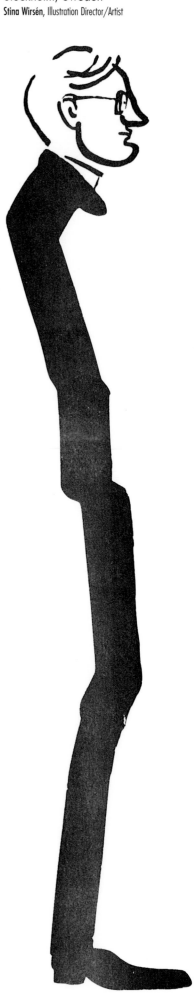

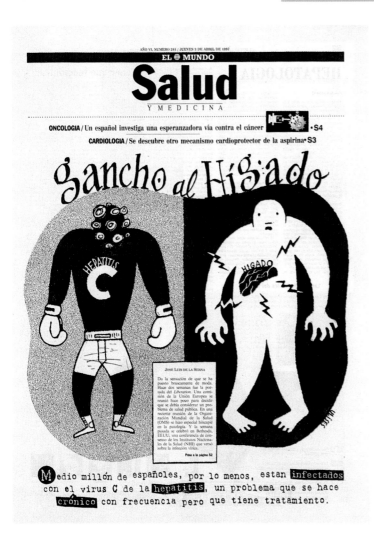

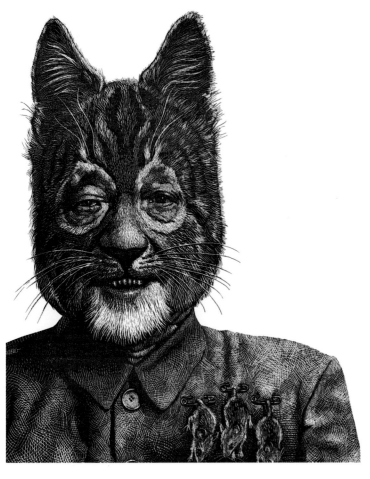

Silver
•Also an **Award of Excellence** for Travel Page
El Mundo Del Siglo XXI
Madrid, Spain
Ulises Culebro, Illustrator & Designer; **Carmelo Caderot**, Design Director;
Manuel de Miguel, Assistant Art Director

Silver
•Also an **Award of Excellence** for Other Page
San Jose Mercury News
San Jose, CA
Rebecca Hall, Illustrator & Designer

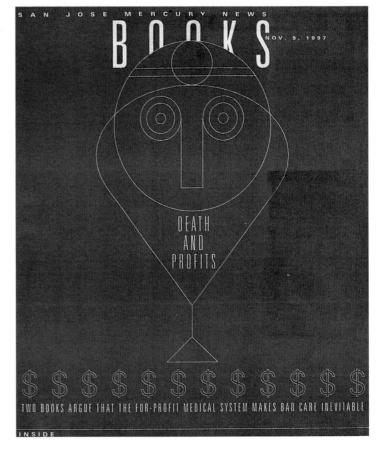

Silver
El Mundo Del Siglo XXI
Madrid, Spain
Ricardo Martínez, Illustrator

Award of Excellence
El Mundo Del Siglo XXI
Madrid, Spain
Ricardo Martínez, Illustrator

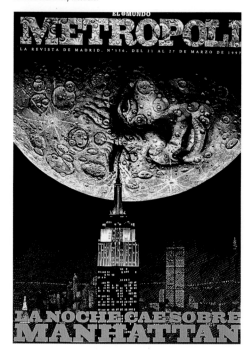

Award of Excellence
Dagens Nyheter
Stockholm, Sweden
Claes Jurander, Freelance Artist

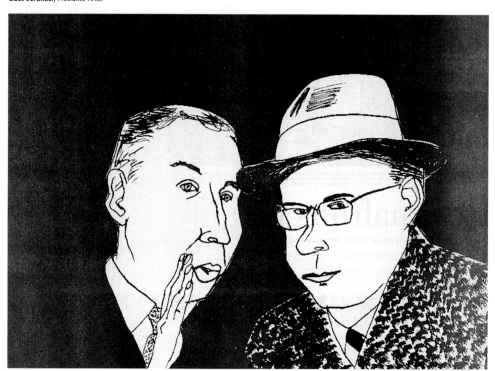

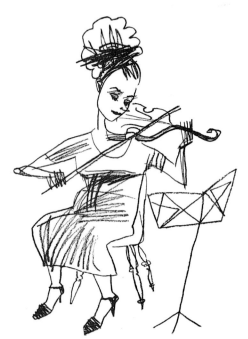

Award of Excellence
Dagens Nyheter
Stockholm, Sweden
Molly Bartling, Freelance Artist

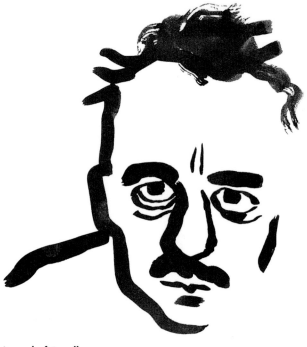

Award of Excellence
Dagens Nyheter
Stockholm, Sweden
Stina Wirsén, Illustration Director/Artist

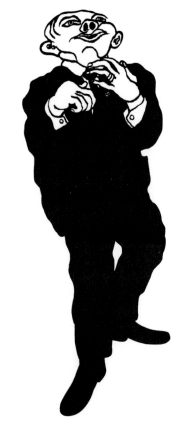

Award of Excellence
Dagens Nyheter
Stockholm, Sweden
Andreas Berg, Freelance Illustrator

Award of Excellence
El Mundo Del Siglo XXI
Madrid, Spain
Ulises Culebro, Illustrator

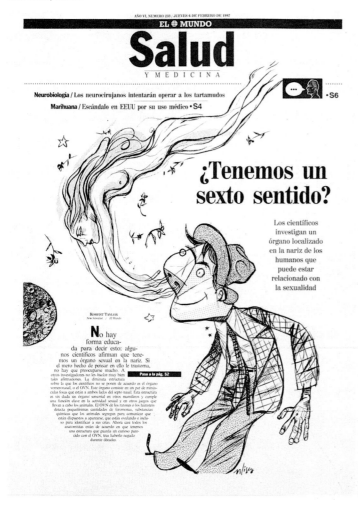

Award of Excellence
El Mundo Del Siglo XXI
Madrid, Spain
Raul Arias, Illustrator

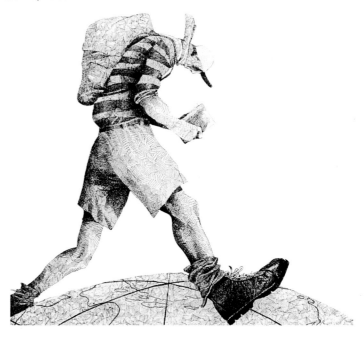

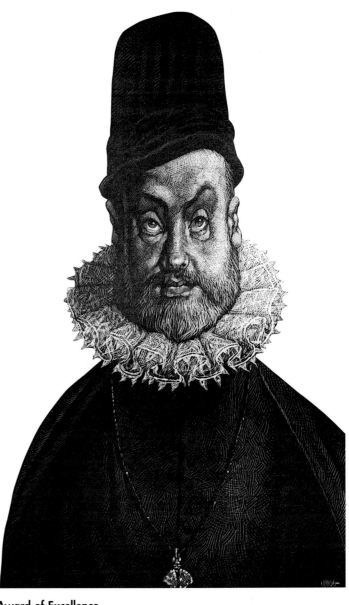

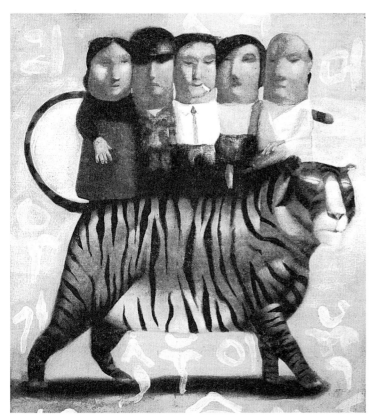

Award of Excellence
Pittsburgh Post-Gazette
Pittsburgh, PA
Stacy Innerst, Illustrator

Award of Excellence
El Mundo Del Siglo XXI
Madrid, Spain
Ricardo Martínez, Illustrator

Gold
Dagens Nyheter
Stockholm, Sweden

Stina Wirsén, Artist

Awarded a **Gold Medal** for its use of white space in this piece of work. Color is not over used, so the tone of the pastels is enhanced. The fine detail also adds strength to the artwork. This is a very witty piece.

● ● ● ● ●

Ganadora de una Medalla de Oro por su uso del espacio en blanco en esta obra. No se abusa del color, por lo que se resalta las tonalidades pastel. El detalle pequeño añade fuerza al trabajo de arte. Un trabajo muy inteligente.

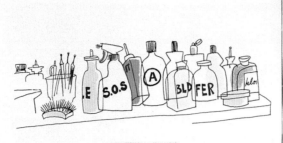

text: ANN PERSSON foto: STINA WIRSÉN

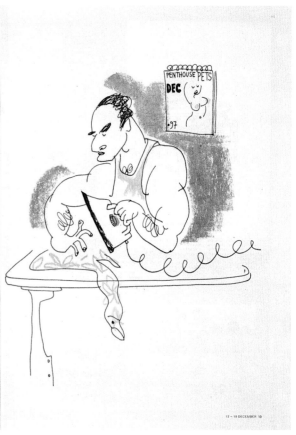

kem

Bland ångrumpor och trasiga armbågar. Efterfrågan står still, men utbudet har exploderat. Stockholms kemtvättar har blivit flera hundra till antalet, till vissas förtret, till andras nödtorft. På stan har gjort en rundvandring i en turbulent bransch på marginalen.

LENNART JACOBSSON HADE de försvunna maskinerna i Europa. I den tvättade han it Olof Palme, kungafamiljen och it vår egen Kennedy, högerpartiets Yngve Holmberg. Då, på sextiotalet, var det modernt med tygor som tappade stilen i vanligt vatten. Kemtvättmaskningen i miljön sat att kjolet var elegant och måste tvättas varsamt.

Skylterna som berättar om Lennart Jacobsson finns kvar i kemtvätten på Kungsholmen. Den tånd de fina kunderna står ondmettällt i fikarummet. Men utre vid kassan har den nuvarande ägaren

Chabo Gabod lätt den förre ägarens optimistiskt tuschretaade skylta hänga kvar. "Vägar du tvätta själv?" "Lätett", på sin tid ett sudervrek, fena också kvar. På den fjerstyrda, rotessade skenor vättar fortfarande pajetklänning ar och fyberveracka på sina ägare. Kostain på inlämningsingskontot rattas in med spokans od kassan. Lnete rutlar och det prasslat i plasfärstraden över de nytvättade kläderna. En dask funkläsning rinner frant. Precis som förr då det var lite rysehigt med kläder som barn hem i plastsäck. Tulen har stätt still och debten finns

kvar, samtidigt som Chabo Gabod meeatavat i en ny stor maskin från kemtvättens quispentland, Tysklnd. Men var finns de nya kunderna? Kemtvättnsjobsheden är en gftkniske förmedvettna måmniskot som tvättar själva. I böjjan av nittiotalet började it långa hem och tillbaka. Några köpte kostymet och oss skjortor, sldatna som pappa bat på bilderna i familjealbunet. Och kostymer från svenska Tiger eller NK Trend kins tne bruntna, tnte ens i trettio grader. Men kemtvättade kläder bäktar fortfarande av gammal uppstoppad fågel, tycker han.

Bara enden, kemisk tvätt, tie en del att tysa. Efterfrågan står still. Men utbudet har exploderat. På Kungsholmen finns minst as ställen som tar emot kläder och skickar it sig den till andra tvätterier. I hela Stockholm har tre-, fyrahundra ställen öppnat. Sveriges Tvätteriförbund har tappat räkningen. Och de är arga. I go-takts början fick var och varannan gatstump en egen kemtvätt. Skräddare från textilfabrikerna i Turkiet, Syrien, Lbanon, Irak och Iran som öppnade eget i

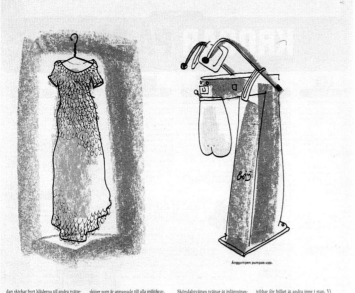

Ånggumpen pumpas upp.

dan skickar bort kläderna till andra tvätterier.
– De förstör branschen, säger en kemtvättare som vill vara anonym.
Kemtvättsbranschen lever på marginalen.
Bo Österlund, ordförande i Stockholms Tvätteriförening, säger:
– Vi i branschen ser vad det kostar att betala miljöavgifter och skatter förstår inte hur de nyetablerade kan hålla så låga priser.
– Det kostar mycket att köpa nya ma-

skiner som är anpassade till alla miljökrav. Men kanske, lägger han till, borde vi också anpassa våra tjänster efter nya behov.
Men Rafael Berjemo, vd på Internationella företagarföreningen som hjälper invandrare att starta eget, ser en konservativ gammal bransch och en skara arbetslösa som vill arbeta.
– Att ta emot kläder i ett hål i väggen och sedan skicka iväg dem till ett större tvätteri ger lägre priser, gynnar konsumenten och är helt rätt i tiden, menar han.
– Golvet är trasigt och bubbligt, säger ägaren Abdul Batti. Jag sa att vi inte har råd att bygga om. Det skulle kosta 50.000 kronor. De som tvättar själva tycker att vi

Sköndalstvätten tvättar åt inlämningsställen. Unga män i shorts och linne stryker med ångande järn. Gamla ångdockor bläser upp sig. Fracken stricker på it över ett stadigt luftbröst. Ångrumpan vässer i ett par byxor så att hänget kan strykas bort.
Sköndalstvätten blev nyligen utestluen ur Sveriges Tvätteriförbund.
– Det är billigt åt andra inne i stan. Vi tvättar åt femton olika ställen.
– Om folk inte tycker att vi tvättar ordentligt får de gå till allmänna reklamationsnämnden, säger Abdul Batti.
I den fridfulla kemtvätten strider en gammal-bransch med nya företagare på liv och död.
Tvätterier borde ha framtiden för sig. Moderna, miljövänliga hjälpinrättningar för ostrukna männskor med konstiga fläckar, som jag.

ANN PERSSON

Vad är kemtvätt?
Engelskans Dry Cleaning bidrar till förvirringen. Man kan väl inte tvätta torrt?
Vid vattentvätt används vatten för att ta bort smuts. Kemtvätten använder lösningsmedel. Det vanligaste är fortfarande perkloretylen. För att undvika klor har en del kemtvättar lösgått till kolväten som förvanaågs alltför brandfarliga. Nu finns nya maskiner som minskar brandrisken.
Det finns numera också maskiner för Kemtvätt i vatten.
– En del miljöorganisationer kräver att vi ska tvätta allt i vatten. Jag tror inte att vatten kan ta bort alla fläckar, säger Bo Österlund, ordförande i Stockholms Tvätteriförening.
De flesta kemtvätterier står inför att lösa valproblem när de ska göra nyinvesteringar de närmaste åren, säger Sveriges Tvätteriförbund.

Rysarfläckarna är:
Det är en fördel om man vet vad man spillt på sig. Fläckar tas bort med olika lösningsmedel som ofta sprutas på plagget med en ångpistol före kemtvätten.

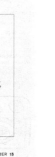

GATUSMUTS OCH SALTSTÄNK
Dessa fläckar har oftast fått torka in i kläderna och måste borstas bort med särskild borste.

BLOD
Oftast har kunden försökt tvätta bort fläckarna hemma, klagar kemtvättaren. Då blir det svårare att få bort fläckarna eftersom höga vattentemperaturer gör att äggvitämnena "brinns" fast i tyget.

GRÄS
I gräs och bärsaft er finns tannin, som gör att dessa fläckar "inte heller är särskilt roliga", enligt kemtvättarna.

BLÄCK
Bläckfläckar är svårast att få bort från kemtvättsyggen där färgen sitter sig fast.

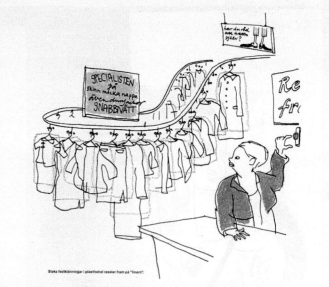

Slaka festklänningar i plastfodral rasslar fram på "linern".

▶ innerstan. De syr på maskiner köpta från den nedlagda tekoindustrin i Borås och tar emot innerstadsbornas samlade ångest. Skor som gått ner sig. nycklar som tappats bort, trasiga blixtlås i dyra barnoveraller, stearin från ifjol på julduken och trasiga armbågar på lammullströjan.
Det finns barnkvevideo, en blomsteraffärer som börjat ta emot tvätt.
En resande affärsman från Norge har inte tid. Han kör sina skjortor hemma i maskinen och lämnar sedan in en plastpåse tygbollar till kemtvätten i kvarteret på

Söder. För femton kronor styck stryker Amin Mohamed dem.
Amin Mohamed talar om hyran. I somras tog han över efter en kille från Syrien, som inte klarade hyran. Innan killen från Syrien kom hit var det en grekisk samlingslokal. Och innan dess ett förlag.
Fanns det mer jobb för familjen för sig. Soldk han kunna dela lokalen med en kompis. Snart får han inte längre "starta eget bidrag" och värden vill ha femtusen mer i månaden. Som 10-åring började Amin Mohamed arbeta i kusinens textilfabrik i Bagdad där man

sydde av tyger från Italien. Han rymde från armén under kriget mot Iran, först till Moskva och sedan kom han till Arlanda 1992.
Mitt i skylfönstret tronar en häst av brons i en förpackning med amerikanska stjärnor. En tändare från tiden då det var status att röka. I spruchen cellofanpåse ligger en nyckelring med en klassisk plast, som den förre ägaren lämnade kvar.
Här kan tioåringen hitta kedjor att fästa i de hängiga byxorna. Och nittiotals-

yuppien finner ungerska skoborstar med 100 procent Rosshaar för att värda fetischerna som köpts snordyrt på Biblioteksgatan.
En upplevn familjefader kommer in med ungen i barnvagn. Snabbt och nu vill han få en nyckelkopia. Han lägger flera minuter av sin dyrbara tid på att förklara hustruns slarv. Mattorna skickar Amin Mohamed till Sundbyberg. Kläderna till ett tvätteri på Kungsholmen.
Tvätteriförbundet har talat om "göra rent hus" med inlämningsställena som se-

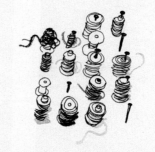

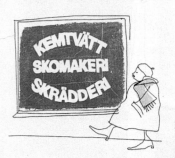

KEMTVÄTT
SKOMAKERI
SKRÄDDERI

Gold
•Also **Silver** for Fashion Page
Dagens Nyheter
Stockholm, Sweden
Stina Wirsén, Illustration Director/Artist; **Anneli Steen**, Designer

Awarded a **Gold Medal**, these pages exhibit a daring use of fashion. They are uniquely modern and set a high standard in editorial illustration. There is a contemporary and original use of illustration, bearing in mind the content.

Ganadoras de una Medalla de Oro estas páginas muestran un osado uso de la moda. Son singularmente modernas y sientan un alto precedente en la ilustración editorial. He aquí un uso de la ilustración contemporáneo y original, que tiene en cuenta el contenido

---

DN Söndag

DAGENS NYHETER SÖNDAGEN DEN 12 OKTOBER 1997 3

MODE

Kläderna som lockar fram
vilddjuret

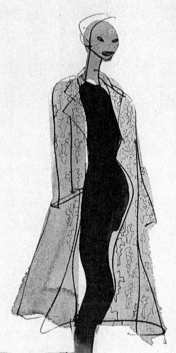

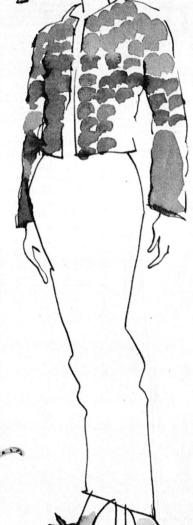

R ovdjur, överallt på Stockholms gator. Varmblodiga vildkatter, kallblodiga reptiler av kvinnokön trängs på bussar och tunnelbanor. I bakhuvudet hör jag Tore Bergers vinylraspigt släpiga stämma sjunga om och om igen att "staden är så full av växter, skogen är så full av skräp..." Jag minns inte hur sången fortsätter, det är någonting om att teaterpjäsens texter fylls av skådespelarknep.

Det skulle kunna vara en ledtråd till varför så många kvinnor samtidigt klär sig i leopard- och ormskinnsmönstrade skor och kläder. Pjäsen de spelar med i år så dålig att de kvinnliga rollerna kräver djurpäls. Kanske har de tagit fram kattungen inom sig, som filmregissören David Lynch rådde skådespelerskan Patricia Arquette inför inspelningen av "Lost Highway".

Kanske vill de inte vara människor längre.

Att djurmönster är modernt, att Hornsgatans skyltfönster är fulla av ozelot- och leopardfläckat, räcker inte te som förklaring. Världen är full av moden som floppat, högar av konstigt skurna och färgade modekläder till reapris i lågprislador. Efterfrågan på djurmönstrat är så stor att leopardfläckarna säljer slut i Hennes & Mauritz butiker. Formgivarna målar päls- och ormmönster på löpande band tills det flimrar framför ögonen. De vill sluta men kan inte, eftersom djurmönstrat säljer.

"Djur ser ju bra ut i päls så varför skulle inte kvinnor göra det?" säger den amerikanske modeskaparen Todd Oldham i en TV-intervju. Valentino trycker leopardfläckar på rockkragar i äkta rävpäls. Alexander McQueens och i synnerhet Jean-Paul Gaultiers av den ryska kejsarinnan Katarina den stora inspirerade haute couture är kallt reptilglatt eller len och klappvänlig som en tigerfäll i syntet. Det allra billigaste, kitschens pinupklassiker, har nu nått modets högst prissatta höjder. Till och med Ikea har börjat, en Disneyfläckad dalmatiner har smugit sig in i möbeljättens föräldralycka och hårat ner soffkuddarna. I TV:s kvällsnyheter räddas en drypande våt kvinna i chica ormskinnsmönstrade långbyxor av

tappra brandmän i något översvämmat område i Frankrike. Hon lyfts bokstavligen ur vattnet, ser ut som en dränkt katt.

Som om alla hade läst pälsfetischisten Léopold von Sacher-Masochs erotiska klassiker "Venus i päls" från 1870. Hans Venus är en sublim, bara nödtorftigt pälsinsvept varelse med marmorkropp och döda förstenade ögon. Grym, både kall och varm, "en stor katt, ett kraftfullt elektriskt batteri..." Det är så hondjuren i kvällsrusningen i tunnelbanan ser ut på väg till kvällsmaten och husslavarna hemma i lägenheten. Jägare och jagade, subjekt och objekt, rovdjur och villebråd i ett.

Fast Jytte Meilvang, designern bakom H&M:s Bib-kollektion för stora kvinnor tar upp mig på markniva igen.

– Djurmönster har varit modernt vartannat till vart tredje år, så länge jag kan minnas, säger hon.

Skillnaden är att det nu trycks fint arbetade naturligt färgade vilddjursmönster på fina tygkvaliteter. Hon påstår att djurmönster är "naturligt" och får det att låta både präktigt och politiskt korrekt för människor som hon själv; som tycker att det är otäckt att äta kött och fel att föda upp djur för att ta deras päls.

Staden är plötsligt full av gräsätare.

Text: Susanne Pagold
Illustration: Stina Wirsén

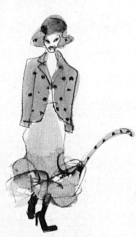

Ormmönstrad kappa från Trussardi.

Fåtöljen "York" från Parker Knoll.

Obestämt djurfläckig kavaj från Moschino.

Krokodilpräglad jacka från Emporio Armani.

Veckan som kommer

Vin, väsen och böcker

Det blir mycket med priser den här veckan också, först ekonomi och sedan kemi och fysik.

Detta när det gäller Nobel och Sverige alltså, om man nu kan räkna ekonomipriset som ett "riktigt" Nobelpris, vilket många inte gör. Komma så där i efterhand och hänga sig på liksom, va? Men kanske är de som klagar över prisets Nobelstatus nu ute i efterhand också – varför se de inte nej till det från början?

I Storbritannien är det dags för prestigefyllda Bookerpriset. Det ges till en skönlitterär författare vare och brukar sprida skadeglädje, hån och bitterhet i skrivande kretsar. Bookerpriset tas på allvar. Att bara vara nominerad gills inte om man inte är debutant. På tisdag blir det klart vem som ska få höra att han/hon givetvis ALDRIG borde ha fått äran.

Av Lena Persson

Samma dag öppnar Bokmässan i Frankfurt, som är årets höjdpunkt för alla som har med böcker i någon form at göra. Ett superjippo av rang som effektivt kan avskaffa alla illusioner om att bokfolk är stillsamma, tillbakadragna och lite musgrå så där. De väsnas väldigt och dricker väldigt mycket vin och rör sig väldigt fort. De som rör sig allra fortast är kvinnliga franska och italienska förlagsredaktörer i skyhöga klackar.

BOKMÄSSAN I FRANKFURT är en upplevelse, men för att kunna njuta av den bör man ligga i träning en månad i förväg och ta semester en vecka efteråt. Man kan ju alltid läsa en bok.

I Sverige är veckan, förutom det här med Nobel, ganska händelsefattig ut. Det vill säga, något kommer ju alltid att hända, antagligen åtskilligt, men ing-

enting som är förutsagt och inbokat på pseudohändelselistorna.

Intressantast verkar kanske LO:s konferens om rapporten "Kultur, Klass, Kön" på torsdag i Stockholm, som handlar om LO-medlemmarnas kulturvanor. "Den goda demensvärden" är det konferens om i två dagar på Karolinska Institutet, det är mässan om "Bättre liv" i Malmö, och i Linköping är det en kurs om smärta och smärtlindring för medicinjournalister. Ekologiska lantbrukare har et seminarium om säker livsmedelsförsörjning, och Röda Korsets Ungdomsförbund ett som heter "Visst kan vi stoppa mobbningen!" och dessutom får vi veta hur Telias nya katalogomslag för 1998 kommer att se ut.

Det låter som en trygg vecka, åtminstone på papperet. En sådan vecka vi alla kan behöva.

Ordet

automatiskt

Vissa ord borde K-märkas. Automatisk, till exempel. Och speciellt om det uttalas så där lite gammaldags: "åtomatisk". Det är ett ord som andas framstegstro och drömmar om ett mindre slitsamt liv. Genast ser man rullband med glasflaskor som fylls med mjölk, finska pinnar som långsamt sänker och hör klappvänlig vare. Jägare och jagade, som fört under mandel- och sockerströare eller konfekt som paketeras i papper.

Numera finns ingenting att se! Ta pengar till exempel. De svischar mellan olika konton, ja hela regnskogar byter ägare i någon abstrakt datorvärld. Frågan är om inte våra hjärnor kände sig alldeles lagom moderna vid ett sävligt åtomatiskt rullband?

Åsa Beckman
litteraturkritiker i DN

Noterat

sexistiskt värre

Svenskar brukar tycka att de politiska debatterna i det brittiska underhuset är uppfriskande med sina verbala rallarsvingar.

Men angreppen kan vara både de grova och kränkande, har Labourpartiets nya kvinnliga parlamentsledamöter upptäckt. I veckan klagade de över alla sexistiska kommentarer som riktas mot dem från Torybänkarna.

– Gå hem och laga mat till din man i stället, skallar ropen från motsatta sidan.

Eller:

– Hon ska ha mens.

Om hon inte påstås vara i klimakteriet, förstås.

Labourkvinnorna betecknar sig för tillmälena, som de antar att Tory-ledamöterna på de bakre bänkarna "har lärt sig på

sina privatskolor". Om inte svinaktigheterna upphör tänker de gå till talmannen, Betty Boothroyd. De hotar också med att nagelfara gamla TV-inspelningar av debatterna i jakt på syndare. Parlamentet får inte vara en drängstuga.

Det har varit svårt att få svar på tal från Tory-sidan, men de som har givits kan sammanfattas med orden: Vad har kvinnorna där att göra om de inte tål tuffa tag?

Underhuset har alltid varit en manliga klubb (om än inte en gentlemansklubb). När Labour vann så stort i våras blev många nya kvinnor invalda, och var femte Labourledamot är en kvinna.

I Tories parlamentsgrupp är inte ens var trettionde kvinna.

Cecilia Jacobsson
DN:s korrespondent i London

Gold
Dagens Nyheter
Stockholm, Sweden
Stina Wirsén, Illustration Director/Artist

Awarded a **Gold Medal**, these pages exhibit a daring use of fashion. They are uniquely modern and set a high standard in editorial illustration. There is a contemporary and original use of illustration, bearing in mind the content.

• • • • •

Ganadoras de una Medalla de Oro estas páginas muestran un osado uso de la moda. Son singularmente modernas y sientan un alto precedente en la ilustración editorial. He aquí un uso de la ilustración contemporáneo y original, que tiene en cuenta el contenido.

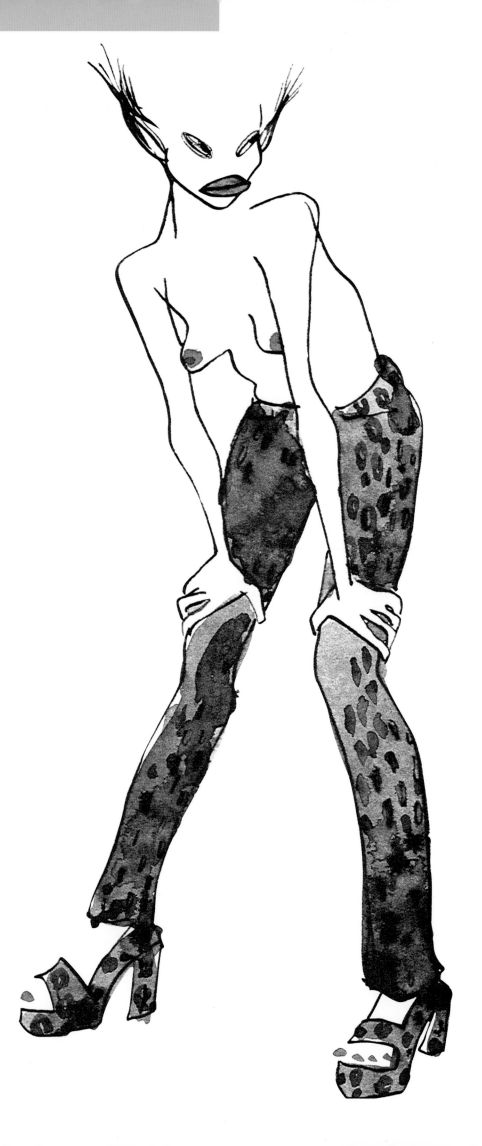

Kittlande lek med nakenhet

Vårmodets spets och chiffong signalerar "se men inte röra"

Silver
Dagens Nyheter
Stockholm, Sweden
Stina Wirsén, Illustration Director/Artist

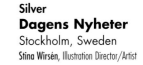

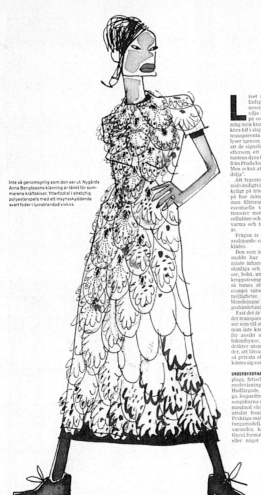

Inte så genomsynlig som den ser ut. Nygårds Anna Bengtssons klänning är tänkt som sommarens kräftskivor. Ytterfodral i stretchig polyesterspets med ett insynsskyddande svart foder i lycrablandad viskos.

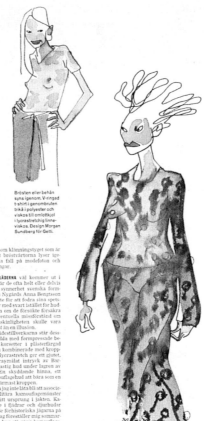

L ivet är en fest i vårmodet. Enligt modeskaparnas prognoser kommer kvinnor att vilja klä sig nakna i vår. Gå på cocktailparty och mottagning men knappast åka buss eller ens köra bil i slöjor och spetsar som är så transparenta att hud och underkläder lyser igenom. I plagg som är så sköra att de signalerar "se men inte röra" eftersom ett barn kan slita sönder tantens dyra klänning i sidenchiffong från Prada bara genom att ta tag i den. Men också att "jag har ingenting att dölja".

Att tygerna är tunna betyder inte nödvändigtvis att det behöver bli kyligt på trädgårdsfesten. Allt beror på hur många lager chiffongtrasor man filtrerar sina bröstvårtor och eventuella tatueringar och operationsärr, för att inte tala om celluliter och fettvalkar. Och hur pass varma och tickande underkläderna är.

Frågan är också vad som är mest avslöjande: ens kropp eller ens underkläder.

Den som är ekonomiskt lagd inser snabbt hur många fler plagg som måste inhandlas ifall alla är genomskinliga och kräver matchande trosor, behå, underklänning, body eller kroppstrumpa. Om klänningarna är så tunna att det krävs minst två ovanpå varandra. Men också vilka möjligheter till färg- och mönsterblandningar lager på lager av gasbindtunna materialen ger.

Fast det är framförallt om trosorna det transparenta modet handlar. Trosor som tål att tittas på av människor man inte känner och heller inte har för avsikt att bli intim med. Inte bikinibyxor, inte shorts eller dansdräkter utan icke-sportiga underkläder, att låtsas avklädd i. Plagg som är så privata att de får betraktaren att känna sig som en inkräktare.

UNDERBYXORNA ÄR VÅRENS stora festplagg, fetisch eller accessoar, enligt modevisningarna i Milano och Paris. Hudfärgade, spetsprydda, skotskrutiga, leopardmönstrade, maskulint kalsongskurna med Y-front för att skapa maximal chockverkan mot de skira, uttalat feminina klänningstygerna. Präktiga midjehöga eller i triangulär tangamodell, kanske flera par ovanpå varandra, kanske med ett G-som-i-Gucci format spänne bak på rumpan, eller något annat dyrt varumärke.

Brösten eller behån syns igenom. V-ringad t-shirt i genombruten trikå i polyester och viskos till omlottkjol i lycrastretchig linneviskos. Design Morgan Sundberg för Getli.

läsbart genom klänningstyget som är så tunt att bröstvårtorna lyser igenom. I alla fall på modefoton och modevisningar.

MEN NÄR KLÄDERNA väl kommer ut i butikerna är de ofta helt eller delvis fodrade. I synnerhet svenska formgivare som Nygårds Anna Bengtsson drar sig inte för att fodra sina spetsklänningar med svart istället för hudfärgat. Som om de försökte försäkra sig mot eventuella missförstånd om att genomskinligheten skulle vara något annat än en illusion.

Underklädestillverkarna står dessutom beredda med formpressade behår och korsetter i plåsterfärgad syntet som kombinerade med kroppstrumpa i lycrastretch ger ett gjutet, nästan spraymålat intryck av Barbiedocksplastig hud under lagren av chiffong. En skyddande hinna, ett slags kamouflagehud att bära som en rustning närmast kroppen.

Själv kan jag inte låta bli att associera till militära kamouflagemönster som har sitt ursprung i jakten. Kamouflerade i fjädrar och djurhudar smög sig de förhistoriska jägarna på sitt byte. Jag föreställer mig sommarens fester, hur ett gäng kamouflagenakna amazoner i chiffong hotfullt närmar sig en oskuldsfullt kostymklädd man. Var ska han fästa blicken någonstans?

Text: Susanne Pagold
Illustration: Stina Wirsén

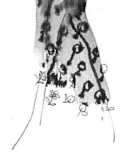

Festfint slöjtunt i transparent jacquardmönstrad viskoscrepe från Bric a brac. Design Malin Isaksson-Engblom, Jeanette Granberg och Christina Wingås. Kjolen säljs med viskosfoder.

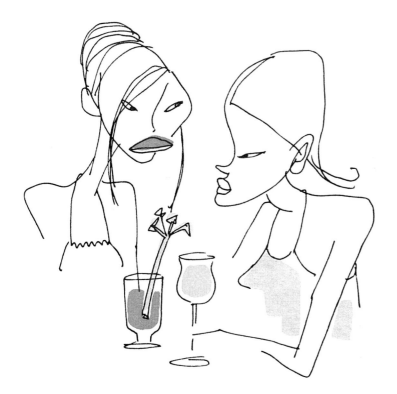

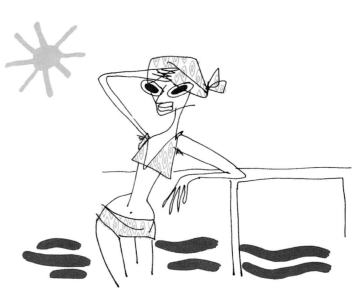

Silver
Dagens Nyheter
Stockholm, Sweden
Stina Wirsén, Illustration Director/Artist

Silver
Dagens Nyheter
Stockholm, Sweden
Stina Wirsén, Illustration Director/Artist

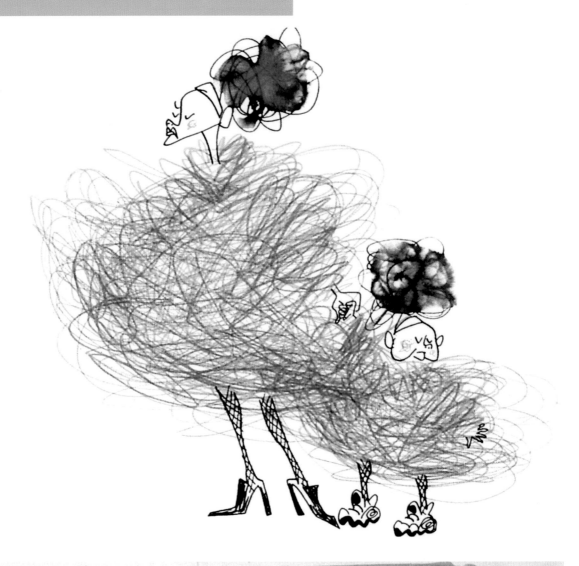

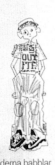

»Kläderna babblar
på oavbrutet. Alla
talar engelska, även
i små storlekar.«

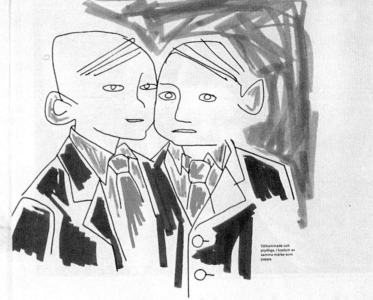

Välkammade och
prydliga, i kostym av
samma märke som
pappa.

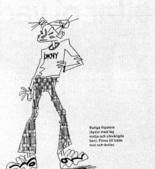

Rutiga hipsters
(byxor med lag
midja och utsvängda
ben). Finns till både
mor och dotter.

»På Stureplan promenerar redan
en och annan tioåring i tröjor med
hennes exklusiva logga, DKNY.«

Många flickor går på
skyhöga Fila-skor, även
små prinsessor. Lila är
höstens färg för flickor.

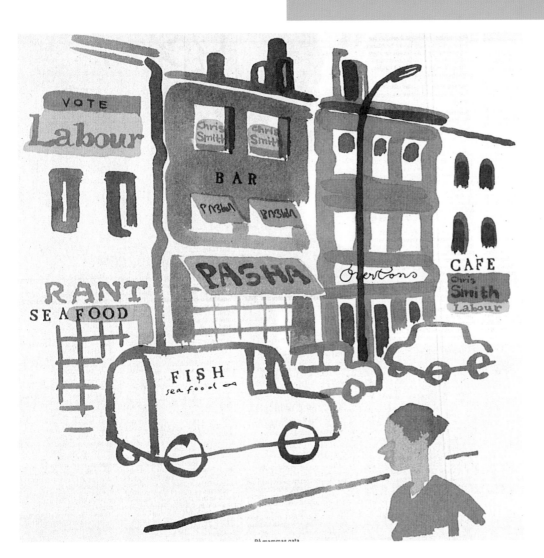

Silver
Dagens Nyheter
Stockholm, Sweden
Stina Wirsén, Illustration Director/Artist

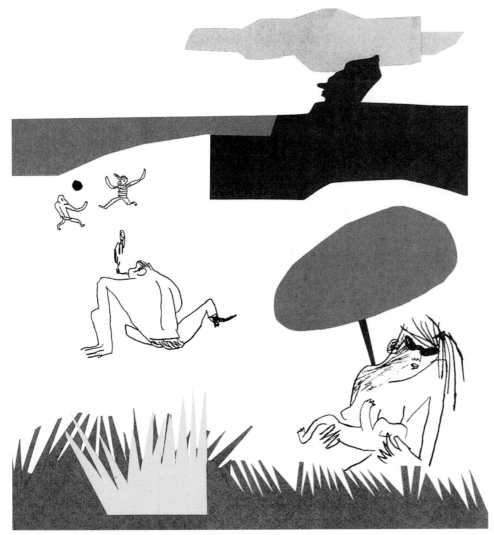

Silver
Dagens Nyheter
Stockholm, Sweden
Sanna Nicklasson, Illustrator

Silver
•Also an **Award of Excellence** for Other Page
El Mundo Del Siglo XXI
Madrid, Spain
Ramon Rodriguez Ramos, Illustrator; **Carmelo Caderot,** Design Director; **Manuel de Miguel,** Assistant Art Director; **Miguel Arzoz,** Designer

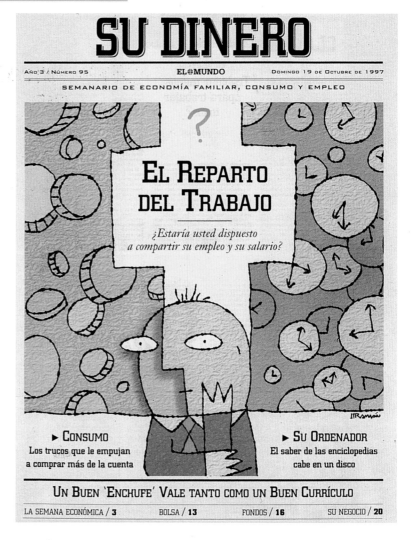

Silver
The New York Times
New York, NY
Anja Kroencke, Illustrator

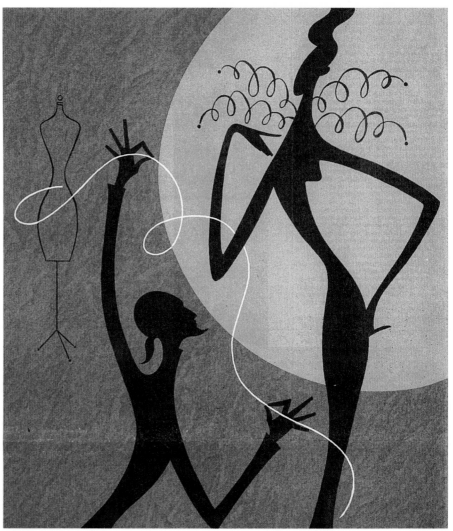

Silver
The New York Times
New York, NY
Caleb Brown, Illustrator

Silver
The New York Times
New York, NY
Nick Dewar, Illustrator

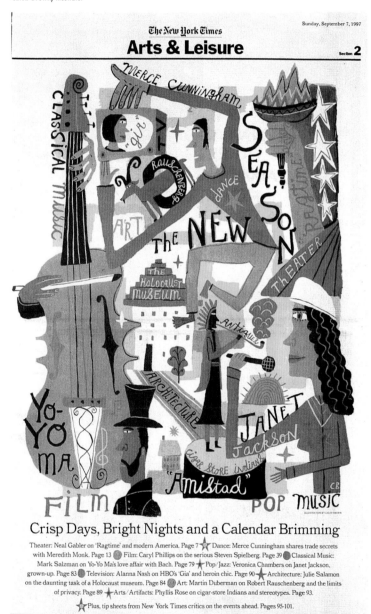

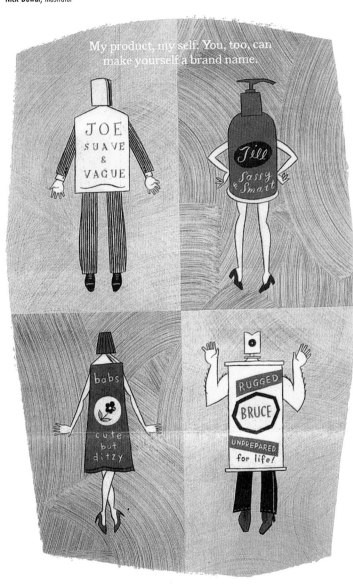

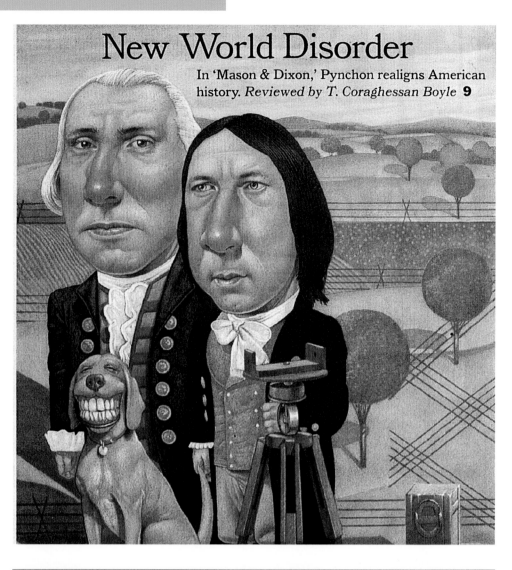

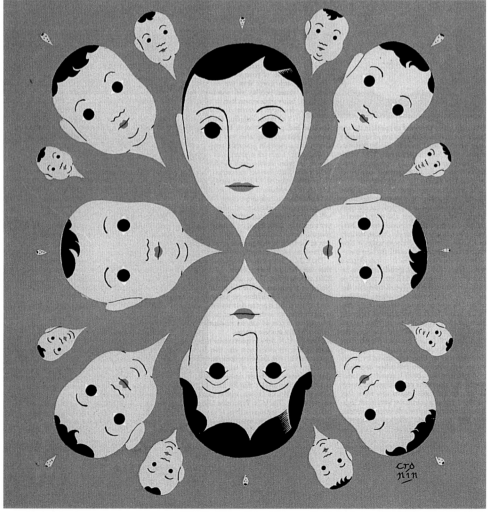

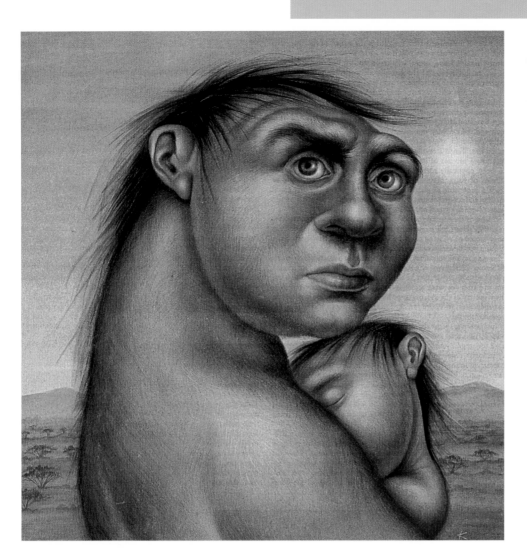

Silver
The New York Times Magazine
New York, NY
Anita Kunz, Illustrator

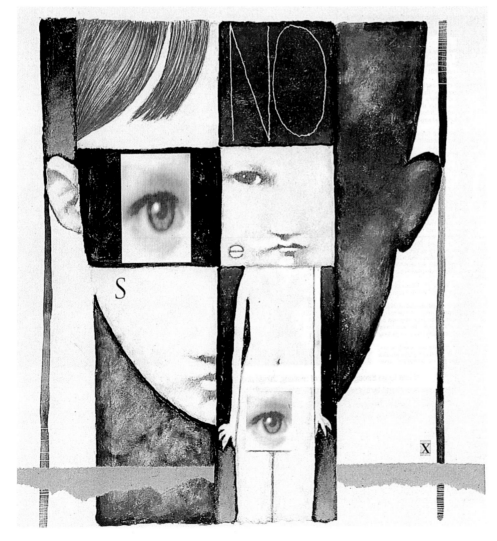

Silver
Sun-Sentinel/Sunshine Magazine
Ft. Lauderdale, FL
Ted Pitts, Illustrator

Silver
The Washington Post Magazine
Washington, DC
Christian Northeast, Illustrator

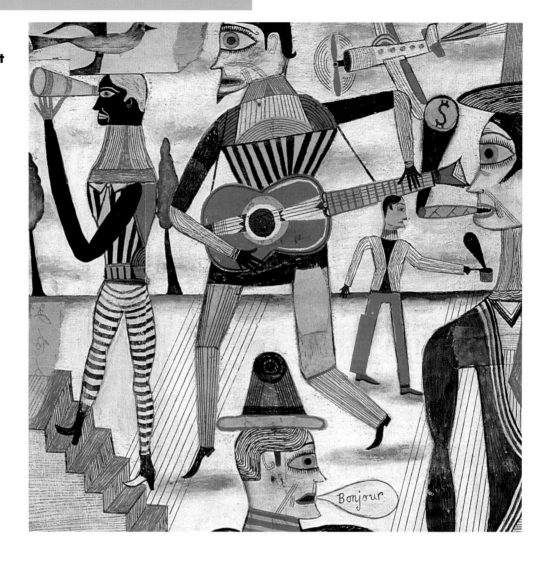

Silver
The Washington Post Magazine
Washington, DC
Kari Alberg, Illustrator

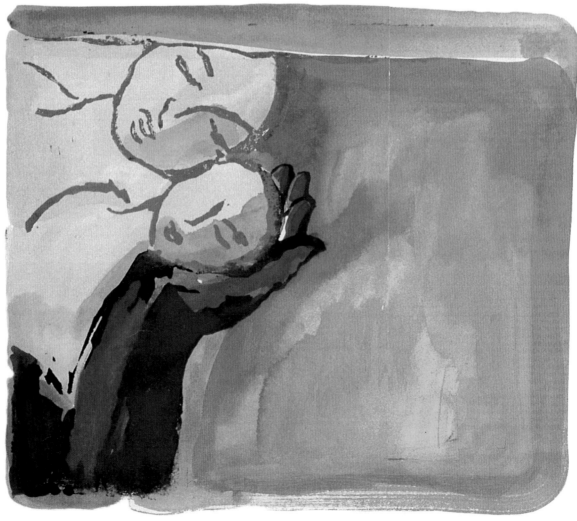

Award of Excellence
Chicago Tribune
Chicago, IL
Greg Clarke, Illustrator

Award of Excellence
Chicago Tribune
Chicago, IL
Heather McAdams, Illustrator

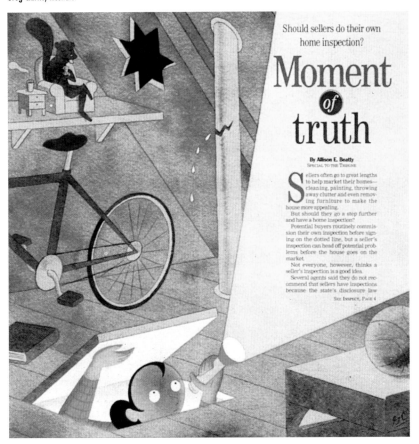

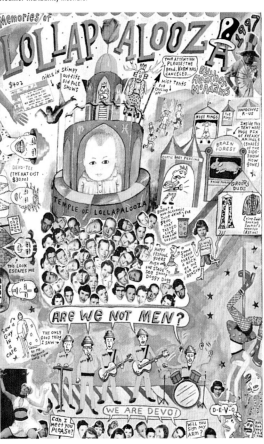

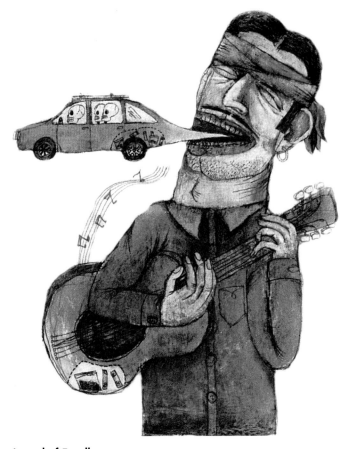

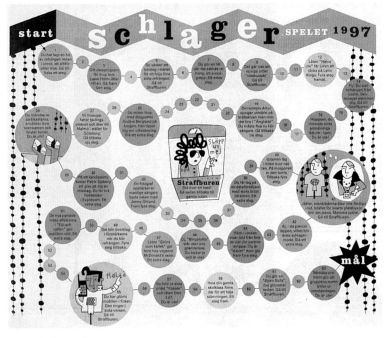

Award of Excellence
Dagens Nyheter
Stockholm, Sweden
Lotta Külhorn, Illustrator; Eva Clementi, Illustrator; Bea Uusma Schyffert, Illustrator

Award of Excellence
Chicago Tribune
Chicago, IL
Tim Hussey, Illustrator

Award of Excellence
Dagens Nyheter
Stockholm, Sweden
Molly Bartling, Freelance Illustrator

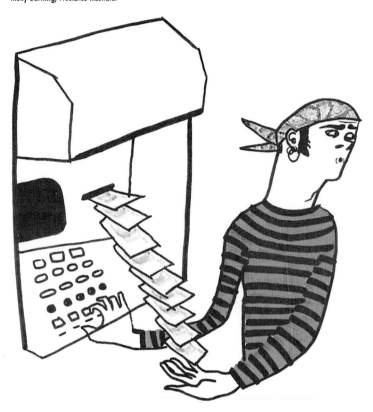

Award of Excellence
Dagens Nyheter
Stockholm, Sweden
Jonas Banker, Freelance Illustrator

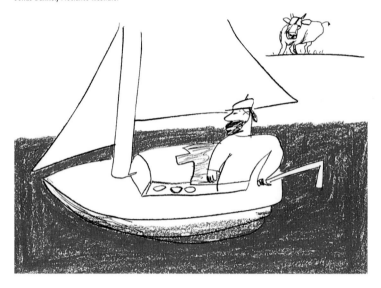

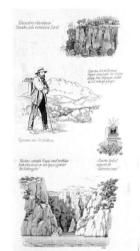
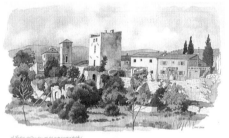
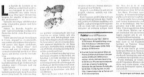

Bergtagen av Provence

Award of Excellence
Dagens Nyheter
Stockholm, Sweden
Jane Bark, Artist

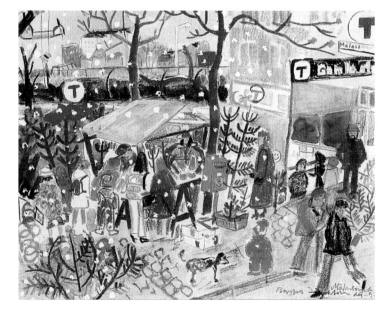

Award of Excellence
Dagens Nyheter
Stockholm, Sweden
Barbro Ingvaldsson, Artist

Award of Excellence
La Gaceta
San Miguel de Tucuman, Argentina
Sebastian Rosso, Illustrator & Designer

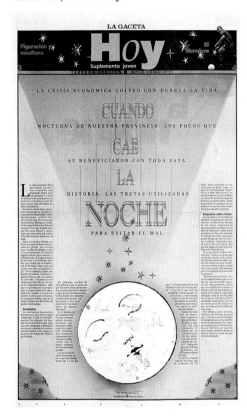

Award of Excellence
Dayton Daily News
Dayton, OH
Tim Borgert, Artist

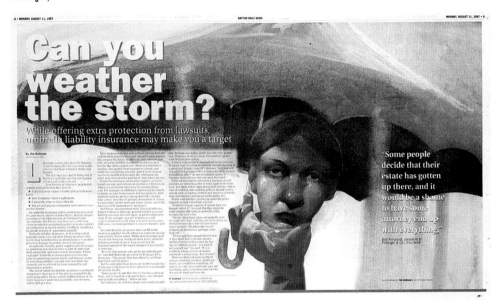

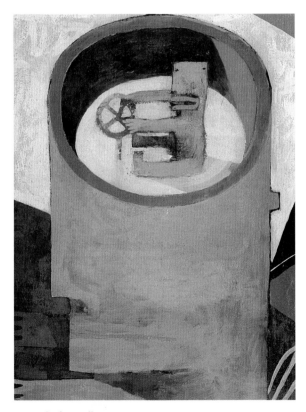

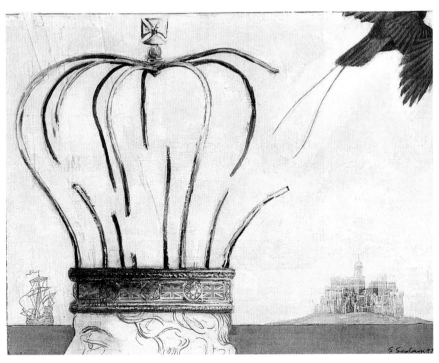

Award of Excellence
Los Angeles Times
Los Angeles, CA
Stephen Sedam, Art Director & Illustrator

Award of Excellence
El Mundo Del Siglo XXI
Madrid, Spain
Raul Arias, Illustrator

Award of Excellence
El Mundo Del Siglo XXI
Madrid, Spain
Toño Benavides, Illustrator

Award of Excellence
El Mundo Del Siglo XXI
Madrid, Spain
Samuel Velasco, Illustrator

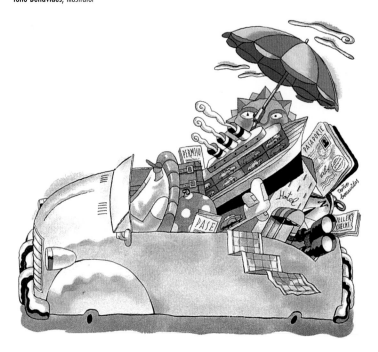

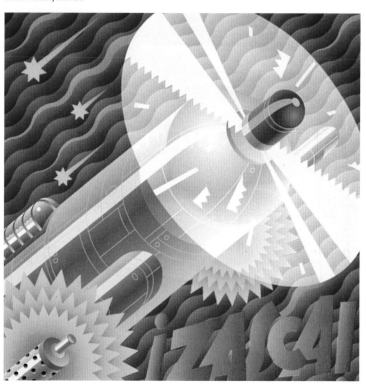

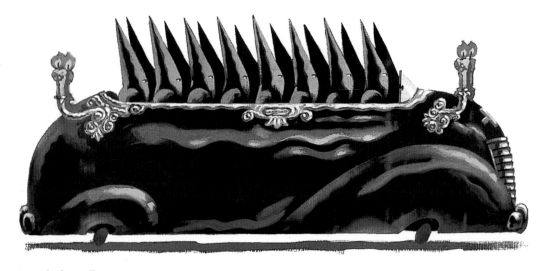

Award of Excellence
El Mundo Del Siglo XXI
Madrid, Spain
Toño Benavides, Illustrator

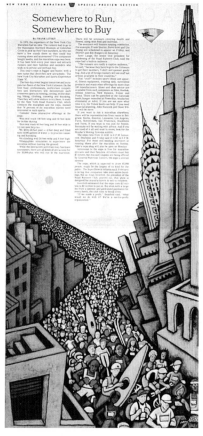

Award of Excellence
The New York Times
New York, NY
Gorka Sampedro, Illustrator

Award of Excellence
The New York Times
New York, NY
Seymour Chwast, Illustrator

Award of Excellence
The New York Times
New York, NY
R.O. Blechman, Illustrator

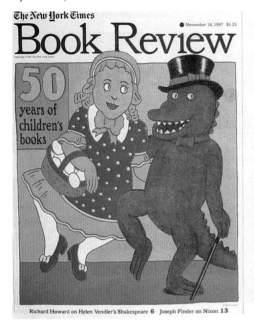

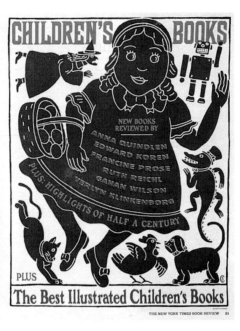

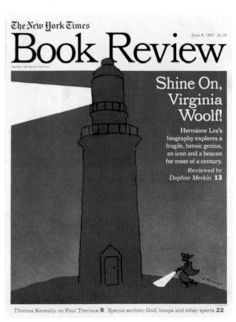

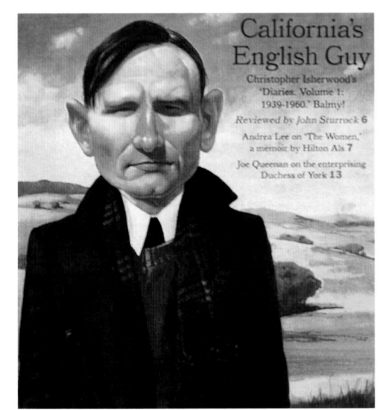

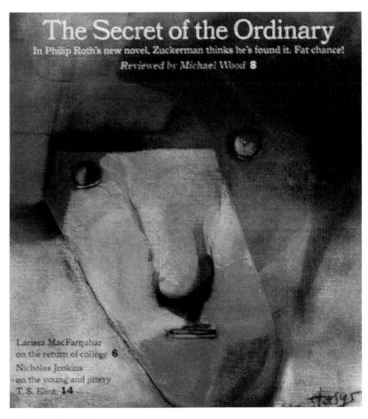

Award of Excellence
The New York Times
New York, NY
C.F. Payne, Illustrator

Award of Excellence
The New York Times
New York, NY
Stasys Eidrigevicius, Illustrator

Award of Excellence
The New York Times
New York, NY
R.O. Blechman, Illustrator

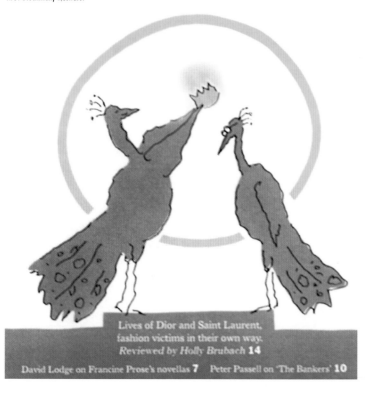

Award of Excellence
The New York Times
New York, NY
Anita Kunz, Illustrator

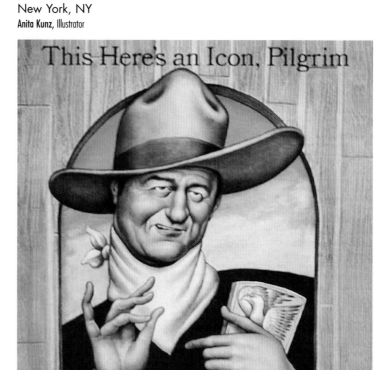

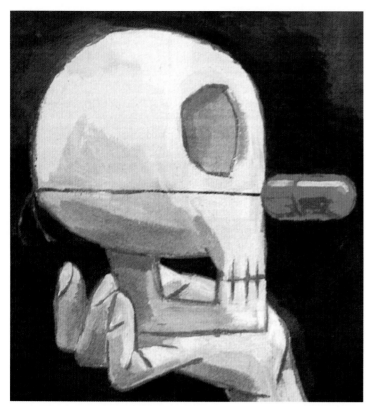

Award of Excellence
The New York Times
New York, NY
Christoph Niemann, Illustrator

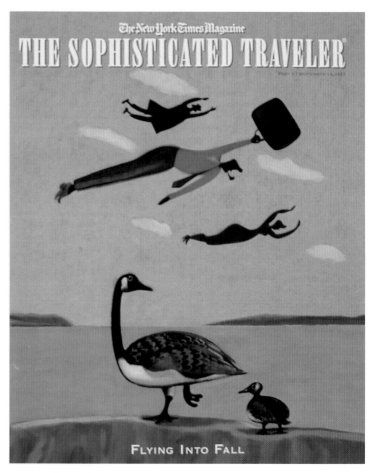

Award of Excellence
The New York Times
New York, NY
Beppe Giacobbe, Illustrator

Award of Excellence
Newsday
Melville, NY
Bob Newman, Illustrator

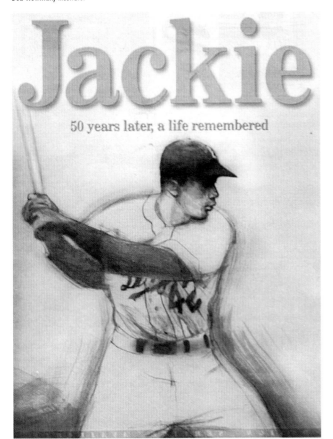

Award of Excellence
Pittsburgh Post-Gazette
Pittsburgh, PA
Stacy Innerst, Illustrator

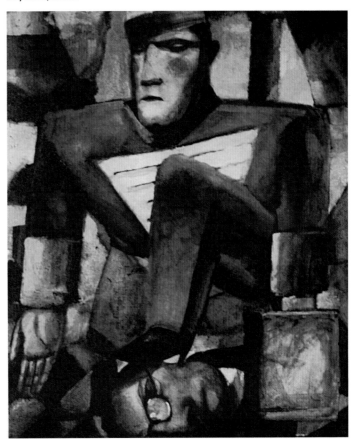

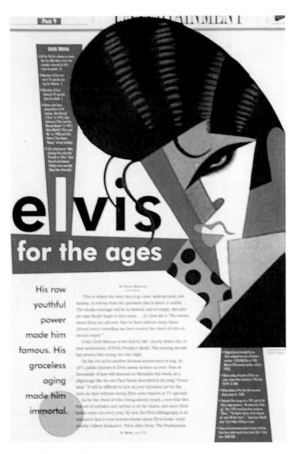

Award of Excellence
The News & Observer
Raleigh, NC
Robin Johnston, Art Director & Designer; David Cowles, Illustrator; Kate Newton Anthony, Features Design Director; Suzanne Brown, Editor

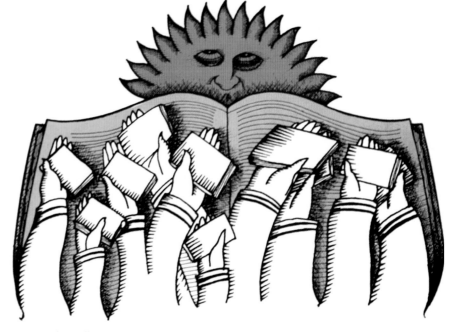

Award of Excellence
Reforma
México City, México
José Luis Barros, Illustrator

Award of Excellence
Reforma
México City, México
Luis Miguel Morales Campero, Illustrator

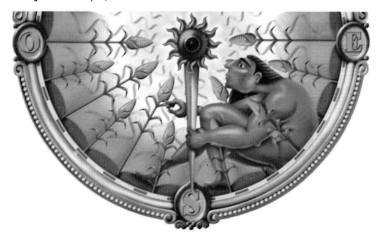

Award of Excellence
San Francisco Examiner
San Francisco, CA
Adam MacCauley, Illustrator

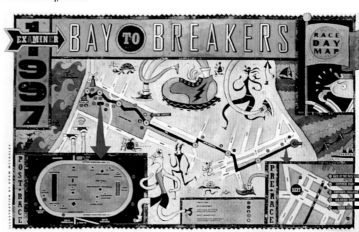

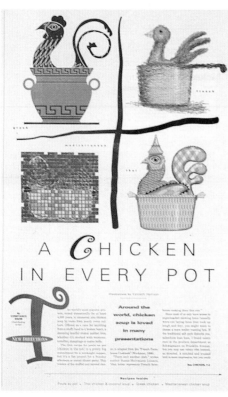

Award of Excellence
The Times-Picayune
New Orleans, LA
Kenneth Harrison, Illustrator

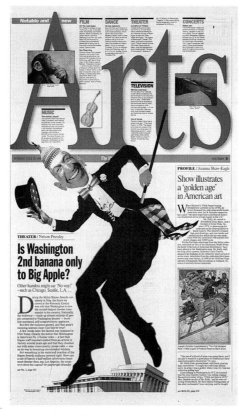

Award of Excellence
The Washington Times
Washington, DC
John Kascht, Illustrator

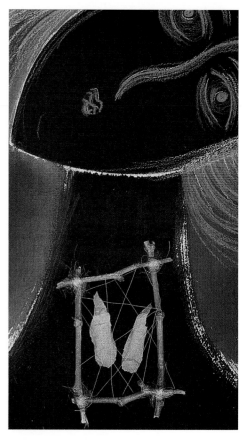

Award of Excellence
San Jose Mercury News
San Jose, CA
Nuri Ducassi, Illustrator

Gold
El Mundo Del Siglo XXI
Madrid, Spain
Toño Benavides, Illustrator

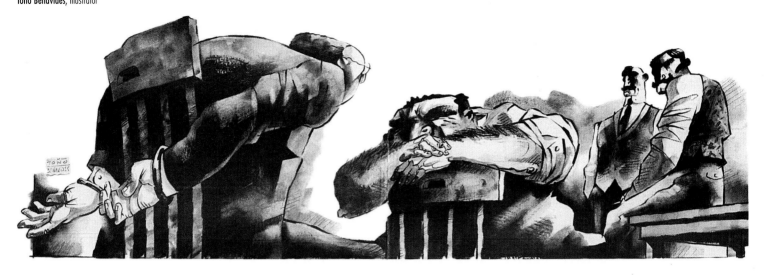

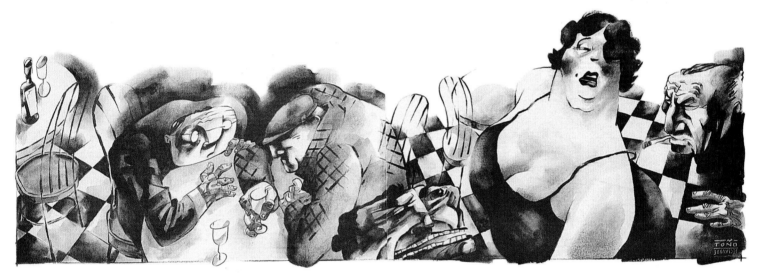

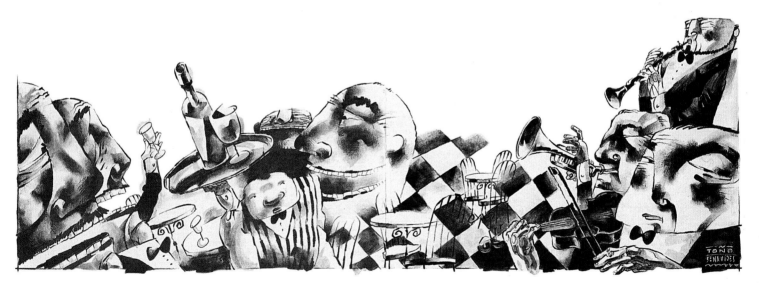

Awarded a **Gold Medal** for the many influences evident throughout these pages. There is a great sense of perspective and the use of gray in the shading is excellent. The unusual movements throughout the illustrations are also well executed.

●●●●●

Ganador de una Medalla de Oro por las muchas influencias evidentes a lo largo de estas páginas. Existe un gran sentido de perspectiva y el uso del gris en el sombreado es excelente. Los movimientos inusuales en todas las ilustraciones también están bien ejecutados.

Gold
El Mundo/La Revista
Madrid, Spain
Ana Juan, Illustrator

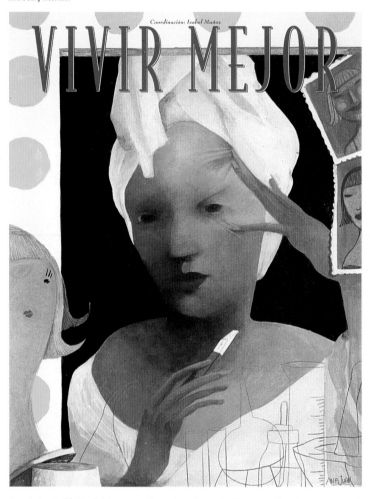

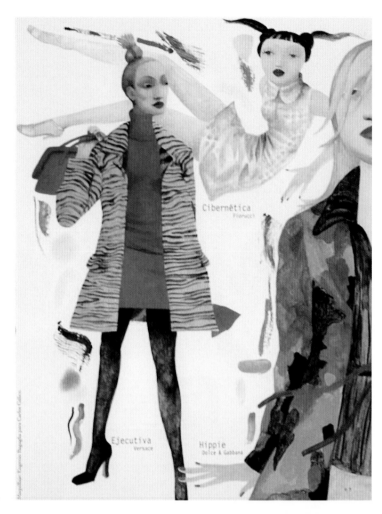

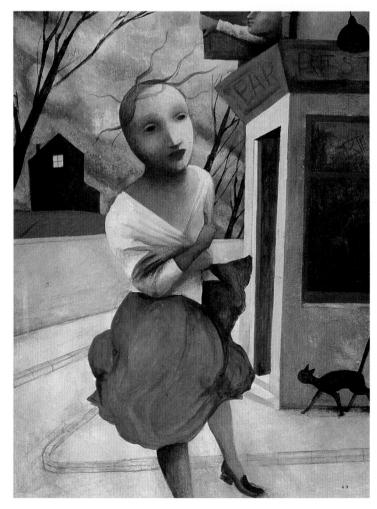

Awarded a **Gold Medal** for its excellent color palette. The illustrator takes chances with a different approach to fashion that we haven't seen before in editorial illustrations.

• • • • •

Ganador de una Medalla de Oro por su excelente gama de colores. El ilustrador toma riesgos y se aproxima a la moda de una manera que nunca hemos visto antes en ilustraciones de editorial.

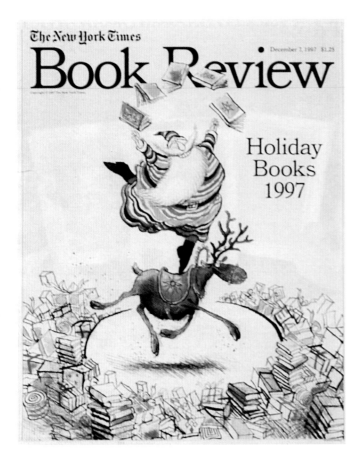

Gold
The New York Times
New York, NY
Ronald Searle, Illustrator

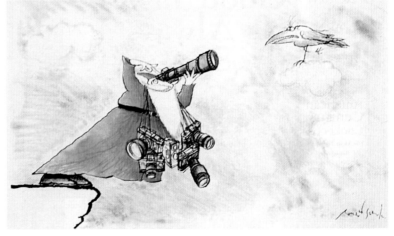

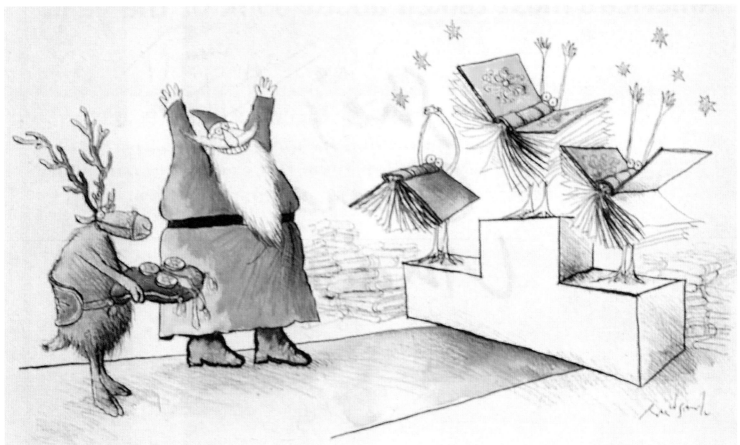

Awarded a **Gold Medal** for pieces that are relentlessly clever. It's a fresh approach with great humor. An absolute delight, and it makes you want to read it all.

• • • • •

Ganadora de una Medalla de Oro por piezas que son inexorablemente ingeniosas. Es un enfoque nuevo con mucho humor. Una delicia absoluta, y hace que uno lo quiera leer todo.

Gold
El Periodico de Catalunya/El Dominical
Barcelona, Spain
El Roto, Illustrator

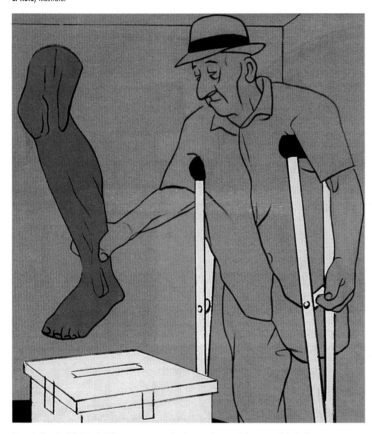

Awarded a **Gold Medal** for its consistently clear and powerful series of dark, humanistic political illustrations. It has a striking use of color which is executed in a direct and uncompromising manner.

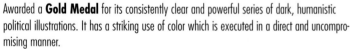

Ganador de una Medalla de Oro por su serie de ilustraciones políticas oscuras y humanísticas siempre claras y potentes. Posee un impactante uso del color el cual es ejecutado de manera directa e intransigente.

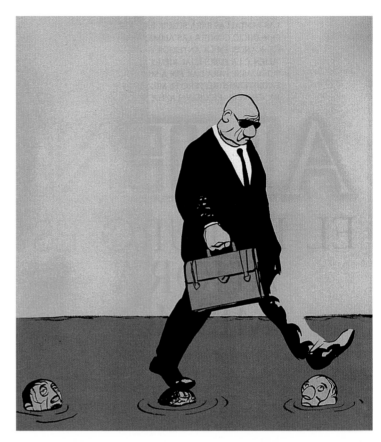

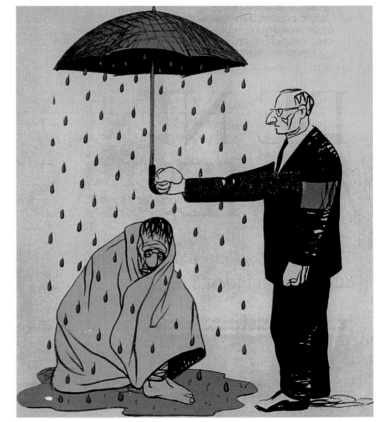

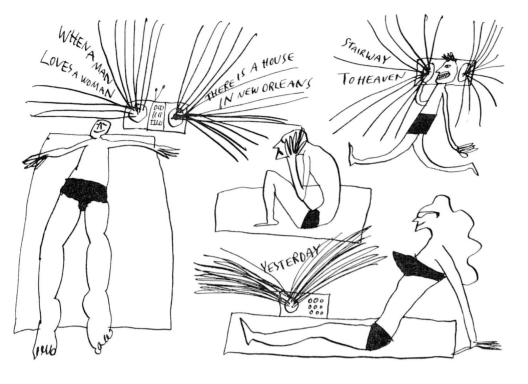

Silver
Dagens Nyheter
Stockholm, Sweden
Klas Fahlén, Illustrator

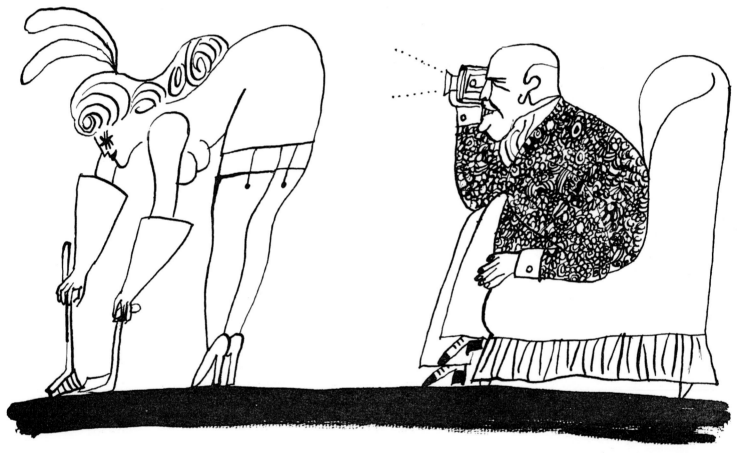

Award of Excellence
El Mundo Del Siglo XXI
Madrid, Spain
Victoria Martos, Illustrator

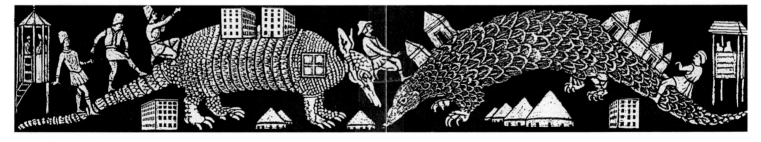

Silver
Dagens Nyheter
Stockholm, Sweden
Jockum Nordstöm, Artist

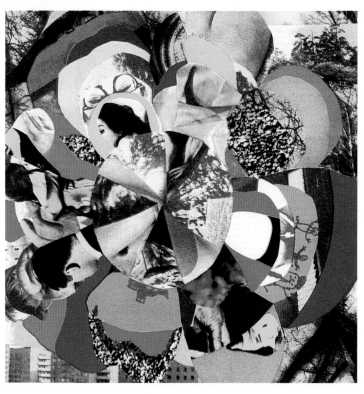

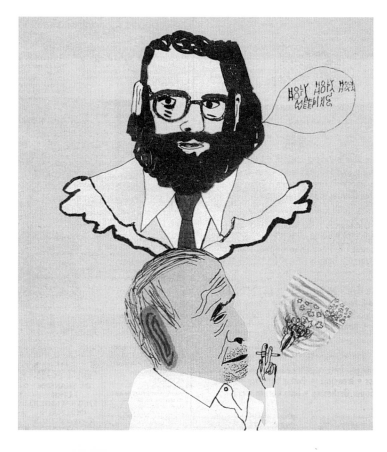

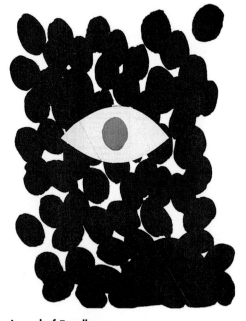

Award of Excellence
Dagens Nyheter
Stockholm, Sweden
Stina Wirsén, Illustration Director/Artist

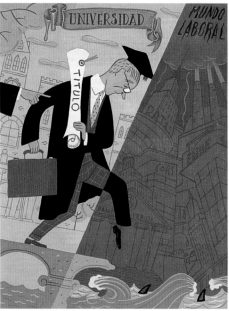

Award of Excellence
La Vanguardia
Barcelona, Spain
Miguel Angel Gallardo, Illustrator

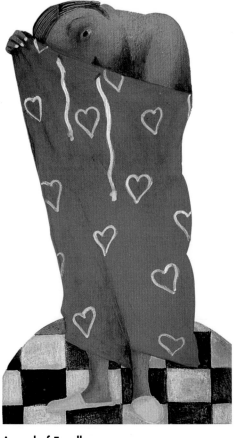

Award of Excellence
El Mundo/La Revista
Madrid, Spain
Ana Juan, Illustrator

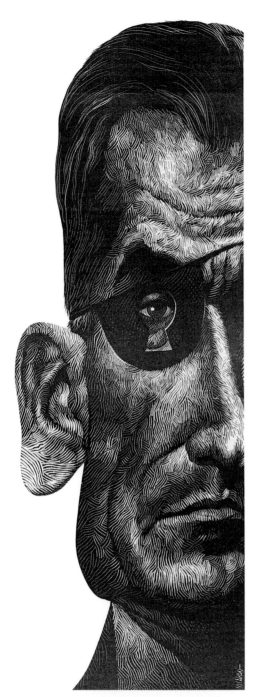

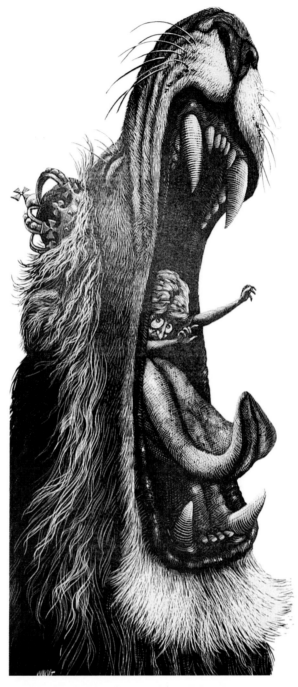

Silver
El Mundo Del Siglo XXI
Madrid, Spain
Ricardo Martinez, Illustrator

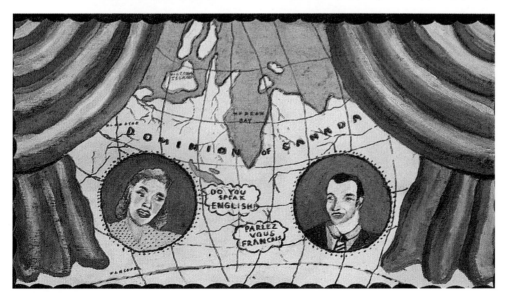

Award of Excellence
The New York Times
New York, NY
Kit Keith, Illustrator

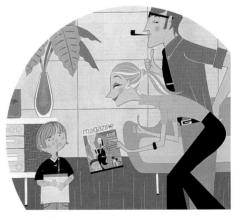

Award of Excellence
La Vanguardia
Barcelona, Spain
Jordi Labanda, Illustrator

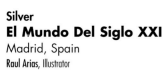

Silver
El Mundo Del Siglo XXI
Madrid, Spain
Raul Arias, Illustrator

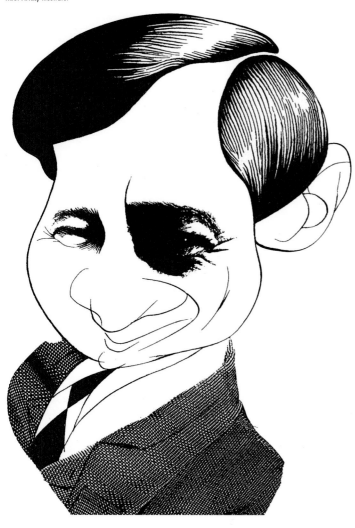

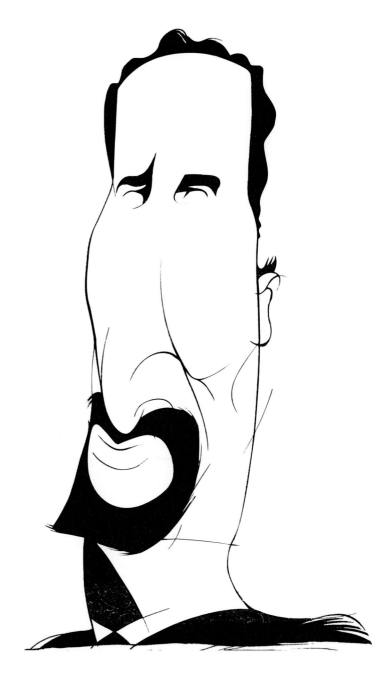

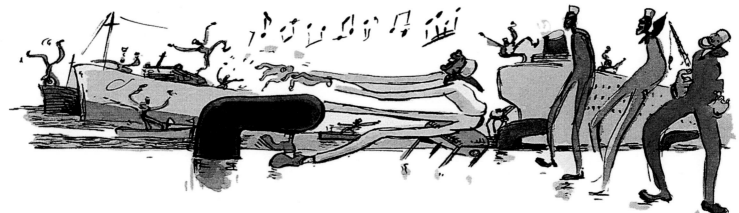

Award of Excellence
La Vanguardia
Barcelona, Spain
Josep M. Rius, Illustrator

Silver
•Also an **Award of Excellence** for Magazine Portfolio
El Mundo Del Siglo XXI
Madrid, Spain
Victoria Martos, Illustrator

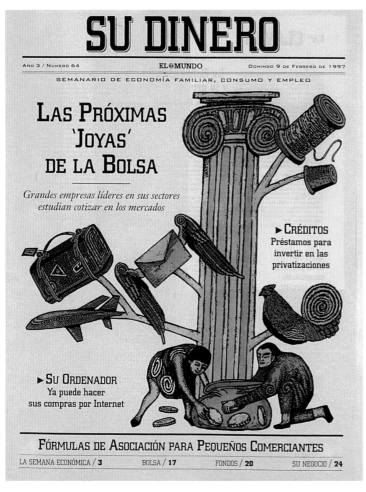

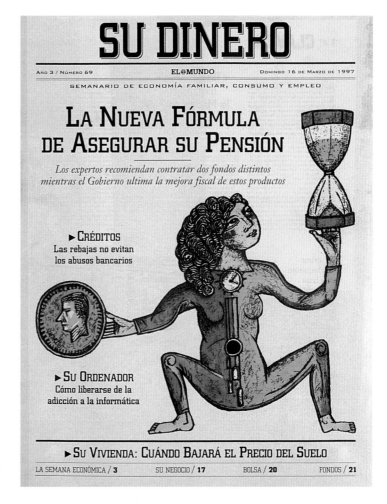

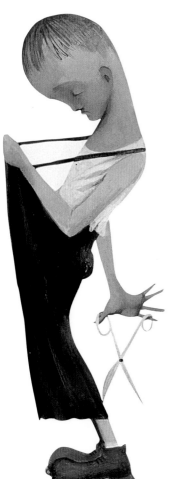

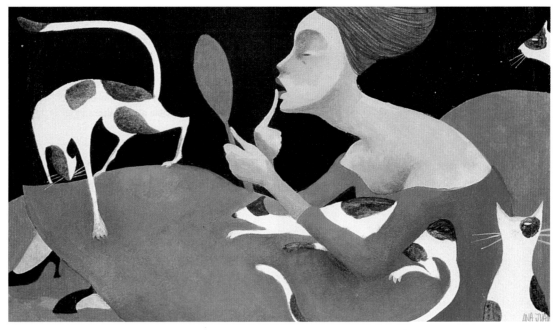

Silver
El Mundo/La Revista
Madrid, Spain
Ana Juan, Illustrator

Silver
The Washington Post Magazine
Washington, DC

Trisha Kraus, Illustrator

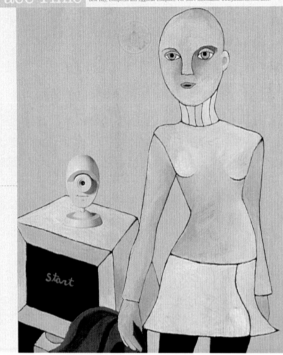

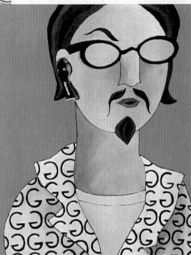

Face Time Picture phones may still be the stuff of science fiction and world's fairs, but as far as video e-mail and teleconferencing go, the future is now. Panasonic's EggCam is a high-resolution color **video camera** with a built-in microphone. It sits on top of your computer monitor on a tilting and swiveling base and records your adorable self, or whatever else you put in front of it. It then prepares your audio-video message for sending as an e-mail attachment; as a thoughtful gesture, it automatically includes the software the recipient will need to play the message back. The egg-size EggCam also comes with CU-SeeMe videoconferencing software, so you can be seen and heard in real time by a group of similarly equipped friends or business associates—all for the price of a local telephone call to your Internet service provider. (Keep in mind, though, that real-time video sent over the Internet has a strobelike, choppy quality.) Will crank calls soon be replaced by video streaming? Panasonic EggCam, about $130 to $280, depending on features included, at Best Buy, CompUSA and Egghead Computer. For more information: www.panasonic.com/olive.

Powered Nap In need of a nap to re-energize your connection with reality? Clip the ingenious Japanese **Earlarm** onto your earlobe, press either the five- or 30-minute button, and begin counting those sheep. After the preset siesta time, a beep—barely audible to anyone more than 10 feet away—will jolt you from your dreams. Available in several colors, the battery-powered Earlarm resembles a hearing aid and is as comfortable as "earbud"-style headphones. Perhaps as grabbing as the gizmo itself is its packaging: The box is adorned with Japanese cartoons of a groggy-eyed salaryman on a bullet train, a delivery-truck driver snoozing in his cab, and a young woman employing the Earlarm as a high-tech kitchen timer. (This is all very responsible—but it ignores the Earlarm's most tempting use: the surreptitious midday nap in a quiet corner of the office.) It comes complete with a tiny faux-velvet pouch. Earlarm, $15, for sale in the United States online at www.2.gol.com/users/aipikilare/fritsk.html.

Smile! Will Web sites replace photo albums? The PowerShot 350 is Canon's second exquisite entry into the **digital camera** market. No film. No developing. Simply point, using the 1.8-inch color screen on the back of the camera, and shoot. The flash is automatic and the photos are stored on a two-megabyte memory card that holds from 11 to 47 images, depending on the resolution you select (the sharpest is 640 x 480). Larger memory cards are also available, and the images are also easily transferred from the camera to your Macintosh or PC via an interface cable and software (both included). Then you can e-mail your snapshots, display them on your home page on the Web, or archive them in digital photo albums to be viewed on your computer screen. Of course, grandparents eager for wallet-size prints can transfer choice images to a floppy and get decent hard-copy results from any copy shop equipped with a color printer. Canon PowerShot 350, about $500 to $600 at Best Buy and Sears. For more information: www.powershot.com.

Technology
With a Human Face

These personal electronic gift ideas offer means
of contact with friends, colleagues and the wider,
wired world By David Pescovitz

Illustrations by Trisha Kraus

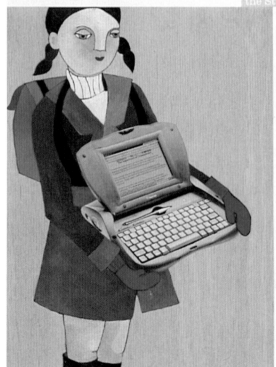

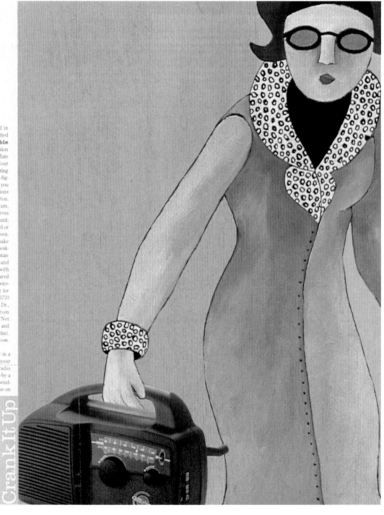

An Apple for the Student If Batman had a kid in college, she'd be outfitted with the stylish Apple eMate **portable computer**. Developed in collaboration with educators, the notebook-size eMate 300 is rugged but weighs only four pounds. Since it uses the same operating system as the Apple Newton personal digital assistant, the eMate 300 will let you run any of the hundreds of applications that have been created for the Newton. A word processor, drawing program, spreadsheet, graphical calculator, address book and calendar are built into the unit; you can access them via the keyboard or by using a stylus on a backlit LCD screen. Expansion and connection ports make it simple for the eMate to talk to a desktop computer, printer and wireless or standard modem for Web browsing and e-mail access. The eMate ships with three megabytes of RAM and an infrared port that will allow you to share files wirelessly. (We know you'd never use it for cheating.) Apple eMate 300, about $770 to $850 at MacHeaven (4500 Daly Dr., Chantilly) and by special order from CompUSA, Friendship Computer/NetData (12313 Wilkins Ave., Rockville) and the Micro Center (3089 Nutley St., Fairfax). For more information: www.apple.com.

Crank It Up No more getting stuck on a boat, or in a blizzard, with dead batteries in your boombox. BayGen's Freeplay 2 radio gets its power the Flintstones way—by a hand crank. Thirty seconds of easy winding provides up to an hour of playtime on this **AM/FM radio**. The sturdy 8-by-11½-by-8-inch unit weighs a little over five pounds and is ideal for campers, beach bums and anyone living in tornado or earthquake country. There's an AC adapter jack for extremely lazy folks, too. The original Freeplay (about $100) also receives shortwave frequencies. BayGen Freeplay 2, about $65 to $80 at Montgomery Ward, the Nature Company and Sports Authority.

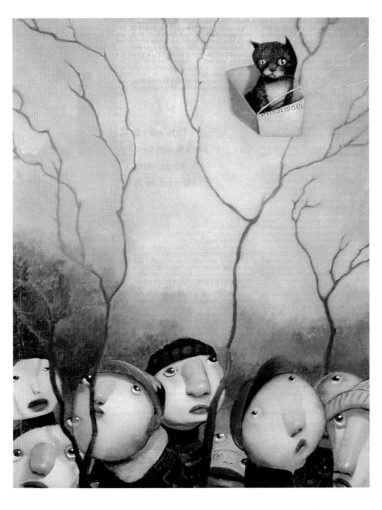

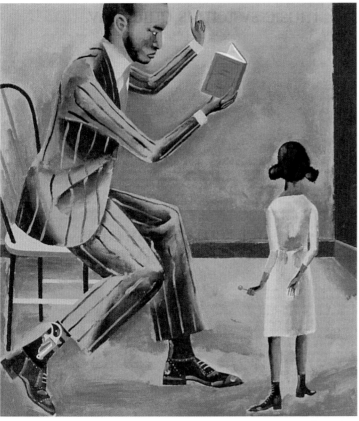

Gold
Philadelphia Inquirer Magazine
Philadelphia, PA
Lisa Nilsson, Illustrator; Alain Pilon, Illustrator; Tom Curry, Illustrator; Amanda Duffy, Illustrator; Anna Kang, Illustrator; Joe Sorren, Illustrator

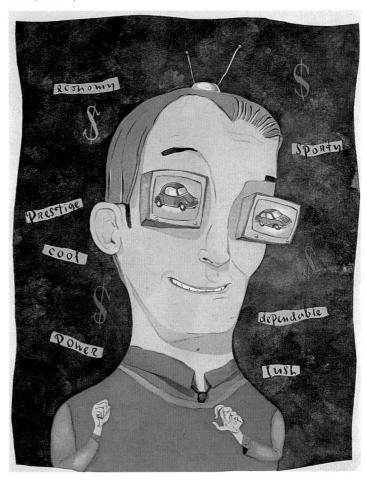

Awarded a **Gold Medal** for these illustrations which contain a high level of sophistication within a large variety of styles. Each one has lots of integrity.

•••••

Ganador de una Medalla de Oro por estas ilustraciones que contienen un alto nivel de sofisticación dentro de una amplia gama de estilos. Cada uno de ellos posee gran integridad.

Silver
The Boston Globe
Boston, MA

Richard Osaka, Illustrator; **Andrea Ventura**, Illustrator

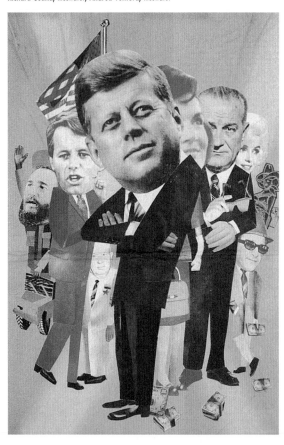

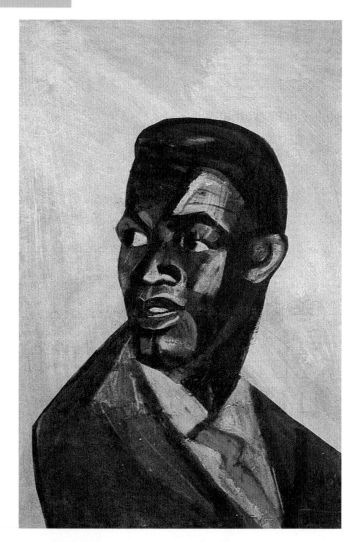

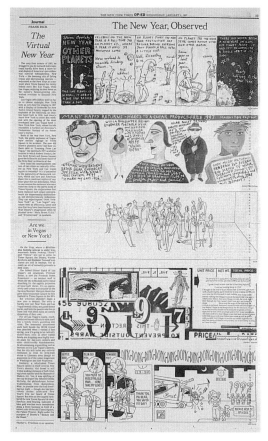

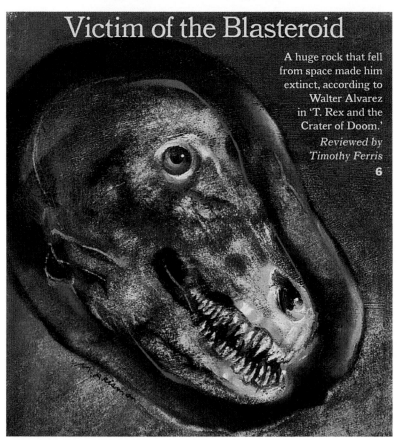

Victim of the Blasteroid

A huge rock that fell from space made him extinct, according to Walter Alvarez in 'T. Rex and the Crater of Doom.'

Reviewed by Timothy Ferris

6

Award of Excellence
The New York Times
New York, NY

Various Illustrators

Award of Excellence
The New York Times
New York, NY

Mirko Ilic, Illustrator; **R.O. Blechman**, Illustrator; **C.F. Payne**, Illustrator; **Marshall Arisman**, Illustrator; **Richard McGuire**, Illustrator; **Brad Holland**, Illustrator

Chapter Nine

PHOTO JOURNALISM

Continuing to pay tribute to the world's best newspaper designs, the 19th edition of The Best of Newspaper Design is a stunning collection of modern work. The included works were selected from more than 10,000 entries submitted by newspapers all over the world. This exceptional collection is an essential reference for anyone involved in print media, graphics, photography, design, journalism, or communications.

The competition, which is sponsored annually by the Society of News Design and the S.I. Newhouse School of Public Communications at Syracuse University, recognizes excellence in newspaper design and graphics. Awards include Best of Show, Gold, Silver, Award of Excellence, Special Recognition, plus the honor of World's Best Designed Newspaper. Categories for judging include overall page design, portfolio, magazine cover design, art and illustration, photo journalism, and informational graphics.

This nineteenth edition presents the finest newspaper design in the field.

Selected by a panel of 21 judges of the Society for News Design, the award-winning publications featured in this nineteenth edition were chosen for excellence in design.

The Best of Newspaper Design, 19th edition, features: Text in English and Spanish; 840 awards: World's Best-Designed Newspapers, Best of Show, Gold medals, Judges' Special Recognition, Silver medals, and Awards of Excellence. More than 12,100 entries were reviewed from hundreds of publications from around the world to select winners from 158 publications. Categories included: Overall design, news, features, portfolios, special coverage, special sections, magazines, art and illustration, photography, informational graphics and redesigns.ign, art and illus

Continuing to pay tribute to the world's best newspaper designs, the 19th edition of The Best of Newspaper Design is a stunning collection of modern work. The included works were selected from more than 10,000 entries submitted by newspapers all over the world. This exceptional collection is an essential reference for anyone involved in print media, graphics, photography, design, journalism, or communications.

The competition, which is sponsored annually by the Society of News Design and the S.I. Newhouse School of Public Communications at Syracuse University, recognizes excellence in newspaper design and graphics. Awards include Best of Show, Gold, Silver, Award of Excellence, Special Recognition, plus the honor of World's Best Designed Newspaper. Categories for judging include overall page design, portfolio, magazine cover design, art and illustration, photo journalism, and informational graphics.

This nineteenth edition presents the finest newspaper design in the field.

Selected by a panel of judges of the Society of News Design, the award-winning newspapers featured in this nineteenth edition were chosen for excellence in design.

The Best of Newspaper Design, 19th edition, features: all text in English and Spanish; more than five hundred awards: Best of Show, Judges' Special Recognition, Gold Medals, Silver Medals, and Awards of Excellence; over five hundred newspapers from all around the world; categories such as overall page design, portfolio, magazine cover design, art and illustration, photo

Continuing to pay tribute to the world's best newspaper designs, the 19th edition of The Best of Newspaper Design is a stunning collection of modern work. The included works were selected from more than 10,000 entries submitted by newspapers all over the world. This exceptional collection is an essential reference for anyone involved in print media, graphics, photography, design, journalism, or communications.

The competition, which is sponsored annually by the Society for News Design and the S.I. Newhouse School of Public Communications at Syracuse University, recognizes excellence in newspaper design and graphics. Awards include Best of Show, Gold, Silver, Award of Excellence, Special Recognition, plus the honor of World's Best Designed Newspaper. Categories for judging include overall page design, portfolio, magazine cover design, art and illustration, photo journalism, and informational graphics.

This nineteenth edition presents the finest newspaper design in the field.

Selected by a panel of 21 judges of the Society for News Design, the award-winning publications featured in this nineteenth edition were chosen for excellence in design.

The Best of Newspaper Design, 19th edition, features: Text in English and Spanish; 840 awards: World's Best-Designed Newspapers, Best of Show, Gold medals, Judges' Special Recognition, Silver medals, and Awards of Excellence. More than 12,100 entries were reviewed from hundreds of publications from around the world to select winners from 158 publications. Categories included: Overall design, news, features, portfolios, special

SPOT NEWS
FEATURE
PHOTO STORY
PHOTO ILLUSTRATION
PORTFOLIO

and illustration, photo journalism, and informational graphics.

This nineteenth edition presents the finest newspaper design in the field.

Selected by a panel of judges of the Society of News Design, the award-winning newspapers featured in this nineteenth edition were chosen for excellence in design.

Selected by a panel of 21 judges of the Society for News Design, the award-winning publications featured in this nineteenth edition were

Continuing to pay tribute to the world's best newspaper designs, the 19th edition of The Best of Newspaper Design is a stunning collection of modern work. The included works were selected from more than 10,000 entries submitted by newspapers all over the world. This exceptional collection is an essential reference for anyone involved in print media, graphics, photography, design, journalism, or communications.

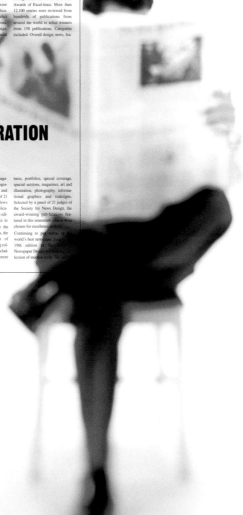

Designed Newspaper. Categories for judging include overall page design, portfolio, magazine cover design, art and illustration, photo journalism, and informational graphics.

This nineteenth edition presents the finest newspaper design in the field.

Selected by a panel of 21 judges of the Society for News Design, the award-winning publications featured in this nineteenth edition were chosen for excellence in design.

The Best of Newspaper Design, 19th edition, features: Text in English and Spanish; 840 awards: World's Best-Designed Newspapers, Best of Show, Gold medals, Judges' Special Recognition, Silver medals, and Awards of Excellence. More than 12,100 entries were reviewed from hundreds of publications from around the world to select winners from 158 publications. Categories included: Overall design, news, features, portfolios, special

coverage, special sections, magazines, art and illustration, photography, informational graphics and redesigns. Selected by a panel of 21 judges of the Society for News Design, the award-winning publications featured in this nineteenth edition were chosen for excellence in design.

Continuing to pay tribute to the world's best newspaper designs, the 19th edition of The Best of Newspaper Design is a stunning collection of modern work. The included works were selected from more

Continuing to pay tribute to the world's best newspaper designs, the 19th edition of The Best of Newspaper Design is a stunning collection of modern work. The included works were selected from more than 10,000 entries submitted by newspapers all over the world. This exceptional collection is an essential reference for anyone involved in print media, graphics, photography, design, journalism, or communications.

The competition, which is sponsored annually by the Society for News Design and the S.I. Newhouse School of Public Communications at Syracuse University, recognizes excellence in newspaper design and graphics. Awards include Best of Show, Gold, Silver, Award of Excellence. Special Recognition, plus the honor of World's Best Designed Newspaper. Categories for judging include overall page design, portfolio, magazine cover design, art and illustration, photo journalism, and informational graphics.

This nineteenth edition presents the finest newspaper design in the field.

Selected by a panel of 21 judges of the Society for News Design, the award-winning publications featured in this nineteenth edition were chosen for excellence in design.

The Best of Newspaper Design, 19th edition, features: Text in English and Spanish; 840 awards: World's Best-Designed Newspapers, Best of Show. Gold medals, Judges' Special Recognition, Silver medals, and Awards of Excellence. More than 12,100 entries were reviewed from hundreds of publications from around the world to select winners from 158 publications. Categories included: Overall design, news, fea-

tures, portfolios, special coverage, special sections, magazines, art and illustration, photography, informational graphics and redesigns. Selected by a panel of 21 judges of the Society for News Design, the award-winning publications featured in this nineteenth edition were chosen for excellence in design.

Continuing to pay tribute to the world's best newspaper designs, the 19th edition of The Best of Newspaper Design is a stunning collection of modern work. The included works were selected from more

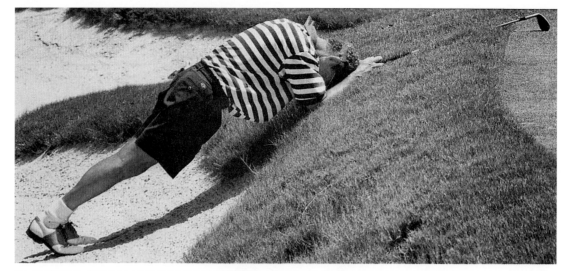

Award of Excellence
The Dallas Morning News
Dallas, TX
Irwin Thompson, Photographer

Award of Excellence
Reforma
México City, México
Emilio Deheza, Art Director; Víctor Cruz, Designer; Julio Candelaria, Photo Editor; Eduardo Danilo, Design Consultant; Roberto Gutiérrez, Section Designer; Guillermo Caballero, Graphic Coordinator; Alejandro González, Editor; Miguel Velazco, Photographer

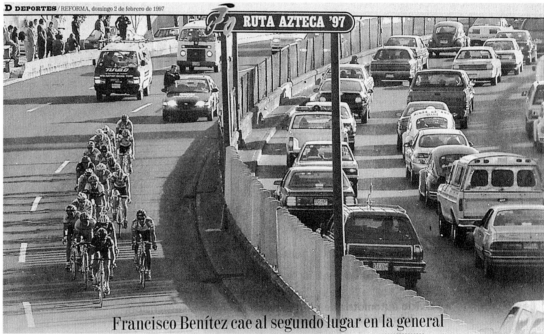

D DEPORTES / REFORMA, domingo 2 de febrero de 1997

RUTA AZTECA '97

Francisco Benítez cae al segundo lugar en la general

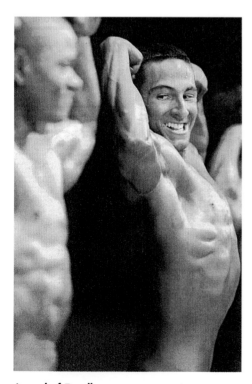

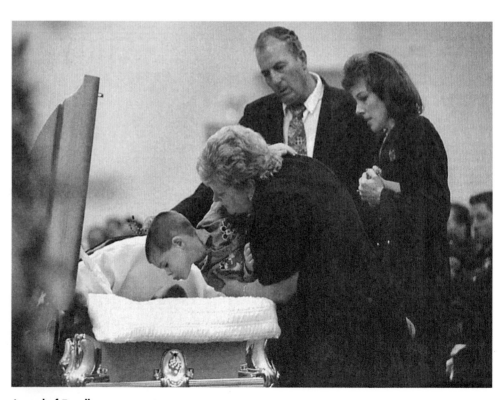

Award of Excellence
The Charlotte Observer
Charlotte, NC
Gary O'Brien, Photographer; Monica Moses, Design Director; Susan Gilbert, Director/Photography

Award of Excellence
Tri-Valley Herald
Pleasanton, CA
Ray Chavez, Photographer; Jane Tyska, Photo Editor; Alan Greth, Director/Photography

Award of Excellence
Winnipeg Free Press
Winnipeg, Canada

Ken Gigliotti, Photographer

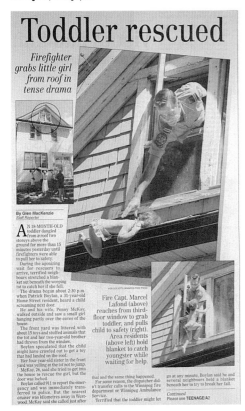

Award of Excellence
The Boston Globe
Boston, MA

Catherine Aldrich, Art Director & Designer; **Mark Wilson**, Photographer

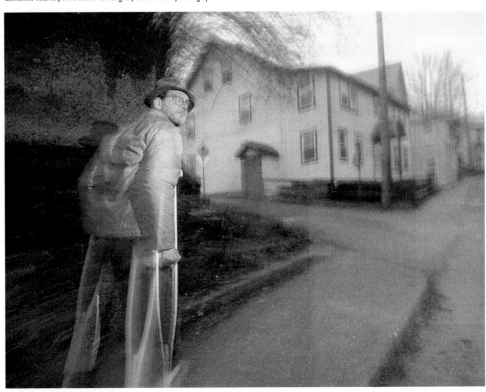

Award of Excellence
The Chilliwack Progress
Chilliwack, Canada

Rick Collins, Photographer & Designer

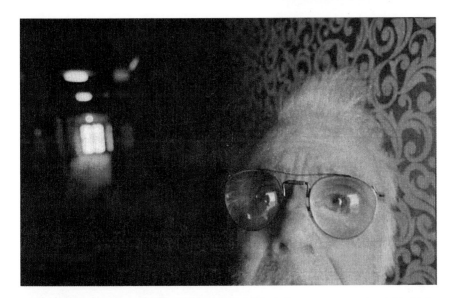

Award of Excellence
El Pais Semanal
Madrid, Spain

David García, Art Director; **Eugenio González**, Design Director; **Maripaz Domingo**, Designer; **Gustavo Sánchez**, Designer; **Alex M. Roig**, Editor-in-Chief; **Francis Giacobetti**, Photographer

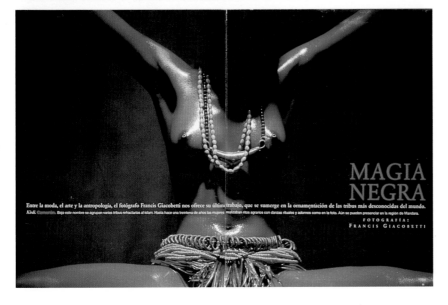

Award of Excellence
Providence Journal-Bulletin
Providence, RI

Glenn Osmundson, Photographer

Award of Excellence
Sun-Sentinel/Sunshine Magazine
Ft. Lauderdale, FL

Greg Carannante, Associate Editor/Design Director; **Susan Stocker,** Photographer

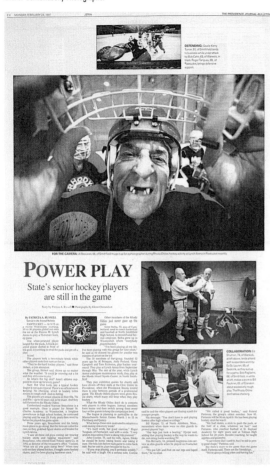

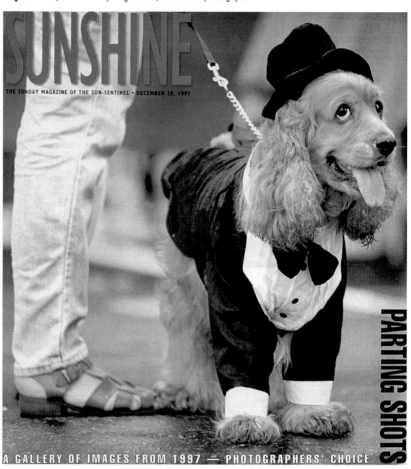

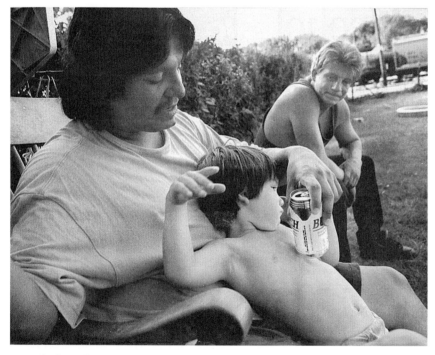

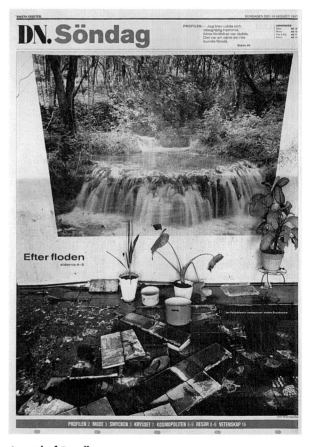

Award of Excellence
The Beacon News
Aurora, IL

Brian Plonka, Photographer

Award of Excellence
Dagens Nyheter
Stockholm, Sweden

Ulla Wingård, Design Director; **John Bark,** Creative Director/Designer; **Peter Hoelstad,** Photographer; **Ylva Magnusson,** Designer

magazine
LA VANGUARDIA

23 de noviembre de 1997

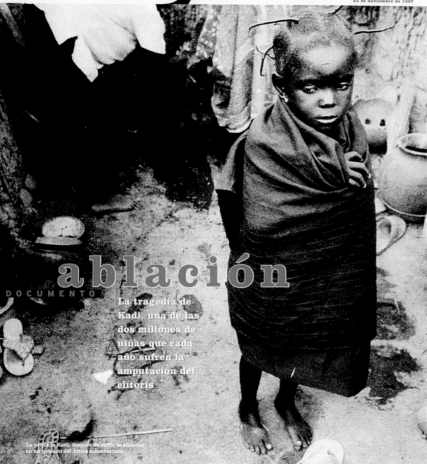

ablación

DOCUMENTO

La tragedia de
Kadi, una de las
dos millones de
niñas que cada
año sufren la
amputación del
clítoris

La pequeña Kadi, después de sufrir la ablación
en un poblado del África subsahariana

Silver
La Vanguardia
Barcelona, Spain

Carlos Pérez de Rozas Arribas, Art Director; **Rosa Mundet Poch**, Graphics Editor; **Ma José Oriol Roca**, Designer; **Mònica Caparrós Bagà**, Designer; **Kim Manresa Miravet**, Photographer; **Antonio Soto**, Design Director

EL DÍA QUE KADI PERDIÓ PARTE DE SU VIDA

La ablación que sufren millones
de mujeres, contada a través de
la tragedia de una niña

FOTOS DE **Kim Manresa**

Dos millones de niñas son sometidas
cada año a la ablación del clítoris.
Unos 130 millones de mujeres
han perdido esa parte de su cuerpo
en una desgarradora amputación.
Un fotógrafo del Magazine ha
conseguido, después de dos años de
trabajo, un documento excepcional e
inédito de un rito que aún se practica
en más de 30 países. La
sobrecogedora historia de la pequeña
Kadi ilustra con toda su crudeza la
pervivencia de unas prácticas que
estremecen al mundo occidental

6.00
Para Kadi es un día más. Al
igual que los adultos, se levanta al amanecer. No tiene
que ponerse más que una
camisa y ya está lista para
salir al exterior.

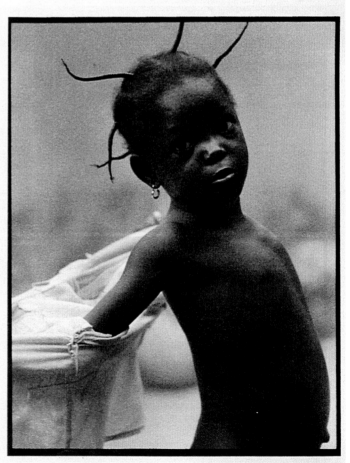

38 MAGAZINE

23 NOVIEMBRE 1997 39

Award of Excellence
•Also an **Award of Excellence** for Magazine Page Design
Philadelphia Inquirer Magazine
Philadelphia, PA

Christine Dunleavy, Art Director; **Susan Syrnick**, Assistant Art Director; **Staff**, Photographer

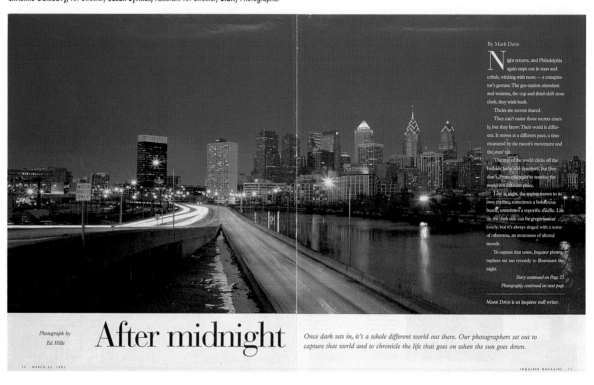

By Mark Davis

Night returns, and Philadelphia again steps out in stars and cobalt, winking with neon — a conspirator's gesture. The gas-station attendant and waitress, the cop and third-shift store clerk, they wink back.

Theirs are secrets shared.

They can't name those secrets exactly, but they know: Their world is different. It moves at a different pace, a time measured by the moon's movement and the stars' tilt.

The rest of the world clicks off the bedside lamp and slumbers, but they don't. From midnight to sunrise, the world is a different place.

Late at night, the region moves to its own rhythm, sometimes a boisterous bustle, sometimes a soporific shuffle. Life on the dark side can be gregarious or lonely, but it's always tinged with a sense of otherness, an awareness of altered moods.

To capture that sense, Inquirer photographers set out recently to illuminate the night.

Story continued on Page 23
Photography continued on next page

MARK DAVIS *is an Inquirer staff writer.*

Photograph by Ed Hille

After midnight

Once dark sets in, it's a whole different world out there. Our photographers set out to capture that world and to chronicle the life that goes on when the sun goes down.

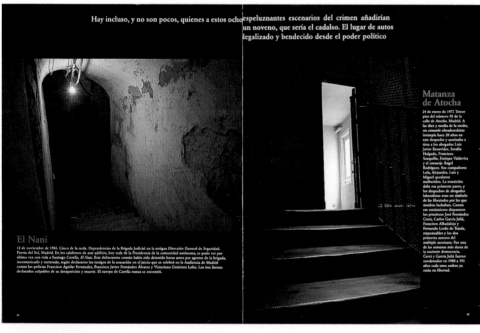

Hay incluso, y no son pocos, quienes a estos ocho espeluznantes escenarios del crimen añadirían un noveno, que sería el cadalso. El lugar de autos legalizado y bendecido desde el poder político

Matanza de Atocha

24 de enero de 1977. Tercer piso del número 55 de la calle de Atocha. Madrid. A las diez y media de la noche, un *comando* ultraderechista irrumpía hace 20 años en este despacho y asesinaba a tiros a los abogados Luis Javier Benavides, Serafín Holgado, Francisco Sauquillo, Enrique Valdevira y el conserje Ángel Rodríguez. Sus compañeros Lola, Alejandro, Luis y Miguel quedaron malheridos. La transición daba sus primeros pasos, y los despachos de abogados laboralistas eran un símbolo de las libertades por las que mucho luchaban. Contra ese sentimiento dispararon los pistoleros José Fernández Cerrá, Carlos García Juliá, Francisco Albaladejo y Fernando Lerdo de Tejada, responsables y los dos primeros autores del múltiple asesinato. Por una de las semanas más duras de la naciente democracia. Cerrá y García Juliá fueron condenados entre 1980 a 193 años cada uno; ambos ya están en libertad.

El Nani

12 de noviembre de 1983. Cinco de la tarde. Dependencias de la Brigada Judicial en la antigua Dirección General de Seguridad. Puerta del Sol, Madrid. En los calabozos de este edificio, hoy sede de la Presidencia de la comunidad autónoma, se pudo ver por última vez con vida a Santiago Corella, El Nani. Este delincuente común había sido detenido horas antes por agentes de la brigada, incomunicado y torturado, según declararon los testigos de la acusación en el juicio que se celebró en la Audiencia de Madrid contra los policías Francisco Aguilar Fernández, Francisco Javier Fernández Álvarez y Victoriano Gutiérrez Lobo. Los tres fueron declarados culpables de su desaparición y muerte. El cuerpo de Corella nunca se encontró.

Award of Excellence
El Pais Semanal
Madrid, Spain

David García, Art Director; **Eugenio González**, Design Director; **Maripaz Domingo**, Designer; **Gustavo Sánchez**, Designer; **Alex M. Roig**, Editor-in-Chief; **José Manuel Navia**, Photographer

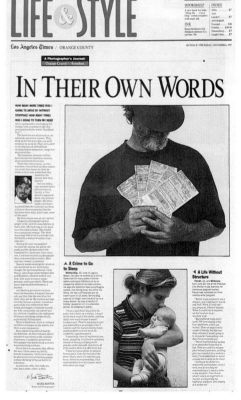

LIFE&STYLE
Los Angeles Times / ORANGE COUNTY

A Photographer's Journal: Orange County's Homeless

IN THEIR OWN WORDS

▲ A Crime to Go to Sleep

◀ A Life Without Structure

Award of Excellence
Los Angeles Times/Orange County Edition
Costa Mesa, CA

Colin Crawford, Director/Photography; **Mark Boster**, Photographer; **Kirk Christ**, Designer

Award of Excellence
Providence Journal-Bulletin
Providence, RI
John Freidah, Photographer

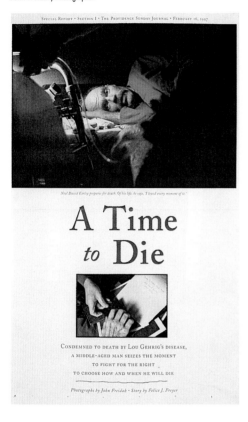

Award of Excellence
The San Diego Union-Tribune
San Diego, CA
Nancee E. Lewis, Photographer; **Drew Silvern**, Reporter; **Chris Ross**, Designer; **Michael Franklin**, Photo Editor

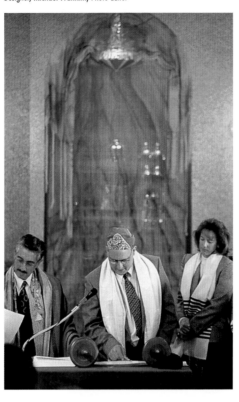

Award of Excellence
The Palm Beach Post
West Palm Beach, FL
Richard Graulich, Photographer; **Mark Edelson**, Photo Editor; **Pete Cross**, Director/Photography; **Michelle Deal Zimmerman**, Assistant Graphics Director

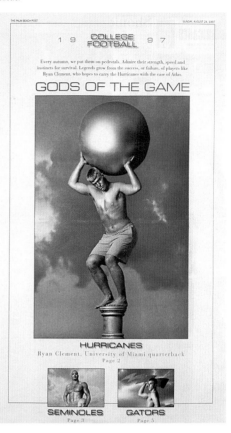

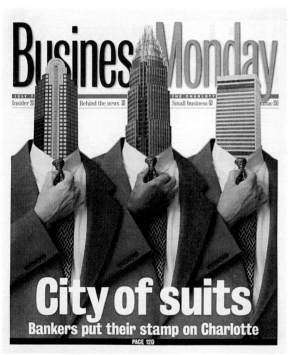

Award of Excellence
The Charlotte Observer
Charlotte, NC
Stephanie Grace Lim, Photographer; **Susan Gilbert**, Director/Photography; **Barry Kolar**, Designer; **Monica Moses**, Design Director

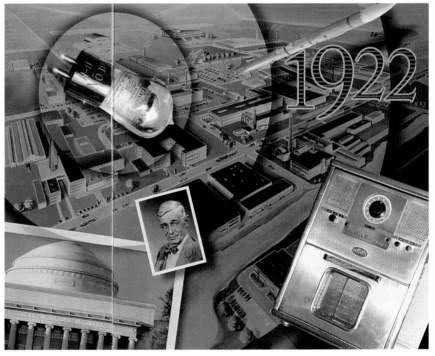

Award of Excellence
The Boston Globe
Boston, MA
Keith A. Webb, Art Director; Designer & Illustrator

Award of Excellence
El Periodico de Catalunya/El Dominical
Barcelona, Spain
Ferran Sendra, Illustrator & Designer

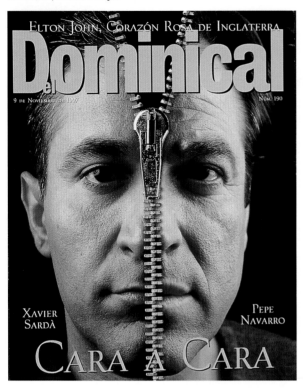

Award of Excellence
The Charlotte Observer
Charlotte, NC
Patrick Schneider, Photographer

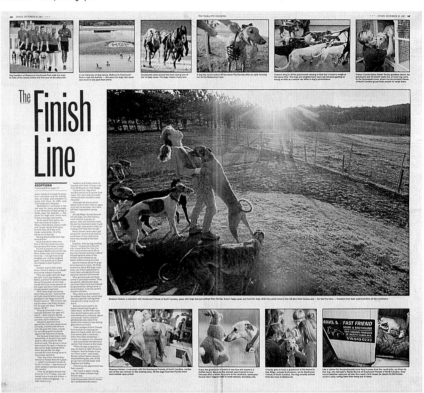

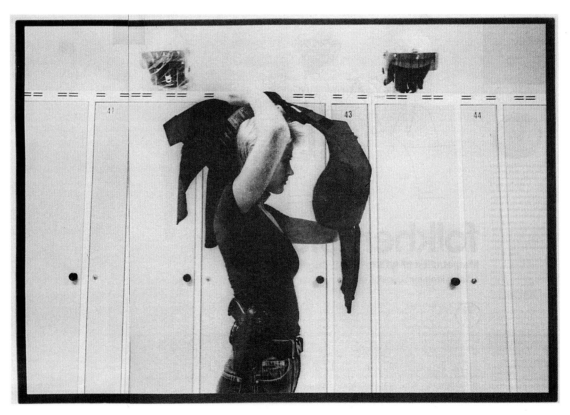

Award of Excellence
DN. på stan
Stockholm, Sweden
Anette Nantell, Photographer

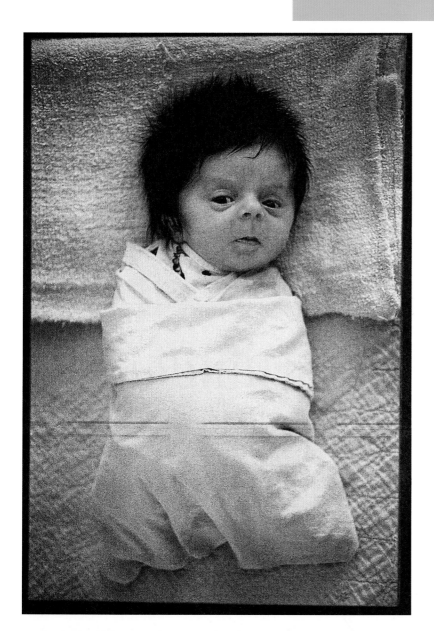

Silver
Goteborgs-Posten
Göteborg, Sweden
Lisa Thanner, Photographer

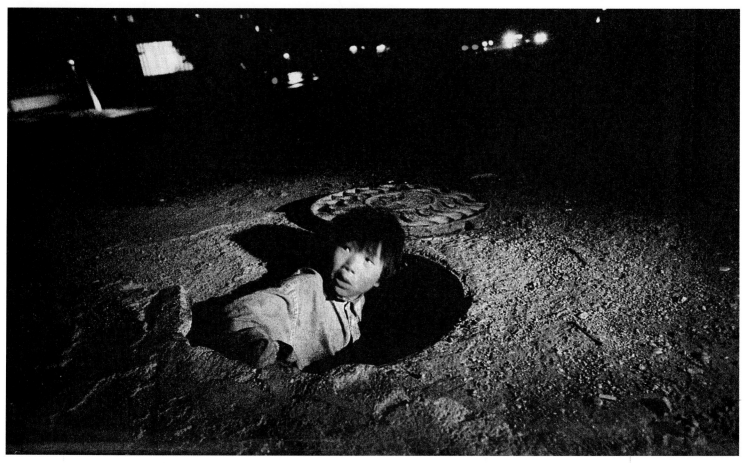

Award of Excellence
The Press Democrat
Santa Rosa, CA
John Burgess, Photographer

Award of Excellence
The Press Democrat
Santa Rosa, CA
Chad Surmick, Photographer

Award of Excellence
The Oregonian
Portland, OR
Serge A. McCabe, Photographer

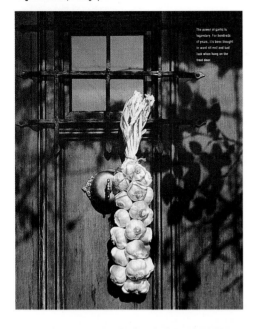

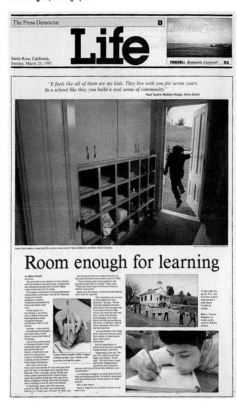

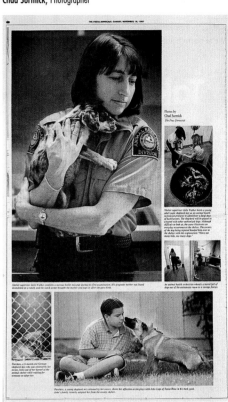

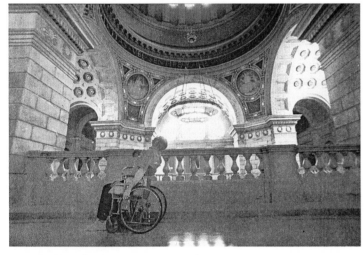

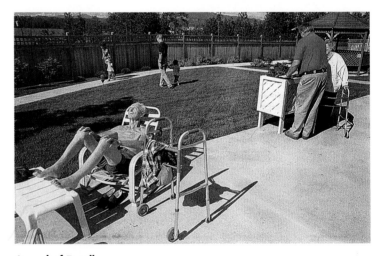

Award of Excellence
Providence Journal-Bulletin
Providence, RI
John Freidah, Photographer

Award of Excellence
The Spokesman-Review
Spokane, WA
Torsten Kjellstrand, Photographer

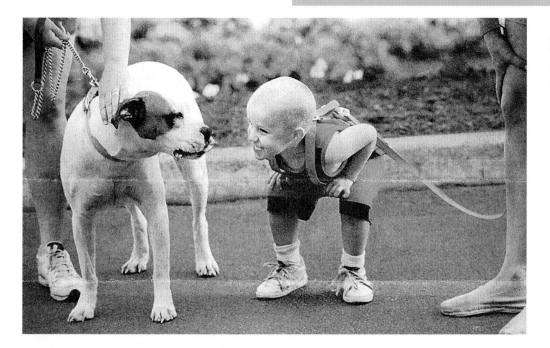

Award of Excellence
The Spokesman-Review
Spokane, WA
Kristy MacDonald, Photographer

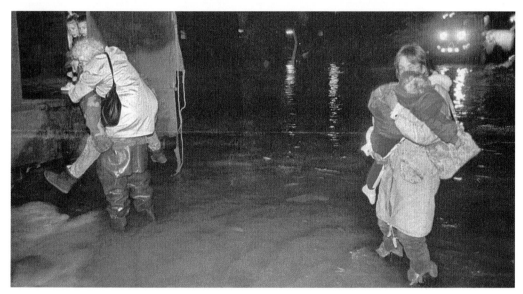

Award of Excellence
St. Paul Pioneer Press
St. Paul, MN
Bill Alkofer, Photographer

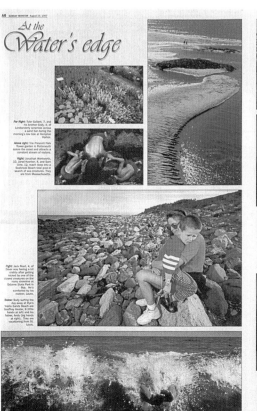
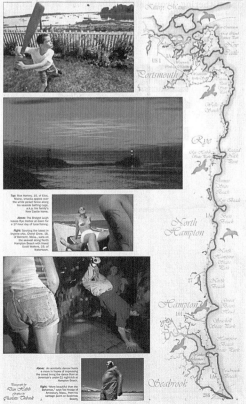

Award of Excellence
Concord Monitor
Concord, NH
A.J. Wolfe, Photographer; Andrea Bruce, Photographer; Ken Williams, Photographer; Romain Blanquart, Photographer; Dan Habib, Photographer; Kim Brent, Photographer

Silver
•Also an **Award of Excellence**
 for Photo Story

**The Press
Democrat**

Santa Rosa, CA

Chad Syrmick, Photographer;
Kent Porter, Photographer;
John Burgess, Photographer;
Mark Aronoff, Photographer;
John Metzger, Photography
Director

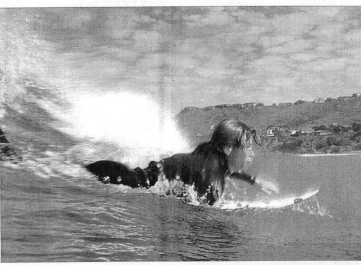
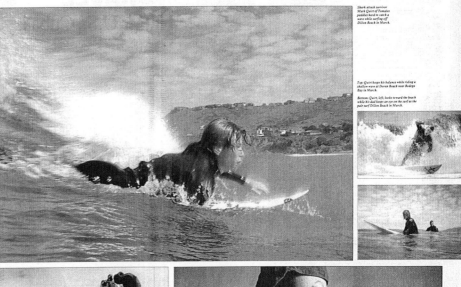

> "A lot of survivors say that eye haunts them. White sharks have no eyelids and the black part is very large in a grey background. I've been underwater in a cage looking into those eyes. They do mean business."
>
> JOHN McCOSKER, SENIOR SCIENTIST
> CALIFORNIA ACADEMY OF SCIENCES

When the shark bites

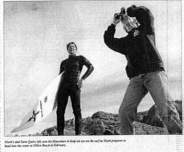

Mark's dad Steve Quirt, left, uses his binoculars to keep an eye on the surf as Mark prepares to head into the water at Dillon Beach in February.

Photos by Chad Surmick
The Press Democrat

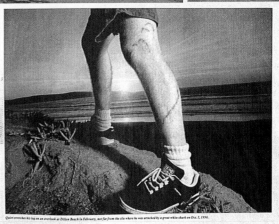

Quirt stretches his leg on an overlook at Dillon Beach in February, not far from the site where he was attacked by a great white shark on Oct. 5, 1996.

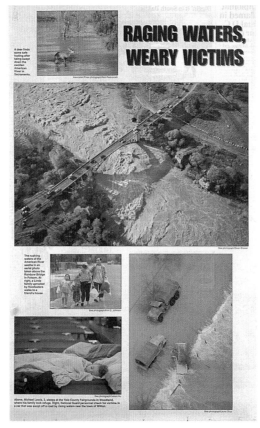

RAGING WATERS, WEARY VICTIMS

Above, Michael Lewis, 3, sleeps at the Yolo County Fairgrounds in Woodland, where his family took refuge. Right, National Guard personnel check for victims in a car that was swept off a road by rising waters near the town of Wilton.

Award of Excellence
The Sacramento Bee

Sacramento, CA

Laura Chun, Photographer; Dick Schmidt, Photographer; Kim D. Johnson, Photographer; Owen Brewer, Photographer; Jay Mather, Photographer; Randy Pench, Photographer

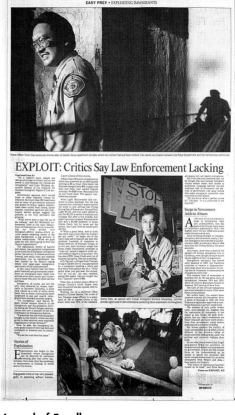

EASY PREY • EXPLOITING IMMIGRANTS

EXPLOIT: Critics Say Law Enforcement Lacking

Award of Excellence
Los Angeles Times/Orange County Edition

Costa Mesa, CA

Geraldine Wilkins-Kasinga, Photographer; Mark Boster, Photographer; Don Bartletti, Photographer; Gail Fisher, Photographer/Photo Editor; Colin Crawford, Director/Photography

INFORMA-TIONAL GRAPHICS

Continuing to pay tribute to the world's best newspaper designs, the 19th edition of The Best of Newspaper Design is a stunning collection of modern work. The included works were selected from more than 10,000 entries submitted by newspapers all over the world. This exceptional collection is an essential reference for anyone involved in print media, graphics, photography, design, journalism, or communications.

The competition, which is sponsored annually by the Society of News Design and the S.I. Newhouse School of Public Communications at Syracuse University, recognizes excellence in newspaper design and graphics. Awards include Best of Show, Gold, Silver, Award of Excellence, Special Recogni-tion, plus the honor of World's Best Designed Newspaper. Categories for judging include overall page design, portfolio, magazine cover design, art and illustration, photo journalism, and informational graphics.

This nineteenth edition presents the finest newspaper design in the field.

Selected by a panel of 21 judges of the Society for News Design, the award-winning pub-lications featured in this nineteenth edition were chosen for excellence in design.

The Best of Newspaper Design, 19th edition, features: Text in English and Spanish; 840 awards: World's Best-Designed Newspapers, Best of Show, Gold medals, Judges' Special Recognition, Silver medals, and Awards of Excel-lence. More than 12,100 entries were reviewed from hundreds of publications from around the world to select winners from 158 publications. Categories included: Overall design, news, features, portfolios, special coverage, special sections, magazines, art and illustration, photography, informational graphics and redesign.ign, art and illustration.

The competition, which is sponsored annually by the Society of News Design and the S.I. Newhouse School

The competition, which is sponsored annually by the Society of News Design and the S.I. Newhouse School of Public Communications at Syracuse University, recognizes excellence in newspaper design and graphics. Awards include Best of Show, Gold.

Silver, Award of Excellence, Special Recogni-tion, plus the honor of World's Best Designed News-paper.Continuing to pay tribute to the world's best newspaper designs, the 19th edition of The Best of Newspaper Design is a stunning collection of modern work. The included works were selected from more than 10,000 entries submitted by newspapers all over the world. This exceptional collection is an essential reference for anyone involved in print media, graphics, photography, design, journalism, or communications.

The competition, which is sponsored annually by the Society of News Design and the S.I. Newhouse School of Public Communications at Syracuse University, recognizes excellence in newspaper design and graphics. Awards include Best of Show, Gold, Silver, Award of Excellence, Special Recogni-tion, plus the honor of World's Best Designed Newspaper. Categories for judging include overall page design, portfolio, magazine cover

Continuing to pay tribute to the world's best newspaper designs, the 19th edition of The Best of Newspaper Design is a stunning collection of modern work. The included works were selected from more than 10,000 entries submitted by newspapers all over the

world. This exceptional collection is an essential reference for anyone involved in print media, graphics, photography, design, journalism, or communications.

The competition, which is sponsored annually by the Society for News Design and the S.I. Newhouse School of Public Communications at Syracuse University, recognizes excellence in newspaper design and graphics. Awards include Best of Show, Gold, Silver, Award of Excellence, Special Recogni-tion, plus the honor of World's Best Designed Newspaper. Categories for judging include overall page design, portfolio, magazine cover design, art and illustration, photo journalism, and informational graphics.

This nineteenth edition presents the finest newspaper design in the field.

Selected by a panel of judges of the Society of News Design, the award-winning newspapers featured in this nineteenth edition were chosen for excellence in design.

Selected by a panel of 21 judges of

This nineteenth edition presents the finest newspaper design in the field.

Selected by a panel of 21 judges of the Society for News Design, the award-winning pub-lications featured in this nineteenth edition were chosen for excellence in design.

The Best of Newspaper Design, 19th edition, features: Text in English and Spanish; 840 awards: World's Best-Designed Newspapers, Best of Show, Gold medals, Judges' Special Recognition, Silver medals, and Awards of Excel-lence. More than 12,100 entries were reviewed from hundreds of publications from around the world to select winners from 158 publications. Categories included: Overall design, news, features, portfolios, special coverage, special sections, magazines, art and illustration, photography, informational graphics and redesigns. Selected by a panel of 21 judges of the Society for News Design, the award-winning pub-lications featured in this nineteenth edition were

The competition, which is sponsored annually by the Society of News Design and the S.I. Newhouse School of Public Communications at Syracuse University, recognizes excellence in newspaper design and graphics. Awards include Best of Show, Gold,

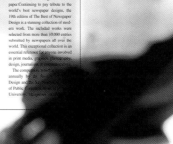

BREAKING NEWS

BLACK AND WHITE AND/OR ONE COLOR

TWO OR MORE COLORS

PORTFOLIO

The competition, which is sponsored annually by the Society of News Design and the S.I. Newhouse School of Public Communications at Syracuse University, recognizes excellence in newspaper design and graphics. Awards include Best of Show, Gold, Silver, Award of Excellence, Special Recogni-tion, plus the honor of World's Best Designed Newspaper. Categories for judging include overall page design, portfolio, magazine cover

Award of Excellence
•Also an **Award of Excellence** for Portfolio More than One Artist
ABC
Madrid, Spain
Fernando Rubio, Editor-in-Chief; **Carlos Aguilera**, Artist; **Staff**

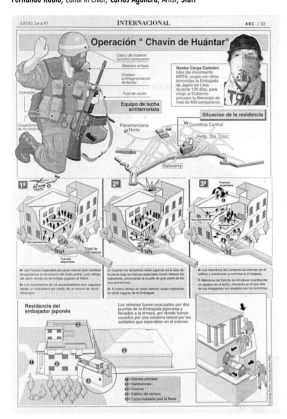

Award of Excellence
ABC
Madrid, Spain
Fernando Rubio, Editor-in-Chief; **Carlos G. Simon**, Artist; **Juan Rodriquez**, Artist

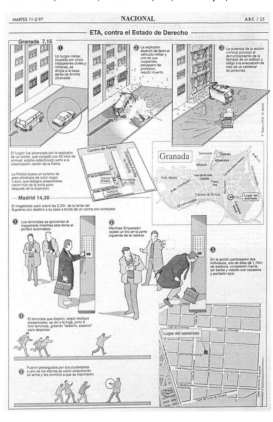

Award of Excellence
The Baltimore Sun
Baltimore, MD
Jerold Council, Graphics Director; **Emily Holmes**, Graphics Editor; **Joseph Hutchinson**, A.M.E. Graphics/Design

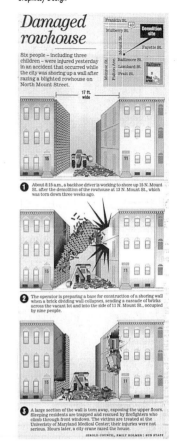

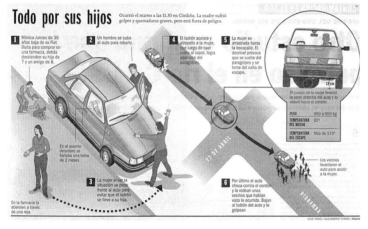

Award of Excellence
Clarin
Buenos Aires, Argentina
Iñaki Palacios, Art Director; **Alejandro Tumas**, Artist; **Jaime Serra**, Artist/Graphics Director

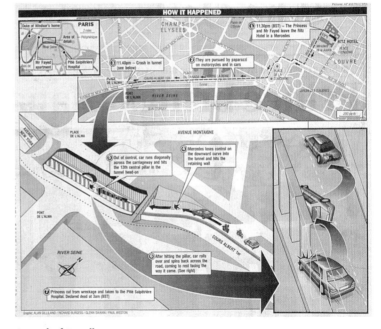

Award of Excellence
The Daily Telegraph
London, England
Alan Gilliland, Graphics Editor/Artist; **Richard Burgess**, Deputy Graphics Editor/Artist; **Paul Weston**, Graphic Artist; **Glenn Swann**, Graphic Artist

Award of Excellence
O Dia
Rio de Janeiro, Brazil
André Barroso, Graphic Artist; **Ary Moraes**, Graphic Artist

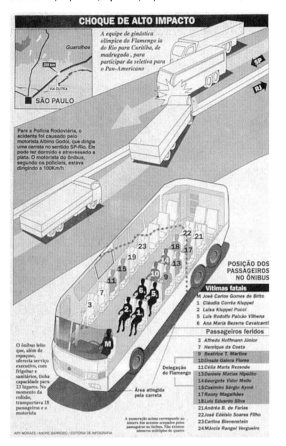

Award of Excellence
The Daily Telegraph
London, England
Alan Gilliland, Graphics Editor/Artist; **Glenn Swann**, Graphic Artist; **Graham Parrish**, Graphic Artist

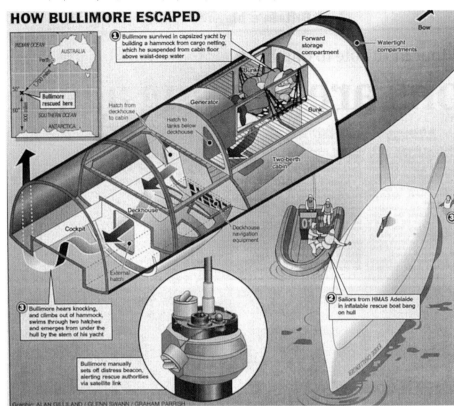

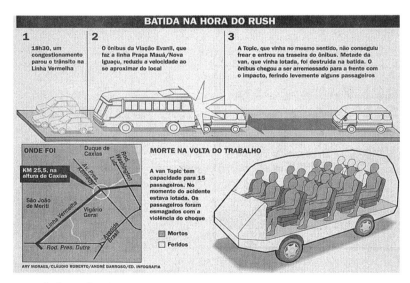

Award of Excellence
O Dia
Rio de Janeiro, Brazil
André Barroso, Graphic Artist; **Ary Moraes**, Graphics Director; **Cláudio Roberto**, Graphic Artist

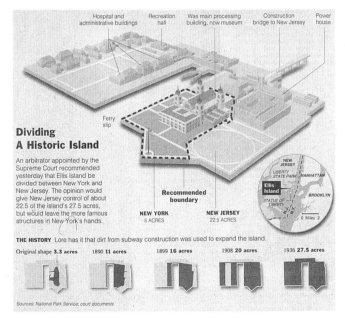

Award of Excellence
The New York Times
New York, NY
Archie Tse, Graphics Editor; **John Papasian**, Graphics Editor

Award of Excellence
The Washington Post
Washington, DC

Laura Stanton, Graphic Artist; **Jackson Dykman**, Art Director

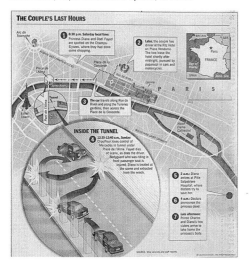

Award of Excellence
The New York Times
New York, NY

Archie Tse, Graphics Editor; **Mika Grondahl**, Graphics Editor

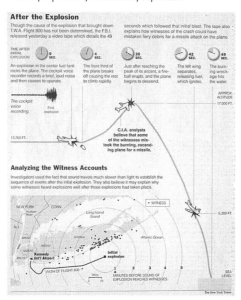

Award of Excellence
ABC
Madrid, Spain

Fernando Rubio, Editor-in-Chief; **Carlos Aguilera**, Artist

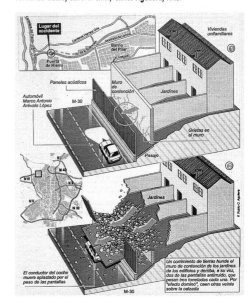

Award of Excellence
The Seattle Times
Seattle, WA

James McFarlane, Graphic Artist; **Chris Soprych**, Graphic Artist; **Karen Kerchelich**, Graphics Editor; **David Miller**, Art Director

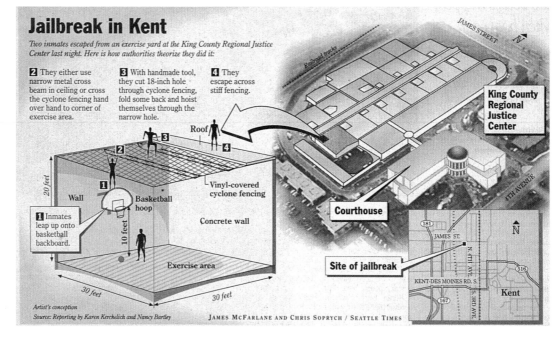

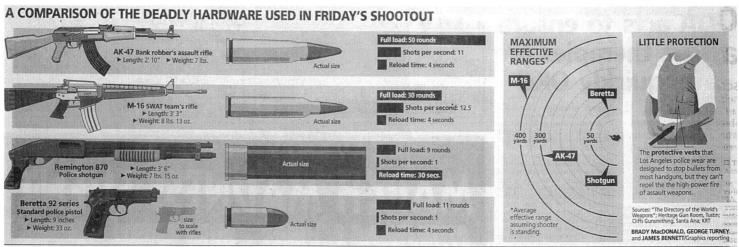

Award of Excellence
The Orange County Register
Santa Ana, CA

James Bennett, Visual Reporter

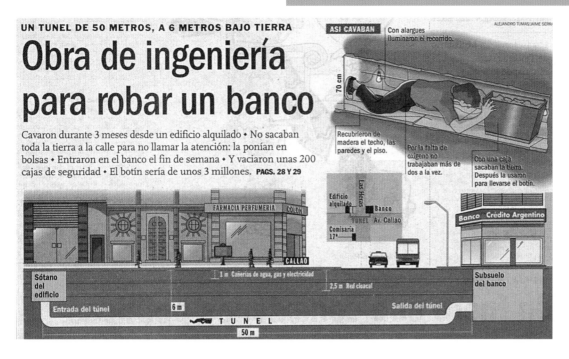

UN TUNEL DE 50 METROS, A 6 METROS BAJO TIERRA

Obra de ingeniería para robar un banco

Cavaron durante 3 meses desde un edificio alquilado • No sacaban toda la tierra a la calle para no llamar la atención: la ponían en bolsas • Entraron en el banco el fin de semana • Y vaciaron unas 200 cajas de seguridad • El botín sería de unos 3 millones. **PAGS. 28 Y 29**

ASI CAVABAN — Con alargues iluminaron el recorrido.

Recubrieron de madera el techo, las paredes y el piso.

Por la falta de oxígeno no trabajaban más de dos a la vez.

Con una caja sacaban la tierra. Después la usaron para llevarse el botín.

Award of Excellence
Clarin
Buenos Aires, Argentina
Iñaki Palacios, Art Director; Alejandro Tumas, Artist; Jaime Serra, Graphics Director

---

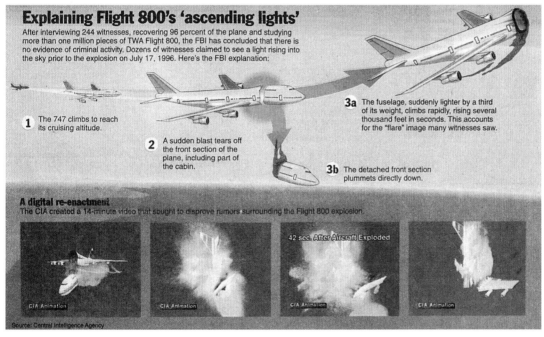

Explaining Flight 800's 'ascending lights'

After interviewing 244 witnesses, recovering 96 percent of the plane and studying more than one million pieces of TWA Flight 800, the FBI has concluded that there is no evidence of criminal activity. Dozens of witnesses claimed to see a light rising into the sky prior to the explosion on July 17, 1996. Here's the FBI explanation:

1. The 747 climbs to reach its cruising altitude.

2. A sudden blast tears off the front section of the plane, including part of the cabin.

3a. The fuselage, suddenly lighter by a third of its weight, climbs rapidly, rising several thousand feet in seconds. This accounts for the "flare" image many witnesses saw.

3b. The detached front section plummets directly down.

A digital re-enactment
The CIA created a 14-minute video that sought to disprove rumors surrounding the Flight 800 explosion.

Source: Central Intelligence Agency

Award of Excellence
The Sacramento Bee
Sacramento, CA
Sean McDade, Graphic Artist/Researcher; Nam Nguyen, Assistant Art Director; Howard Shintaku, Art Director; Pam Dinsmore, Executive News Editor; Mort Saltzman, A.M.E. Graphics; Rick Rodriguez, M.E.; Gregory Favre, Executive Editor

---

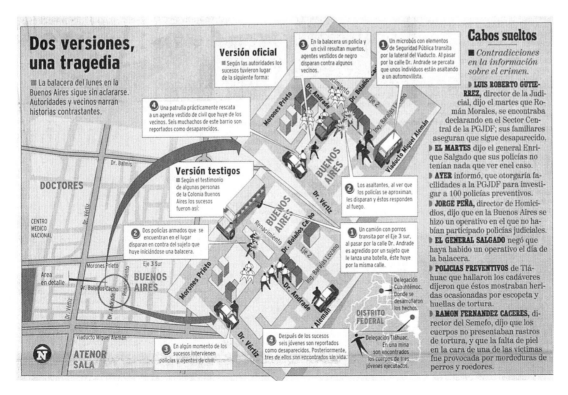

Dos versiones, una tragedia

■ La balacera del lunes en la Buenos Aires sigue sin aclararse. Autoridades y vecinos narran historias contrastantes.

Versión oficial
■ Según las autoridades los sucesos tuvieron lugar de la siguiente forma:

Versión testigos
■ Según el testimonio de algunas personas de la Colonia Buenos Aires los sucesos fueron así:

Cabos sueltos
■ *Contradicciones en la información sobre el crimen.*

Award of Excellence
Reforma
México City, México
Emilio Deheza, Art Director; Juan Jesús Cortés, Illustrator; Oscar Yañez, Section Designer; Eduardo Danilo, Design Consultant; Daniel Esqueda Guadalajara, Graphics Coordinator; Héctor Zamarrón, Section Editor

Award of Excellence
El Mundo Del Siglo XXI
Madrid, Spain

Juancho Cruz, Graphic Journalist

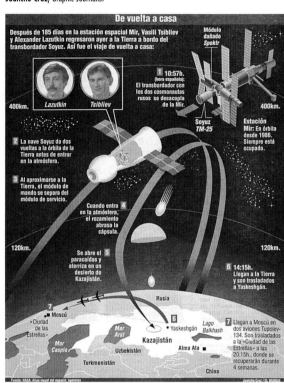

Award of Excellence
Savannah Morning News
Savannah, GA

Drew Martin, Graphic Artist

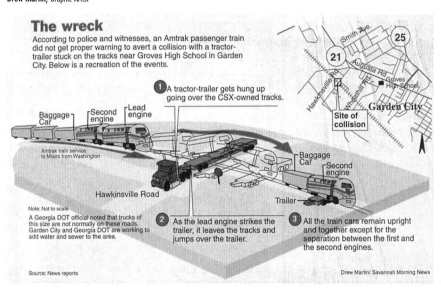

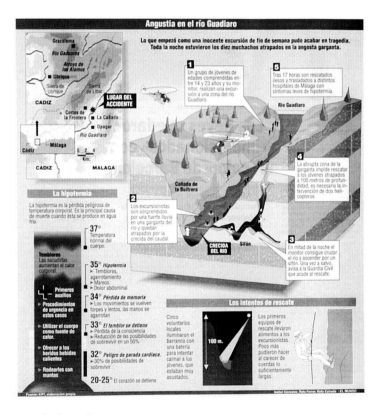

Award of Excellence
El Mundo Del Siglo XXI
Madrid, Spain

Dina Sanchez, Graphic Artist; Isabel Gonzalez, Graphic Artist; Rodrigo Silva, Graphic Artist; Rafa Estrada, Graphic Artist; Rafa Ferrer, Graphic Artist; Juantxo Cruz, Graphic Artist; Chema Matia, Graphic Artist; Modesto J. Carrasco, Graphic Artist

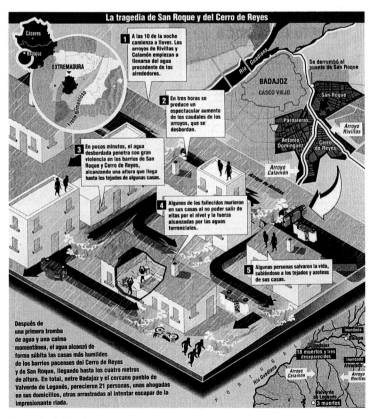

Award of Excellence
El Mundo Del Siglo XXI
Madrid, Spain

Dina Sanchez, Graphic Artist; Isabel Gonzalez, Graphic Artist; Rodrigo Silva, Graphic Artist; Rafa Estrada, Graphic Artist; Rafa Ferrer, Graphic Artist; Juantxo Cruz, Graphic Artist; Chema Matia, Graphic Artist; Modesto J. Carrasco, Graphic Artist

Award of Excellence
La Nacion

Buenos Aires, Argentina

Horacio Corsini, Infographic Designer; Eduardo Jose Perez, Infographic Designer; Cristian Werb, Infographic Designer; Jose Corsetti, Infographic Designer; Marcelo Regalado, Infographic Designer; Tomas Ondarra, Infographic Editor

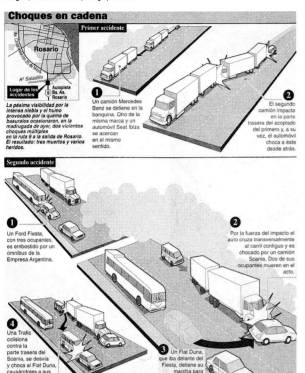

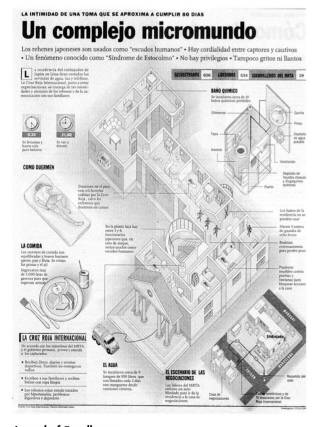

Award of Excellence
Clarin

Buenos Aires, Argentina

Iñaki Palacios, Art Director; Stella Bin, Researcher; Jaime Serra, Graphics Director; Paula Simonetti, Artist

Award of Excellence
El Mundo Del Siglo XXI

Madrid, Spain

Dina Sanchez, Graphic Artist; Isabel Gonzalez, Graphic Artist; Rodrigo Silva, Graphic Artist; Rafa Estrada, Graphic Artist; Rafa Ferrer, Graphic Artist; Juantxo Cruz, Graphic Artist; Chema Matia, Graphic Artist; Modesto J. Carrasco, Graphic Artist

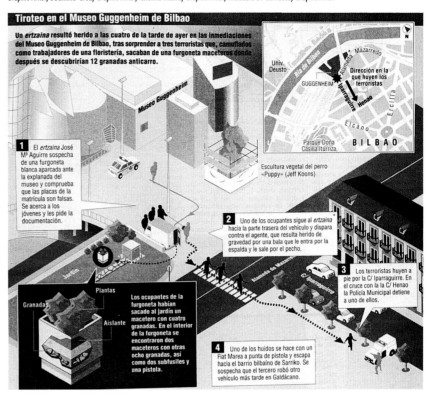

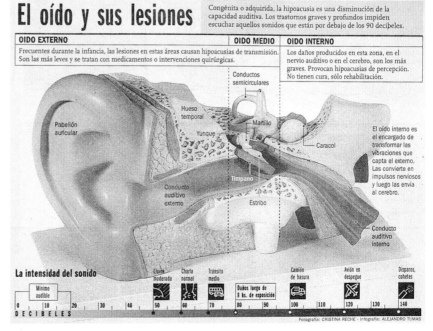

Award of Excellence
Clarin

Buenos Aires, Argentina

Iñaki Palacios, Art Director; Alejandro Tumas, Artist; Jaime Serra, Artist/Graphics Director; Cristina Reche, Photographer

Silver
•Also an **Award of Excellence** for Science/ Technology Page
The New York Times
New York, NY
Michael Valenti, Art Director; **Juan Velasco**, Graphics Editor/Illustrator

Award of Excellence
The Detroit News
Detroit, MI
Chris Kozlowski, A.M.E. Graphics/Design; **David Kordalski**, Graphics/Design Editor; **Shanna Flowers**, Deputy City Editor/Sunday; **Michael Hodges**, Reporter; **Satoshi Toyoshima**, Graphic Artist

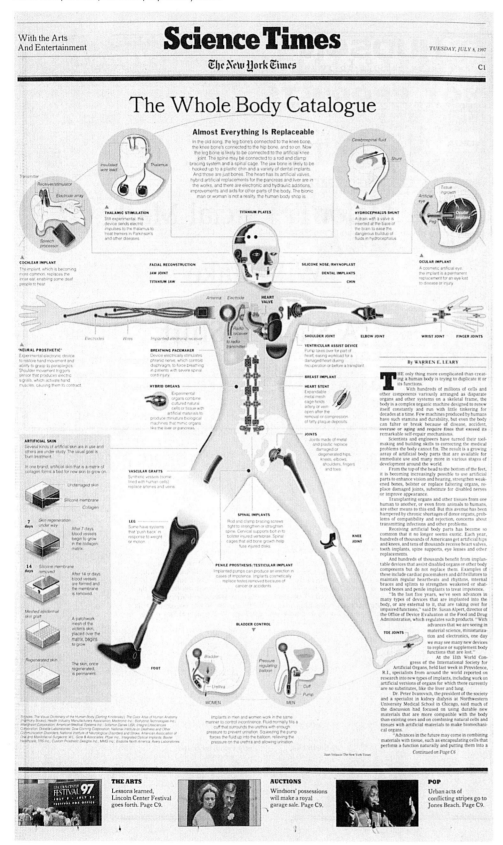

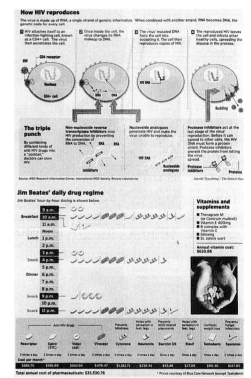

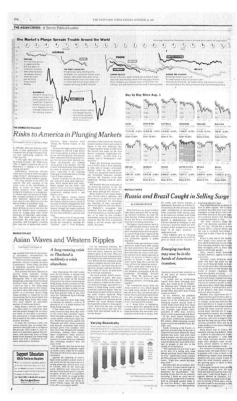

Award of Excellence
The New York Times
New York, NY
Patrick J. Lyons, Graphics Editor

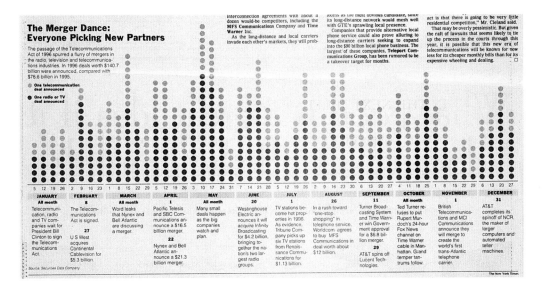

Award of Excellence
The New York Times
New York, NY

Tim Oliver, Presentation Editor; Kris Goodfellow, Graphics Editor

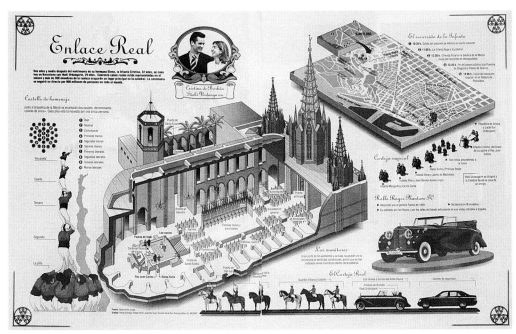

Award of Excellence
El Mundo Del Siglo XXI
Madrid, Spain

Rodrigo Silva, Graphic Artist; Rafa Estrada, Graphic Artist; Rafa Ferrer, Graphic Artist; Juantxo Cruz, Graphic Artist; Ricardo de la Paz, Graphic Artist

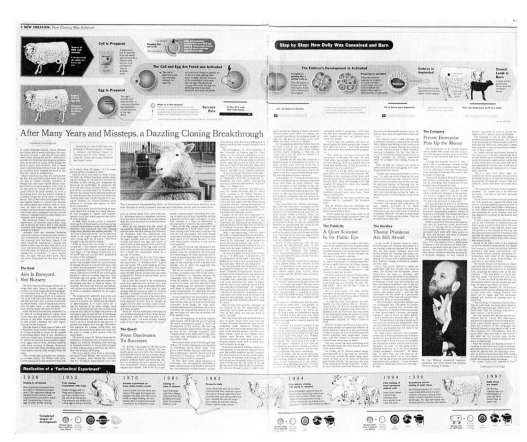

Award of Excellence
The New York Times
New York, NY

Charles M. Blow, Graphic Designer

Award of Excellence
The San Diego Union-Tribune
San Diego, CA

Mark Nowlin, Graphic Journalist; **Dave Hardman,** Graphics Editor; **Bill Gaspard,** Senior Editor/Visuals

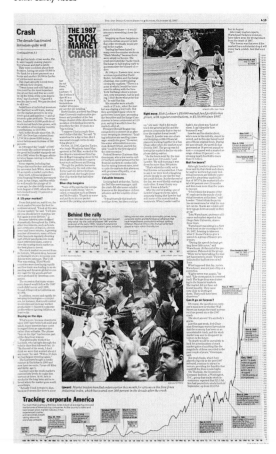

Award of Excellence
The San Diego Union-Tribune
San Diego, CA

Paul Horn, Graphic Journalist; **Dave Hardman,** Graphics Editor

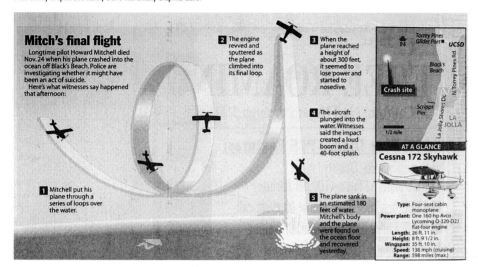

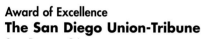

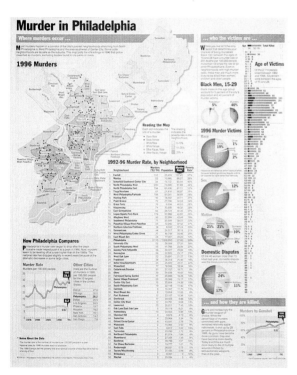

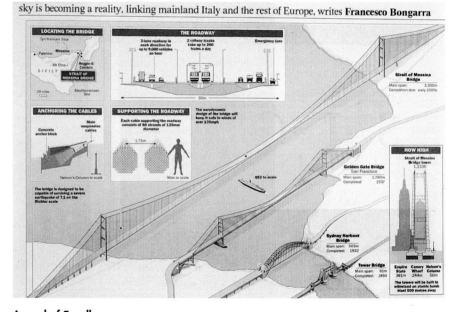

Award of Excellence
The Times
London, England

Geoffrey Sims, Graphics Editor; **Tony Garrett; Fiona Plumer; Paul Bryant**

Award of Excellence
The Philadelphia Inquirer
Philadelphia, PA

Matthew Ericson, Graphic Artist; **David Milne,** A.M.E. Design; **Bill Marsh,** Design Director

Silver
Clarin
Buenos Aires, Argentina
Iñaki Palacios, Art Director; **Lucas Varela**, Artist; **Jaime Serra**, Artist/Graphics Director; **Luis Young**, Artist/Researcher; **Aldo Chippe**, Artist

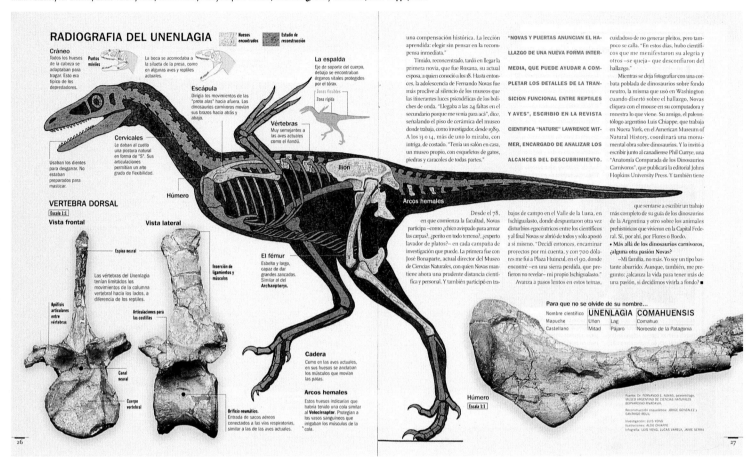

RADIOGRAFIA DEL UNENLAGIA

Huesos encontrados · Estudio de reconstrucción

Cráneo Todos los huesos de la cabeza se adaptaban para tragar. Esto era típico de los depredadores.

Puntos móviles La boca se acomodaba a la silueta de la presa, como en algunas aves y reptiles actuales.

Cervicales Le daban al cuello una postura natural en forma de "S". Sus articulaciones permitían un alto grado de flexibilidad.

Usaban los dientes para desgarrar. No estaban preparados para masticar.

Escápula Dirigía los movimientos de las "proto alas" hacia afuera. Los dinosaurios carnívoros movían sus brazos hacia atrás y abajo.

La espalda Eje de soporte del cuerpo, debajo se encontraban órganos vitales protegidos por el tórax.

Zonas flexibles · Zona rígida

Vértebras Muy semejantes a las aves actuales como el ñandú.

Ilión

Húmero

Arcos hemales

VERTEBRA DORSAL
Escala 1:1
Vista frontal · **Vista lateral**

Espina neural

Las vértebras del Unenlagia tenían limitados los movimientos de la columna vertebral hacia los lados, a diferencia de los reptiles.

Inserción de ligamentos y músculos.

Apófisis articulares entre vértebras · **Articulaciones para las costillas**

Canal neural · Cuerpo vertebral

El fémur Esbelto y largo, capaz de dar grandes zancadas. Similar al **Archaeopteryx**.

Cadera Como en las aves actuales, en sus huesos se anclaban los músculos que movían las patas.

Arcos hemales Estos huesos indicarían que habría tenido una cola similar al **Velocirraptor**. Protegían a los vasos sanguíneos que irrigaban los músculos de la cola.

Orificio neumático. Entrada de sacos aéreos conectados a las vías respiratorias, similar a las de las aves actuales.

Húmero
Escala 1:1

una compensación histórica. La lección aprendida: elegir sin pensar en la recompensa inmediata."

Tímido, reconcentrado, tardó en llegar la primera novia, que fue Roxana, su actual esposa, a quien conoció a los 18. Hasta entonces, la adolescencia de Fernando Novas fue más proclive al silencio de los museos que las itinerantes luces psicodélicas de los boliches de onda. "Llegaba a las 24 faltas en el secundario porque me venía para acá", dice, señalando el piso de cerámica del museo donde trabaja, como investigador, desde 1989. A los 13 o 14, más de uno lo miraba, con intriga, de costado. "Tenía un salón en casa, un museo propio, con esqueletos de gatos, piedras y caracoles de todas partes."

Desde el 78, en que comienza la facultad, Novas participa –como ¿chico avispado para armar las carpas?, ¿perito en todo terreno?, ¿experto lavador de platos?– en cada campaña de investigación que puede. La primera fue con José Bonaparte, actual director del Museo de Ciencias Naturales, con quien Novas mantiene ahora una prudente distancia científica y personal. Y también participó en trabajos de campo en el Valle de la Luna, en Ischigualasto, donde despuntaron otra vez disturbios egocéntricos entre los científicos y al final Novas se abrió de todos y sólo apostó a sí mismo. "Decidí entonces, encaminar proyectos por mi cuenta, y con 700 dólares me fui a Plaza Huincul, en el 90, donde encontré –en una sierra perdida, que prefieron no revelar– mi propio Ischigualasto."

Avanza a pasos lentos en estos temas,

cuidadoso de no generar pleitos, pero tampoco se calla. "En estos días, hubo científicos que me manifestaron su alegría y otros –se queja– que desconfiaron del hallazgo."

Mientras se deja fotografiar con una corbata poblada de dinosaurios sobre fondo neutro, la misma que usó en Washington cuando disertó sobre el hallazgo, Novas cliquea con el mouse en su computadora y muestra lo que viene. Su amigo, el paleontólogo argentino Luis Chiappe, que trabaja en Nueva York, en el American Museum of Natural History, coordinará una monumental obra sobre dinosaurios. Y lo invitó a escribir junto al canadiense Phil Currie, una "Anatomía Comparada de los Dinosaurios Carnívoros", que publicará la editorial Johns Hopkins University Press. Y también tiene que sentarse a escribir un trabajo más completo de su guía de los dinosaurios de la Argentina y otro sobre los animales prehistóricos que vivieron en la Capital Federal. Sí, por ahí, por Flores o Boedo.

• **Más allá de los dinosaurios carnívoros, ¿alguna otra pasión Novas?**

–Mi familia, no más. Yo soy un tipo bastante aburrido. Aunque, también, me pregunto: ¿alcanza la vida para tener más de una pasión, si decidimos vivirla a fondo? ■

Para que no se olvide de su nombre...

Nombre científico	UNENLAGIA	COMAHUENSIS
Mapuche	Uñen	Lag	Comahue
Castellano	Mitad	Pájaro	Noroeste de la Patagonia

Fuente: Dr. FERNANDO E. NOVAS, paleontólogo. MUSEO ARGENTINO DE CIENCIAS NATURALES BERNARDINO RIVADAVIA.
Reconstrucción esquelética: JORGE GONZALEZ y SANTIAGO REUIL.
Investigador: LUIS YONG.
Ilustraciones: ALDO CHIPPE.
Infografía: LUIS YONG, LUCAS VARELA, JAIME SERRA.

El hombre
QUE HIZO VOLAR
a los dinosaurios

dinosaurio no era ningún gigante: unos 2,30 de largo por 1,20 de alto, pero con algo del feroz velocirraptor de Spielberg en "Parque Jurásico". Y si bien no acaba con el misterio del nacimiento de las aves, lo achica bastante. No lo dice él, que desde hace un año y medio vive si se quiere obsesionado con la entidad de estos huesos parecidos a la estructura ósea de un avestruz, pero con 90 millones de años de historia. "El descubrimiento puede ayudar a entender los detalles de la transición funcional entre reptiles y aves", escribió Lawrence Witmer, el científico que analizó críticamente el trabajo de Novas en la prestigiosa revista "Nature".

A las cinco de la tarde, la oficina de Novas, un recoveco de dos metros por cinco, comienza a poblarse de manera desmesurada. Llegan casi todos los jóvenes que participaron en la expedición que regresó con la novedad científica. De fondo, suena una música leve, que puede ser Vangelis o algo así, nada que despabile demasiado los sentidos. Está Sebastián Apesteguía, un estudiante de Paleontología de 20 años, que toma apuntes de pie. El dibujante Jorge González, de 18, en un rincón, busca encontrar, sobre el papel, posibles gestos de caza del dinosaurio casi pájaro. Agustín Scanferla, estudiante secundario todavía, que tiene definida su vida y vivirá –seguro– entre huesos fósiles, escribe en una computadora. Fue Agustín el que se encontró con una vértebra del Unenlagia, el 9 de enero de 1996, en una sierra cerca de Plaza Huincul, en la provincia de Neuquén. "Vení, Agustín. Contá cómo fue...", lo invita Novas. "Había poca luz, era de mañana...", dice el chico, algo nervioso por el grabador encendido. "Había poca luz, pero porque estaba por anochecer", lo corrige el resto. La carcajada es más o menos general.

Hay buen clima. Sólo faltan del equipo el fundamental Pablo Puertas, técnico que trabaja en el Museo Paleontológico "Edigio Feruglio", de Trelew, quien firmó como coautor la investigación publicada en "Nature". Y tampoco están Santiago Reuil, de 18, que se encargó de realizar la réplica de los huesos de Unenlagia; y Adriana Mancuso, casi bióloga, que ajusta detalles todo el tiempo. "Fuimos a la sierra –bromean– con un jeep y dos camionetas que eran, de verdad, prehistóricas."

No fue sólo el dinosaurio más parecido a un pájaro el único acierto de aquella expedición. Volvieron también con una pata casi integra de un nuevo dinosaurio carnívoro: el Araucanorraptor, lo llamaron. "Y tenemos –augura en tono firme Novas, ahora decididamente ganador– un as en la manga que todavía no podemos mostrar, porque se lo debe•

Tal vez haya sido una lección que Fernando Novas no olvidó. Pero hasta los 5 años, su destino y primera inclinación tenía los colores azul y amarillo. "De Boca", decía el pibe, ante la pregunta inevitable. Pero a los 6, en 1966, Racing arma aquel notable equipo de Pizzutti y el chico, seducido por el éxito, se hace de la Academia. "Y no ganamos –se lamenta– ningún campeonato más." Muchos años después, ya crecido, asegura que en la Universidad de La Plata eran sólo dos personas las que cursaban Paleontología –él y Pablo Pandolfi, recuerda con precisión– nunca dudó de su elección profesional. Y le salió bien. "¿Quién iba a pensar que el tema de los dinosaurios iba a ejercer la seducción y atracción de estos años?", se pregunta. Y él mismo, por su cuenta, asocia una cosa con la otra. "Debe ser –dice•

El dinosaurio que quería volar

Es el eslabón perdido entre los dinosaurios y las aves. Los 22 huesos encontrados permiten conjeturar cómo vivía y mataba el Unenlagia Comahuensis hace 90 millones de años.

EL PICO El **Unenlagia Comahuensis** debió tener un "pico" parecido al del **Archaeopteryx**.

1 · Archaeopteryx · Dientes · Hocico recubierto de piel escamosa.
2 · La piel se cornifica formando una sustancia semejante a nuestras uñas.
3 · Los dientes desaparecen.
Ave moderna A través de millones de años el pico fue cubriendo al "hocico".

LAS PLUMAS La aparición de plumas tendría como objetivo regular la temperatura corporal.

PROTO ALAS Ayudaban a mantener su equilibrio e incrementar su velocidad. Para reconocimiento e intimidación.

LA COLA La usaba para mantener el cuerpo en equilibrio. Como antecesor del **Archaeopteryx**, el pájaro conocido más antiguo, la evidencia sugiere la posibilidad de que el Unenlagia debía tener pequeñas plumas en la cola.

El **Archaeopteryx** poseía una cola desarrollada, larga y emplumada que actuaba como un timón durante el vuelo.

El paso intermedio Unenlagia 90 millones de años. Las "proto alas" le permiten aletear y controlar el movimiento al correr y saltar.

Descendiente del **Velocirraptor** y antecesor del **Archaeopteryx**, ambos depredadores, se cree que esta especie también lo era, aunque no se han encontrado restos de dientes.

DE BRAZOS A ALAS
Antiguos depredadores Velocirraptor 210 millones de años. Los brazos le permitían la captura y manipulación de las presas.

Sus movimientos estaban limitados por el tipo de articulación del hombro. Los brazos colgaban debajo del cuerpo.

Elevaba los brazos con una mayor amplitud que los dinosaurios primitivos.

Profunda modificación en la orientación de la cavidad articular del hombro.

Los huesos del brazo están más desarrollados.

Aves actuales Las alas están totalmente adaptadas para el vuelo. Mayor movilidad del brazo sobre el hombro. Gran desarrollo de las alas.

LAS PATAS Posterior al **Velocirraptor**, se presume que ambos tenían un dedo con una larga uña diseñada para desgarrar a sus presas.

Caminaban apoyando sus dedos de las patas.
LINEA DE TIERRA

Almohadilla · Dedos

Todos los dinosaurios, aun los más gigantes, como el Brachiosaurus, sólo apoyaban los dedos de las patas en el suelo.

Comparación de tamaño

Silver
The New York Times
New York, NY

Charles M. Blow, Graphics Director; **Michael Valenti**, Art Director

Award of Excellence
Asbury Park Press
Neptune, NJ

Andrew Prendimano, Art & Photo Director, Designer; **Harris G. Siegel**,
M.E./Design & Photography; **Ed Gabel**, Infographics Artist

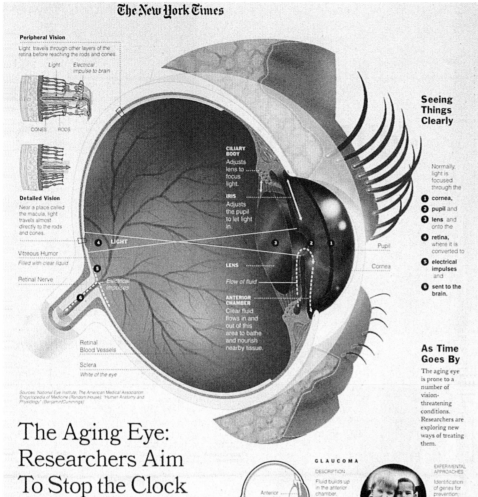

The Aging Eye: Researchers Aim To Stop the Clock

By JANE E. BRODY

New treatments and ways to stop trouble before it starts are sought.

AGING Americans expect more from their eyes these days than ever before. People in their 70's and 80's want to be able to drive, play cards, recognize people on the street, travel with their grandchildren, take advantage of senior discounts in the movies and read the books they missed while working full time.

But eyes have a way of aging that can render such expectations unrealistic. Far worse than the loss of visual acuity that prompts most middle-aged people to resort to magnifying lenses are sight-robbing diseases like glaucoma, cataracts, age-related macular degeneration, diabetic retinopathy and other retinal disorders that afflict tens of millions of Americans, usually after age 50.

The incidence of such potentially blinding disorders is increasing rapidly as the number of older people grows. Experts predict, for example, that by the year 2030, 6.3 million older Americans will develop macular degeneration, up from 1.7 million in 1995. It is a still-irreversible disorder that robs people of the central vision needed to drive, read, watch television, recognize faces, play cards or do any fine work. If Grandma Moses had had macular degeneration, her artistic talents would never have been noticed.

Fortunately, research is progressing on a number of promising new treatments, including low doses of

radiation, and a combination of lasers and light-activated chemicals, both of which are used for some particularly hard-to-treat forms of macular degeneration. Other research is concentrating on how to stop toxins that damage the eye in glaucoma, and the genetics of several different eye diseases.

"Older Americans today expect to enjoy their retirement with the same visual capacity that they had in their younger years," said Dr. Harold Spalter, professor of ophthalmology at Columbia-Presbyterian Medical Center in New York. But, alas, as was apparent at a four-day seminar that Dr. Spalter chaired here last month, researchers are still a long way from knowing how to reverse most blinding eye disorders.

Still, major progress in understanding and treating these conditions — and perhaps detecting them early enough to blunt their effects — was evident at the seminar, organized by Research to Prevent Blindness, a New York-based voluntary organization. Unfortunately, though, many elderly Americans cannot afford the early detection procedures

Continued on Page 6

Award of Excellence
Chicago Tribune
Chicago, IL

Celeste Bernard, Graphics Coordinator; **Kevin Hand**, Graphics Artist;
Therese Shechter, Associate Graphics & Design Editor

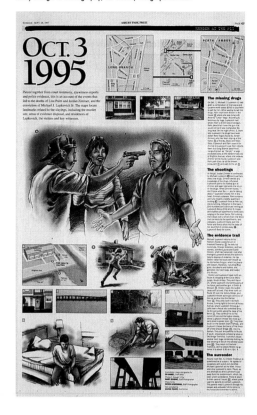

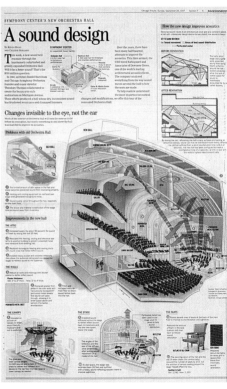

Award of Excellence
• Also an **Award of Excellence** for Special Section Without Ads

The Baltimore Sun
Baltimore, MD

Lamont W. Harvey, Graphic Artist; **Emily Holmes**, Graphics Editor; **Joseph Hutchinson**, A.M.E. Graphics/Design; **Jerold Council**, Graphics Director; **Steve Marcus**, Assistant Sports Editor

Award of Excellence
Clarin
Buenos Aires, Argentina

Iñaki Palacios, Art Director; **Alejandro Tumas**, Artist; **Jaime Serra**, Graphics Director; **Stella Bin**, Researcher

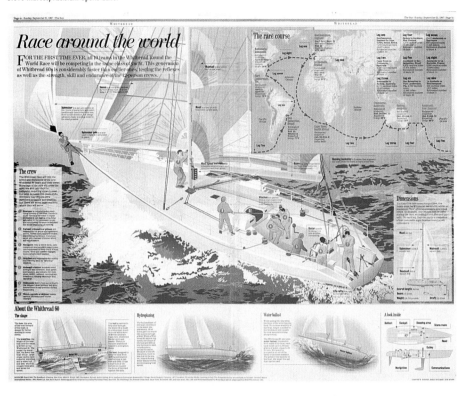

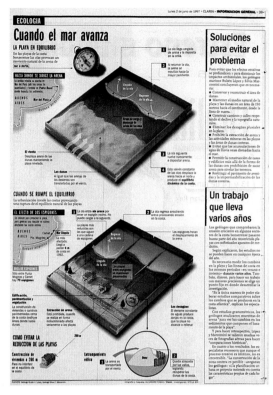

Award of Excellence
Clarin
Buenos Aires, Argentina

Iñaki Palacios, Art Director; **Lucas Varela**, Artist; **Jaime Serra**, Artist/Graphics Director

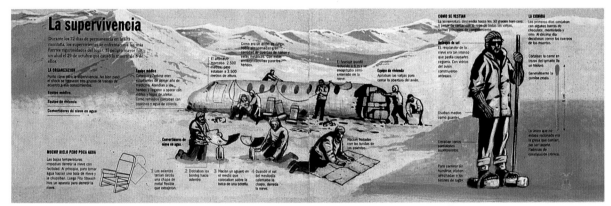

Award of Excellence
Clarin
Buenos Aires, Argentina

Iñaki Palacios, Art Director; **Lucas Varela**, Artist; **Jaime Serra**, Graphics Director; **Stella Bin**, Researcher

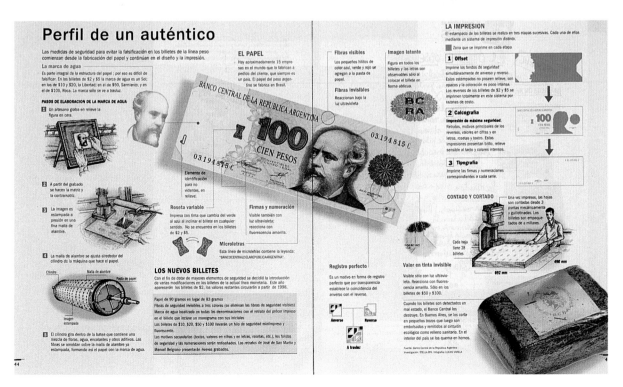

Award of Excellence
The New York Times
New York, NY

Jan Staller, Photographer; Janet Froelich, Art Director

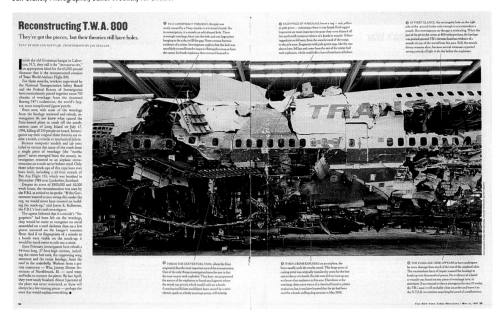

Reconstructing T.W.A. 800
They've got the pieces, but their theories still have holes.

Award of Excellence
Los Angeles Times
Los Angeles, CA

Rebecca Perry, Artist; Victoria McCargar, Graphics Editor

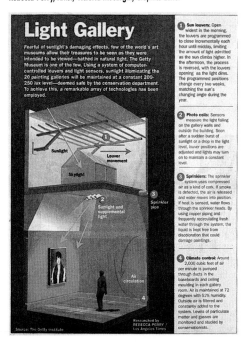

Light Gallery

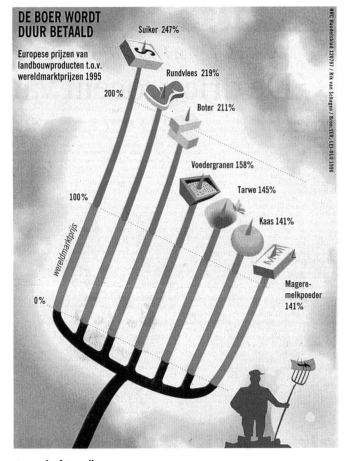

**DE BOER WORDT
DUUR BETAALD**

Europese prijzen van
landbouwproducten t.o.v.
wereldmarktprijzen 1995

Suiker 247%
Rundvlees 219%
Boter 211%
Voedergranen 158%
Tarwe 145%
Kaas 141%
Magere-
melkpoeder 141%

Award of Excellence
NRC Handelsblad
Rotterdam, The Netherlands

Rik van Schagen, Graphic Artist

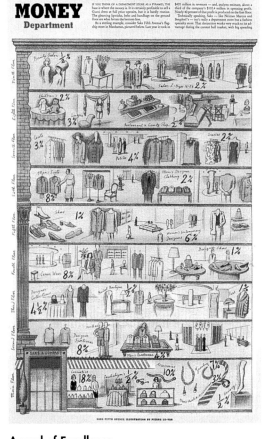

The
MONEY
Department

Award of Excellence
The New York Times Magazine
New York, NY

Janet Froelich, Art Director; Nancy Harris, Designer; Pierre Le-Tan, Illustrator

Award of Excellence
Omaha World-Herald
Omaha, NE

Dean Weinlaub, Infographics Artist; **Mike Drummy**, Art Director; **Laura Ruel**, Presentation Editor

Award of Excellence
The Sacramento Bee
Sacramento, CA

Edie Lau, Researcher; **Nam Nguyen**, Assistant Art Director; **Howard Shintaku**, Art Director; **Gregory Favre**, Executive Editor; **Mort Saltzman**, A.M.E. Graphics; **Rick Rodriguez**, M.E.

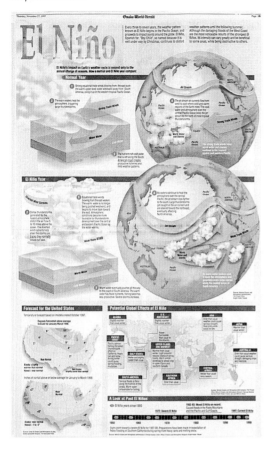

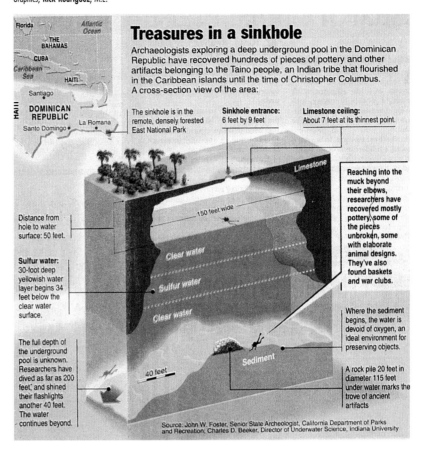

Treasures in a sinkhole

Archaeologists exploring a deep underground pool in the Dominican Republic have recovered hundreds of pieces of pottery and other artifacts belonging to the Taino people, an Indian tribe that flourished in the Caribbean islands until the time of Christopher Columbus. A cross-section view of the area:

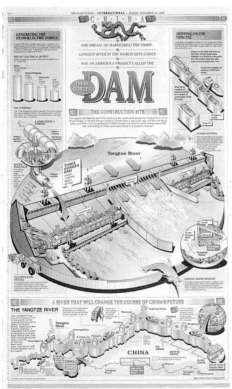

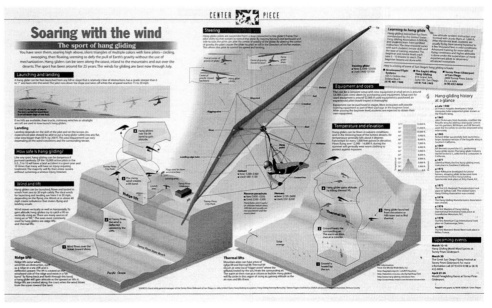

Award of Excellence
The San Diego Union-Tribune
San Diego, CA
Mark Nowlin, Graphic Journalist; **Dave Hardman**, Graphics Editor

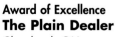

Award of Excellence
The Plain Dealer
Cleveland, OH
James Owens, Artist

Award of Excellence
Star Tribune
Minneapolis, MN

Ray Grumney, Graphics Director; **Greg Branson**, Graphic Artist; **Dean Rebuffoni**, Environmental Reporter; **Samantha Branson**, Copy Editor; **Howard Sinker**, State Team Leader; **Bill Dunn**, Visual Content Editor

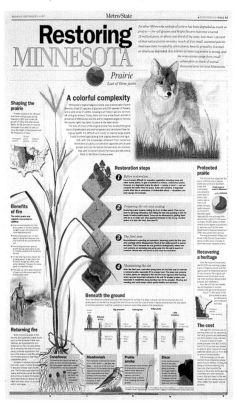

Award of Excellence
St. Petersburg Times
St. Petersburg, FL

Cristina Martinez, Artist

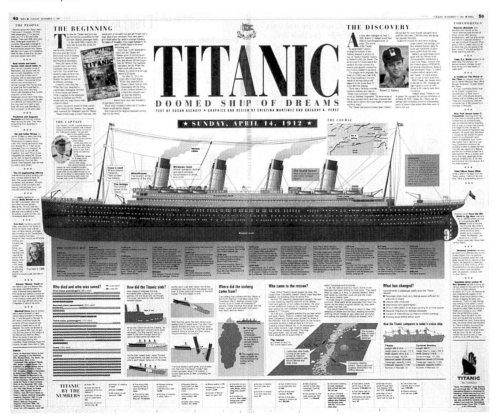

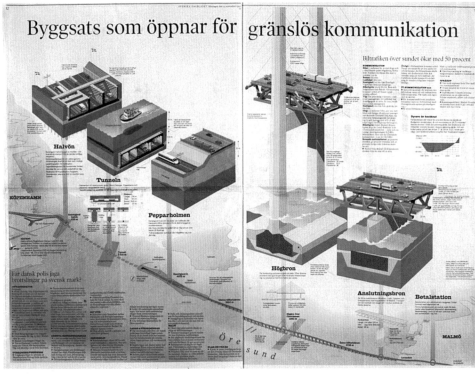

Award of Excellence
Svenska Dagbladet
Stockholm, Sweden
Staff

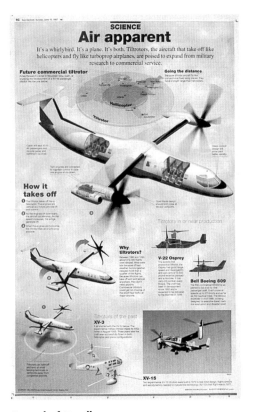

Award of Excellence
Sun-Sentinel
Ft. Lauderdale, FL

R. Scott Horner, Assistant Graphics Editor; **Kristen Walbolt**, Graphic Researcher; **Leavett Biles**, Graphics Director

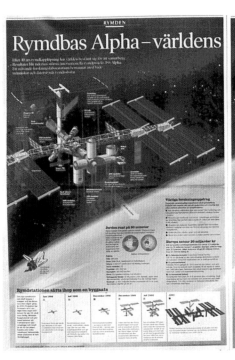

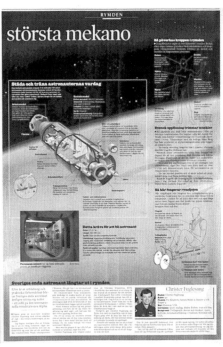

Award of Excellence
Svenska Dagbladet
Stockholm, Sweden
Staff

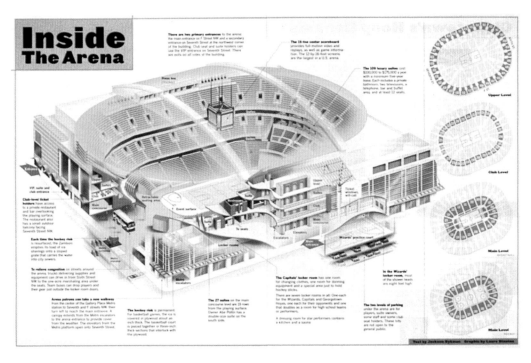

Award of Excellence
The Washington Post Magazine
Washington, DC
Laura Stanton, Graphic Artist; **Jackson Dykman**, Graphics Director; **Kelly Doe**, Magazine Art Director

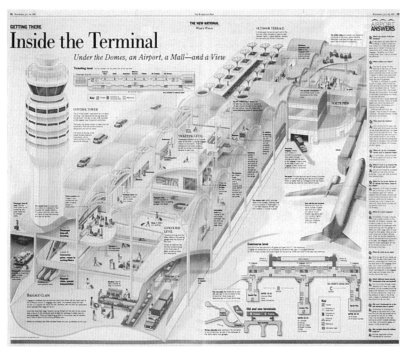

Award of Excellence
The Washington Post
Washington, DC
Laura Stanton, Graphic Artist; **Jackson Dykman**, Graphics Director

Silver
The New York Times
New York, NY

Juan Velasco, Graphics Editor

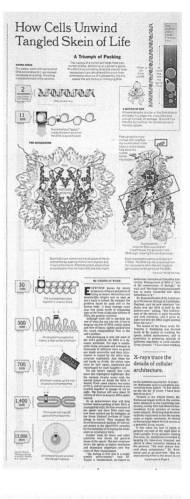

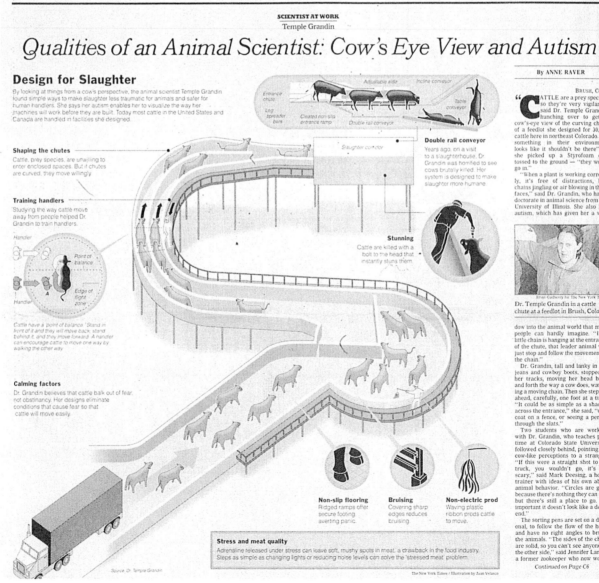

Better Weapons Emerge For War Against Mines

By WARREN E. LEARY

WASHINGTON

THEY lurk underground like alien predators in a science fiction film. From countless locations they spring unexpectedly, snatching an arm, or a hand, or a leg, or a life.

But unlike movie monsters, they are actually here. They are real and they kill or wound every day all over the world. They are land mines.

Most of the world's nations have agreed to stop manufacturing, shipping or using land mines, but the political struggle to ban the explosive devices may have been the easiest part of the battle against these remnants of war.

Scientists and engineers say the really tough work is going to be finding and destroying the more than 110 million mines the United Nations estimates are buried around the world in as many as 70 countries.

"We're at the beginning of a long, complex process, but at least we've started," said Dr. Kosta Tsipis, an arms expert at the Massachusetts Institute of Technology. "If we are fortunate, we will get 80 percent of these mines out of the ground in 20 to 25 years, but it's going to take an international effort and new technology."

The global struggle against these weapons took a significant turn this month when representatives of some 125 nations met in Ottawa to sign a treaty banning antipersonnel land mines, a type designed to wound or kill people. The United States refused to endorse the pact, saying such mines were still needed to protect American troops in Korea. But President Clinton said the United States would help lead an effort to remove mines from the rest of the world, doing such things as developing and deploying new technology to find and destroy these munitions.

The need is urgent because of continued human suffering. The International Committee of the Red Cross estimates that land mines kill 8,000 to 10,000 people a year and seriously injure at least twice as many more, often destroying hands and limbs. Most of the victims are civilians and many are children, experts say.

The United Nations estimates that using cur-

Worldwide, more than 110 million buried mines remain a threat.

---

rent technology, it would take $33 billion and 1,100 years to clear all the mined areas of the world. These areas include countries in Europe, like Croatia and Bosnia and Herzegovina; in Africa, like Angola, the Sudan and Somalia; in the Middle East, like Egypt, Iran and Iraq; in Central America, like Honduras and El Salvador; and in Asia, including Laos, Cambodia and China.

Humanitarian mine removal is the process of carefully clearing mines after a conflict, in contrast to how advancing armies and their special tanks and bulldozers try to cut their way rapidly through mine fields during a battle. And while the humane work results in the removal of about

Continued on Page 7

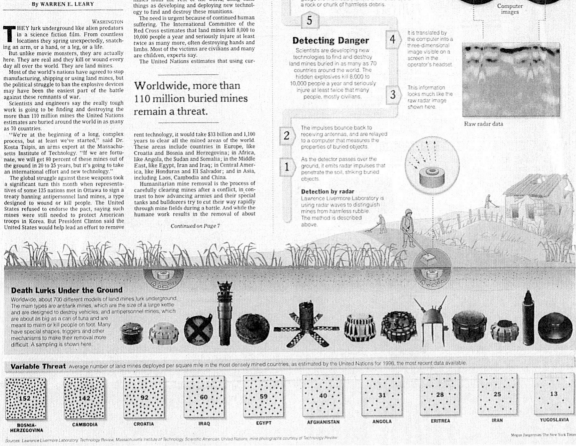

6 The image may also give clues to the type of mine — antipersonnel or antitank — information that could be critical in removing it safely.

The image lets the operator visualize the rough size, shape and depth of the object, and to gauge the likelihood that it is a mine rather than a rock or chunk of harmless debris.

Computer images

5

Detecting Danger

Scientists are developing new technologies to find and destroy land mines buried in as many as 70 countries around the world. The hidden explosives kill 8,000 to 10,000 people a year and seriously injure at least twice that many people, mostly civilians.

4 It is translated by the computer into a three-dimensional image visible on a screen in the operator's headset.

3 This information looks much like the raw radar image shown here.

Raw radar data

2 The impulses bounce back to receiving antennas, and are relayed to a computer that measures the properties of buried objects.

1 As the detector passes over the ground, it emits radar impulses that penetrate the soil, striking buried objects.

Detection by radar

Lawrence Livermore Laboratory is using radar waves to distinguish mines from harmless rubble. The method is described above.

Death Lurks Under the Ground

Worldwide, about 700 different models of land mines lurk underground. The main types are antitank mines, which are the size of a large kettle and are designed to destroy vehicles, and antipersonnel mines, which are about as big as a can of tuna and are meant to maim or kill people on foot. Many have special shapes, triggers and other mechanisms to make their removal more difficult. A sampling is shown here.

Variable Threat Average number of land mines deployed per square mile in the most densely mined countries, as estimated by the United Nations for 1996, the most recent data available.

152	142	92	60	59	40	31	28	25	13
BOSNIA-HERZEGOVINA	CAMBODIA	CROATIA	IRAQ	EGYPT	AFGHANISTAN	ANGOLA	ERITREA	IRAN	YUGOSLAVIA

Sources: Lawrence Livermore Laboratory, Technology Review, Massachusetts Institute of Technology, Scientific American, United Nations; mine photographs courtesy of Technology Review

Megan Jaegerman/The New York Times

Silver
The New York Times
New York, NY

Megan Jaegerman, Graphics Editor

•Also an **Award of Excellence** for Informational Graphics

Life: Start Here ...

A woman's life cycle can sometimes seem like an obstacle course in which she must dodge an increasing number of health threats. In reality, as medical experts point out, every stage in a woman's life has its health benefits. Indeed, women typically pass through long periods of essentially good health. Risks can be reduced if good habits are nurtured early on. And even late in the game, women can undertake preventive measures that improve the quality of life. *MARGOT SLADE*

BIRTH

AGE 1 2 3 4 5 6 7

▶ **CHILDHOOD**
BIRTH THROUGH AGE 6
Girls tend to be healthier than boys during the first six months of life. Language and reading skills develop earlier, as does some physical prowess, especially during the first year.

For many women, adjusting to middle age means restructuring their physical and sexual identities.

▼ **LATE MIDDLE AGE**
60 THROUGH 65
Adjustment to middle age is completed, and just in time to enjoy a period of generally good health. Women may feel less obliged to care for others, but many find they have a husband who needs to be cared for.

Growth spurt

▶ **PREPUBERTY**
7 THROUGH 11
A major growth spurt marks the premenstrual years. And with physical development often outpacing intellectual and emotional maturity, girls may feel uneasy with who they are and what they look like.

Body image

● The most rapid loss of bone mineral occurs in the first few years after menstruation stops.

Bone loss

● **PUBERTY**
12 THROUGH 17
Girls are building bones for a healthy adulthood; calcium and exercise are vital.

● **Eating disorders** begin most often between ages 14 and 18, when body image can become an obsession.

● **Sexually-transmitted diseases** pose a greater risk to teen-agers than to adults because the still-developing cervix is easily infected.

Pregnancy risk is high, but teen-agers do as well as, and often better than, women during labor and delivery.

Overtraining in athletics can interrupt the menstrual cycle, depleting estrogen and, over the long term, bone mass.

▶ **YOUNG ADULTHOOD**
18 THROUGH 25
The good news: Young women, a generally healthy lot, are usually not at risk for ovarian and breast cancer. But they are increasingly smoking, putting themselves at risk for lung cancer – the leading cancer among women – later in life.

▶ **TYPICAL CHILDBEARING YEARS**
25 THROUGH 35
These women have a lower risk of gonorrhea and chlamydia. Pregnancy now confers health benefits that include lower risk for breast and ovarian cancer.

MENOPAUSE AND SOON AFTER
50 THROUGH 59
One event defines menopause: no more menstruation; no more worries about birth control either, which many women applaud and some bemoan as they adjust to being middle aged and no longer child-bearing age. But in the aftermath of menopause may come distressing hot flashes, night sweats and sleep disturbances.

LATE CHILDBEARING YEARS
36 THROUGH 50
Older mothers tend to be better equipped as parents: calmer, more self-aware, settled. But women in midlife are at higher risk of auto-immune diseases like lupus.

"YOUNG" OLD
65 THROUGH 80
"Physiologic reserve" – the ability to tolerate stresses – is fairly high. The effect of preventive measures increases as the risk of disease, including cancer and heart disease, increases with age.

A time marked by an appreciation of the moment, value of the self.

Obesity risk increases, especially between ages 65 and 74, when many women are at their most sedentary. Accumulation of fat around the midsection carries a high risk of heart attack.

Heart alert

Pear shape: Low health risk
Apple shape: High health risk

Fracture risk

OLD
81 PLUS
Diversity is the hallmark of this age group – diversity of health, mood, cognition. For many conditions – hypertension, for example, or diabetes – it is never too late to treat.

Indeed, simple measures, like moderate exercise or diet changes, can yield enormous benefits.

Illustration by Megan Jaegerman/The New York Times

Award of Excellence
Clarin
Buenos Aires, Argentina
Lucas Varela, Artist

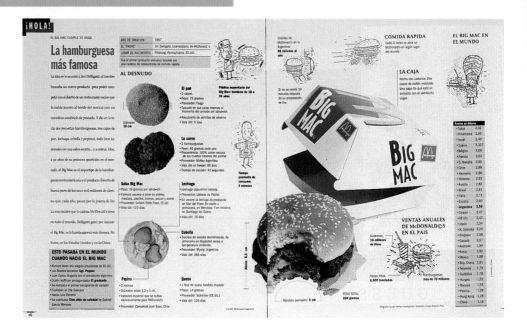

Award of Excellence
Clarin
Buenos Aires, Argentina
Luis Young, Artist

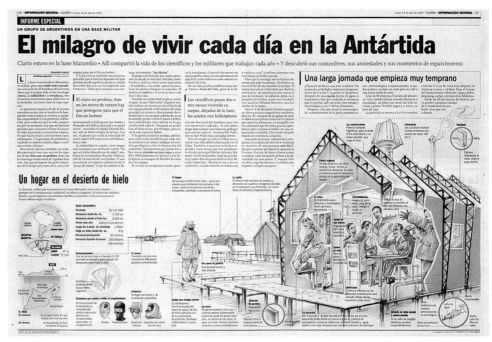

Award of Excellence
• Also an **Award of Excellence** for Informational Graphics
El Mundo Del Siglo XXI
Madrid, Spain
Juancho Cruz, Graphic Journalist

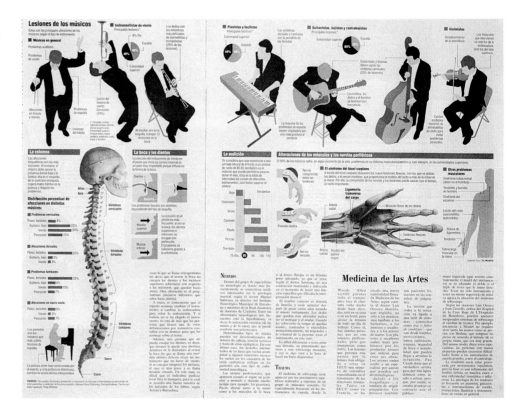

Award of Excellence
Clarin
Buenos Aires, Argentina

Jaime Serra, Artist

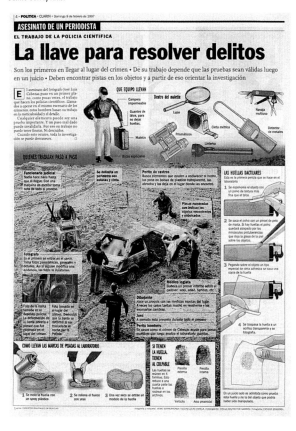

Award of Excellence
The New York Times
New York, NY

Frank O'Connell, Graphics Editor

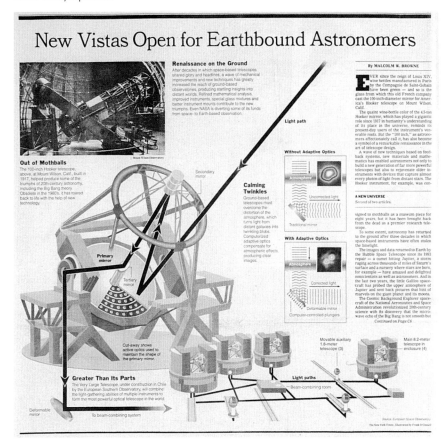

Award of Excellence
•Also an **Award of Excellence** for Informational Graphics

The Washington Post
Washington, DC

Laura Stanton, Graphic Artist

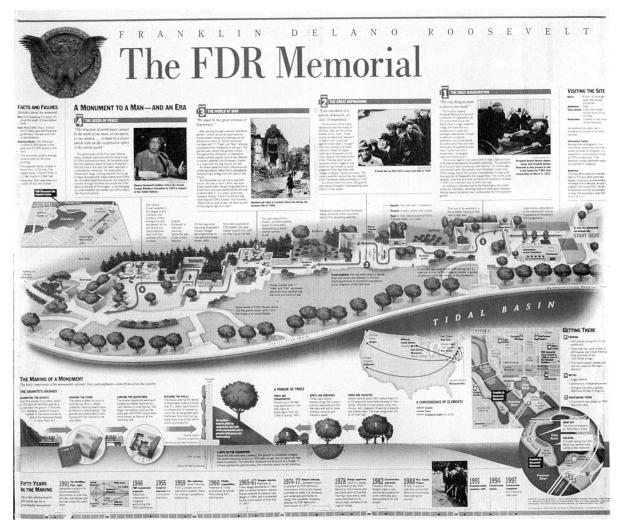

Gold
Clarin

Buenos Aires, Argentina

Jaime Serra, Artist/Graphics Director;
Iñaki Palacios, Art Director

Awarded a **Gold Medal** for its new ground-breaking presentation of graphic information. It represents a new sophisticated melding of art and journalism. Beginning with an ingenious concept, the artist takes graphic conventions such as bar charts and time lines and marries them with every day objects and fine art textures. The graphics demonstrate mastery of typography, photography, composition and design. It is breakthrough work.

●●●●●

Ganador de una Medalla de Oro por su presentación revolucionaria de la información gráfica y representa una nueva amalgama sofisticada de arte y periodismo. A partir de un concepto ingenioso, el artista hace uso de convenciones gráficas tales como las tablas de barras y las líneas de tiempo y las fusiona con elementos cotidianos y finas texturas de arte. Los gráficos demuestran una maestría de la tipografía, fotografía, composición y diseño. Un trabajo innovador.

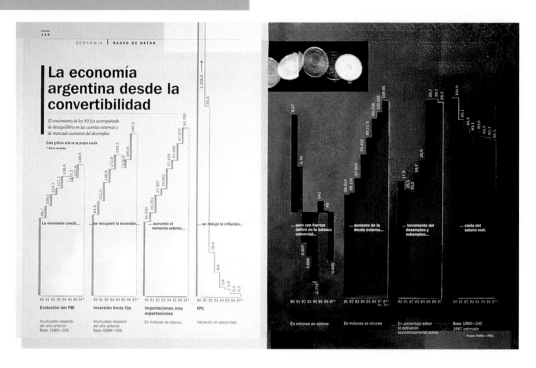

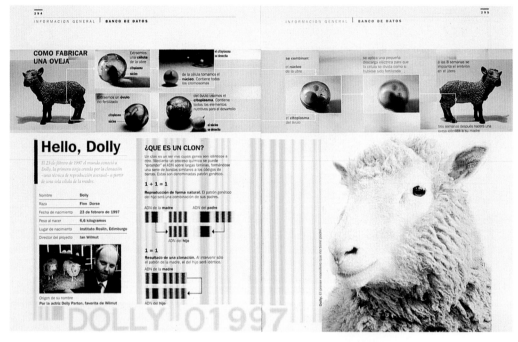

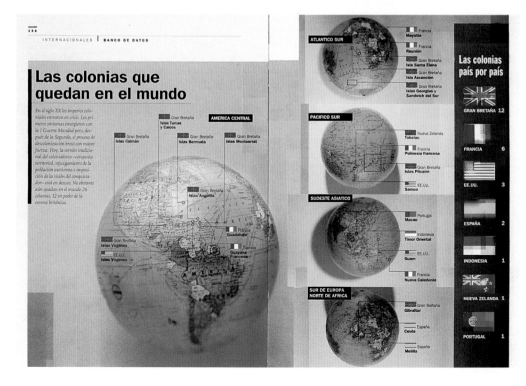

Silver
•Also an **Award of Excellence** for Informational Graphics
The New York Times
New York, NY
Charles M. Blow, Graphics Director; **Staff**

Saving the Ship That Revolutionized War at Sea

By WILLIAM J. BROAD

Raising the Monitor

After 135 years of undersea decay, and 24 years of expert study, the Union warship Monitor is in need of rescue. A new plan calls for important parts of the ironclad to be raised for conservation and museum display.

THE RECOVERY GEAR

Civil War Battle of the Ironclads

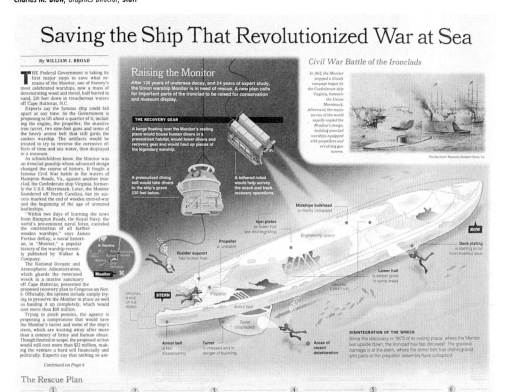

The Rescue Plan

| 1 Recovering small artifacts | 2 Bracing port side | 3 Removing propulsive gear | 4 Clearing turret area | 5 Lifting turret | 6 Stabilizing remains |

Dainty Worm Tells Secrets Of the Human Genetic Code

By NICHOLAS WADE

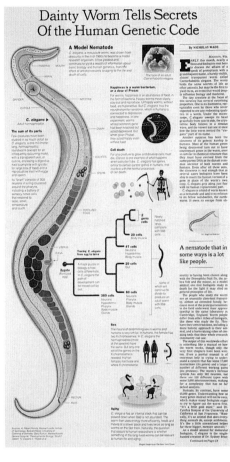

A nematode that in some ways is a lot like people.

¡HOLA!

"Buenos Aires también es ese árbol"
JORGE LUIS BORGES

El gomero y la historia

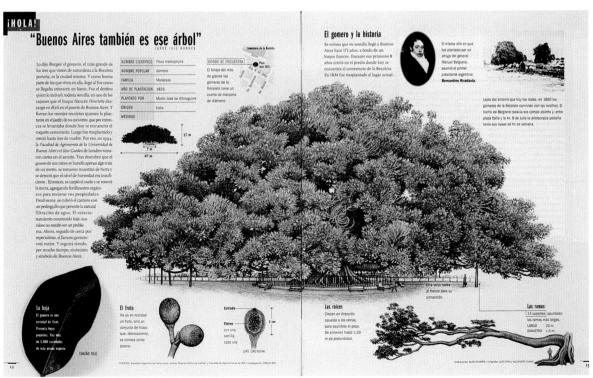

Award of Excellence
Clarin
Buenos Aires, Argentina
Iñaki Palacios, Art Director; Stella Bin, Researcher; Jaime Serra, Graphics Director; Alejandro Tumas, Artist; Luis Young, Artist

Award of Excellence
Clarin

Buenos Aires, Argentina

Jaime Serra, Artist; **Gerardo Morel**, Artist; **Alejandro Tumas**, Artist; **Iñaki Palacios**, Art Director

Award of Excellence
The Guardian

London, England

Paddy Allen, Graphics Editor; **Steve Villiers**, Deputy Graphics Editor; **Finbarr Sheehy**, Designer; **Chris Madden**, Designer; **Michael Agar**, Designer; **John Elsey**, Designer

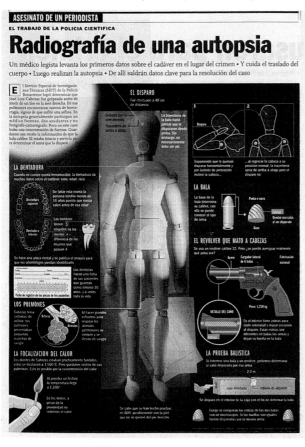

ASESINATO DE UN PERIODISTA
EL TRABAJO DE LA POLICIA CIENTIFICA

Radiografía de una autopsia

Un médico legista levanta los primeros datos sobre el cadáver en el lugar del crimen • Y cuida el traslado del cuerpo • Luego realizan la autopsia • De allí saldrán datos clave para la resolución del caso

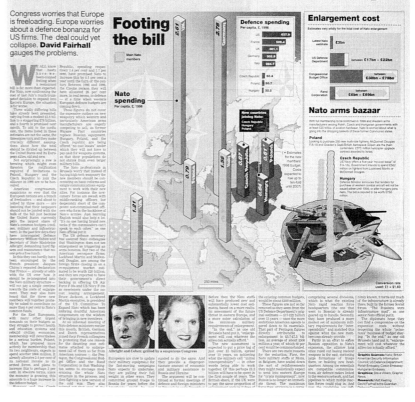

No free launch for the new boys

Congress worries that Europe is freeloading. Europe worries about a defence bonanza for US firms. The deal could yet collapse. **David Fairhall** gauges the problems.

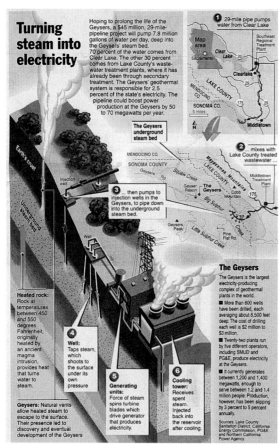

Turning steam into electricity

Hoping to prolong the life of the Geysers, a $45 million, 29-mile-pipeline project will pump 7.8 million gallons of water per day, deep into the Geysers' steam bed. 70 percent of the water comes from Clear Lake. The other 30 percent comes from Lake County's waste-water treatment plants, where it has already been through secondary treatment. The Geysers' geothermal system is responsible for 2.5 percent of the state's electricity. The pipeline could boost power production at the Geysers by 50 to 70 megawatts per year.

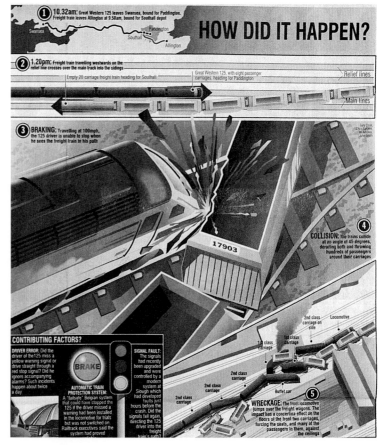

HOW DID IT HAPPEN?

Award of Excellence
The Sacramento Bee

Sacramento, CA

Pam Dinsmore, Executive News Editor; **Nam Nguyen**, Assistant Art Director; **Howard Shintaku**, Art Director; **Gregory Favre**, Executive Editor; **Mort Saltzman**, A.M.E. Graphics; **Rick Rodriguez**, M.E.

Award of Excellence
The Sunday Times

London, England

Gary Cook, Graphics Editor; **Chris Sargent**, Deputy Graphics Editor; **Ian Moores**, Graphic Artist; **John Smith**, Graphic Artist; **Jenny Preece**, Graphic Artist; **Julian Osbaldstone**, Graphic Artist; **Roy Cooper**, Graphic Artist; **Clare Harrison**, Graphic Artist

Chapter Eleven

MISCELLA- NEOUS

Continuing to pay tribute to the world's best newspaper designs, the 19th edition of The Best of Newspaper Design is a stunning collection of modern work. The included works were selected from more than 10,000 entries submitted by newspapers all over the world. This exceptional collection is an essential reference for anyone involved in print media, graphics, photography, design, journalism, or communications.

The competition, which is sponsored annually by the Society of News Design and the S.I. Newhouse School of Public Communications at Syracuse University, recognizes excellence in newspaper design and graphics. Awards include Best of Show, Gold, Silver, Award of Excellence, Special Recogni-tion, plus the honor of World's Best Designed Newspaper. Categories for judging include overall page design, portfolio, magazine cover design, art and illustration, photo journalism, and informational graphics.

This nineteenth edition presents the finest newspaper design in the field.

Selected by a panel of 21 judges of the Society for News Design, the award-winning pub-lications featured in this nineteenth edition were chosen for excellence in design.

The Best of Newspaper Design, 19th edition, features: Text in English and Spanish; 840 awards: World's Best-Designed Newspapers, Best of Show, Gold medals, Judges' Special Recognition, Silver medals, and Awards of Excel-lence. More than 12,100 entries were reviewed from hundreds of publications from around the world to select winners from 158 publications. Categories included: Overall design, news, features, portfo-lios, special coverage, special sections, magazines, art and illustration, photog-raphy, informational graphics and

Selected by a panel of 21 judges of the Society for News Design, the award-winning pub-lications featured in this nineteenth edition were chosen for excellence in design.Continuing to pay tribute to the world's best newspa-per designs, the 19th edition of The Best of Newspaper Design is a stun-ning collection of modern work. The included works were selected from more than 10,000 entries submitted by newspapers all over the world. This exceptional collection is an essential reference for anyone involved in print media, graphics, photography, design,

Selected by a panel of 21 judges of the Society for News Design, the award-winning pub-lications featured in this nineteenth edition were chosen for excellence in design.Continuing to pay tribute to the world's best newspa-per designs, the 19th edition of The Best of Newspaper Design is a stun-ning collection of modern work. The included works were selected from more than 10,000 entries submitted by newspapers all over the world. This exceptional collection is an essential reference for anyone involved in print media, graphics, photography, design, journalism, or communications.

The competition, which is sponsored annually by the Society of News Design and the S.I. Newhouse School of Public Communications at Syracuse University, recognizes excellence in newspaper design and graphics. Awards include Best of Show, Gold, Silver, Award of Excellence, Special Recogni-tion, plus the honor of World's Best Designed Newspaper. Categories for judging include overall page design, portfolio, magazine cover design, art and illustration, photo jour-nalism, and informational graphics.

This nineteenth edition presents the finest newspaper design in the field.

Selected by a panel of judges of the Society of News Design, the award-winning newspapers featured in this nineteenth edition were chosen for excellence in design.

Selected by a panel of 21 judges of the Society for News Design, the award-winning pub-lications featured in this nineteenth edition were chosen for excellence in design.

The Best of Newspaper Design, 19th edition, features: all text in English and Spanish; more than five hundred awards: Best of Show, Judges' Special Recognition, Gold Medals, Sil-ver Medals, and Awards of Excellence; over five hundred newspa-pers from all around the world; cate-gories such as overall page design, portfolio, magazine cover design, art and illustration, photo journalism, and informational graphics

Selected by a panel of 21 judges of the Society for News Design, the award-winning pub-lications featured in this nineteenth edition were chosen for excellence in design.Continuing to pay tribute to the world's best newspa-per designs, the 19th edition of The Best of Newspaper Design is a stun-ning collection of modern work. The

Continuing to pay tribute to the world's best newspaper designs, the 19th edition of The Best of Newspaper Design is a stunning collection of mod-ern work. The included works were selected from more than 10,000 entries submitted by newspapers all over the world. This exceptional collection is an essential reference for anyone involved in print media, graphics, photography, design, journalism, or communica-tions.

The competition, which is sponsored annually by the Society for News Design and the S.I. Newhouse School of Public Communications at Syracuse University, recognizes excellence in newspaper design and graphics. Awards include Best of Show, Gold, Silver, Award of Excellence, Special Recogni-tion, plus the honor of World's Best Designed Newspaper. Categories for judging include overall page design, portfolio, magazine cover design, art and illustration, photo jour-nalism, and informational graphics.

This nineteenth edition presents the finest newspaper design in the field.

Selected by a panel of judges of the Society of News Design, the award winning newspapers featured in this nineteenth edition were chosen for excellence in design.

Selected by a panel of 21 judges of the Society for News Design, the award-winning pub-lications featured in this nineteenth edition were chosen for excellence in design.

The Best of Newspaper Design, 19th edition, features: Text in English and Spanish; 840 awards: World's Best-Designed Newspapers, Best of Show, Gold medals, Judges' Special Recognition, Silver medals, and Awards of Excel-lence. More than 12,100 entries were reviewed from hundreds of publications from around the world to select winners from 158 publications. Categories included: Overall design, news, features, portfo-lios, special coverage, special sections, magazines, art and illustration, photog-raphy, informational graphics and redesigns.

Selected by a panel of 21 judges of the Society for News Design, the award-winning pub-lications featured in this nineteenth edition were chosen for excellence in design.Continuing to pay tribute to the world's best newspa-per designs, the 19th edition of The Best of Newspaper Design is a stun-ning collection of modern work. The

Selected by a panel of 21 judges of the Society for News Design, the award-winning pub-lications featured in this nineteenth edition were chosen for excellence in design.Continuing to pay tribute to the world's best newspa-per designs, the 19th edition of The Best of Newspaper Design is a stun-ning collection of modern work. The included works were selected from more than 10,000 entries submitted by newspapers all over the world. This exceptional collection is an essential reference for anyone involved in print media, graphics, photography, design, journalism, or communications.

The competition, which is sponsored annually by the Society for News Design and the S.I. Newhouse School of Public Communications at Syracuse University, recognizes excellence in newspaper design and graphics. Awards include Best of Show, Gold, Silver, Award of Excellence, Special Recogni-tion, plus the honor of World's Best Designed Newspaper. Categories for judging include overall page design, portfolio, magazine cover design, art and illustration, photo jour-nalism, and informational graphics.

This nineteenth edition presents the finest newspaper design in the field.

Selected by a panel of 21 judges of the Society for News Design, the award-winning pub-lications featured in this nineteenth edition were chosen for excellence in design.

The Best of Newspaper Design, 19th edition, features: Text in English and Spanish; 840 awards; World's Best-Designed Newspapers, Best of Show, Gold medals, Judges' Special Recognition, Silver medals, and

REDESIGN
REPRINTS
JUDGES
INDEX

Awards of Excel-lence. More than 12,100 entries were reviewed from hundreds of publications from around the world to select winners from 158 publications. Categories included: Overall design, news, features, portfo-lios, special coverage, special sections, magazines, art and illustration, photog-raphy, informational graphics and redesigns. Selected by a panel of 21 judges of the Society for News Design, the award-winning pub-lications fea-

The competition, which is spon-sored annually by the Society for News Design and the S.I. Newhouse School of Public Communications at Syracuse University, recognizes excellence in newspaper design and graphics. Awards include Best of Show, Gold, Silver, Award of Excellence, Special Recogni-tion, plus the honor of World's Best Designed Newspaper. Categories for judging include overall page design, portfolio, magazine cover design, art and illustration, photo journalism, and informational graphics.

This nineteenth edition presents the finest newspaper design in the field.

Selected by a panel of 21 judges of the Society for News Design, the award-winning pub-lications featured in this nineteenth edition were chosen for excellence in design.

The Best of Newspaper Design, 19th edition, features: Text in English and Spanish; 840 awards: World's Best-Designed Newspapers, Best of Show, Gold medals, Judges' Special Recognition, Silver medals, and Awards of Excel-lence. More than 12,100 entries were reviewed from hundreds of publications from around the world to select winners from 158 publications. Categories included: Overall design, news, features, port-folio, special coverage, special sec-tions, magazines, art and illustration, photography, informational graphics and redesigns. Selected by a panel of 21 judges of the Society for News Design, the award-winning pub-lica-tions featured in this nineteenth edi-tion were chosen for excellence in design.

Continuing to pay tribute to the world's best newspaper designs, the 19th edition of The Best of Newspaper Design is a stunning col-lection of modern work. The included works were selected from more than 10,000 entries submitted by newspa-pers all over the world. This excep-tional collection is an essential refer-ence for anyone involved in print media, graphics, photography, design, journalism, or communications.

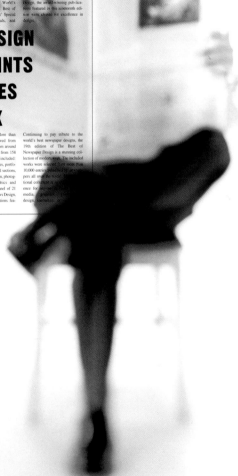

Gold
The European
London, England

John Belknap, Art Director; **Ally Palmer,** Group Art Director; **Alex Evans,** Designer

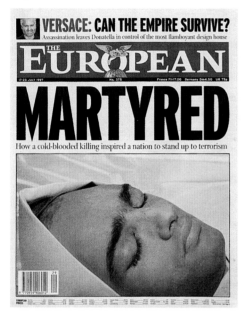

After

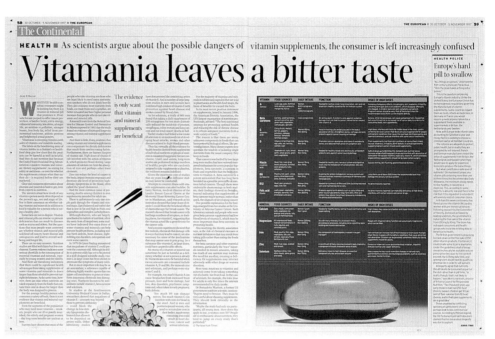

After

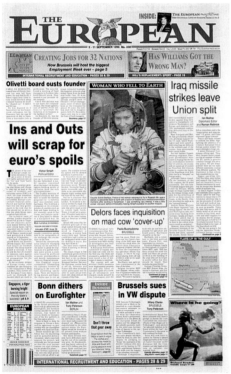

Before

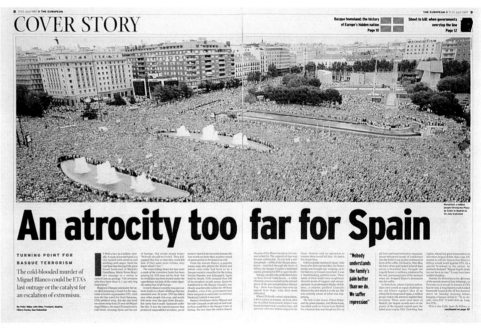

After

Awarded a **Gold Medal** for its redesign. The change from broad sheet to tab is an important one. This is elegant and has a distinctive personality. There is a great deal of attention to detail.

Ganador de la **Medalla de Oro** por su nuevo diseño. El cambio de tamaño sábana a tabloide es importante. Es elegante y con una personalidad característica. Gran detalle.

Award of Excellence
The Gainesville Sun
Gainesville, FL

Mary Holdt, Design Director; **Jacki Levine,** A.M.E.; **Rob Mack,** Graphics Artist/Designer; **Robert Holst,** Group Graphics Coordinator; **Staff**

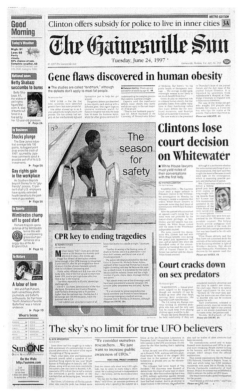

Before

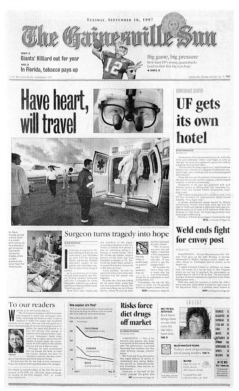

After

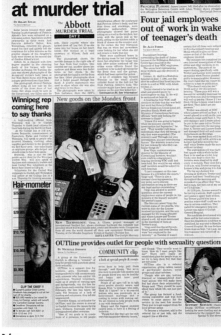

Before

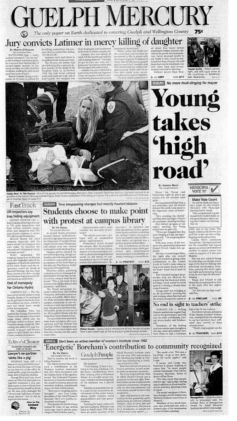

After

Award of Excellence
The Guelph Mercury
Guelph, Canada
Staff

Award of Excellence
El Pais de las Tentaciones
Madrid, Spain

David Garcia, Art Director; **Nuria Muiña,** Art Editor; **Tori Alimbau,** Art Editor; **Fernando Gutierrez,** Graphic Designer; **Cesar Paredes,** Art Dept.; **Guillerolo Trigo,** Art Dept.; **Jose Guillermo Abad,** Art Dept.; **Julian Arroyo,** Art Dept.

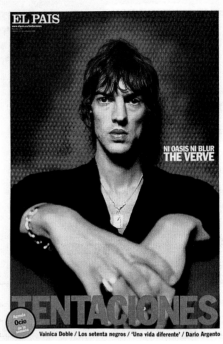

Before

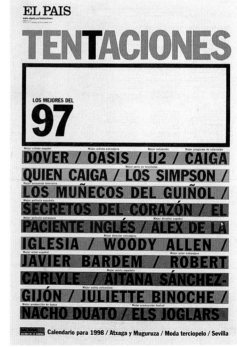

After

Silver
DN. på stan
Stockholm, Sweden

Peter Alenas, Art Director; **Pompe Hedengren,** Art Director; **John Bark,** Creative Director; **Martin Vardstedt,** Editor

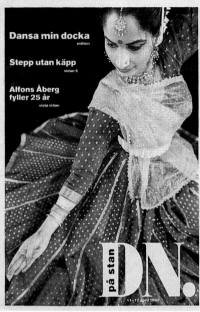

Before

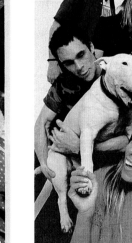

After

Award of Excellence
El Periódico Mediterráneo
Castellón de la Plana, Spain

José Manuel Martos, Designer; **Ricard Sans,** Designer; **Mireia Armengol,** Designer; **Miquel Llargués,** Art Director; **Jesús Montesinos,** Editor in Chief

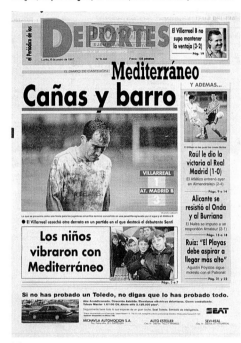

Before

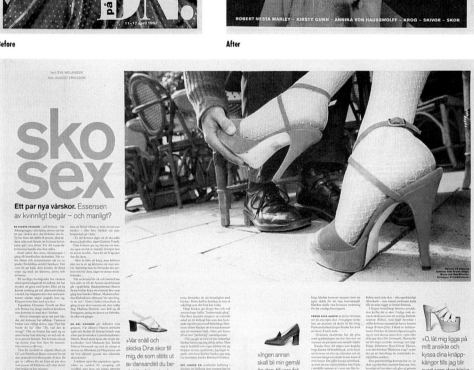

After

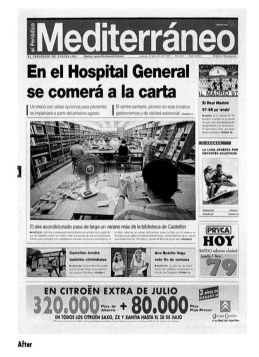

After

Silver
The New York Times
New York, NY

Sam Reep, Art Director & Designer; Suzanne Richie, Photo Editor; Barbara Graustark, Editor; Tom Bodkin, Associate M.E.

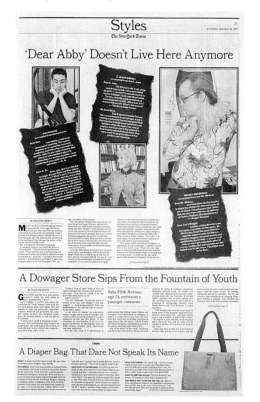

Before

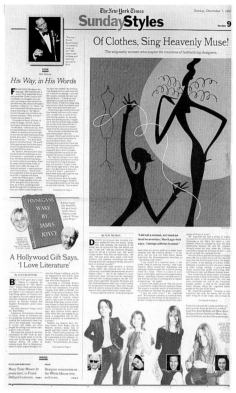

After

After

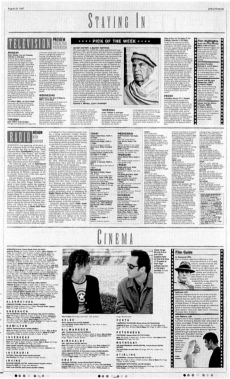

Before

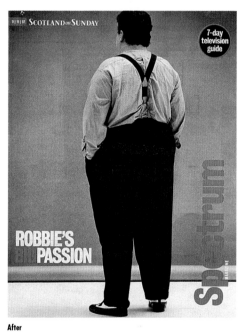

After

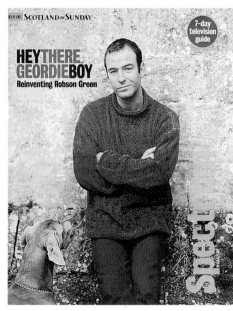

After

Silver
Scotland on Sunday
Edinburgh, Scotland

Sandra Colamartino, Design Editor; Gavin Munro, Deputy Design Editor;
Ally Palmer, Company Art Director; Kayt Turner, Picture Editor

Award of Excellence
Clarin

Buenos Aires, Argentina

Iñaki Palacios, Art Director; Tea Alberti, Design Editor; Oscar Bejarano, Graphic Designer; Alejandro Lo Celso, Graphic Designer; Omar Olivella, Graphic Designer; Matilde Oliveros, Graphic Designer; Pablo Ruiz, Graphic Designer; Carolina Wainsztok, Graphic Designer

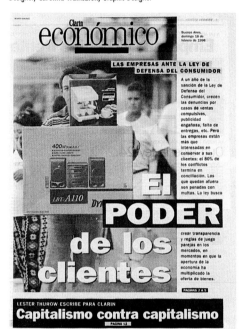

Before

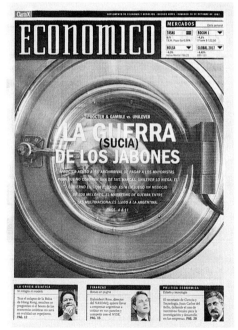

After

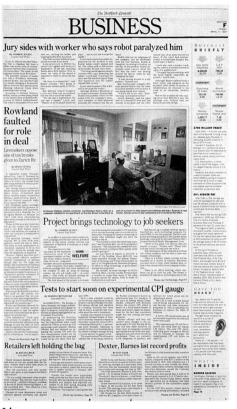

Before

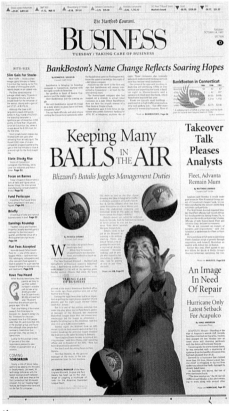

After

Award of Excellence
The Hartford Courant

Hartford, CT

Christian Potter Drury, Art Director; Toni Kellar, Photo Editor; Melanie Shaffer, Designer; Christopher Moore, Designer

Award of Excellence
Lideres/El Comercio

Quito, Ecuador

Ponto Moreno, Graphics Director; Velasco Edison, Designer; Corral Guillermo, Photo Editor; Cajas Francisco, Infographic Editor

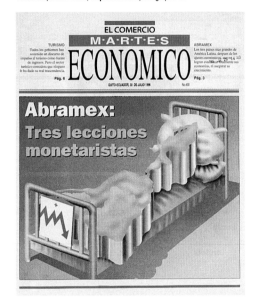

Before

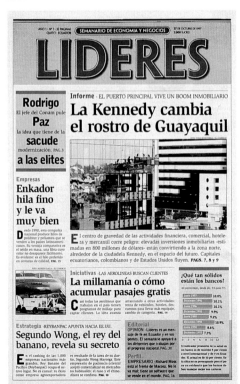

After

Award of Excellence
El Mundo
Madrid, Spain

Carmelo Caderot, Design Director; **Jose Carlos Saiz**, Designer; **Manuel de Miguel**, Assistant Art Director

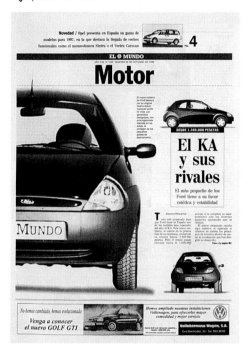

Before

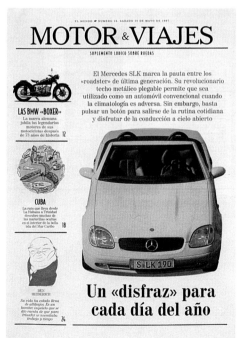

After

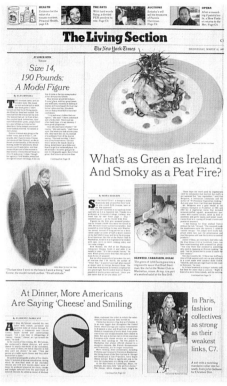

Before

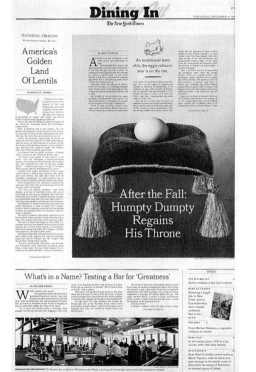

After

Award of Excellence
The New York Times
New York, NY

Sam Reep, Designer; **Corinne Myller**, Designer; **Richard Aloisio**, Art Director; **Tom Bodkin**, Associate M.E.

Award of Excellence
The New York Times
New York, NY

Sam Reep, Designer; **Nancy Kent**, Art Director; **Barbara Graustark**, Editor; **Tom Bodkin**, Associate M.E.

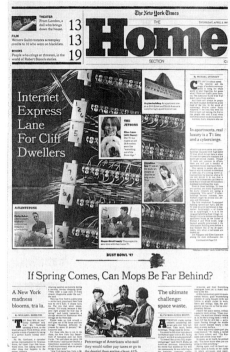

Before

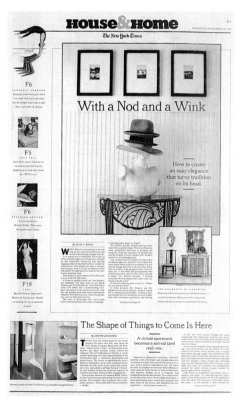

After

Award of Excellence
The San Diego Union-Tribune
San Diego, CA

Bill Gaspard, Designer; **Channon Seifert,** Designer

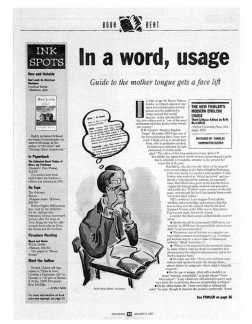

Before

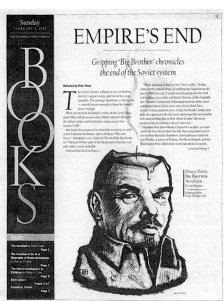

After

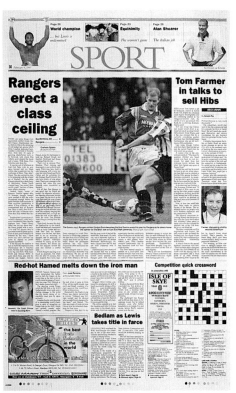

Before

Award of Excellence
Scotland on Sunday
Edinburgh, Scotland
Staff

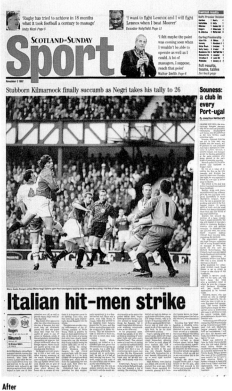

After

Award of Excellence
The Washington Post
Washington, DC

Marty Barrick, Re-Designer; **Alice Kresse,** Designer; **Kathy Legg,** Photo Editor

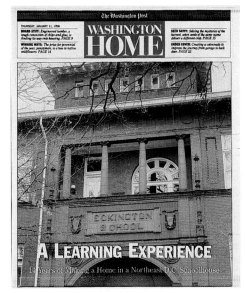

Before

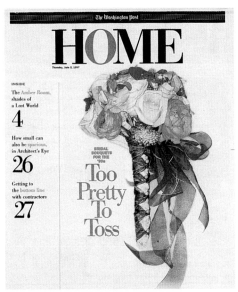

After

Award of Excellence
Chicago Tribune
Chicago, IL

Steve Layton, Graphic Artist; Stacy Sweat, Graphics and Design Editor; Tom Skilling, Meteorologist

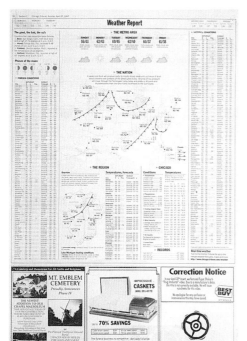

Before

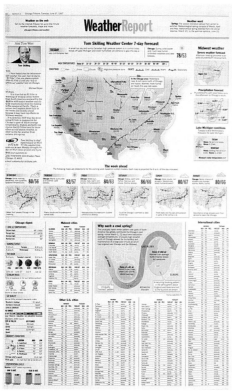

After

Silver
The Charlotte Observer
Charlotte, NC

Monica Moses, Design Director/Designer; Jon Talton, Business Editor; Barry Kolar, Designer; John D. Simmons, Photo Editor; Stephanie Grace Lim, Photographer; Al Phillips, Illustrator

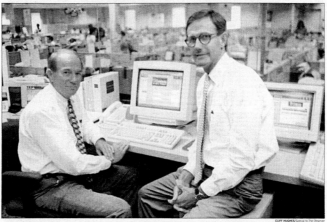

Centura Chairman Bob Mauldin (left) and President Cecil Sewell visit the company's on-line banking center. The bank hopes being aggressive with technology will help it stay independent.

MIDSIZE BANKS ON THE BRINK
4 North Carolina-based banks may not survive battle with giants **PAGE 8D**

CAROLINAS INK
Moon Pie's first advertising campaign comes with something to drink
PAGE 3D

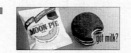

WORKPLACE
Employment will continue to rise in the next 10 years, but where will the jobs be?
PAGE 6D

Before

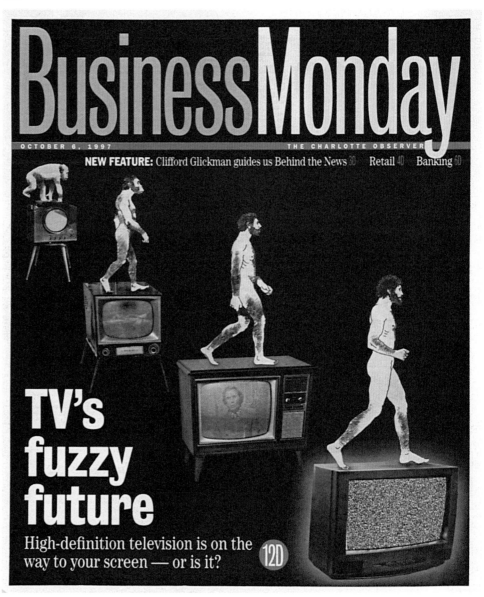

After

Award of Excellence
The Gainesville Sun
Gainesville, FL

Mary Holdt, Design Director; **Jacki Levine**, A.M.E.; **Rob Mack**, Graphics Artist/Designer; **Robert Holst**, Group Graphics Coordinator; **Jeff Tudeen**, Day Desk Editor; **Diane Chun**, Features Editor

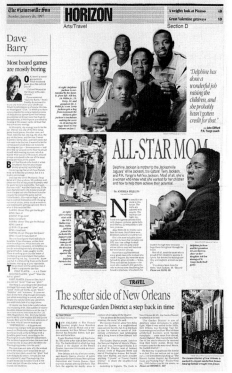

Before

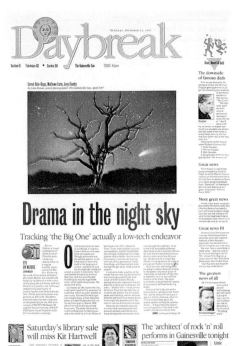

After

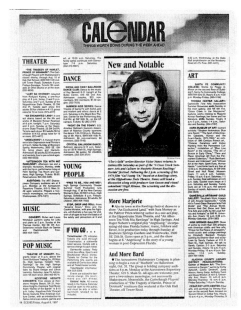

Before

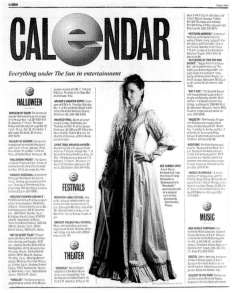

After

Award of Excellence
The Gainesville Sun
Gainesville, FL

Mary Holdt, Design Director; **Jacki Levine**, A.M.E.; **Rob Mack**, Graphics Artist/Designer; **Robert Holst**, Group Graphics Coordinator; **Bill DeYoung**, Scene Editor

Award of Excellence
The Gainesville Sun
Gainesville, FL

Mary Holdt, Design Director; **Jacki Levine**, A.M.E.; **Rob Mack**, Graphics Artist/Designer; **Noel Nash**, Sports Editor

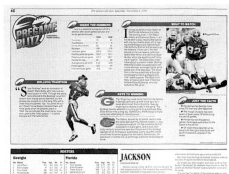

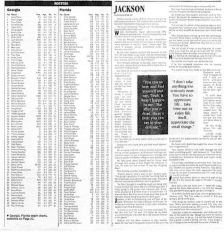

Before

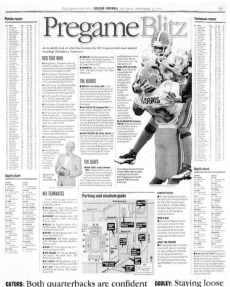

After

Award of Excellence
The Gainesville Sun
Gainesville, FL

Mary Holdt, Design Director; **Jacki Levine,** A.M.E.; **Rob Mack,** Graphics
Artist/Designer; **Robert Holst,** Group Graphics Coordinator

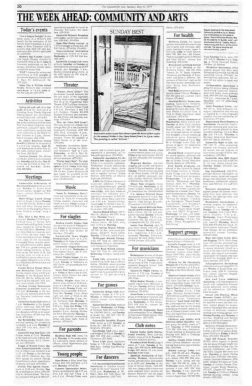

Before

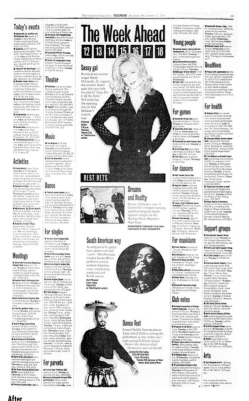

After

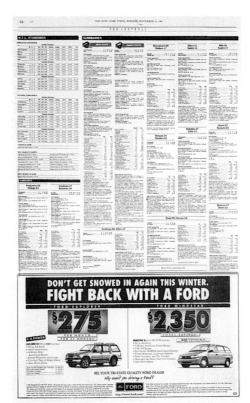

Before

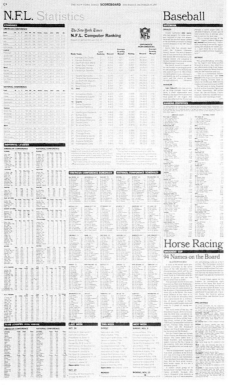

After

Award of Excellence
The New York Times
New York, NY

Wayne Kamidoi, Designer; **Ted Williamson,** Technology; **Sports Staff**

Award of Excellence
The State Journal-Register
Springfield, IL

David Ahntholz, Art Director; **Ted Wolf,** Day News Editor; **Kathleen Riley,**
Illustrator/Designer

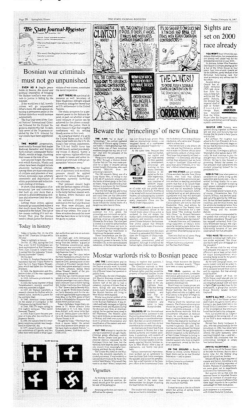

Before

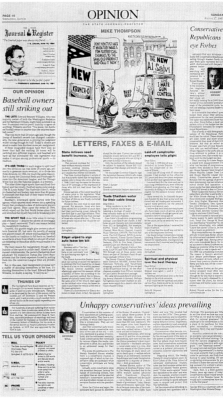

After

Award of Excellence
El Tiempo
Santa Fe de Bogota, Colombia

Beiman Pinilla, Graphics Editor; **Mario Garcia,** Design Consultant; **Carlos Morales,** Illustrator

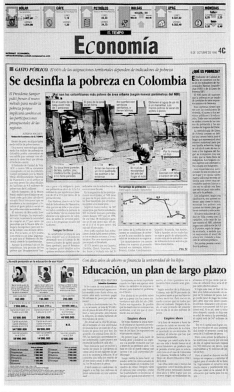

Before

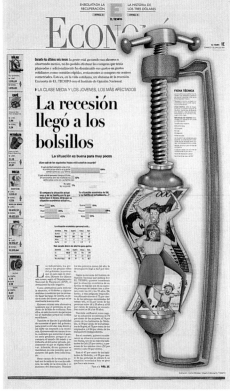

After

Award of Excellence
The Philadelphia Inquirer
Philadelphia, PA

Matthew Ericson, Designer/Graphic Artist; **David Milne,** A.M.E. Design; **Peter Tobia,** Photographer/Photo Editor; **Mark Bowden,** Reporter; **David Zucchino,** Foreign Editor

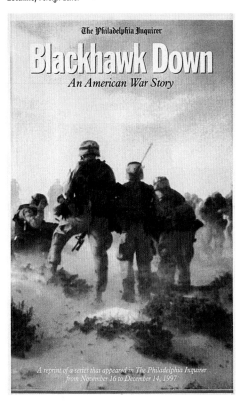

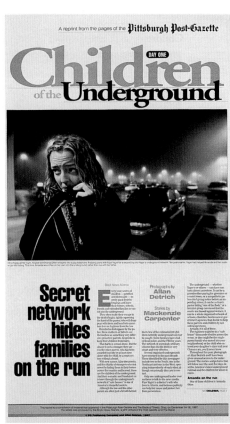

Award of Excellence
Pittsburgh Post-Gazette
Pittsburgh, PA

Curt Chandler, Associate Editor/Photography; **Christopher Pett-Ridge,** A.M.E. Graphics; **Mandy Ross,** M.E.; **Anita Dufalla,** Art Director; **Allan Detrich,** Photographer; **Bill Pliske,** Associate Editor/Graphics

Award of Excellence
Asbury Park Press
Neptune, NJ

Andrew Prendimano, Art & Photo Director, Designer; **Harris G. Siegel,** M.E./Design & Photography; **Noah K. Murray,** Photographer; **Arlene Schneider,** Editor

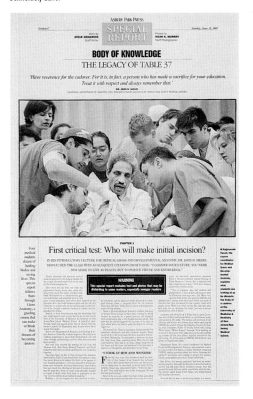

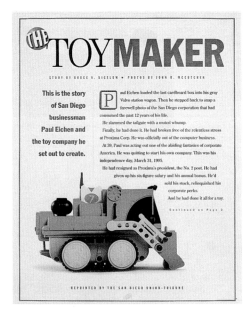

Award of Excellence
The San Diego Union-Tribune
San Diego, CA

Stacy Seifert, Designer; **Kris Lindblad,** Designer; **Bruce V. Bigelow,** Reporter; **Michael Franklin,** Photo Editor; **John R. McCutchen,** Photographer; **Susan White,** Editor; **Elizabeth Bacon,** Copy Editor;

Award of Excellence
St. Petersburg Times
St. Petersburg, FL

Patty Cox, Designer; Neville Green, M.E./Tampa; Cherie Diez, Photographer; Sonya Doctorian, A.M.E. Photography; Don Morris, Art Director

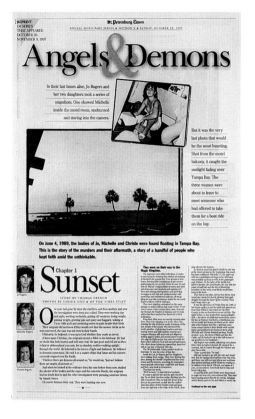

Award of Excellence
The Star-Ledger
Newark, NJ

Linda Grinbergs, Designer; Pablo Colon, Art Director; Helen Driggs, Graphics Arts Director; Jerry McCrea, Photographer; Andre Malok, Graphic Artist

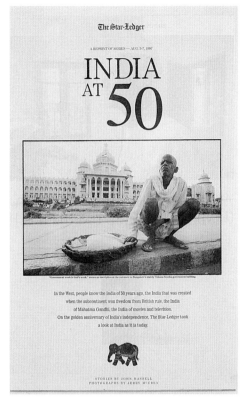

Award of Excellence
Sun-Sentinel
Ft. Lauderdale, FL

Bill McDonald, Assistant News Editor/Design; Joe Raedle, Photographer

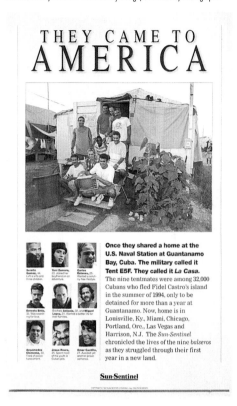

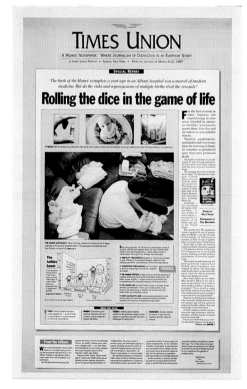

Award of Excellence
Times Union
Albany, NY

Sharon Okada, Artist; Richard Stoddard, Artist; Richard Lovrich, Artist; Monica Bartoszek, Executive News Editor; Paul Buckowski, Photographer

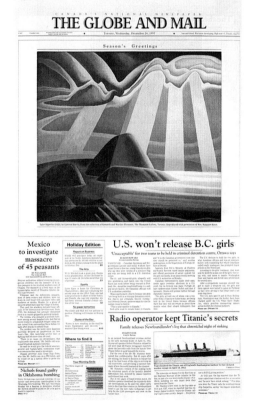

Award of Excellence
The Globe & Mail
Toronto, Canada

Eric Nelson, Art Director; William Thorsell, Editor

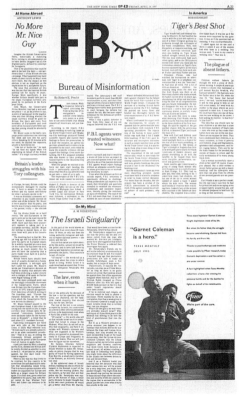

Award of Excellence
The New York Times
New York, NY

Nicholas Blechman, Art Director; Art Hughes, Illustrator

Silver
Goteborgs-Posten
Göteborg, Sweden
Ulf Sveningson, Illustrator; **Lisa Thanner**, Photographer

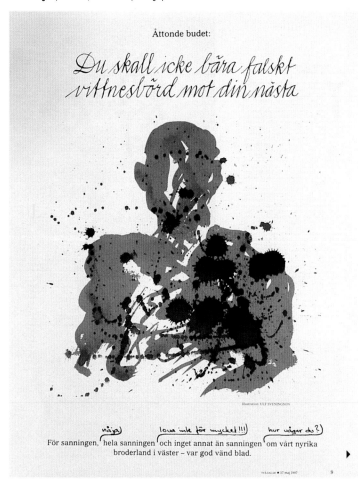

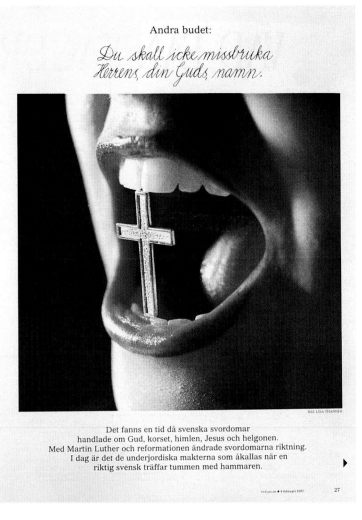

Award of Excellence
Newsday
Melville, NY

Ned Levine, Art Director; **Bill Zimmerman**, Editor; **Peggy Brown**, Writer; **Yancy Labat**, Comics Artist; **Frank Springer**, Comics Artist; **Steve Geiger**, Comics Artist; **Bozena Syska**, Student Briefing Page Designer; **Jonalyn Schuon**; Copy Editor

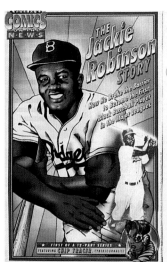

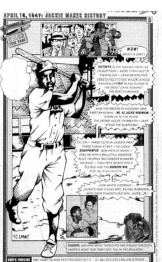

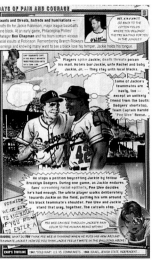

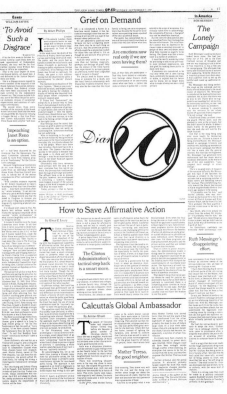

Award of Excellence
The New York Times
New York, NY

Nicholas Blechman, Art Director; **Chip Kidd**, Illustrator

Two groups of judges at competition / Dos jurados en el certamen

The first group of 16 judges was organized much as in past competitions: three groups of five judges with a "floater judge" to solve conflicts and act as a backup to the three groups. These judges begin on page 268.

The second group of five judges (this page) looked at only the competition's overall design category 1, studying newspapers as a whole. They determined the top overall newspapers for information and design presentation in all 20 categories of the competition in three circulation sizes. Thus, they decided the World's Best-Designed Newspapers winners.

● ● ● ● ●

El primer grupo de 16 jueces fue organizado de manera similar a los concursos pasados: tres grupos de cinco jueces con un juez "flotante" para resolver conflictos y actuar como suplente para los tres grupos. Estos jueces comienzan en la página 268.

El segundo grupo de cinco jueces (en esta página) juzgaron solamente la categoría diseño general del certamen, estudiando los periódicos como un todo. Ellos fueron quienes seleccionaron los principales periódicos en general en cuanto a presentación de información y diseño en las 20 categorías que integraban el concurso en tres tamaños de circulación. Por ende, eligieron los ganadores de los Periódicos Mejor Diseñados del Mundo.

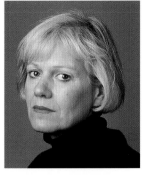

Lynn Staley began working at Newsweek in May 1995 as the director of design, responsible for the art, cover and graphics departments. She was promoted to assistant managing editor and given oversight responsibility for photo in January 1996. Before that she joined the Boston Globe in 1980 as an editorial designer, serving later as art director of the Sunday magazine, assistant managing editor and deputy managing editor. She led a total redesign of the Globe in 1989. She also has served as design director for Inc. Magazine and art director of the Real Paper. She is currently the SND president.

● ● ● ● ●

Lynn Staley comenzó a trabajar en Newsweek en mayo de 1995 como directora de diseño, a cargo de los departamentos de arte, tapa y gráficos. Fue ascendida a subeditora general y se hizo cargo de fotografía en enero de 1996. Antes de eso se unió al Boston Globe en 1980 como diseñadora editorial, para pasar a desempeñarse luego como directora de la revista del domingo, subeditora general y vicedirectora general. Estuvo a cargo del rediseño total del Globe en 1989. También se ha desempeñado como directora de diseño para Inc. Magazine y directora de arte del Real Paper. Actualmente es presidenta de SND.

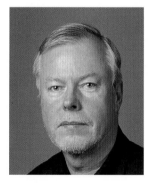

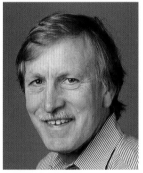

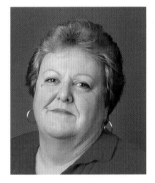

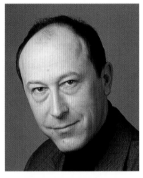

Carl Henning is assistant managing editor/design of the largest Scandinavian daily, Helsingin Sanomat, in Helsinki, Finland, where he has worked since 1965. As an active member of the Society of Newspaper Design/Scandinavia he has served as a frequent judge both in national and Scandinavian newspaper design contests.

● ● ● ● ●

Carl Henning es subbdirector administrativo de diseño del mayor diario escandinavo, Helsingin Sanomat, de Helsinki, Finlandia, donde trabaja desde 1965. Como miembro activo de la Sociedad de Diseño de Periódicos para Escandinavia ha sido juez frecuentemente en los concursos de diseño tanto de su país como del resto de Escandinavia.

Heath Meriwether, publisher of the Detroit Free Press, used to be called a "word guy." But he loves what the "visual" people do. He hopes he has convinced most of those he has worked with at The Miami Herald and the Detroit Free Press that we're all on the same team, on the same page, and that content is king.

● ● ● ● ●

Heath Meriwether, editor del Detroit Free Press, a quien llamaban un "hombre de palabras," pero él ama lo que hace la gente de artes visuales. Espera haber convencido a la mayoría de quienes han trabajado con él en The Miami Herald y Detroit Free Press que todos pertenecemos al mismo equipo, trabajamos en la misma página y que el contenido es rey.

Joette Riehle, assistant to the publisher, Akron Beacon Journal, Akron, Ohio, has done just about everything: from reporter/photographer to copy editor, wire editor and news editor to assistant managing editor and managing editor at five newspapers. She was night national editor at The Detroit News before moving to Knight Ridder's Akron Beacon Journal as deputy managing editor/operations. In 1995, she became assistant to the publisher.

● ● ● ● ●

Joette Riehle, asistente del editor, del Akron Beacon Journal de Akron, Ohio, ha hecho prácticamente de todo: desde reportera/fotógrafa hasta correctora, editor de cables y de noticias hasta subeditora general y editora en jefe de cinco periódicos. Fue editora nacional nocturna de The Detroit News antes de pasarse al Knight Ridder's Akron Beacon Journal como viceeditora general de operaciones. En 1995, pasó a ser asistente del director.

Stephen Ryan, editorial consultant to The Irish Times, has worked for a variety of media as a journalist and editor over the past 15 years. His work as an art director for The Sunday Business Post and The Sunday Tribune has been recognized in SND competitions and the British Newspaper Design Awards. He is married to political journalist and author, Emily O'Reilly. They have four children.

● ● ● ● ●

Stephen Ryan, asesor editorial de The Irish Times, ha trabajado para una diversidad de medios como periodista y editor durante los últimos 15 años. Su trabajo como director de arte de The Sunday Business Post y The Sunday Tribune ha sido reconocido en los concursos de SND y los Premios al Diseño de Periódicos Británicos. Está casado con una periodista política y escritora, Emily O'Reilly. Tienen cuatro hijos.

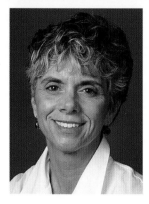

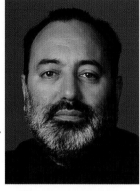

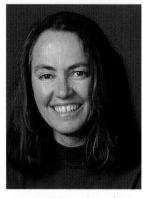

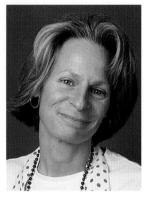

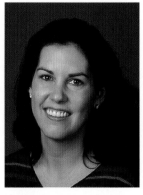

Kate Newton Anthony is features design director at the News & Observer in Raleigh, N.C., where she has worked since 1988. Before that she was a features page designer at The Providence Journal. She has won a number of awards from the SND competition. She was co-editor of SND's Design magazine from 1985-1987.

Kate Newton Anthony es directora de diseño de secciones especiales del News & Observer de Raleigh, Carolina del Norte, donde trabaja desde 1988. Anteriormente se desempeñaba como diseñadora de la página de artículos especiales del The Providence Journal. Ha ganado una serie de premios del concurso SND. Fue coeditora de la revista Design de SND de 1985 a 1987.

Carlos Pérez de Rozas Arribas is art director of La Vanguardia. In 1989 he assisted in the redesign of La Vanguardia. Because of this project and his art department's work, he was granted two Laus de Oro and several SND and Malofiej awards. He is the art & photo director in Journalism Studies at Pompeu Fabra University in Barcelona. He is a founding member of the SND chapter in Spain.

Carlos Pérez de Rozas Arribas es director de arte de La Vanguardia. En 1989 colaboró en el nuevo diseño de La Vanguardia. Por este proyecto y la totalidad del trabajo de su departamento de arte ganó dos Laus de Oro y varios premios de SND y Malofiej. Es director de arte y fotografía de Estudios Periodísticos de la Universidad Pompeu Fabra en Barcelona. Es miembro fundador de la filial de SND en España.

Diane Benefiel is art director for the Jackson Hole News, Jackson, Wyo., where she has worked since 1977. She was appointed art director in 1990. Her newspaper was named one of the World's Best-Designed Newspapers for 1996 by SND.

Diane Benefiel es directora artística del Jackson Hole News, de Jackson, Wyoming, en donde trabaja desde 1977. Fue nombrada directora de arte en 1990. Su periódico fue nombrado uno de los Periódicos Mejor Diseñados del Mundo en 1996 por SND.

Christian Potter Drury is art director at The Hartford Courant. Before that she worked at The Providence Journal and The Litchfield County Times. She studied painting and printmaking at Sir John Cass School of Art in London before she began her newspaper career.

Christian Potter Drury es director de arte de The Hartford Courant. Anteriormente trabajo en The Providence Journal y The Lichfield County Times. Estudió pintura e impresión en la escuela de arte Sir John Cass de Londres antes de comenzar su carrera periodística.

Christine Dunleavy is art director of The Philadelphia Inquirer's Sunday Magazine. Before being promoted to that position, she was design director for the magazine. Prior to that she designed features fronts for The Inquirer. She has worked as features designer at the Asbury Park Press and as art director at the Atlantic City Sun.

Christine Dunleavy es directora artística del The Philadelphia Inquirer's Sunday Magazine. Antes de ser ascendida a este cargo, se desempeñaba como directora de diseño para la revista. Antes de ello diseñaba las cubiertas de secciones especiales para The Inquirer. Ha trabajado como diseñadora de artículos especiales en el Asbury Park Press y como directora de arte en el Atlantic City Sun.

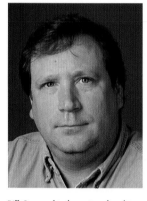

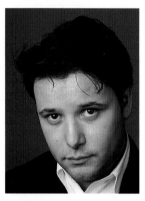

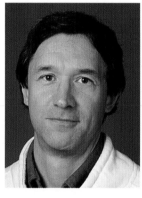

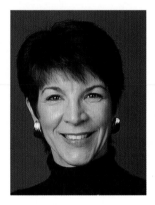

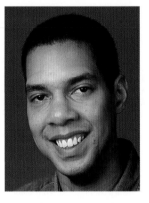

Bill Gaspard is the senior editor/visuals for The San Diego Union-Tribune, supervising the design, photo and graphics departments. He has been with the paper since 1989. Prior to San Diego, he was art director of The Kansas City Times and The Kansas City Star Sunday Magazine. He has consulted on redesign projects with several newspapers.

Bill Gaspard es el editor en jefe de artes visuales de The San Diego Union-Tribune, a cargo de la supervisión de los departamentos de diseño, fotografía y gráfica. Trabaja en este periódico desde 1989. Antes de trabajar en el San Diego, fue director de arte de The Kansas City Times y The Kansas City Star Sunday Magazine. Se ha desempeñado como asesor en los proyectos de nuevo diseño de varios periódicos.

Fernando Gutiérrez is a design consultant for El Pais, Barcelona, Spain. He has brought innovative and commercial approaches to wide-ranging projects: preparing film promotions, designing a weekly supplement to attract younger readers to El Pais, producing MATADOR, a highly visual annual publication published in Madrid devoted to the passions of international leading artists and thinkers.

Fernando Gutiérrez es asesor de diseño de El País, de Barcelona, España. Ha llevado enfoques innovadores y comerciales a proyectos de gran envergadura: preparación de promociones de películas, diseño de un suplemento semanal para atraer a los lectores jóvenes a El País, producción de MATADOR, una publicación anual altamente visual publicada en Madrid dedicada a las pasiones de los principales artistas y pensadores nternacionales.

Tim Harrower is an educator, consultant and author of The Newspaper Designer's Handbook. Since 1985, he has been a designer, feature editor and daily columnist at The Oregonian, Portland, Ore. SND named his newspaper one of the World's Best-Designed Newspapers for 1995 and 1996.

Tim Harrower es un educador, consultor y autor de The Newspaper Designer's Handbook. Desde 1985, ha sido diseñador, editor de secciones especiales y columnista diario de The Oregonian, de Portland, Oregon. SND nombró su periódico como uno de los Periódicos Mejor Diseñados del Mundo en 1995 y 1996.

Mary Holdt is design director of The New York Times Regional Newspaper Group where she has worked with small and mid-sized newspapers for 18 years. Her newspapers have received numerous design awards from SND including one being named the World's Best-Designed Newspaper in 1995.

Mary Holdt es directora de diseño de The New York Times Regional Newspaper Group en donde ha trabajado con periódicos pequeños y medianos durante 18 años. Sus periódicos han recibido numerosos premios al diseño de SND incluyendo el de Periódico Mejor Diseñado del Mundo en 1995.

Monica Moses is design director at The Charlotte Observer, where she supervises 25 news and feature page designers. She has been in charge of art and design departments at four newspapers and won numerous design awards from SND and other organizations. She has also been a copy editor and assistant features editor.

Monica Moses es directora de diseño de The Charlotte Observer, donde supervisa a 25 diseñadores de noticias

Joseph Hutchinson is the assistant managing editor/design and graphics for The Baltimore Sun where he oversees the news design, features design and graphics desks. He was part of the team that worked to redesign The Sun. He has won numerous awards for design and graphics from SND and other organizations.

Joseph Hutchinson es el subdirector general de diseño y gráficas de The Baltimore Sun donde supervisa el diseño de las noticias, de los artículos especiales y de gráficos. Integró el equipo que re-diseñó The Sun. Ha ganado numerosos premios al diseño y los gráficos de SND y otras organizaciones.

y de la página de artículos especiales. Ha estado a cargo del departamento de arte y diseño en cuatro periódicos y ha ganado muchos premios al diseño de SND y otras organizaciones. También se ha desempeñado como correctora y subeditora de artículos especiales.

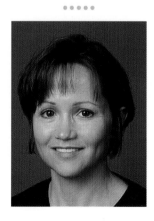

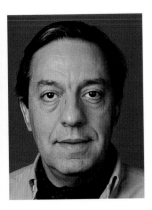 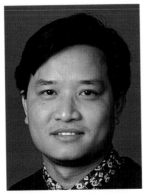 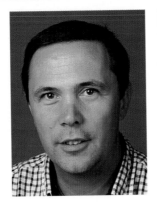 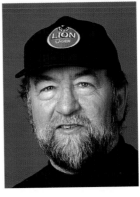 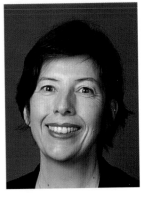

Carlos Mutto was a copy editor and columnist and is now editor in info-graphics services at Agence France Presse, Paris, France. He has won many awards for his work and has been a judge for the Malofiej Awards. He has worked for both newspapers and maga-zines in Argentina, England and Mexico.

• • • • •

Carlos Mutto fue corrector y columnista y ahora es editor de servicios infográficos de Agence France Presse, París, Francia. Ha ganado muchos premios por su trabajo y ha sido juez de los Premios Malofiej. Ha trabajado tanto para periódicos como para revistas en Argentina, Inglaterra y México.

Nam Nguyen is editorial assistant art director and head of the news-graphics department at The Sacramento Bee. Before joining The Bee he worked at the News & Observer, Raleigh, N.C., and The Orange County Register, Santa Ana, Calif., as a graphics artist/illustra-tor. His work has received many awards from SND, Malofiej and other organiza-tions.

• • • • •

Nam Nguyen es subdirector de arte editorial y jefe del departamento de noticias gráficas en The Sacramento Bee. Antes de unirse a The Bee se desempeñó como artista/ilustrador gráfico en News & Observer de Raleigh, Carolina del Norte y The Orange County Register, de Santa Ana, California. Su trabajo ha recibido muchos premios de SND, Malofiej y otras organizaciones.

Gonzalo Peltzer is a professor and consultant on newspaper design. He is the former dean of Austral University's School of Mass Communication. He has a Ph.D. from the University of Navarra in Spain where he was the founder and first director of the Media Design Laboratory.

• • • • •

Gonzalo Peltzer es profesor y consultor de diseño de periódicos. Fue decano de la Escuela de Comunicación Masiva de la Universidad Austral. Tiene un doctorado de la Universidad de Navarra en España donde fue fundador y primer director del Laboratorio de Diseño de Medios.

Tony Sutton is president of News Design Associates, editorial and publica-tion design consultants of Georgetown, Ontario, Canada and editor of SND's Design magazine. Previously, he was design director of Toronto's Globe and Mail, executive editor of Drum maga-zine in South Africa and worked as an editor on magazines and newspapers in Britain.

• • • • •

Tony Sutton es presidente de News Design Associates, una firma de consultoría sobre diseño editorial y publicación de Georgetown, Ontario, Canadá y editor de la revista Design de SND. Anteriormente se desempeñó como director de diseño del Globe and Mail de Toronto, editor ejecutivo de la revista Drum de Sudáfrica y trabajó como editor de revistas y periódicos en Gran Bretaña.

Kerstin Wigstrand is head of the news graphic department at Dagens Nyheter, Stockholm, Sweden. Before that she was feature design director and responsible for the art department at the newspaper. She is one of the founders of the Society of Newspaper Design/Scandinavia.

• • • • •

Kerstin Wigstrand es directora del departamento de noticias gráficas del Dagens Nyheter en Estocolmo, Suecia. Anteriormente fue directora de diseño de secciones especiales y responsable del departamento de arte del periódico. Es una de las fundadoras de la Sociedad de Diseño de Periódicos para Escandinavia.

supplier	M Howard
catalogue	5 04 01
process	AJR
tag	AJR
spine	MJ
cover	✓
memo	
barcode	R62175
final check	✓